The Appalachian Long Distance Hikers Association

Appalachian Trail
Thru-Hikers' Companion

Robert Sylvester

Editor

APPALACHIAN TRAIL
CONSERVANCY

Harpers Ferry

Cover photograph: Mahoosuc Notch, Maine © Jerry and Marcy Monkman
Back-cover photograph: Mt. Rogers, Virginia © Jody Stickle

Maps © 2009 David Miller

Seventeenth edition

Published by the Appalachian Trail Conservancy
799 Washington Street (P.O. Box 807)
Harpers Ferry, West Virginia 25425-0807
<www.appalachiantrail.org>

ISBN 978-1-889386-69-0

The sunrise logo on the previous page and the back cover is a registered trademark of
the Appalachian Trail Conservancy.

Mixed Sources

Product group from well-managed
forests, controlled sources and
recycled wood or fiber
www.fsc.org   Cert no. SW-COC-002553
© 1996 Forest Stewardship Council

FSC

Contents

Foreword

Welcome to the seventeenth edition of the *Appalachian Trail Thru-Hikers' Companion*! Each year, our field editors go out searching for the new hostels, businesses, and town changes so that you can be assured that you have the most up-to-date information on the various changes that the occur on a regular basis along the Appalachian Trail. Those changes could include new town services, shelters built, or trail relocated.

The 2010 *Companion* has been carefully compiled and reviewed. We thank you for purchasing this edition. We hope that you, the Appalachian Trail hiker, will find it to be a great accompaniment to the various maps and guides that you have to make important decisions regarding your hike. From post offices and hostels to town services, this book will provide you with the necessary information needed to make your hike a success.

This book is made possible by the more than thirty ALDHA field editors and ATC staff members who have volunteered countless hours to ensure the information contained is as accurate and up-to-date as possible. Thanks to the many folks who contributed to the successful publication of this book.

Please remember on your journey that this guidebook, not unlike the Trail, is as ever changing as the seasons. You may discover something new or something that has changed since publication. To make this a better guidebook for you and other hikers in the future, we would like hear about any of your discoveries and suggestions for inclusion in the next edition. All comments and/or corrections are welcome and can be sent to us at ALDHA *via* <companion@aldha.org> or <coordinator@aldha.org>.

Remember, the journey is the destination, so
Savor the Moments!

Jojo Smiley
ALDHA Coordinator

About the *Companion*

The *Companion* is compiled, written, and edited by volunteers of the Appalachian Long Distance Hikers Association (ALDHA) and published by the Appalachian Trail Conservancy (ATC) as a service to those seeking to explore the Trail. It is intended for those making thru-hikes but is also valuable for those taking shorter section-hikes or overnight backpacking trips. The *Companion* provides you with details on shelters, water sources, post offices, hostels, campgrounds, lodging, groceries, restaurants, outfitters, and other related services along the Trail. In addition, the *Companion* offers information of historical significance about places you pass through while hiking the A.T. Unlike commercial guides, this book benefits from the latest information from volunteers who measure, maintain, and manage the Trail and those who hike it regularly.

Due to publication deadlines, we cannot guarantee that the information in this book will not change by the time you arrive in an area, despite the efforts of volunteers to acquire the most up-to-date information. Businesses close or change hours, hostels change rates and policies, and the Trail itself is subject to relocation. This edition was produced in the fall of 2008.

As you walk, talk to other hikers, and read shelter registers. The Conservancy's Web site periodically posts updates at <www.appalachiantrail.org/companionupdates>.

Inclusion in this book is not an endorsement by ALDHA or ATC, but rather a listing of services available. Likewise, the businesses listed in this book do not pay for "advertisements" but are listed because of their proximity to the Trail.

ALDHA members do field research for each section of the Trail and are instrumental in gathering information. Without the hard work of the following ALDHA field editors, other volunteers, and ATC staff members, this book would not have been possible: **Georgia and North Carolina**—Scott Dowling (Pilgrim), Ann W. Thomas (Timberpixie); **North Carolina and Tennessee**—Lamar Powell (Hopeful), Judy Young (GrayJay), Sue Kanoy (Bearcharmer); **Southwest Virginia**—Sue Kanoy (Bearcharmer); **Central Virginia**—Charles Davidson (Chase), Laurie Foot (Happy Feet), Leonard Adkins (Habitual Hiker); **Northern Virginia**—David Hennel (Gourmet Dave), Sue Hennel (The Real Gourmet), Gary Ticknor (Greenbriar), Jim Austin (Skyline), Rodney Ketterman; **West Virginia**—ATC Information Services Manager Laurie Potteiger; **Maryland**—Mike Wingeart (Wingheart); **Southern Pennsylva-

nia—Bob and Tricia Dudley (Greyowl), ATC Mid-Atlantic Office Manager John
Luthy; **Northern Pennsylvania**—Mary Ann Nissley (M.A. from Pa.), Sarah Stafford
(Rainbow Brite), Aaron Safford (Mountain Dew); **New Jersey**—Robert Cunningham;
New York—Mark Hudson (Skeeter); **Massachusetts**—Kevin Reardon (Slider), Han-
nah Reardon (Catamount); **Vermont**—Cindy Taylor-Miller (Mrs. Gorp), Smith
Edwards (Old Ridgerunner), Pete Antos-Ketchum, Kathy Krevetski; **New Hamp-
shire**—Art Cloutman (Gabby); **Maine**—J.W. Gordon (Teej), Sandie Sabaka (Blue-
bearee), Christopher Keene (Kineo Kid), Kathy Preble (Boarstone), Jaime Renaud
(NaviGator). ATC Information Assistant John Fletcher also provided valuable information on town and Trail changes. Mileage figures are based on information
from the 2010 edition of the *Appalachian Trail Data Book*. Special thanks to David
Miller (AWOL) for the complete set of new town maps for this edition.

TRAIL-MAINTAINING CLUBS AND REGISTERS

Trail-maintaining clubs are listed throughout the book. You may use the addresses
provided to contact the clubs with any comments, suggestions, or feedback. Although
often a thru-hiker will leave an additional one, the official shelter registers are the
property of the maintaining club and should not be removed by hikers. The register
is a useful tool for information on Trail conditions and other things that are hap-
pening in its section of the A.T. It may also help locate a hiker in case of an emergency. If you wish to donate a register (assuming that one doesn't already exist), you
should include a note asking the maintaining club to forward it to you when it's
filled.

GETTING TO THE TRAIL

Section-hikers looking for shuttle services should check the business and individual listings for the area in which they plan to hike. Also, check with ATC at (304)
535-6331, <info@appalachiantrail.org>, or check the ATC's A.T. shuttle and public-
transportation list available at <www.appalachiantrail.org/shuttles>. (See page 1 for
an important note on shuttles.) This same Web site will link to information on
Trailhead parking.

Using the *Companion*

MAKING THE COMPANION YOUR OWN

Do not be afraid to abuse your paper *Companion*. While it has considerable information, it has been suggested that it could be made smaller. Unfortunately, no one agrees on what should be left out. So, here is an idea—do your own editing. Rip out what you don't want, use a hole-punch, a pair of scissors, or a highlighter. Send sections ahead to mail drops; mail completed sections home. Do some old-fashioned cut-and-paste. Make this book your own. Or, go to ALDHA's Web site, <www.aldha.org>, download an electronic copy of the *Companion* (in Adobe Acrobat PDF format), and print out only the pages you need.

READING THE COMPANION

 Road-crossings and Trailheads with significant services nearby are indicated in south-to-north order.

Towns and post offices (including P.O. hours) are printed in **bold type**. A listing of post offices can also be found on page 273.

East and West—Regardless of compass direction, "**east**" or "E" and "**west**" or "W" are used as they are in the *A.T. Data Book and the series of 11 A.T. guides*: "East" is to the northbounder's right and the southbounder's left, when referring to the Trail.

Services—Major categories are indicated with *bold italics*, specifically *groceries, lodging, hostels, campgrounds, doctors or hospitals, restaurants, Internet access, laundries, veterinarians, and outfitters.*

Trail-Maintaining Clubs—Information is provided at the southern end of their sections and is offset by two rules.

Abbreviations—

In the body of the text:

M—Monday	F—Friday
Tu—Tuesday	Sa—Saturday
W—Wednesday	Su—Sunday
Th—Thursday	

FedEx—Federal Express

USPS—U.S. Postal Service

UPS—United Parcel Service

a/c—air conditioning

AYCE—all-you-can-eat

B/L/D—breakfast/lunch/dinner

CATV—cable television

EAP—each additional person

D—double

PP—per person

S—single

T—triple

In the tables at beginning of each chapter:

C—campground, campsites

cl—coin laundry

D—doctor, medical

f—fuel

G—groceries, supplies

H— hostels

L— lodging

m—miles

M—meals; restaurants

O—outfitter

P.O.—post office

R—road access

S—shelter

sh—shower

nw—no potable water

V—veterinarian

w—water

@—Internet

Elevation—The elevation column refers to the approximate elevation (in feet) of the landmark.

Comma—Services separated by commas are in the same location. For example, E–1.5m P.O., G means that the post office and grocery store are both located 1.5 miles east.

Parentheses—Services separated by parentheses are not all in the same location. For example, (E–0.2m C, S) (W–0.1m w) means that the campsite and shelter are east 0.2 mile, and the water source is west 0.1 mile from the Trailhead.

Shelters—May also be referred to in New England as lean-tos. Shown in **bold print**, with distance and direction off Trail, water-source location, and distance to the next shelter (in italics, both north and south). **The distance to the next north and south shelter shown in the *Companion* includes the side-trail(s) distance from one to the other.**

Issues on the Trail

2,000-MILER CERTIFICATES

ATC recognizes anyone who reports completion of the entire Trail as a "2,000-Miler" with a certificate. The term "2,000-Miler" is a matter of tradition and convenience, based upon the original estimated length of the Trail. ATC policy is to operate on the honor system, assuming that those who apply for 2,000-Miler status have hiked all of the A.T. between Katahdin and Springer, not just 2,000 miles of it. In the event of an emergency, such as a flood, forest fire, or an impending storm on an exposed high-elevation stretch, blue-blazed trails or officially required roadwalks are considered viable substitutes for the white-blazed route. Issues of sequence, direction, speed, length of time, or whether one carries a pack or not are not considered. ATC assumes that those who apply have made an honest effort to walk the entire Trail.

HUNTING SEASONS

Hunters are rarely an issue for northbounders, but southbounders need to be aware of the hunting seasons, which may begin as early as mid-Oct, as you progress south toward Springer Mountain. Hunting is legal along many parts of the Trail, and ATC's Web site lists local hunting seasons. Wearing bright ("blaze") orange is a necessity in fall, winter, and spring.

SAFETY—OTHER HUMANS

If you tell friends you are planning a long-distance hike on the A.T., one of the first questions is likely to be, "Aren't you afraid? What will you do to protect yourself?" There are dangers in the backcountry, but, because of mass-media publicity and the popularity of backpacking, your friend was likely speaking of the dangers posed by other humans. Violent crimes have occurred on the Trail, but with a frequency rate of less than two every ten years, on a footpath that more than three million people use each year.

The difference on the A.T. and in any wilderness setting—other than people's expectations—is that you only have yourself and your instincts for protection. That means you must use common sense to avoid potential dangers.

It is best not to hike alone, but, if you choose to, a few precautions can help keep you safe:

- Don't tell strangers where you are headed or plan to camp for the night; don't post plans in real time on on-line journals or blogs.

- If you run into a suspicious person, consider moving on to another location.

- Avoid camping or staying at shelters that are within a mile of a road crossing.

- Leave an itinerary of your trip with family or friends.

- If you use a Trail name, make sure the folks back home know what it is.

- Even with a partner, don't be lulled into a false sense of security. Two or more can also be vulnerable.

- Trust your gut. Always.

Eliminate opportunities for theft. Don't bring jewelry. Keep wallets and money on your person rather than in your pack or tent. Leaving a pack unattended at trailheads or shelters is risky, even when it is hidden, and also may attract wildlife in search of food.

ATC and most long-distance hikers strongly discourage the carrying of a gun on the Trail. Guns are restricted on national park lands (40 percent of the route) and in many other jurisdictions through which the Trail passes. Report any crime or harassment immediately to the local police and ATC. Contact ATC at (304) 535-6331 or <incident@appalachiantrail.org>.

SAFETY—MOTHER NATURE

While natural dangers are inherent to backpacking, many of the dangers are misunderstood. For some, a hike in the woods conjures images of snakebites and bear attacks—both rare.

BEARS

Black bears live along many parts of the Trail and are particularly common in Georgia, the Shenandoah and Great Smoky Mountains national parks, and north of Shenandoah on into New York. While attacks on humans are rare, a startled bear or a female with cubs may react aggressively. The best way to avoid an encounter while you are hiking is to make noise by whistling, talking, *etc.*, to give the bear a chance to move away before you get close enough to make it feel threatened. If you encounter a bear and it does not move away, you should back off, and avoid making eye contact. Do not run or "play dead," even if a bear makes a "bluff charge."

The best preventive defense against bears showing up in camp is preparing and storing food properly:

- Cook and eat meals away from your tent or shelter so food odors do not linger;

- Hang food, cookware, toothpaste, personal hygiene items, water bottles with drink mixes in a sturdy bag from a strong tree branch 10 feet off the ground, 6 feet from the tree, and away from your campsite;

- Use bear boxes, poles, or cable systems where provided;

- Never feed bears or leave food behind for them;

- A bear that enters a campsite or cooking area should be considered predatory. Yelling, making loud noises, throwing rocks may frighten it away, however you should be prepared to fight back if necessary.

- If you are attacked by a bear, fight for all you are worth with anything at hand— rocks, sticks, fists.

Less dramatic threats to safety, such as contaminated water, dehydration, and hypothermia, afflict far more hikers—particularly those who are unprepared.

If you are unfamiliar with backcountry travel, ask questions, and read and learn about backpacking safely. Learn about dehydration, heat exhaustion, and hypothermia; learn safe ways of fording rivers and purifying water; learn how to avoid lightning, rabies, and Lyme disease—the most common threats to a hiker's well-being. A good resource for learning more about these topics is the ATC publication *Step by Step: An Introduction to Walking the A.T.* Before starting an end-to-end hike, take shorter backpacking trips until you feel confident in the backcountry. Finally, information and experience are useless if you forget one thing—common sense.

LYME DISEASE

Ticks that transmit disease may be anywhere there is vegetation. In the South, ticks can be active year-round. In the Northeast, the heightened risk for Lyme disease (LD) is Apr to Jul and Oct to Nov, which coincide with the timeframe thru-hikers pass through the states with the highest reported cases of the disease. Cases have been reported in all fourteen Trail states.

LD is a bacterial infection transmitted to humans by the bite of infected black-legged ticks (formerly known as "deer" ticks). Hikers should watch carefully for symptoms of LD, which may include "flu-like" reactions of fever, headache, chills, and fatigue and a characteristic "bulls-eye" skin rash, called *erythema migrans,* at the site of the tick attachment. Hikers should seek immediate medical attention for treatment. If left untreated, infection can spread to joints, the heart, and the nervous system. Most cases of LD can be treated successfully with a few weeks of antibiotics.

Steps hikers can take to prevent LD include using insect repellent with Deet for exposed skin; spraying clothing items with the insecticide permethrin; removing ticks promptly; conducting a daily full-body tick check, including the head, underarms, and groin area; minimizing contact with high grass, brush, and woody shrubs; wearing long pants tucked into your socks; and wearing long sleeves, tucking your shirt into your pants to keep ticks off your torso.

LEAVE NO TRACE

Each year, more people venture into the woods to escape the stresses of modern life. Unfortunately, this puts greater pressure on our fragile natural areas. In order to preserve and protect our wilderness, please follow guidelines developed by Leave No Trace, Inc., and endorsed by ATC and ALDHA.

• *Plan ahead and prepare.* You're more likely to damage natural areas if you haven't brought the right equipment or planned where you're going to stay and go. Know local regulations. Remember: Shelters may be full, so bring a tent or tarp.

• *Travel and camp on durable surfaces.* Stay on the Trail, and don't cut switchbacks. Keep off fragile trailside areas such as those in alpine zones. Camp in designated campsites. If you must camp elsewhere, do so out of sight of any trails, and find a spot that has not been used before, at least 200 feet from lakes and streams, being sure to leave it the way you found it. Camping in undesignated areas that show signs of use destroys ground cover and compacts soil, increasing erosion and damaging habitat.

• *Dispose of waste properly.* Pack out all trash and food waste, *including that left behind by others.* Do not bury trash or food, and do not try to burn packaging materials in campfires. Bury human and pet waste six inches deep in a "cathole" at least 200 feet from trail or water. All toilet paper and feminine-hygiene products should be packed out. Avoid using soap to wash yourself or your equipment. When using soap, use biodegradable soap, and dispose of the "gray water" at least 200 feet from open water.

• *Leave what you find.* Don't take flowers or other sensitive natural resources. Don't disturb historical artifacts, such as cellar holes, arrowheads, *etc.*

• *Minimize campfire impacts.* Know local regulations, which may prohibit campfires. Use a portable stove instead of a fire. If you must build a fire, make a low-impact fire, use only downed wood, use existing designated fire pits or rings, and don't add rocks to existing rings. Extinguish the fire before breaking camp. Drown out fires, and empty the fire pit. Scatter leaves and twigs to remove any signs that you have been there.

- *Respect wildlife.* Don't feed or disturb wildlife. Store food properly to avoid attracting bears and rodents. If you bring a pet, keep it leashed.

- *Be considerate of other visitors.* Limit overnight groups to 10 or fewer persons; 25 on day trips. Minimize noise and intrusive behavior (including cellphone chats at shelters). Share shelters and other facilities.

More than three million people use a portion of the Trail each year, and, unfortunately, not all of them are aware of the Leave No Trace camping ethic. Those who are less knowledgeable will observe you (respecting you as a long-distance hiker and, supposedly, an expert wilderness traveler) and your practices. Set a good example. If you see an opportunity to teach others, do so. If Leave No Trace camping is not practiced by all, the A.T. will quickly lose its beauty.

KENNEBEC RIVER FERRY SERVICE AND BAXTER STATE PARK

It is your responsibility to honor the established hours of operation for the free ferry service across the Kennebec River between mid-May and Oct 12, 2010; see page 256 for further details. Do not call from the Trail on your cellphone and expect "special" off-hours service or service out of the range of set dates. Due to weather concerns, hikers should do their parts and plan accordingly to reach Baxter State Park as early as possible. We suggest reaching BSP by Oct 1. After Oct 15, there is no camping inside BSP. See page 266 for posted park cut-off times and further information.

TOWN CONDUCT

As a result of tension between hikers and some communities adjacent to the Trail, ALDHA implemented an "Endangered Services Campaign" to educate hikers to be responsible for their actions. In town, consider yourself a walking, talking billboard for all backpackers and the Trail. Your individual actions have a direct impact on the businesses that provide services for the long-distance hiking community.

The Endangered Services Campaign

The success of a thru-hiker's journey depends on Trail towns and the services they provide. Remember that you are a guest of the community, no matter how large or small, even though you may be pumping money into the local economy. Be courteous to those who earn their livelihood there, and remember that your conduct will have a bearing on how well—or badly—the next hiker is treated. As with so many other things in life, we are never truly alone. You are an ambassador for all those who follow you on the Trail. Nothing can turn a person or town against backpacking and the Trail quicker than an arrogant, smelly, and ill-behaved hiker.

In recent years, some business owners have reduced services or closed their doors to hikers simply because some hikers wouldn't respect their rules. Be a part of the movement that will reverse this practice and ensure that no one closes another door because of bad hiker behavior.

DONATIONS

Many of the hostels listed in this book suggest donations for the services provided. This means that the service should not be considered a gift or that it costs the provider nothing. The honor system of the Trail requires that you leave something.

GIVING BACK

If you would like to give back what was freely given to you by those who maintain the Trail or while you stayed in Trail towns, volunteer your time, effort, or money to the services and people who supported you. Consider contacting a Trail-maintaining club and working with them to organize or participate in a work trip, Trail-construction project, or regular maintenance. Every year, ALDHA sponsors work trips to Trail establishments. The Konnarock and other ATC crews seek volunteers during the summer, and you often will pass a Trail club working busily as you head along the path. Be sure to acknowledge their work with your thanks and respect. Giving back to the Trail and community helps keep the Trail safe and services available.

HITCHHIKING

Hitchhiking is illegal in certain states. It is your responsibility to know the motor-vehicle law as it applies to hitchhiking for the state through which you are hiking, to avoid being fined or hitching into worse trouble. Hitchhiking poses the risk of being picked up by an unsafe driver or by someone who is personally dangerous. Hitchhiking is prohibited on interstate highways, the Blue Ridge Parkway, and Skyline Drive in Shenandoah National Park.

HIKING WITH DOGS

If you choose to hike with your canine companion, treat your dog as another back-packer. That means bury its waste as you would your own, and carry a water bowl so your dog won't drink directly from Trailside water sources. You are responsible for your dog, and you will be held accountable if it decides to steal another hiker's food or flop its wet body on another hiker's equipment. Keep your pet under control in camp, on the Trail, and in towns. Many hostels and other accommodations don't allow dogs, and, in those that do, a dog does not belong in the communal kitchen and sleeping areas. Closely monitor your pet's feet for torn flesh, bleeding, and other sores. After the weather warms up, check for ticks. It is best to keep your dog on a leash at all times; on national-park lands (40 percent of the Trail), regulations require it. Most post offices allow only guide dogs inside. Carry current rabies-vaccine certification papers in addition to a tag on the dog's collar. Dogs are prohibited in the Great Smoky Mountains National Park, the zoo area of Bear Mountain State Park in New York, and Maine's Baxter State Park. (For information on kennels near GSMNP and BSP, see entries for those sections.)

APPALACHIAN TRAIL MUSEUM SOCIETY

Efforts are underway to open an Appalachian Trail museum in June 2010 in Pine Grove Furnace State Park near the Trail's midpoint. A group has been working on this project for several years and, in 2002, formed the Appalachian Trail Museum Society (ATMS). The group includes representatives of ATC and ALDHA and also is working with the National Park Service. The society is collecting items for eventual display in the museum and monetary donations. They are also in need of volunteers to help in many areas. Please contact ATMS, if you'd like to help, at <www.atmuseum.org>.

APPALACHIAN LONG DISTANCE HIKERS ASSOCIATION

The Appalachian Long Distance Hikers Association (ALDHA) is a nonprofit organization founded in 1983 to promote the welfare of the Appalachian Trail and the Trail community. ALDHA conducts work weekends on the Trail, speaks out on issues concerning the A.T. and its environs, and collects the information for this book. In past years, the group has tackled such issues as backpacker etiquette and environmental threats. More recently, it has worked with various clubs and hostels to maintain areas widely used by hikers. ALDHA is open to anyone (even if your longest hike is a walk around the block). To find out more, e-mail ALDHA at <aldha@aldha.org>, or write to 10 Benning Street, PMB 224, West Lebanon, NH 03784. Visit our Web site at <www.aldha.org>. A membership form is included at the back of this book.

THE GATHERING

Folks who want to learn what it takes to thru-hike the Appalachian Trail can find out everything they need to know at the fall Gathering. If you are already thru-hiking the Trail this year, the Gathering is also the place to find out what's next for your worn-in hiking boots. Slide shows and how-to workshops on the Pacific Crest Trail, Continental Divide, and other major foot trails help fill the weekend event. The 29th Gathering will be Oct. 15–17, 2010, at Concord University in Athens, West Virginia. Camping will be at the Folklife Center in nearby Pipestem. Registration fees are $10 per family or individual and include the annual membership directory and quarterly newsletter. Send a check with the registration form on page 288 to ALDHA, 10 Benning St. PMB 224, West Lebanon, NH 03784.

AN INVITATION

This is the seventeenth edition of the *A.T. Thru-Hikers' Companion,* and ALDHA will again depend on comments, suggestions, and volunteers to update it in the fall of 2010. If you see information that needs correcting or come across information that should be included, or would like to be a volunteer field editor, please contact the editor at <companion@aldha.org>.

For additional information about the Appalachian Trail and a complete list of guidebooks, maps, and thru-hiking publications, contact the Appalachian Trail Conservancy at P.O. Box 807, Harpers Ferry, WV 25425-0807, or call (304) 535-6331, Monday through Friday except federal holidays, between 9 a.m. and 5 p.m. Eastern time. The e-mail address is <info@appalachiantrail.org>; the Web address is <www. appalachiantrail.org>. For direct access to the Ultimate A.T. Store, e-mail sales@ appalachiantrail.org>, call (888) 287-8673 weekdays before 4:30 p.m., or visit <www. atctrailstore.org>.

Getting to the Termini

An important note about shuttle services

Beginning in 1995, USDA Forest Service law-enforcement rangers in the South—who report to the regional office rather than the supervisor of an individual forest—began enforcing agency regulations on "special-use permits." The regulations say anyone taking money for a service involving Forest Service lands (including roads) must obtain a permit to do so; profit is not a factor. Permit-holders must pay a fee (up to $75) and, more prohibitively, carry high-premium insurance. Some A.T. shuttlers have been fined. Responding to questions from ATC and its Park Service partners, regional officials made it clear they will continue to enforce the policy and cited directives stating that it is to be enforced consistently and nationally. The A.T. crosses six national forests in the South and two in New England. ATC will continue to provide names of shuttle services, but keep that policy in mind—**call ahead to ensure the person is still performing this service.** You can check the ATC Web site, www.appalachiantrail.org/shuttles, for a downloadable copy of that list, or write ATC, Attn.: Shuttle List (address on page ii), for a copy by first-class mail.

Getting to Amicalola Falls State Park, Georgia

No public transportation is available to or from Amicalola Falls State Park, but hikers have several options from Atlanta, Gainesville (located 40 miles southeast of the park), and the mountain town of Dahlonega (located 16 miles east of Amicalola Falls).

LEAVING ATLANTA

If you fly into Atlanta, you can take Atlanta's rapid-transit trains (MARTA) from the airport to either the Greyhound bus station or the Amtrak station. To reach either station, take the MARTA train north from MARTA's airport station ($1.75 fare). To reach the Greyhound bus station, exit the train at Garnett Station. The bus station is located at 232 Forsyth Street, within sight of the entrance to the MARTA station. To get to the Amtrak station, continue north on the train to the Arts Center Station. From the Arts Center Station, bus No. 23 (departing the station every 10 minutes) will take you to the Amtrak station, located about 10 blocks north on Peachtree. If you wish to walk to the Amtrak station, follow Peachtree Street approximately one mile north; the station is on the left (west) at 1688 Peachtree NW. For more information, call MARTA, (404) 848-4711. Other options from the airport to the bus and train stations include taxis and the Atlanta Airport Shuttle, (404) 524-3400, a privately owned bus service. Atlanta Airport Shuttle vans leave the airport every 15 minutes, from south baggage claim, bound for the bus station and Amtrak station ($18.50 fare). In addition, AAA Airport Express, (800) 354-7874, <www.aaaairportexpress.com>, from space 10 of the pink aisle in the ground-transportation area, offers rides from the airport to Gainesville hotels, $40. The shuttle leaves the airport every two hours from 6:30 a.m. to 10:30 p.m. Reservations recommended.

ATLANTA TO GAINESVILLE

Two buses and one Amtrak train leave daily from Atlanta for Gainesville. At publication time, Greyhound buses, (800) 229-9424, <www.greyhound.com>, departed the Atlanta station for Gainesville at 7:45 a.m. and 3:15 p.m. ($11.88 M–Th, $14 F–Su) and arrived in Gainesville at 9:20 a.m. and 4:55 p.m. Buses departed Gainesville for Atlanta at 10:25 a.m. and 6:55 p.m. However, Greyhound routinely revises its schedule; call for current information. Amtrak's train was scheduled to depart from Atlanta daily at 8:08 p.m. and arrive in Gainesville at 9:03 p.m. ($11). A train was scheduled to depart Gainesville for Atlanta daily at 7:08 a.m. Reservations are required. Call (800) 872-7245, or log on to <www.amtrak.com>.

Gainesville—*Lodging:* Motel 6, (770) 532-7531, $47.95S $48.59D weekdays, $45.99S $49.99D weekends, $3EAP, pet-friendly n/c; Lanier Center Best Western, (800) 782-8966, $99.95D, no dogs, hot B; Ramada Limited, (770) 287-3205, $59, B buffet, small pets $10; Hampton Inn, (770) 503-0300, $115, no pets, hot B; Best Value Inn, (770) 534-0303, $55–$65, no pets. All are within four miles of the bus and train stations.

GAINESVILLE TO AMICALOLA FALLS STATE PARK

UNITAXI, (770) 534-5355 or (770) 297-0255, offers service to Amicalola Falls State Park ($65 fare); transports dogs and accepts only cash. Service to the Trailheads at Nimblewill Gap and USFS 42 available at an additional cost.

GAINESVILLE TO DAHLONEGA

Some hikers choose to stay in Dahlonega rather than Gainesville. The site of the country's first gold rush, in the 1830s, Dahlonega sits 16 miles east of Amicalola Falls and offers all major services. UNITAXI (see above) offers service to Dahlonega.

Dahlonega—*Hostel:* A.T. Hiker Hostel run by Josh and Leigh Saint, (770) 312-7342, <www.hikerhostel.com>, <hikerhostel@yahoo.com>, by reservation; $70 thru-hiker's special includes pick-up at North Springs MARTA station in Atlanta or bus/train station in Gainesville, bunk, fuel, stop at outfitters if needed, B, and shuttle to Springer or Amicalola. Gear shipment to hostel available. Bunk & B $16, private room & B $38D. Fuel (white gas & alcohol), shuttle service, free Internet access. See Web site or contact hostel for shuttle rates. *Lodging:* Hotel rates in Dahlonega vary with the season. After May 1 and on weekends, expect listed rates to increase. Holiday Inn Express, (706) 867-7777, $79–$109, $5EAP, includes hot B, no pets; Super 8, (706) 864-4343, $55D, includes B, $10 for dogs, WiFi; Days Inn, (706) 864-2338, newly renovated, $49–$70, one room for pets, B, WiFi; Econo Lodge, (706) 864-6191, $50–$80, includes B, pets <20 pounds, Internet access; Smith House, (800) 852-9577, <www.smithhouse.com>, $139–$269, includes B, no dogs. The Smith House Restaurant, in operation since 1922, is famous for its family-style AYCE fare: L (beginning in April) Tu–F 11–3, D Tu F 4 8, Sa Su 11–8. Hours are seasonal and may vary. Call ahead.

ALTERNATIVES

Several Trail enthusiasts in the Atlanta area offer shuttles from Atlanta to the park and Springer Mountain. The ATC is continually updating its list. Many people who offer shuttles do so on their time off; arrangements are best made at least a week or two in advance. See above for shuttle services.

AMICALOLA FALLS APPROACH TRAIL

Miles from Springer	Features	Services	Elev.	Miles from AFSP
8.8	Amicalola Falls State Park; Visitors Center; **AFSP Shelter** *0.0mS; 7.3mN*	R, C, L, M, S, sh, cl, w (W–19 m O)	1,700	0.0
7.6	Amicalola Lodge Rd	R, L, M, w	2,550	1.2
7.4	+Len Foote Hike Inn Trail	E–5m L, M	2,600	1.4
5.6	High Shoals Rd	R	2,800	3.2
4.0	Frosty Mtn	C, w	3,382	4.8
4.5	+Len Foote Hike Inn	E–1m L,M	3,310	5.3
3.7	Frosty Mtn. Rd USFS 28	R	3,192	5.1
2.8	Nimblewill Gap, USFS 28	R	3,100	6.0
1.5	**Black Gap Shelter** *7.3mS; 1.7mN*	C, S, w	3,300	7.3
0.0	Springer Mountain		3,782	8.8

+ Fee charged

THE APPROACH TRAIL

Amicalola Falls State Park—Its facilities nestled almost nine miles southwest of Springer Mountain, the park is the gateway to the southern terminus of the A.T. Scales to weigh packs and showers are located near the center entrance, as well as a restroom, pay phone, snack machines, and water fountain. The visitors center sells guidebooks, maps, and gift items. The park holds UPS and USPS packages sent c/o Amicalola Falls State Park, 240 Amicalola Falls State Park Rd., Dawsonville, GA 30534. Indicate on the box to hold the package at either the visitors center or the lodge. The visitors center, (706) 265-4703, is open 8:30–5 daily. While at the park, sign the hiker register inside the visitors center. Long-distance hikers may leave vehicles only in the parking area opposite the visitors center. A $5-per-vehicle user fee is charged to all park visitors. Dogs must be on a leash within the park. ■ *Camping:* The park also offers campsites and cabins: campsites $23 with shower, coin laundry, 1- to 3-bedroom cabins (2-night minimum) $80–$160. ■ *Lodging:* The desk at Amicalola Lodge, (706) 265-8888, (800) 573-9656, <www.gastateparks.org>, is staffed around the clock; rooms $75–$200, B included. Reservations suggested for cabins, campsites, and the lodge. ■ *Restaurant:* The lodge houses the Maple Restaurant, daily buffets, continental B 7–10:30, L 11:30–3, D 5–8.

West 19 miles to *Outfitters:* North Georgia Mountain Outfitters, Collin and Gil Carter, (706) 698-4453, fax (706) 698-4454, <www.hikenorthgeorgia.com>, <info@hikenorthgeorgia.com>, 1215 Industrial Blvd., East Ellijay, GA 30540, closed Tu–W; open M, Th, F 10–6; Sa 9–6; Su 12–6; full-service outfitter, Coleman and alcohol fuels by the ounce, canister fuels, short-term food resupply; will hold packages w/o fee; possible shuttles to Atlanta Airport, Amicalola, Springer Mountain, and Neels Gap; call for possible delivery of packages and store items. Ellijay Outfitters, Sa–Su 10–6, 10 N. Main St., Ellijay, GA 30540; (706) 698-GEAR, <www.ellijayoutfitters. com>, <info@ellijayoutfitters.com>. Mark (Trail Trucker, '01) and Anne Micallef can shuttle as time allows.

Amicalola Falls State Park Shelter (1993)—Located 50 yards behind the visitors center, sleeps 12, and available to thru-hikers at no charge. Built by a group of Trail backpacking enthusiasts from nearby Canton in memory of their friend, Max Epperson. The "A.T. Gang" spent 800 hours constructing the facility. Epperson hiked the Trail as far north as Connecticut before his health failed. Afterward, he continued to offer shuttles and support for his hiking friends. Water source and restroom 50 yards away at visitors center.

Approach Trail to Springer Mountain—From the park visitors center, it is an 8.8-mile trek to the first white blaze, most of it uphill. To cut off the steep, one-mile ascent of the falls, catch a ride to the top of the falls, and pick up the blue blazes there. The southern end was recently relocated just past its start at the visitor center.

Approach Trail *via* Nimblewill Gap—This alternative puts you 2.2 miles south of Springer Mountain on the Approach Trail but requires a bumpy, muddy drive up Forest Service roads. From the park entrance, go east 9.5 miles on Ga. 52 to abandoned Grizzles Store. Turn left on Nimblewill Road, and continue past Nimblewill Church at 6.6 miles. Just beyond the church, pass a road on the left where the pavement ends. Continue to the right on the unpaved road, and reach Nimblewill Gap at 14 miles. This is a very rough road and probably should not be attempted unless you have a vehicle with high ground clearance.

From Amicalola Falls to Springer Mountain *via* Forest Service roads—The easiest and quickest route takes you within one mile of the Springer summit. From the park, go west on Ga. 52 for 13.6 miles to Roy Road, at Cartecay Church and Stanley's Store. Turn right, and proceed 9.5 miles to the second stop sign. At the stop sign, bear right, and go 2.3 miles to Mt. Pleasant Church on the left. Across from the church, turn right onto unpaved Forest Service Road 42. This well-graded gravel road, suitable for all vehicles, winds 6.6 miles to the A.T. crossing at Big Stamp on the north side of the road. To reach the summit of Springer Mountain, walk 0.9 mile south. If you don't want to retrace your steps on the A.T., an alternative is to continue 1.7 miles past the A.T. crossing to USFS 42's intersection with the Benton MacKaye Trail (BMT). The BMT leads 1.5 miles up Springer and joins the A.T. just north of the southern terminus.

Len Foote Hike Inn—(800) 581-8032, <www.hike-inn.com>. This $1-million lodge is similar to the huts in New Hampshire's White Mountains. The 40-bed, 20-room inn is approximately 5.0 miles north of Amicalola Falls State Park facilities and 4.5 miles south of the Springer Mountain summit. The yellow-blazed Hike Inn Trail creates a loop with the blue-blazed Approach Trail that leads from Amicalola Falls State Park to Springer. Overnight stays, which include family-style B/D, are $97S, $140D, rates subject to change; no dogs allowed. Amenities include linens, hot showers, composting toilets, and electricity (outlets in bath house only). Owned by the Georgia Department of Natural Resources, the inn is operated by the Appalachian Education and Recreation Services, Inc., a nonprofit corporation affiliated with the Georgia Appalachian Trail Club. Walk-ins are allowed, subject to availability. Registration is at the Amicalola Falls State Park visitor center, where you can check on room availability. Open year-round, guest rooms in the bunkhouse are heated. Sleeping bags recommended Nov–Mar.

Black Gap Shelter (1953/1995)—Sleeps 8. privy. Once the Springer Mountain Shelter, before being dismantled and moved to its present location in 1995. This shelter is 1.5 miles south of the summit of Springer Mountain on the Approach Trail. Water is located 300 yards downhill to the right of the shelter.

Getting to Baxter State Park, Maine

No public transportation is available to or from Baxter State Park, but arrangements can be made to conclude or begin your journey with little difficulty. This usually means going through Boston, Portland, and/or Bangor, then to Medway, and then to Millinocket, still 20 miles southeast of the park. The nearest airport is in Bangor; the Portland airport is said to have more competitive rates, and Boston more so. For services and accommodations in Bangor, see page 272. Bus transportation is available from Portland to Medway and also from Boston to Portland.

LEAVING BANGOR

Cyr Bus Lines of Old Town, Maine, (207) 827-2335, (207) 827-2010, or (800) 244-2335, <www.cyrbustours.com>, <info@cyrbustours.com>, serves northern Maine. A bus leaves Bangor Greyhound bus station at 6:00 p.m. and Concord–Trailways bus station at 6:30 p.m. and arrives at Medway at 7:40 p.m. A bus leaves Medway at 9:30 a.m. and arrives at Concord-Trailways station at 10:50 a.m. and at Bangor Greyhound station at 11:10 a.m. ($11.50 fare). The A.T. Lodge in Millinocket, (207) 723-4321, shuttles.

MEDWAY TO MILLINOCKET

From Medway, in the past, you would have to hitch on Maine 157 or call a taxi to go to either Millinocket, 10 miles to the west, or Baxter State Park, about 30 miles away. Town Taxi, (207) 723-2000, charges $55 to Baxter State Park (BSP) gate and to Katahdin Stream Campground. Today, however, transportation is available to and from BSP *via* shuttle from the A.T. Lodge in Millinocket. The A.T. Lodge also offers a SOBO special: pick-up in Medway, bed in the bunkroom, breakfast at the A.T. Café, and shuttle to Katahdin Stream Campground; $70. For more information on that and other lodging and facilities near Baxter State Park in Medway and Millinocket, please see the entries on pages 269-270.

Baxter State Park—The park, (207) 723-5140, has 10 campgrounds available May 15–Oct 15 by reservation on a first-come, first-served basis, $10PP, two-person minimum ($20 per site) except at the Birches. The Birches campsite, near Katahdin Stream Campground, is intended for long-distance hikers who have hiked 100 miles or more on their current trip. Hikers staying at the Birches must sign up at the information kiosk just north of Abol Bridge. Please see the entry for Baxter on page 264 for more information and details about camping and regulations near Katahdin. Southbound hikers should reserve a regular lean-to or tentsite at Katahdin Stream or Abol campgrounds. Reservations may be made by telephone four months in advance of the date you wish to stay in the park and can be made using a credit card. More information and a chart outlining when reservations can be made is available at <www.baxterstateparkauthority.com>. Inside the park, ranger stations do NOT accept credit cards. Every hiker must register *with a ranger* upon entering Baxter. Information kiosks are located at Abol Stream and Katahdin Stream campgrounds.

Pets—No dogs or other pets are allowed; see Medway and Millinocket entries for kennels (pages 269-270).

Parking—No long-term parking is available, and parking at all trailheads and campgrounds is at a premium and controlled by permits issued at the entrance gates; when the space is gone, that specific parking lot is closed. Plan ahead!

APPROACH TO KATAHDIN

A note for would-be southbounders—Katahdin is no stroll in the park. The profile and topo on the MATC's maps only give you a hint of what to expect—the single greatest sustained climb on the A.T. Get yourself physically prepared before you start at Baxter State Park (you will be on your own once you get past the ranger station). Northbounders routinely leave their full packs on the ranger's porch and hike up with daypacks provided there for that purpose. Every year, several stubborn southbounders, invariably much less-conditioned than seasoned northbounders, insist on carrying their fully loaded packs up the A.T. beyond Katahdin Stream Campground. This results in knee injuries and aborted climbs or even entire A.T. hiking plans. Take a hint from the northbound veterans: Hike Katahdin with a day pack, and pick up your full pack on your way back through the campground—you will still be a thru-hiker, and you will enjoy your day, rather than suffer the entire time and predispose yourself to any number of injuries or the need for a rescue on your first Trail day. The footpath below treeline is more rocks and roots than soil—no problem for the hikers who have been rock-hopping for 2,000 miles, but not a pleasant journey straight from the desk chair.

Above treeline, you pull yourself over rocks in a few places and walk across slanted, roof-sized boulders in others. The climb is tough, even without a pack. The park recommends you bring or borrow a day pack (plenty of water, lots of snacks, sunscreen, a first-aid kit, gloves, hat, and extra layers of clothing). If you don't want to retrace your steps, you might consider going up the Abol Trail (part of which is referred to as the "Abol Slide," because of the loose rocks and steepness formed by a nineteenth-century landslide) and down the Hunt Trail (A.T.). That requires a two-mile walk or ride from Katahdin Stream along the Perimeter Road to Abol Campground before starting your hike. The Abol Trail usually opens after the Hunt Trail; until the sandy, gravelly soils dry out, the trail is slippery, and boulders can become dislodged.

"Weather permitting," you can begin a southbound hike as early as May 31. Before then, trails are so wet, even without snow and ice, that foot traffic would irreparably harm the alpine and subalpine areas. However, even for the following few weeks, the tiny, biting blackflies can drive you out of the woods in agony and frustration, leaving behind a contribution of your blood to the North Woods ecosystem. Overnight camping season in Baxter is May 15–Oct 15. Baxter State Park posts daily weather reports at the Trailheads at 7 a.m. during the hiking season. Categories tell you what is to be expected for the day:

- *Class I*—Recommended for hiking above treeline.

- *Class II*—Not recommended for hiking above treeline.

- *Class III*—Not recommended for hiking above treeline, with the following trails closed (specified trails will be listed).

- *Class IV*—All trails closed at the trailhead. A hiker who climbs Katahdin on a Class IV day is subject to a court summons, fine, seizure of equipment, and permanent revocation of park privileges.

Georgia

Miles from Katahdin	Features	Services	Elev.	Miles from Springer
2,179.1	Springer Mtn		3,782	0.0
2,178.9	**Springer Mtn Shelter**... *1.9mS; 3mN*	E–0.2m S, C, w	3,730	0.2
2,178.1	USFS 42	R	3,350	1.0
2,176.3	**Stover Creek Shelter**... *3mS; 5.4mN*	E–0.2m S, w	2,870	2.8
2,175.3	Stover Creek	w	2,660	3.8
2,174.8	Three Forks, USFS 58	R, C, w	2,530	4.3
2,174.0	Trail to Long Creek Falls	w	2,800	5.1
2,173.1	Logging Rd	R	3,000	6.0
2,171.3	**Hawk Mtn Shelter**... *5.4mS; 7.6mN*	W–0.2m S; 0.4m w	3,200	7.8
2,170.8	Hightower Gap, USFS 42/69	R	2,854	8.3
2,168.9	Horse Gap	R	2,673	10.2
2,167.9	Sassafras Mtn		3,300	11.2
2,167.3	Cooper Gap, USFS 42/80	R	2,800	11.8
2,166.7	Justus Mtn		3,224	12.4
2,165.3	Justus Creek	C, w	2,550	13.8
2,164.0	**Gooch Mtn Shelter**... *7.6mS; 12.5mN*	W–0.1m S, w	3,000	15.1
2,162.6	Gooch Gap, USFS 42	R, w	2,784	16.5
2,160.4	Ramrock Mtn		3,260	18.7
2,159.0	Ga. 60, Woody Gap **Suches, GA 30572**	R (W–0.1m w; 2m PO G, C, D, cl, sh, f) (E–7m H, f, @)	3,150	20.1
2,158.0	Big Cedar Mtn		3,737	21.1
2,156.7	Dan Gap		3,300	22.4
2,153.9	Burnett Field Mtn		3,480	25.2
2,153.4	Jarrard Gap	W–0.3m w; 1m C, sh, w; 2m M	3,250	25.7
2,152.1	**Woods Hole Shelter**... *12.5mS; 1.8mN*	W–0.5m S, w	3,600	27.0
2,152.0	Bird Gap, Freeman Trail		3,650	27.1
2,151.6	Slaughter Creek Campsite	C, w	3,800	27.5

Miles from Katahdin	Features	Services	Elev.	Miles from Springer
2,150.8	Blood Mtn, **Blood Mtn Shelter**... *1.8mS; 9.8mN*	S, nw	4,450	28.3
2,149.4	Flatrock Gap, Trail to Byron Reece Memorial	W–0.2m w	3,450	29.7
2,148.4	U.S. 19 & 129, Neels Gap	R, H, O, cl, sh, f, @ (E–0.3m L) (W–3m C, G, cl, sh; 3.5m C, L, cl, sh)	3,125	30.7
2,147.3	Bull Gap	C, w	3,690	31.8
2,146.9	Levelland Mtn		3,942	32.2
2,146.3	Swaim Gap		3,470	32.8
2,145.6	Rock Spring Top	w	3,520	33.5
2,145.1	Corbin Horse Stamp		3,620	34.0
2,145.0	Wolf Laurel Top		3,766	34.1
2,144.2	Baggs Creek Gap	C, w	3,800	34.9
2,143.7	Cowrock Mtn		3,842	35.4
2,142.9	Tesnatee Gap, Ga. 348	R	3,138	36.2
2,142.4	Wildcat Mtn		3,500	36.7
2,142.2	**Whitley Gap Shelter**... *9.8mS; 5.8mN*	E–1.2m S; 1.5m w	3,370	36.9
2,142.0	Hogpen Gap, Ga. 348	R, w	3,450	37.1
2,141.1	White Oak Stamp		3,470	38.0
2,140.1	Poor Mtn		3,620	39.0
2,138.4	Sheep Rock Top		3,600	40.7
2,137.6	**Low Gap Shelter**... *5.8mS; 7.2mN*	S, w	3,050	41.5
2,136.2	Poplar Stamp Gap	C, w	2,990	42.9
2,133.8	Cold Springs Gap		3,300	45.3
2,132.6	Chattahoochee Gap	E–0.5m w	3,500	46.5
2,132.0	Red Clay Gap		3,485	47.1
2,131.3	Campsite	C	3,600	47.8
2,131.1	Spring	w	3,500	48.0
2,130.4	**Blue Mtn Shelter**... *7.2mS; 8.0mN*	S, w	3,900	48.7
2,129.6	Blue Mtn		4,025	49.5

Miles from Katahdin	Features	Services	Elev.	Miles from Springer
2,128.2	Ga. 75, Unicoi Gap **Helen, GA 30545**	R (E−9m PO G, M, L, cl, @) (W−3.8m C, L, G, cl, f, @)	2,949	50.9
2,127.6	Stream	w	3,300	51.5
2,126.9	Rocky Mtn	C	4,017	52.2
2,125.6	Indian Grave Gap, USFS 283	R	3,113	53.5
2,124.9	Tray Mtn Rd, (USFS 79)	R	3,580	54.2
2,124.6	Cheese Factory Site	C, w	3,590	54.5
2,123.8	Tray Gap, Tray Mtn Rd, (USFS 79)	R	3,847	55.3
2,123.0	Tray Mtn		4,430	56.1
2,122.6	**Tray Mtn Shelter...** *8.0mS; 8.0mN*	W−0.2m S; 0.3m w	4,200	56.5
2,119.0	Swag of the Blue Ridge		3,400	60.1
2,117.8	Sassafras Gap	w	3,500	61.3
2,117.0	Addis Gap	E−0.5m C, w	3,304	62.1
2,116.0	Kelly Knob		4,276	63.1
2,115.1	**Deep Gap Shelter...** *8.0mS; 8.5mN*	E−0.3m S, w	3,550	64.0
2,114.0	McClure Gap	C	3,650	65.1
2,113.8	Powell Mtn		3,850	65.3
2,112.8	Moreland Gap		3,200	66.3
2,112.2	Streams	w	2,650	66.9
2,111.6	U.S. 76, Dicks Creek Gap **Hiawassee, GA 30546**	R, w (W−1.5m H, f; 3.5m H, f, cl; 11m PO, G, M, L, D, V, cl, sh, @)	2,675	67.5
2,110.5	Campsite	C, w	3,150	68.6
2,109.8	Cowart Gap		2,900	69.3
2,108.3	Bull Gap		3,690	70.8
2,107.1	**Plumorchard Gap Shelter...** *8.5mS; 7.5mN*	E−0.2m S, w	3,050	72.0
2,106.4	As Knob		3,460	72.7
2,105.8	Blue Ridge Gap		3,020	73.3
2,104.8	Campsite	C, w	3,500	74.3
2,104.6	Rich Cove Gap		3,390	74.5
2,102.7	Ga.−N.C. State Line		3,825	76.4

Springer Mountain by Van Hill

The Trail begins in Georgia at Springer Mountain and follows a rugged, often rocky terrain, reaching a height of more than 4,461 feet and never dipping below 2,500 feet. It passes through five major gaps and more than 25 smaller ones. Thru-hikers starting their journey in March or April will probably see snow, which can add to the difficulty. Spring melts give way to many of the wildflowers common throughout the mountains, including bloodroot, trillium, and azalea. Forests are mostly second-growth hardwoods of hickory, oak, and poplar.

Georgia Appalachian Trail Club—GATC maintains the 76.5 miles from Springer Mountain to Bly Gap, just over the North Carolina line. Correspondence should be sent to GATC, P.O. Box 654, Atlanta, GA 30301; (404) 634-6495; <trails_supervisor@georgia-atclub.org>.

Chattahoochee National Forest—The Trail in Georgia winds through the Chattahoochee National Forest, created by Congress in 1936. By that time, much of the land had been laid bare from intensive timber harvesting. Today, little virgin timber remains, but the hardwoods have reestablished themselves with the help of 73 years of management and protection. Half of the Trail lies within five designated wilderness areas in the forest.

Bear problems—With the loss of habitat from development in the mountains, black bears are roaming farther in search of food. To combat this problem, the GATC and the USFS are placing bear cables for hanging food at the shelters most affected. If bear cables are not available, secure food using bear-proof techniques.

Springer Mountain—Springer has served as the A.T.'s southern terminus since 1958. Before that, Mt. Oglethorpe, to the southwest, was the southern terminus. In 1993, GATC members and the Forest Service installed a new plaque marking the Trail's southernmost blaze. The hiker register is located within the boulder on which the plaque is mounted. The origin of the mountain's name is a bit foggy. The best guess is that it was named in honor of William G. Springer, a settler who, in 1833, was appointed by the Georgia governor to implement legislation to improve conditions for North Georgia Indians. The original bronze plaque marking the southern terminus, one of three intended for road crossings, was created in 1934 by GATC member and amateur sculptor George Noble at a cost of $20—a hefty amount in those days. Warner Hall, the club's second president, served as Noble's model and coined the phrase, "A footpath for those who seek fellowship with the wilderness." That plaque was moved to the mountain in May 1959; keep an eye out for the other two plaques at road crossings along the Trail in Georgia. The overlook at the 3,782-foot summit provides views to the west—a nice sunset spot.

Springer Mountain Shelter (1993)—Sleeps 12. Privy. Near the summit, about 250 yards north of the bronze plaque, then east on a blue-blazed side trail about 200 yards. Use the designated tentpads in this heavily trafficked area, and use the food-hoist cables to discourage local bears. Water source is a spring located 80 yards on a blue-blazed trail in front of the shelter; spring may go dry in times of drought.

Stover Creek Shelter (2006)—Sleeps 16. Privy, tentpads, bear cables. The fourth incarnation, this nearby alternative to the often-crowded Springer Mountain Shelter was built in 2006. Water source is the creek. No tenting near water.

Hawk Mountain Shelter (1993)—Sleeps 12. Privy. Army Rangers from nearby Camp Frank D. Merrill use the area for training exercises and have been spotted all times of the day and night. Food-hoist cables available; bear activity often reported. Water source is located 300 yards on a blue-blazed trail behind the shelter.

Gooch Mountain Shelter (2001)—Sleeps 14. Privy. Nearly 2,000 volunteer hours were spent constructing this double-decker shelter and nearby tentpads. Additional tenting space farther north at Gooch Gap, near the old shelter site. Food-hoisting cables. Excellent water source is 100 yards behind the shelter.

Ga. 60/Woody Gap/Suches—At the gap are picnic tables and a privy. A spring is on a poorly marked side trail west of the A.T. on the northern side of the gap.
East 7 miles to *Hostel:* A.T. Hiker Hostel run by Josh and Leigh Saint, (770) 312-7342, <www.hikerhostel.com>, <hikerhostel@yahoo.com>. Bunk & B $16, private & B $38D; 5 p.m. pick-up at Woody Gap, Feb 26–Apr 29. Fuel (white gas, canister & alcohol), shuttle service (call for pick-up outside period of 2/22 to 4/25), free Internet; see Web site or contact for shuttle rates.
West 2 miles to **Suches, Ga. [P.O. ZIP 30572: M–F 7:30–11:30 & 1–4:30, Sa 7:30–11:30; (706) 747-2611].** ■ *Camping:* Two Wheels Only, (706) 747-5151, tentsite $7PP, hot showers, L 11–2 Sa, Su; D 6–8:30 F, Sa; open Apr–Oct. ■ *Groceries:* Suches General Store (short-term resupply), (706) 747-3325, Coleman fuel and alcohol by the ounce, B and L, holds UPS packages shipped to 12905 Wolf Pen Gap Rd., Suches, GA 30572. Open M–Th 7–7, F–Sa 7–8. ■ *Other services:* Don L. Pruitt, M.D., (706) 747-1421, open M–Th 9–4, walk-ins 9–11. Jim and Ruth Ann Miner, (706) 747-5434, live in town and are available if you need help. ■ *Shuttles:* Wes Wisson, (706) 747-2671; <dwisson@windstream.net>.

Jarrard Gap—A blue-blazed trail to the west leads 1 mile to USFS Lake Winfield Scott Recreation Area, which offers tentsites, showers, $12; dogs must be leashed. Lenny's Grill, hours F, Sa 4–9, Su 10:30–3; turn left at LWS entrance, and continue 1 mile.

Woods Hole Shelter (1998)—Sleeps 7. Privy. Located 0.4 mile west on a blue-blazed side trail, this "Nantahala design" shelter is named in honor of the late Tillie and Roy Wood, operators of the Woodshole Hostel near Pearisburg, Virginia. Food-hoist cables available. Water source is an unreliable spring along the trail to the shelter.

Bird Gap—From here, the Freeman Trail leads 1.7 miles around the south slope of Blood Mountain and rejoins the A.T. 1.1 miles from Neels Gap. Those who choose this blue-blazed route miss the climb to the Trail's high point in Georgia; it serves as a foul-weather route around Blood Mountain.

Slaughter Gap—Reached by a side trail (after a major relocation to restore this over-used area), tentsites have been built near Slaughter Creek to ease the load on Blood Mountain.

Blood Mountain—According to tales of the Creek and Cherokee, a battle between the two nations on the slopes of the mountain left so many dead and wounded that the ground ran red with blood, which inspired the name. Blood Mountain is the most-visited spot on the A.T. south of Clingmans Dome, and the impact of more than 40,000 visitors a year has taken its toll. Vandalism in and around the shelter has been a chronic problem. In an effort to counter visitor impact, fires have been banned along a 3.3-mile section between Slaughter Gap and Neels Gap.

Blood Mountain Shelter (1934)—Sleeps 8. Privy. Located atop the highest peak on the A.T. in Georgia (4,461 feet), this historic two-room stone structure was last refurbished in 1981. No water or firewood available; no fires permitted. Northbounders can get water from a stream 0.3 mile north of Bird Gap or on a blue-blazed side trail at Slaughter Gap, 0.9 mile from the shelter. Southbounders can get water at Neels Gap or at a spring located on the blue-blazed trail to Byron Reece Memorial, 0.2 mile from where the trail joins the A.T., 2.4 miles south of Neels Gap.

U.S. 19 & 129/Neels Gap—Mountain Crossings at Walasi-Yi Center is a full-service *Outfitter* with all stove fuels and gift shop (short-term resupply) operated by Winton Porter, (706) 745-6095; open daily 8:30–6. UPS and USPS packages held, $1 donation. Ship packages to 9710 Gainesville Hwy., Blairsville, GA 30512. ■ *Hostel:* Walasi-Yi, <www.mountaincrossings.com>, open year-round, $15PP, with shower, coin laundry, nonguest shower $3.50, pets outside. Call for possible cabin rentals (available by reservation), up to 8 people (2 minimum), $30 PP. ■ *Shuttles:* Tom Bazemore, (706) 265-9454; "Cool Breeze," (813) 470-9777.

East 0.3 mile to *Lodging:* Blood Mountain Cabins, (800) 284-6866, <www.blood-mountain.com>. Cabins with showers, kitchens, and satellite TV sleep 4; thru-hiker rate $60, no pets. A trail leads from the Walasi-Yi Center to the resort office.

West 3 miles to *Camping:* Vogel State Park, (800) 864-7275, <www.gastateparks.org>. Tentsites with shower $12–$23, showers only $3. Other park services include a camp store (short-term resupply), coin laundry (detergent 75¢), and rental cabins; reservations are suggested for tentsites and cabins. Leash dogs inside the park.

West 3.5 miles to *Lodging:* Goose Creek Cabins, (706) 745-5111, <www.goose-creekcabins.com>. Owners Keith and Retter Bailey offer free shuttles from Neels Gap with cabin or tentsite rental. Special hiker rates for cabin begin at $25PP; dogs permitted. Tentsites with shower, $10PP. Amenities include laundry ($5/load), CATV, WiFi, and shuttles to a nearby restaurant each evening. UPS packages can be shipped to Goose Creek Cabins, 7061 U.S. 19/129S, Blairsville, GA 30512; <goose-creek@alltel.net>.

Whitley Gap Shelter (1974)—Sleeps 6. Privy. This shelter is located 1.2 miles east of the A.T. down a steep side trail. Food-hoist cables available. Water source is a spring 0.3 mile behind the shelter.

Low Gap Shelter (1953)—Sleeps 7. Privy. Food-hoist cables available. Water source is crossed at the shelter; a second source can be found 30 yards in front of the shelter.

Chattahoochee Gap—A blue-blazed side trail leads east to Chattahoochee Spring, source of the Chattahoochee River, which supplies drinking water to Atlanta and almost half of the state's population. Some 500 miles from this point, the river empties into the Gulf of Mexico. Springs rising on the other side of the continental divide flow to the Tennessee River and eventually to the Mississippi.

Blue Mountain Shelter (1988)—Sleeps 7. Privy. Located on a short side trail, this shelter is notorious for cold north winds that blow up Blue Mountain from the gap below. Food-hoist cables available. Water source is a spring on the A.T. 0.1 mile south of the shelter.

Ga. 75/Unicoi Gap—East 9 miles to **Helen, Ga. [P.O. ZIP 30545: M–F 9–5, Sa 9–12; (706) 878-2422]**, Georgia's "Gatlinburg." The town's year-round population of 300 can play host to as many as 30,000 people in a day, so there are many motels and restaurants from which to choose. A good place to start in town is the visitors center, found behind the post office, which has a map and free phone from which to call motels to find the best rates. Rates vary greatly according to season but are generally at their lowest Jan–Mar. Expect rates to increase after Apr 1 and on the weekends and for Oktoberfest (held early Sep–Oct). Retail shops abound as well. ■ *Lodging:* Hofbrau Riverfront Hotel, (800) 830-3977, $80–125, small pets $17.25, ATM, B, microwave, refrigerator; Helendorf River Inn, (800) 445-2271, $75, coin laundry, detergent $1, dogs $10, B, heated pool; Econolodge, (706) 878-8000, $50–$159, $10EAP, B, pets under 8 lbs. in selected rooms $20; Super 8 Motel, (800) 535-1251, next to laundromat, hiker rates ($35s) exclude weekends, B, microwave, refrigerator, no pets, WiFi, Internet access, heated pool; Best Western, (800) 435-3642, $45, WiFi, hot B, no pets, free possible shuttles to Trail M–F; Motel 6, (706) 878-8888, $28–$60,

$6EAP, pets allowed; Ramada Limited, (706) 878-1451, $50–$179D, B, no pets; Quality Inn, (706) 878-2268, $39–$69, $10EAP, B, pets under 20 lbs. $10, WiFi, possible shuttle to Trail; Days Inn, (706) 878-4079, $39–$149D, B, pets $10 and less than 25 lbs. in limited rooms; RiverBend, (706) 878-2155, hiker rate $39–$69, $10EAP, cabins up to 4 people $99–250, pets $12.50; Rodeway Inn, (706) 878-2141, $30–$60 in off-season, $10EAP, pets less than 15 lbs. $12.50, heavier $15, B; Helen accommodations, <www.helenga.org>. ■ *Groceries:* Betty's Country Store and Deli (long-term resupply), open daily 7–8. ■ *Restaurants:* numerous. ■ *Internet access:* White County Library, Helen Branch. ■ *Other services:* bicycle rentals available at Woody's Mountain Bikes, (706) 878-3715; pharmacy. ■ *Shuttles:* Mall Shuttle Transport Service, (706) 219-1653.

East 17 miles to *Medical:* Cleveland, Ga., Neighborhood Health Care, (706) 865-1234, M–F 8:15–5.

West 1.3 miles, then left 2.5 miles on Ga. 180 to *Lodging:* Enota Mountain Retreat, (800) 990-8869, <www.enota.com>; waterfalls, organic gardens, and an animal sanctuary; $10 membership per visit and $5 campfire fee; tentsites $20, bunkhouse $25, cabins $100–$165, dogs $5. Amenities include free long-distance phone, coin laundry with soap, B 8–10:30 with advance notice, L/D, satellite TV, video library, Internet access, Jacuzzis in some cabins, massage 1½ hours $100, possible shuttle to Trail for fee. General store (short-term resupply) open 8:30–8, including Coleman, alcohol, and canister fuels. Enota holds packages, for guests only, mailed to 1000 Hwy. 180, Hiawassee, GA 30546.

Cheese Factory Site—In the mid-1800s, an eccentric New Englander established a dairy near Tray Mountain, about 15 miles from the nearest farmhouse. Other Georgians, who received parcels in the mountains after a government survey of former Indian lands in the 1830s, opted to sell their land to speculators rather than attempt to tame the untamable. For several years, the man ran his dairy successfully and reportedly produced a superior cheese that won several awards at state agricultural fairs. Little evidence of the dairy remains today, although the spot is a designated campsite with a spring.

Tray Mountain—Spectacular views from the 4,430-foot summit and probably the southernmost breeding area in the United States for Canada warblers. These small, active songbirds may be spotted in the rhododendron thickets along the southern approach to the summit. Males are blue-gray above and yellow throughout the chest. Look for the distinctive "necklace" on both the males' and females' chests. The Canada warbler's song is an irregular burst of beautiful notes.

Tray Mountain Shelter (1971)—Sleeps 7. Privy. Food-hoist cables. Excellent overnight spot for taking in the sunset and sunrise from the summit or from viewpoints along the 0.2-mile trail to the shelter. Water source is a spring located 260 yards behind the shelter.

Deep Gap Shelter (1983)—Sleeps 12. Privy. Food-hoist cables. Shelter is designed like the Springer Mountain Shelter and located on a 0.3-mile side trail to the east. Water source is on the blue-blazed trail to the shelter.

 U.S. 76/Dicks Creek Gap/Hiawassee—At road are parking lot, picnic tables, and small creek.

West 3.5 miles to *Hostel:* Blueberry Patch Hiker Hostel, a Christian ministry owned by '91 thru-hiker Gary Poteat and his wife, Lennie. Look for the Blueberry Patch sign on the left side of the highway as you descend from Dicks Creek Gap; (706) 896-4893. Evenings are the best time to reach the Poteats. If you can't reach them, keep trying; they cannot return long-distance calls. Open Feb 15–May 1. Hostel remains open by generosity of hiker donations. Includes shower, laundry service, B, and shuttle back to the Trail at 9:30 a.m. Bunks for 7 with accommodations for up to 10. Please arrive no earlier than 10 a.m. and no later than 6 p.m. Coleman fuel by the ounce. The Poteats hold UPS and USPS packages mailed to 5038 U.S. Hwy. 76, Hiawassee, GA 30546. NO pets, alcohol, drugs, or tobacco products.

West 11 miles to **Hiawassee, Ga. [P.O. ZIP 30546: M–F 8:30–5:30, Sa 8:30–12; (706) 896-3632].** ■ *Lodging:* Mull's Motel, (706) 896-4195, $55 and up, holds packages for guests only, no dogs, 213 N. Main St., Hiawassee, GA 30546; Hiawassee Inn, (706) 896-4121, $39.95D, $5EAP each, tent set-up with shower $10, one evening restaurant shuttle, laundry with detergent $3, shower only $3, free shuttle from/to Trail at Dicks Creek or Unicoi gaps Mar–Apr only, $5 per person other months, holds UPS packages only for guests, 193 East Main St., Hiawassee, GA 30546; Holiday Inn Express, <www.hiexpress.com/hiawasseega>, (706) 896-8884, special hiker rates of $69–$120, $6EAP, no pets, B included, coin laundry with free detergent, indoor whirlpool, free bicycle use, possible shuttle to Trail for a fee, Internet access, will hold UPS packages, 300 Big Sky Dr., Hiawassee, GA 30546. ■ *Groceries:* Dill's Food City, Ingles, both long-term resupply. ■ *Restaurants:* Georgia Mountain Restaurant, B only on weekends, L/D; Shoney's, AYCE buffet, B/L/D (about one mile from the town center); Subway; China Grill AYCE; Dairy Queen; Monte Alban Mexican, L/D; Daniel's Steakhouse, L/D AYCE; Corner Café; Huddle House; Smoke Rings BBQ; various other fast-food places. ■ *Internet access:* Towns County Public Library. ■ *Other services:* Western Union; coin laundry; Chatuge Regional Hospital, (706) 896-2222, known for treatment of blisters; Open Door Clinic on Thursdays, (706) 896-6241, 120 River St., fee based on income; pharmacy; dentist; banks with ATM; hardware store; Hiawassee Animal Hospital, (706) 896-4173. ■ *Shuttles:* Hiawassee Inn, (706) 896-4121.

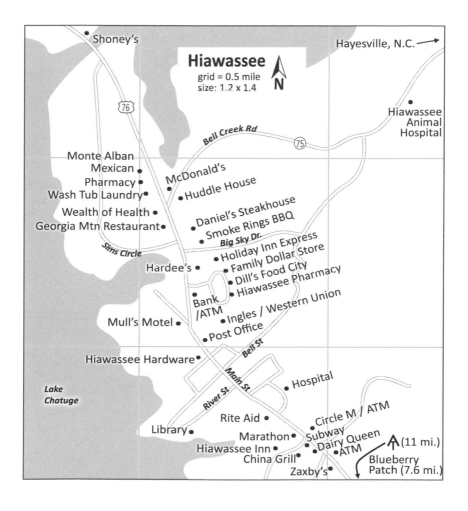

Plumorchard Gap Shelter (1993)—Sleeps 14. Privy. The stump in front of the shelter has been a residence of copperhead snakes. Water source is a creek that crosses the trail to the shelter or a spring located 200 yards west of the A.T., opposite the shelter trail. Food-hoisting cables.

Bly Gap—If you are thru-hiking, it is time to celebrate your first (or last) state line. When you see the gnarled oak in a clearing, you're officially in North Carolina. The gap, with its grassy area and views to the northwest, makes a good campsite. Water can be obtained from a spring about 100 yards south on the A.T.

North Carolina

Miles from Katahdin	Features	Services	Elev.	Miles from Springer
2,102.7	N.C.-Ga. State Line		3,825	76.4
2,102.6	Bly Gap	C, w	3,840	76.5
2,100.7	Sassafras Gap		4,300	78.4
2,099.8	**Muskrat Creek Shelter...** *7.5mS; 4.9mN*	S, w	4,600	79.3
2,099.0	Whiteoak Stamp		4,620	80.1
2,098.8	Chunky Gal Trail		4,700	80.3
2,097.9	Watcroak Gap		4,490	81.2
2,095.8	Deep Gap, USFS 71, Kimsey Creek Trail	R, w (W–3.7m C, G, sh)	4,341	83.3
2,094.9	**Standing Indian Shelter...** *4.9mS; 7.6mN*	S, w	4,760	84.2
2,093.4	Lower Trail Ridge Trail, Standing Indian Mtn	(E–0.2m summit) (W–0.2m w)	5,498	85.7
2,090.5	Beech Gap	C, w	4,460	88.6
2,087.7	Timber Ridge Trail		4,700	91.4
2,087.3	**Carter Gap Shelter...** *7.6mS; 6.8mN*	S, w	4,540	91.8
2,083.6	Betty Creek Gap	C, w	4,300	95.5
2,082.7	Mooncy Gap, USFS 83	R	4,400	96.4
2,082.5	Spring	w	4,500	96.6
2,081.4	Bearpen Trail, USFS 67	R	4,790	97.7
2,081.1	Albert Mtn		5,250	98.0
2,080.5	**Big Spring Shelter...** *6.8mS; 5.3mN*	S, w	4,940	98.6
2,077.7	Glassmine Gap		4,160	101.4
2,075.2	**Rock Gap Shelter...** *5.3mS; 8mN*	S, w	3,760	103.9
2,075.1	Rock Gap; Wasilik Poplar; Standing Indian Campground	R (W–1.5m C, G, sh)	3,750	104.0
2,074.5	Wallace Gap, Old U.S. 64	R	3,738	104.6
2,071.4	Winding Stair Gap, U.S. 64 **Franklin, NC 28734**	R, w (W–10m PO, G, M, L, O, D, V, cl, f, @)	3,770	107.7
2,070.5	Campsite	C, w	3,970	108.6

Miles from Katahdin	Features	Services	Elev.	Miles from Springer
2,070.3	Swinging Lick Gap		4,100	108.8
2,069.4	Panther Gap		4,480	109.7
2,067.7	**Siler Bald Shelter**... *8mS; 7.88mN*	E–0.5m S, w	4,600	111.4
2,065.5	Wayah Gap, S.R. 1310	R	4,180	113.6
2,063.7	USFS 69	R, w	4,900	115.4
2,063.2	Wine Spring	C, w	5,290	115.9
2,061.3	Wayah Bald	R	5,342	117.8
2,060.9	Campsite	C, w	5,200	118.2
2,060.4	**Wayah Shelter**... *7.8mS, 4.8mN*	Sw		118.7
2,059.1	Licklog Gap	W–0.5m w	4,440	120.0
2,056.8	Burningtown Gap, S.R. 1397	R	4,236	122.3
2,055.6	**Cold Spring Shelter**... *4.8mS; 5.8mN*	C, S, w	4,920	123.5
2,054.9	Copper Ridge Bald Lookout		5,080	124.2
2,053.7	Trail to Rocky Bald Lookout		5,030	125.4
2,053.4	Spring	w	4,900	125.7
2,052.0	Tellico Gap, S.R. 1365	R	3,850	127.1
2,050.6	Wesser Bald Observation Tower		4,627	128.5
2,049.9	Spring	w	4,100	129.2
2,049.8	Wesser Creek Trail, **Wesser Bald Shelter**... *5.8mS; 4.9mN*	C, S, w	4,115	129.3
2,048.2	Jump-up Lookout		4,000	130.9
2,044.9	**A. Rufus Morgan Shelter**... *4.9mS; 7.7mN*	S, w	2,300	134.2
2,044.1	U.S. 19, U.S. 74, Nantahala River, Nantahala Outdoor Center, Wesser, N.C. **Bryson City, NC 28713**	R, G, L, M, O, cl, sh, f (E–1m C, G, L; 13m PO, G, M, L, D, cl) (S–1m C, sh)	1,723	135.0
2,042.5	Wright Gap	R	2,390	136.6
2,041.0	Grassy Gap		3,050	138.1
2,038.1	Swim Bald		4,710	141.0
2,037.2	**Sassafras Gap Shelter**... *7.7mS; 9.1mN*	S, w	4,330	141.9

Miles from Katahdin	Features	Services	Elev.	Miles from Springer
2,036.0	Cheoah Bald		5,062	143.1
2,033.6	Locust Cove Gap	C, w	3,690	145.5
2,032.6	Simp Gap		3,700	146.5
2,030.5	Stecoah Gap, N.C. 143	R, w	3,165	148.6
2,029.5	Sweetwater Gap		3,270	149.6
2,028.1	**Brown Fork Gap Shelter...** *9.1mS; 6.1mN*	S, w	3,800	151.0
2,027.9	Brown Fork Gap		3,600	151.2
2,026.1	Hogback Gap		3,540	153.0
2,025.3	Cody Gap	C, w	3,600	153.8
2,022.9	Yellow Creek Gap, S.R. 1242 (Yellow Crk Mtn Rd)	R	2,980	156.2
2,022.0	**Cable Gap Shelter...** *6.1mS; 6.6mN*	S, w	2,880	157.1
2,020.6	Black Gum Gap		3,490	158.5
2,019.2	Walker Gap, Yellow Creek Trail	W–2.5m PO, G, L, M, O, cl, f	3,450	159.9
2,019.0	Campsite	C, w	3,200	160.1
2,016.5	N.C. 28 **Fontana Dam, NC 28733**	R (E–0.6m L, f, @) (W–1.8m PO, G, L, M, O, cl, f)	1,810	162.6
2,015.4	**Fontana Dam Shelter...** *6.6mS; 11.3mN*	R, S, w	1,775	163.7
2,015.1	Fontana Dam Visitor Ctr	R, sh, w	1,700	164.0

At Bly Gap, northbounders enter the Nantahala National Forest with 4,000-foot gaps and 5,000-foot peaks. Nantahala is Cherokee for "land of the noonday sun." Long climbs between the Stecoah–Cheoah Mountain area and Cheoah Bald offer panoramic views of western North Carolina. Don't rush; enjoy the landscape from an observation tower or two. Take a pit stop at the NOC playground on the Nantahala River for some food and a rafting trip.

Nantahala Hiking Club—NHC maintains the 58.5 miles between Bly Gap and the Nantahala River. Correspondence should be sent to NHC, 173 Carl Slagle Rd., Franklin, NC 28734; <www.maconcommunity.org/nhc/>.

No road access to the A.T. is available between Bly Gap and Rock Gap during Jan, Feb, and part of Mar. The Forest Service closes USFS 71 to all vehicular traffic until Mar 1 and USFS 67 until Mar 15. Frequently used Trailheads at Deep Gap, and others, are inaccessible.

Muskrat Creek Shelter (rebuilt 1995)—Sleeps 8. Moldering privy. Birthplace of "The Old Pros," a legendary backpacking group that included Ron Tipton (now SVP of the National Parks Conservation Association), Dave Sherman (retired from the Forest Service Washington lands office), and the late Ed Garvey. This shelter uses the "Nantahala design." Water source is just south and visible from the shelter.

Deep Gap—From here, the Kimsey Creek Trail leads 3.7 miles to the Forest Service's Standing Indian Campground (see next page).

Standing Indian Shelter (1996)—Sleeps 8. Privy. "Nantahala design" shelter east of the A.T. Water source is a stream opposite the side trail to the shelter. Recent bear sightings; _use bear-proofing techniques._

Standing Indian Mountain—The 5,498-foot summit of the mountain 0.2 mile east is reached _via_ a blue-blazed side trail. Cliff-top views to the south gave it the nickname, "Grandstand of the Southern Appalachians." According to Cherokee legend, a great winged monster once inhabited the mountain, and, during the monster's reign, warriors were posted on the mountain as lookouts. As the story goes, a tremendous bolt of lightning shattered the mountain and killed the monster. During the strike, a lone Cherokee sentinel was hit by the bolt and turned into stone, supposedly for being a poor sentry. Remnants of the stone "Standing Indian" are visible today. At the top are flat areas for camping and views south toward Blood Mountain. A spring is located 0.2 mile downhill on an unmarked trail near the A.T. junction with Lower Trail Ridge Trail. Please tread lightly if you choose to camp here; the area receives tremendous use.

Carter Gap Shelter (1959 old/1998 new)—Two shelters, the old and the new. Old shelter sleeps 6; new shelter sleeps 8. Privy. The new shelter uses the "Nantahala design." Water source is a spring located downhill behind the old shelter, on the west side of the Trail.

Mooney Gap—This gap has been identified as among the wettest places in the eastern U.S., with an estimated annual precipitation of 93.5 inches.

Big Spring Shelter (1959)—Sleeps 8. Privy. Food-hoist cables available. Water source is Big Spring, behind and to the left of the shelter.

Rock Gap Shelter (1965)—Sleeps 8. Privy. Located only 0.5 mile from the road. Food-hoist cables available. Water source is a spring to the left and behind the shelter.

Rock Gap/Standing Indian Campground—West 1.5 miles on a paved road to the Forest Service campground with tentsites $16, restroom, warm showers ($2 shower only), and pay phone; small campstore open Memorial Day–Nov 30; opens according to weather but usually weekend before Easter. *Note: Closed for construction until May 1, 2010.*

Wasilik Poplar—At Rock Gap, a blue-blazed side trail leads **East** 0.5 mile to the second-largest poplar tree in the United States, now dead. In 1996, the tree measured 27 feet in circumference, 8.6 feet in diameter, and 125.5 feet in height (to a broken-off top). In the early 1900s, when logging companies began cutting the timber in this area, workers cut down another poplar similar in size to the Wasilik. However, its weight so badly strained the oxen transporting the tree the lumberjacks decided against harvesting this one.

U.S. 64/Winding Stair Gap—East 10 miles to **Franklin, N.C. [P.O. ZIP 28734: M–F 8:45–12 & 1:15–5, Sa 8:30–10; (828) 524-3219].** Although a bit spread out, most major services are within walking distance along Business U.S. 441; <www.franklinchamber.com>. ■ *Lodging:* Franklin Motel, (800) 433-5507, $39.99S/D, $5EAP, microwave, refrigerator, will hold packages for guests, 17 West Palmer St., fuel by the ounce, laundry including detergent $3, pets allowed $10, shuttle list available; Haven's Budget Inn, (828) 524-4403, <tiamalle@aol.com>, $39.99S/D $5EAP, free a.m. Mar–Apr shuttle to town (donations accepted), outfitter, and Trail, pets welcome with $50 deposit/pet, in-room phone, free local calls, laundry room with free detergent, Internet access, will hold packages, 433 E. Palmer St.; Microtel Inn & Suites, (828) 349-9000, $40–$54, pets allowed free, free long-distance phone (U.S.), B, Internet access, has a local shuttle list. ■ *Groceries:* Ingles Supermarket (long-term resupply). ■ *Restaurants:* Shoney's, AYCE; Cody's Roadhouse; Huddle House; Rathskeller Snack, Lunch and Coffee Shop, Tu–Th 11–7, F–Sa 11–11, Internet access; and various other restaurants. ■ *Outfitter:* Three Eagles Outfitters, (828) 524-9061, open M–Sa 10–6, Su 12–4, full-service outfitter; Coleman and alcohol fuel by the ounce, Esbit and canisters; will ship and hold packages, 78 Siler Rd., 1 Three Eagles Place. ■ *Internet access:* Macon County Library, Rathskeller. ■ *Other services:* UPS Store,

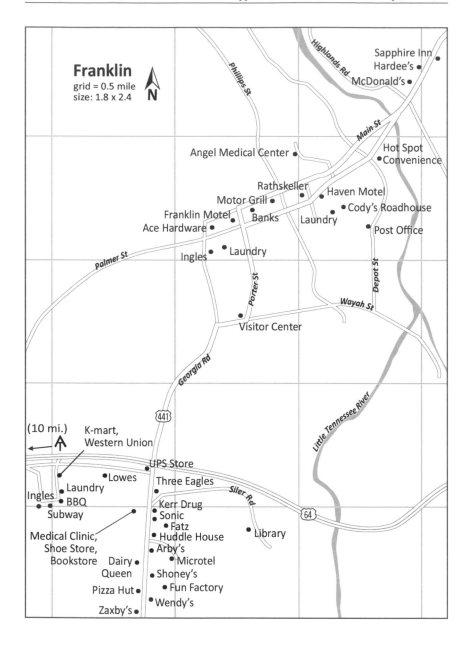

Franklin
grid = 0.5 mile
size: 1.8 x 2.4 **N**

Highlands Rd
Phillips St
Main St

Sapphire Inn
Hardee's
McDonald's

Angel Medical Center
Hot Spot
Convenience

Rathskeller
Motor Grill
Franklin Motel
Ace Hardware
Banks
Haven Motel
Cody's Roadhouse
Laundry
Post Office

Palmer St
Ingles
Laundry
Porter St
Depot St
Wayah St

Visitor Center

Georgia Rd

Little Tennessee River

(10 mi.)
K-mart,
Western Union

441

UPS Store

Lowes
Three Eagles
Ingles
Laundry
BBQ
Subway
Siler Rd
64

Kerr Drug
Sonic
Fatz
Huddle House
Arby's
Microtel
Shoney's
Fun Factory
Wendy's
Library

Medical Clinic,
Shoe Store,
Bookstore
Dairy
Queen
Pizza Hut
Zaxby's

(828) 524-9800, M–F 8–6, Sa 9–1; coin laundry; cobbler; hospital; Angel Urgent Care Center, (828) 369-4427, M–F 8–6, Sa–Su 10–4; pharmacy; veterinarian; banks with ATM; City Taxi, (828) 369-5042 until 6 p.m., after 6 p.m. by appointment; visitors center, (866) 372-5546, M–Sa 9–5. ■ *Shuttles:* Roadrunner Driving Services, (706) 201-7719, <where2@mac.com>.

Siler Bald Shelter (1959)—Sleeps 8. Privy. Located 0.5 mile on a blue-blazed loop. Food-hoist cables available. Water source is 80 yards down a blue-blazed trail from the shelter.

Wayah Bald—John B. Byrne Memorial Tower. The stone observation tower at the summit of Wayah Bald (5,342 ft.) was built in 1937 by the CCC and renovated in 1983. Byrne was the supervisor of the Nantahala National Forest who first proposed the route of the Appalachian Trail in this area. Wayah is Cherokee for "wolf."

Wayah Shelter (2007)—Nantahala-type shelter sleeps 8 with overhang for cooking shelves and seating. Privy. Five tentsites and fire ring near shelter. Water source is Little Laurel Creek, 600 feet west of A.T. on blue-blazed trail. This shelter was built by NHC in memory of Ann and Larry McDuff, thru-hikers and ALDHA members who were killed about a year apart in eerily similar accidents, hit by vehicles while riding bikes near home.

Cold Spring Shelter (1933)—Sleeps 6. Privy. Food-hoist cables available. Shelter built by the CCC. Tentsites are reached *via* a trail on the east side of the Trail 200 yards north on the A.T. Water source is 5 yards in front of the shelter.

Wesser Bald—Formerly a fire tower, the structure atop Wesser Bald is now an observation deck offering panoramic views. The Great Smoky Mountains and Fontana Lake dominate the view to the north.

Wesser Bald Shelter (1994)—Sleeps 8. No privy. This was the first of the "Nantahala design" shelters. Food-hoist cables available. Tentsites available in clearing where the blue-blaze heads to the shelter. Water source is a spring 0.1 mile south on the A.T., then 75 yards on a blue-blazed trail.

Rufus Morgan Shelter (rebuilt 1989)—Sleeps 6. No privy. Located in a small cove, this shelter is named after the Nantahala club's founder. The water source is a stream across the A.T. from the shelter.

U.S. 19/Nantahala River/Nantahala Outdoor Center—At U.S. 19, the A.T. passes through the Nantahala Outdoor Center (NOC), (828) 488-2175 or (800) 232-7238, <www.noc.com>, an outdoor-adventure center with many services for backpackers; call ahead for shuttles. Between the store and River's End Restaurant, the A.T. crosses a pedestrian bridge over the Nantahala River. ■ *Lodging:* NOC, office hours Sep–Apr 8–5, May–Aug 8–9; after hours, go to Base Camp (behind Relia's Garden Restaurant), a winterized hostel that may be full on weekends, $17 for bunk space; motel rooms $44–$94. NOC Nantahala Inn, $59–$99, satellite TV, pets in two rooms only, cabins $99–$379 with free cleaning. ■ *Groceries:* Wesser General Store (short-term resupply), M–F 8 a.m.–10 p.m., Sa–Su 11–11. ■ *Restaurants:* River's End Restaurant (8–7) serves B/L/D; Relia's Garden and Sloe Joe's Café, L until 4 (outdoors), open seasonally. ■ *Outfitter:* NOC Outfitters (short-term resupply), 8–8, offers backpacking gear, Coleman and alcohol fuel by the ounce, Esbit and canisters, ATM, stamps, laundry detergent, ATC publications. Pay phone, coin laundry with detergent by the scoop during office hours, restroom, and shower with towel $2 (except with bunkroom) are located on the southern side of U.S. 19. NOC accepts USPS, UPS, and FedEx packages sent to 13077 Hwy. 19W, Bryson City, NC 28713. Check with the front desk; packages must be marked "Hold for A.T. Hiker." NOC can ship packages; extra charge on weekends.

South 1 mile to *Camping:* Lost Mine Campground, (828) 488-6445, across from NOC on Silvermine Road, sites $16 Apr–Oct, showers, pay phone, dogs on leash.

East 1 mile to *Groceries:* Nantahala Food Mart with ATM (short-term resupply), daily 7 a.m.–9 p.m. ■ *Lodging:* Carolina Outfitters Cottages, (800) 468-7238, <www. carolinaoutfitters.com>, check-in at Nantahala Food Mart, $50D, $10EAP, kitchen, satellite TV, no pets, shuttle to/from Trail. ■ *Camping:* Nantahala Wesser Campground, (828) 488-8708, located near Nantahala Food Market on Wesser Rd; turn right at gem-mine sign; tentsite $7PP, showers, open Apr–Oct.

East 13 miles on U.S. 19 to **Bryson City, N.C. [P.O. ZIP 28713: M–F 8:30–12 & 12:30–4, closed Sa; (828) 488-3481].** Bryson City is a large town with many services, including Ingles Supermarket (long-term resupply), pharmacy, coin laundry, several restaurants, banks with ATM, Western Union, hospital, and several hotels.

Whitewater Rafting—The Nantahala marks the northbounder's first chance at Trailside whitewater rafting. The French Broad River in Hot Springs, N.C., and the Nolichucky River in Erwin, Tenn., are also whitewater hot-spots. Guided tours on the Nantahala are available through NOC for about $25 on nonpeak days, but you can rent a raft or "ducky" for less, with shuttles to the put-in point upstream included. Mountain biking and horseback riding also available.

Smoky Mountains Hiking Club—SMHC maintains the 101 miles between the Nantahala River and Davenport Gap. Correspondence should be sent to the SMHC, P.O. Box 1454, Knoxville, TN 37901; <www.smhclub.org>.

Sassafras Gap Shelter (2002)—Sleeps 14. Privy. Located in a ravine 100 yards in on a blue-blazed side trail, this wood-framed shelter features a covered porch and benches. Water source is a reliable spring in front of the shelter.

N.C. 143/Stecoah Gap—A good spring can be found by following the paved road west 200 feet to an overgrown logging road. Spring is located down the logging road on the left.

Brown Fork Gap Shelter (1996)—Sleeps 6. Privy. Constructed by the SMHC, Konnarock Crew, and the USFS. Water source is a reliable spring to the right of the shelter.

Cable Gap Shelter (1939/1988)—Sleeps 6. Privy. Shelter originally built by the CCC. The water source is a reliable spring in front of the shelter.

Walker Gap—The Yellow Creek Trail leads 2.5 miles west to Fontana Village. However, it is a poorly marked, difficult short-cut to the resort.

N.C. 28/Fontana Dam—East 6 miles to *Lodging:* The Hike Inn, (828) 479-3677, <www.thehikeinn.com>, <hikeinn@graham.main.nc.us>. A hikers-only inn, owned and operated by Jeff and Nancy Hoch. Open Feb 15–July 10, Sep 1–Dec 1, other dates by reservation only. For pick-up, continue north on the A.T. to the Fontana Dam Visitors Center (see below), and call from the pay phone. Thru-hikers, call from NOC or Hot Springs for reservations. Five rooms with max 2 per room. No credit cards. Thru-hiker/long-distance-hiker package reservations required (check in by 4 p.m., check-out 9 a.m. firm), $60s, $75D. Rate includes shuttle to and from dam, one load of laundry, evening shuttle to Robbinsville (5–7 p.m.) for dinner and supplies. Section-hikers, $40s/D (room only). Packages accepted for guests only c/o Hike Inn, 3204 Fontana Rd., Fontana Dam, NC 28733. Shuttles, slack-pack, Coleman and alcohol fuel.

West 2 miles to Fontana Village Resort. **Fontana Dam, N.C. [P.O. ZIP 28733: M–F 8:30–12 & 12:30–4:30, closed Sa; (828) 498-2315],** is located 2 miles from Fontana Dam within the Fontana Village Resort. *Please note: Some services may close or be under* *reduced hours during off-season, and supplies are limited; most services available by Apr 1.* Constructed in 1946 for TVA workers building Fontana Dam, the village is now a seasonal recreational area and resort using many of the original buildings. ■ *Lodging:* Fontana Lodge, <www.fontanavillage.com>, (800) 849-2258, $69D, EAP up to 4 no charge; cabins also available, Apr–Oct $99 & up, Nov–Mar $59 & up. ■ *Groceries:* Fontana General Store (short-term resupply). ■ *Outfitter:* Hazel Creek Outfitter, limited hiker gear and all stove fuels, shuttles available. ■ *Other services:* restaurant, ATM, Internet access, coin laundry, detergent available at outfitters 50¢, ice cream/soda fountain (open in May), mountain-bike rentals, and fitness center. Shuttle to and from Fontana Marina for $3; dial 265 from the boat-dock house phone. Backcountry permits available.

Fontana Dam Shelter (1982)—Sleeps 24. Restroom with showers and water located at shelter. Known as the "Fontana Hilton," this spacious shelter is located 0.3 mile south of the dam on TVA land. Pay phone and shower facilities are located at the dam; see below.

Fontana Dam—At 480 feet, Fontana Dam is the highest dam in the eastern United States. This facility offers a visitors center with restrooms and shower that is normally open May–Nov, 9–7.

Great Smoky Mountains National Park

Miles from Katahdin	Features	Services	Elev.	Miles from Springer
2,015.1	Fontana Dam Visitors Ctr	R, sh, w	1,700	164.0
2,014.7	Little Tennessee River, Fontana Dam; southern boundary, Great Smoky Mtns. National Park	R	1,740	164.4
2,010.7	Shuckstack		3,800	168.4
2,009.5	Birch Spring Gap	C, w	3,680	169.6
2,007.2	Doe Knob		4,520	171.9
2,005.8	Ekaneetlee Gap	w	3,842	173.3
2,004.1	**Mollies Ridge Shelter**... *11.3mS; 2.5mN*	S, w	4,570	175.0
2,004.0	Devils Tater Patch		4,775	175.1
2,002.4	Little Abrams Gap		4,120	176.7
2,001.6	**Russell Field Shelter**... *2.5mS; 3.1mN*	S, w	4,360	177.5
1,998.7	Eagle Creek Trail to **Spence Field Shelter**... *3.1mS; 6.5mN*; Bote Mtn Trail	E–0.2m S, w	4,915	180.4
1,997.5	Rocky Top		5,440	181.6
1,996.9	Thunderhead (east peak)		5,527	182.2
1,996.6	Beechnut Gap	w	4,920	182.5
1,995.9	Mineral Gap		5,030	183.2
1,993.5	Sugar Tree Gap		4,435	185.6
1,992.4	**Derrick Knob Shelter**... *6.5mS; 5.5mN*	S, w	4,880	186.7
1,992.2	Sams Gap	w	4,995	186.9
1,989.6	Buckeye Gap	w	4,817	189.5
1,986.9	**Silers Bald Shelter**... *5.5mS; 1.7mN*	S, w	5,460	192.2
1,986.7	Silers Bald		5,607	192.4
1,985.2	**Double Spring Gap Shelter**... *1.7mS; 6.8mN*	S, w	5,505	193.9
1,982.7	Clingmans Dome	E–0.5m R, w	6,643	196.4
1,981.1	Mt. Love		6,446	198.0

Miles from Katahdin	Features	Services	Elev.	Miles from Springer
1,978.9	**Mt. Collins Shelter...** *6.8mS; 8mN*	W–0.5m S, w	5,870	200.2
1,976.1	Indian Gap	R	5,286	203.0
1,974.4	U.S. 441, Newfound Gap **Gatlinburg, TN 37738**	R, w (W–15m PO, G, L, M, O, D, f) (E–18m PO, G, L, M, D, f)	5,045	204.7
1,971.7	Boulevard Trail to Mt. LeConte	W–5m L, M	5,695	207.4
1,971.4	**Icewater Spring Shelter...** *8mS; 7.8mN*	S, w	5,920	207.7
1,970.6	Charlies Bunion		5,905	208.5
1,968.6	Porters Gap, The Sawteeth		5,577	210.5
1,965.3	Bradley's View		5,200	213.8
1,964.0	**Peck's Corner Shelter...** *7.8mS; 5.6mN*	w (E–0.4m S, w)	5,280	215.1
1,961.3	Mt. Sequoyah		6,069	217.8
1,959.8	Mt. Chapman		6,417	219.3
1,958.8	**Tri-Corner Knob Shelter...** *5.6mS; 7.7mN*	S, w	5,920	220.3
1,957.6	Guyot Spur		6,360	221.5
1,957.0	Guyot Spring	w	6,150	222.1
1,956.9	Mt. Guyot Side Trail		6,395	222.2
1,955.0	Snake Den Ridge Trail		5,600	224.1
1,951.6	Cosby Knob		5,150	227.5
1,951.1	**Cosby Knob Shelter...** *7.7mS; 7.1mN*	S, w	4,700	228.0
1,948.3	Side Trail to Mt. Cammerer Fire Tower	W–0.6m	5,000	230.8
1,947.8	Spring	w	4,300	231.3
1,946.2	Spring	w	3,700	232.9
1,944.0	**Davenport Gap Shelter...** *7.1mS; 10.7mN*	S, w	2,600	235.1
1,943.1	Davenport Gap, Tenn. 32, N.C. 284; eastern boundary, Great Smoky Mtns. National Park	R (E–1.3m Ranger Station; 2.3m C)	1,975	236.0

Established in 1934, the Smokies is the most visited of the traditional national parks; for this reason, it is especially important to practice Leave No Trace in this area. The highest elevation on the A.T. is here at Clingmans Dome at 6,643 feet. The Smokies also has the most rainfall and snowfall on the A.T. in the South, and many hikers are caught off-guard by the snow and cold temperatures that the high elevation means. On the other hand, extreme drought in 2007 left many water sources extraordinarily low or dry.

Great Smoky Mountains National Park—<www.nps.gov/grsm>. The Trail through the park officially begins for northbounders on the northern side of Fontana Dam; for southbounders, Davenport Gap is the beginning. In recent years, the park has hosted more than nine million visitors annually. Home to the most diverse forest in North America, the park includes more than 100 species of trees, 1,570 species of flowering plants, 60 species of mammals, more than 25 different salamanders, and 2,000 varieties of mushrooms.

Seasonal and temporary closures can be found at <www.nps.gov/grsm>.

Backcountry Permits—Backcountry permits must be obtained before entering the park. A self-registration facility is located near the pay phone at the Fontana Dam visitors center (page 30). Forms and a deposit box are also available at the "Fontana Hilton" for northbounders. Southbounders—if you do not get a permit at Bluff Mountain Outfitters in Hot Springs, you must trek 1.3 miles east on Tenn. 32 from Davenport Gap to the park's Big Creek Ranger Station. Section-hikers (considered to be anyone not beginning and ending a hike 50 miles outside the park) can make reservations by calling the GSMNP Reservations Office at (865) 436-1231. Anyone caught without a permit will be issued a $125 ticket!

Human Waste and Privies—In past years, the park's administration shunned privies at backcountry facilities. Instead, "toilet areas" were designated where backpackers are supposed to dig cat holes and bury their waste. In the 1990s, a privy-building campaign, underwritten by ATC and SMHC, resulted in new facilities at the more heavily used shelters. Although privies mainly provide an aesthetically acceptable way to deal with many hikers' refusal to use proper Leave No Trace methods, they are costly to maintain and a management last resort. The best decision is to do your business away from the shelter area before you get to camp or after you leave. Pick a spot far from any trails and 200 feet or more from any water, and practice Leave No Trace methods.

Horses—Within the park, half of the A.T. is open to horseback riding; horse users may also share A.T. shelters. SMHC and ATC have made a concerted effort to resolve issues with the horse users, who have helped with major rehabilitation and other projects along the Trail in that half.

Bears—Between 400 and 600 bears reside in the park. They become more active in the early spring and remain active through the fall. Following a few simple guidelines can help keep bears and other animals away from people and safe within the park. Be sure to hang food on the provided bear-bag system, and do not feed or leave food for these wild creatures to eat. Many shelters no longer have chain-link fences to keep bears out. Whenever possible, eat away from the shelters.

Dogs—Dogs are not permitted on trails in the park. Hikers violating this rule will be fined up to $500. Those hiking with dogs should arrange to board their pets. Several kennels provide this service. Contact Standing Bear Farm Hiker Hostel, (423) 487-0014, <curtisvown@gmail.com>, for its details. Loving Care Kennels, (865) 453-2028, in Pigeon Forge, Tenn.; owner Lida O'Neill will pick up and drop off your dog at Fontana Dam and Davenport Gap for $250 for one dog, $400 for two dogs. Rippling Water Kennels, <www.ripplingwaterkennel.com>, (828) 488-2091, will pick up, board, and deliver pets for $250, up to 7 days; $50 deposit, reservations necessary.

Pests and Disease—At Clingmans Dome and throughout the park, you will witness changes in the Smokies' ecosystem. The most obvious has been the death of conifers at higher elevations. Atmospheric pollution weakens the trees, which makes it easier for the balsam woolly adelgid to attack and eventually kill the park's Fraser firs. The small, waxy insects attack the firs, which then overreact to the feeding aldegids, clogging their own transport tissues. Trees die within five years of infestation. Other pests and diseases affecting the park's ecosystem include chestnut blight, southern pine beetle, hemlock woolly adelgid, and dogwood anthracnose.

Air Pollution—This is one of the Smokies' most conspicuous problems. Pollution can drop visibility from 93 to 22 miles on an otherwise clear day. Ironically, this effect enhances sunset colors. Along with sulfur, nitrogen provides the basis for acid deposition, which includes acid rain. Ozone can make breathing difficult and causes visible damage to black cherry, milkweed, and thirty other species of plants in the park. The park's ozone, nitrogen, and sulfur levels are among the nation's highest and often remain high longer than in nearby urban communities.

Shelter Renovation/Replacement—The SMHC and the ATC are working to rebuild or replace all the shelters in the Smokies. Work has been completed at Double Spring Gap, Mollies Ridge, Spence Field, Derrick Knob, Silers Bald, Icewater Springs, Pecks Corner, Tricorner Knob, Cosby Knob, and Davenport Gap shelters. To improve shelter sanitation, the rebuilt shelters do not have chain-link fencing separating shelter users from park wildlife. Keep a clean camp!

Shelter Policy—Park regulations require that you stay in a shelter. While other backpackers must make reservations to use backcountry shelters, thru-hikers are exempt from this regulation, and, from Mar 15 to Jun 15, four spaces at each A.T. shelter are reserved for thru-hikers. If the shelter is occupied by reservation and four thru-hikers, however, additional thru-hikers should tent close by and use the bear cables. Because only thru-hikers are permitted to tent-camp at shelters, the burden is on them to make room inside shelters for others who have reserved space.

Shelters South of Newfound Gap—Seven shelters and a campsite are located between the Little Tennessee River (Fontana Dam) and Newfound Gap.

Birch Spring Campsite—Former shelter site with water, bear cables, and tentpads.

Mollies Ridge Shelter (1961/2003)—Sleeps 12. No privy. Food-hoist cables available. Legend says the area was named for a Cherokee maiden who froze to death looking for a lost hunter and that her ghost still haunts the ridge. Water source is a somewhat reliable spring 200 yards to the right of the shelter.

Russell Field Shelter (1961)—Sleeps 14. No privy. This section of Trail is popular with riders. Food-hoist cables available. Water source is a spring 150 yards down the Russell Field Trail toward Cades Cove. A short walk beyond the spring is an open, grassy area with views into Cades Cove; the Russell Gregory family grazed stock here in the 1800s.

Spence Field Shelter (1963/2005)—Sleeps 12. Privy. Shelter is located 0.2 mile east on the Eagle Creek Trail. Food-hoist cables available. This section of Trail is popular with riders and bears. Spence Field, to the north of the shelter, offers azaleas, blueberries, and open views into North Carolina and Tennessee from the largest grassy bald in the Smokies. James Spence cleared 100 acres here in the 1830s for cattle grazing. Water source is a reliable spring 150 yards down the Eagle Creek Trail.

Derrick Knob Shelter (1961)—Sleeps 12. No privy. Food-hoist cables available. Water source is a reliable spring near the shelter.

Silers Bald Shelter (1961/2001)—Sleeps 12. No privy. Food-hoist cables available. Named for Jesse Siler, who once grazed stock here. The increasingly overgrown bald 0.3 mile north of the shelter offers views of Clingmans Dome and sunsets over Cove Mountain. Water source is to the right; a trail leads 75 yards to a reliable spring.

Double Spring Gap Shelter (1963)—Sleeps 12. Privy. Food-hoist cables available. Two unfortunate hikers were killed by lightning inside this shelter in 1980. Gap was named to indicate the existence of two springs, one on each side of the state line and both now unreliable. The better water source is on the North Carolina side, 15 yards from the crest; second source is on the Tennessee side, 35 yards from the crest.

Clingmans Dome—At 6,643 feet, this is the highest point on the A.T. There are no feet-on-the-ground views from the tree-clad summit, but the observation tower provides 360-degree views. The summit is usually busy; a park road leads to within 0.5 mile of the tower. Restroom and water are available near the day-hiker parking lot. From here to the northern end of the park, Fraser firs and red spruce are now dying *en masse*—a dramatic change from the southernmost 30 miles of the park.

Mt. Collins Shelter (1960)—Sleeps 12. Privy. Food-hoist cables available. Nestled in spruce thicket, this mountain is named for Robert Collins, who guided geographer Arnold Guyot's explorations in the Smokies in the 1850s. Water source is a small spring 200 yards beyond the shelter on the Sugarland Mountain Trail.

U.S. 441/Newfound Gap—The only road crossing along the Trail in the Smokies. Great Smoky Mountain National Park shuttle, (828) 497-5296, makes regularly scheduled stops at Newfound Gap, Gatlinburg, Tenn., and Cherokee, N. C. (May–Dec); hiker drop-off/pick-up at any GSMNP pull-over by arrangement; $12 round-trip cash or travelers checks, $7 one-way; purchase tickets from driver or at welcome center on Tsali Blvd./U.S. 441N. A North Carolina state grant to the Cherokee makes the shuttle possible.

    East 18 miles to **Cherokee, N.C., [P.O. ZIP 28719: M-F 9-4:30, Sa 10-11:30; (828) 497-3891]**, <www.cherokee-nc.com>, home of the Eastern Band of the Cherokee and its reservation, with more than 40 motels and most major services. Attractions include the Museum of the Cherokee Indian, Unto These Hills Mountainside Theatre, and Qualia Arts & Crafts center.

West 15 miles to the resort town of **Gatlinburg, Tenn. [P.O. ZIP 37738: M–F 9–5, Sa 10–11; (865) 436-3229],** <www.gatlinburg.com>, with most major services. Most current information on hiker-friendly services is available at the Happy Hiker or Smoky Mountain Outfitters. There's plenty of traffic through Newfound Gap, with its large parking lot, shuttle (see above), and scenic overlook; usually an easy hitch into Gatlinburg. Once in town, a trolley service, Nov–Mar 10–6, Apr–Oct 8–12, takes you to most services and costs a quarter. ■ *Lodging:* Grand Prix Motel, (865) 436-4561, <www.grandprixmotel>, 235 Ski Mountain Road, Gatlinburg, TN 37738, near edge of town closest to the park, hiker rate, B, Internet access, laundry, shuttles to Trail, accepts mail drops. Nearly 100 other hotels and motels are in Gatlinburg. ■ *Restaurants:* More than 70, including Shoney's, with AYCE B and soup/salad bar, and most fast-food chains. ■ *Groceries:* Battle's Food Center and Food City (both long-term resupply). ■ *Outfitters:* The Happy Hiker, (800) HIKER01 or (865) 436-6000, <www.happyhiker.com>, open 9–5 daily, fuel and denatured alcohol by the ounce, holds packages and will ship packages for you *via* UPS or other means. Send packages to the Happy Hiker, 905 River Rd., Suite 5, Gatlinburg, TN 37738. To get to the Happy Hiker, turn left at the first stop light as you enter town, then walk one block to the small shopping center. Smoky Mountain Outfitters, (865) 430-2267, 9–6 M–Sa, 9–5 Su, canister fuel, white gas, and denatured alcohol by the ounce, holds mail drops, 453 Brookside Village Way, Gatlinburg, TN 37738. Take the "blue trolley" to Winery Square. ■ *Other services:* Banks with ATM, doctor. ■ *Dog shuttle/kennel:* A Walk in the Woods, <www.awalkinthewoods.com>, (865) 436-8283, dog-shuttling and boarding.

Boulevard Trail—This side trail, located 2.7 miles north of Newfound Gap, leads 5 miles to the summit of Mt. LeConte. A shelter and LeConte Lodge, (865) 429-5704, <www.lecontelodge.com>, are located at the top (reservations required; $116PP includes B/D). The 10-mile round-trip to this spectacular mountain may be worth it, if you have the time.

Shelters North of Newfound Gap—GSMNP has five shelters between Newfound Gap and Davenport Gap.

Icewater Spring Shelter (1963/1999)—Sleeps 12. Privy. Food-hoist cables available. Water source for this heavily used shelter is 50 yards north on the A.T.

Charlies Bunion—Views of Mt. LeConte to the west. It got its name on a hike in 1929, when Charlie Conner and Horace Kephart, an A.T. pioneer and famed writer/conservationist of the period, discovered this feature, created by a landslide after a disastrous rain the same year. The two decided the rocky outcropping stuck out like a bunion on Charlie's foot. The narrow path was blasted out by the Park Service.

Pecks Corner Shelter (1958/2000)—Sleeps 12. Privy. Food-hoist cables available. Follow the Hughes Ridge Trail 0.4 mile to a junction with the side trail to the shelter. This shelter gets its name from a corner marker for two state land grants to the Peck family. Water source is in front of the shelter 50 yards.

Tri-Corner Knob Shelter (1961/2004)—Sleeps 12. Privy. Located on the North Carolina side of the A.T., this is the most remote shelter in the GSMNP. The water source for this shelter is a reliable spring 10 yards in front of the shelter. In wet weather, this shelter may be a very soggy place.

Cosby Knob Shelter (1959)—Sleeps 12. Privy. Shelter is located 100 yards east down a side trail. Food-hoist cables available. Water source is a reliable spring 35 yards downhill and in front of the shelter.

Mt. Cammerer Side Trail—This trail to the west leads 0.6 mile to the Mt. Cammerer firetower, a historic stone-and-timber structure originally built in 1939 by the CCC and rebuilt in 1994. Panoramic views from its platform.

Davenport Gap Shelter (1961/1998)—Sleeps 12. No privy. Named for William Davenport, who surveyed the state line in 1821. Your last, or first, GSMNP A.T. shelter, dubbed the "Smokies Sheraton." Water source is a spring to the left of the shelter.

Tenn. 32, N.C. 284/Davenport Gap—East 1.3 miles to Big Creek Ranger Station, (828) 486-5910, with phone and self-registration backcountry permits (southbounders—see note on page 33 about registration); 1 mile farther to the station's seasonal campsites, $12 per site, no showers. The Chestnut Branch Trail leads out from the ranger station and, in two miles, meets the A.T. one mile south of Davenport Gap Shelter.

North Carolina & Tennessee Border

Miles from Katahdin	Features	Services	Elev.	Miles from Springer
1,943.1	Davenport Gap, Tenn. 32, N.C. 284; eastern boundary, Great Smoky Mtns. National Park	R (E–1.3m Ranger Station; 2.3m C)	1,975	236.0
1,941.8	State Line Branch	C, w	1,600	237.3
1,941.6	Pigeon River	R	1,400	237.5
1,941.2	I-40	R	1,500	237.9
1,940.7	Green Corner Rd	R (W–0.1m H, G, cl, sh, f, @)	1,800	238.4
1,938.4	Painter Branch	C, w	3,100	240.7
1,937.5	Spanish Oak Gap		3,730	241.6
1,936.0	Snowbird Mtn		4,263	243.1
1,935.5	Campsite	C, w	4,100	243.6
1,933.5	Deep Gap, **Groundhog Creek Shelter**... *10.7mS; 8.4mN*	E–0.2m S, w	2,850	245.6
1,930.6	Brown Gap	R, C, w	3,500	248.5
1,927.9	Max Patch Rd; N.C. 1182	R	4,380	251.2
1,927.1	Max Patch Summit		4,629	252.0
1,925.3	**Roaring Fork Shelter**... *8.4mS; 4.9mN*	S, w	3,950	253.8
1,921.7	Lemon Gap, N.C. 1182, Tenn. 107	R	3,550	257.4
1,920.4	**Walnut Mtn Shelter**... *4.9mS; 9.9mN*	S, w	4,260	258.7
1,918.0	Bluff Mtn		4,686	261.1
1,916.4	Big Rock Spring	w	3,730	262.7
1,913.9	Garenflo Gap	R	2,500	265.2
1,910.5	**Deer Park Mtn Shelter**... *9.9mS; 14.2mN*	S, w	2,330	268.6
1,907.3	U.S. 25 & 70, N.C. 209 **Hot Springs, NC 28743**	R, PO, H, C, G, L, M, O, cl, sh, f, @	1,326	271.8
1,905.9	Lovers Leap Rock		1,820	273.2
1,904.0	Pump Gap		2,130	275.1
1,902.4	Campsite	C, w	2,490	276.7
1,901.4	U.S. 25 & 70 overpass, Tanyard Gap	R	2,270	277.7

Miles from Katahdin	Features	Services	Elev.	Miles from Springer
1,899.1	Rich Mtn Fire Tower Side Trail	C, w	3,600	280.0
1,898.0	Hurricane Gap	R	2,900	281.1
1,896.3	**Spring Mtn Shelter...** *14.2mS; 8.6mN*	S, w	3,300	282.8
1,894.8	Spring	w	3,190	284.3
1,892.6	Allen Gap, N.C. 208, Tenn. 70	R, w (Paint Creek W–350 yds)	2,234	286.5
1,891.0	Log Cabin Drive	R (W–0.7m C, L, G, sh, f, @)	2,560	288.1
1,887.7	**Little Laurel Shelter...** *8.6mS; 6.8mN*	S, w	3,620	291.4
1,886.4	Camp Creek Bald, side trail to fire tower	R	4,750	292.7
1,884.7	Spring	w	4,390	294.4
1,884.4	Blackstack Cliffs		4,420	294.7
1,883.4	Big Firescald Knob	w	4,360	295.7
1,880.9	**Jerry Cabin Shelter...** *6.8mS; 5.9mN*	S, w	4,150	298.2
1,879.0	Big Butt	C	4,750	300.1
1,877.7	Spring	w	4,480	301.4
1,877.4	Shelton Graves		4,490	301.7
1,875.0	**Flint Mtn Shelter...** *5.9mS; 8.9mN*	S, w	3,570	304.1
1,874.1	Campsite	C, w	3,400	305.0
1,872.3	Devil Fork Gap; N.C. 212	R	3,100	306.8
1,871.8	Rector Laurel Rd	R	2,960	307.3
1,869.0	Frozen Knob		4,579	310.1
1,868.4	Big Flat	C, w	4,160	310.7
1,867.4	Rice Gap	R	3,800	311.7
1,866.2	**Hogback Ridge Shelter...** *8.9mS; 10.2mN*	E–0.1m S; 0.3m w	4,255	312.9
1,865.6	High Rock		4,460	313.5
1,863.8	Sams Gap, U.S. 23, I-26	R	3,850	315.3
1,863.1	Springs	w	4,000	316.0
1,861.4	Street Gap		4,100	317.7
1,860.1	Low Gap	C, w	4,300	319.0

Miles from Katahdin	Features	Services	Elev.	Miles from Springer
1,858.1	Spring	w	4,850	321.0
1,857.3	Big Bald	(C, w N on A.T. 0.2m then W 0.3m)	5,516	321.8
1,857.0	Big Stamp	W–0.3m C, w	5,300	322.1
1,856.1	**Bald Mtn Shelter...** *10.2mS; 10.6mN*	S, w	5,100	323.0
1,855.7	Campsite	C, w	4,890	323.4
1,854.7	Little Bald		5,220	324.4
1,852.7	Whistling Gap	C, w	3,650	326.4
1,852.4	Trail to High Rocks		4,100	326.7
1,850.9	Campsite	C, w	3,490	328.2
1,850.4	Spivey Gap, U.S. 19W	R	3,200	328.7
1,849.8	Ogelsby Branch	w	3,800	329.3
1,845.7	Spring	w	3,300	333.4
1,845.5	**No Business Knob Shelter...** *10.6mS; 10.5mN*	S, w	3,180	333.6
1,843.1	Temple Hill Gap		2,850	336.0
1,839.2	Chestoa Bridge, Nolichucky River **Erwin, TN 37650**	R (W–3.8m PO, C, H, G, M, L, cl, sh, f)	1,700	339.9
1,837.9	Nolichucky River Valley	R	1,780	341.2
1,835.0	**Curley Maple Gap Shelter...** *10.5mS; 12.8mN*	S, w	3,070	344.1
1,830.9	Indian Grave Gap, Tenn. 395, N.C. 197	R (W–7m Erwin, Tenn.)	3,350	348.2
1,829.8	USFS 230	R	3,980	349.3
1,828.6	Beauty Spot		4,437	350.5
1,828.1	Beauty Spot Gap	R, C, w	4,120	351.0
1,827.1	Deep Gap	C, w	4,100	352.0
1,826.5	USFS 230	R	4,660	352.6
1,825.5	Unaka Mtn		5,180	353.6
1,825.2	Spring	w	4,750	353.9
1,826.3	Low Gap	w	3,900	352.8
1,822.2	**Cherry Gap Shelter...** *12.8mS; 9.3mN*	S, w	3,900	356.9

Miles from Katahdin	Features	Services	Elev.	Miles from Springer
1,819.1	Iron Mtn Gap, Tenn. 107, N.C. 226 **Unicoi, TN 37692**	R (E–3m G, f) (W– 4.7m G, M; 10.3m PO, G, M, D)	3,723	360.0
1,817.8	Campsite	C, w	3,950	361.3
1,814.9	Greasy Creek Gap	R (E–0.6m H, G, C, M, sh, f, @) (W– 0.2m w)	4,034	364.2
1,814.1	Campsite	C, w	4,110	365.0
1,813.0	**Clyde Smith Shelter**... *9.3mS; 6.5mN*	W–0.1m S, w	4,400	366.1
1,812.1	Little Rock Knob		4,918	367.0
1,809.9	Hughes Gap	R	4,040	369.2
1,808.1	Ash Gap	C, w	5,350	371.0
1,807.3	Trail to Roan High Bluff, Rhododendron Gardens	R, w	6,200	371.8
1,806.6	**Roan High Knob Shelter**... *6.5mS; 5mN*	S, w	6,275	372.5
1,805.1	Carvers Gap, Tenn. 143, N.C. 261	R, w	5,512	374.0
1,803.2	Trail to Grassy Ridge	E–0.5m C, w	5,770	375.9
1,801.6	**Stan Murray Shelter**... *5mS; 2mN*	S, w	5,050	377.5
1,799.9	Yellow Mtn Gap, **Overmountain Shelter**... *2mS; 9mN*	C (E–0.2m w; 0.3m S)	4,550	379.2
1,798.3	Little Hump Mtn		5,459	380.8
1,797.0	Bradley Gap	C, w	4,950	382.1
1,796.1	Hump Mtn		5,587	383.0
1,793.7	Doll Flats, N.C.–Tenn. State Line	C, w	4,600	385.4
1,791.3	Spring	w	3,060	387.8
1,791.2	**Apple House Shelter**... *9mS; 9.3mN*	S, w	3,000	387.9
1,790.7	U.S. 19E **Elk Park, NC 08622; Roan Mtn, TN 37687**	R (E–0.5m M; 2.5m PO, G, M; 9m PO, G, M, f, cl, @) (W–0.3m H, C, L, f, sh; 3.4m PO, G, M, D, V; 7.5m C)	2,895	388.4

This section has plentiful 360-degree views and ever-changing scenery flowing from rich mountain coves, boreal forests, and heath balds. Highlights are Max Patch, Big Bald, Beauty Spot, Unaka Mountain, Roan Mountain at 6,285 feet (where an annual rhododendron festival is held), and the open, grassy bald of Hump Mountain.

Carolina Mountain Club—CMC maintains the 92.7 miles between Davenport Gap and Spivey Gap. Send correspondence to CMC, P.O. Box 68, Asheville, NC 28802; <www.carolinamtnclub.com>.

Due to trailhead vandalism, the supervisor of trails for the CMC advises, "We do not recommend leaving cars at trailheads for anything more than a day trip."

Water sources—Several water sources are located between Davenport Gap and Deep Gap. State Line Branch may be polluted.

Green Corner Road—West 0.1 mile to *Hostel:* Standing Bear Farm Hiker Hostel, (423) 487-0014, <www.standingbearfarm.com>, <curtisvowen@gmail.com>; operated by Maria Guzman and Curtis Owen; $20PP cabin, $15 bunkhouse or tentsite, includes hot shower, laundry, phone, kennel services (call for details), Internet $5/hour, kitchen; campstore with enough Trail foods and supplies to get you to Hot Springs or Fontana, including stove fuels by the ounce plus cook-your-own pizzas and sand-wiches; dogs outside $5/night; shuttles available; parking $2 per day; debit and credit cards accepted; for all services without stay, donations accepted. Holds packages sent to 4255 Green Corner Rd., Hartford, TN 37753. Unclaimed parcels will go into the hiker box. *Directions:* After walking under I-40, continue north on the A.T. 1.0 mile beyond the stone stairs to the first gravel road (Green Corner Rd.), turn left, walk 200 yards to white farmhouse.

Groundhog Creek Shelter (1939)—Sleeps 6. Privy. Stone shelter located 0.2 mile on a blue-blazed side trail. Water source is a reliable spring to the left of the shelter.

Max Patch—The site of an old homestead and logging camp, Max Patch was origi-nally forested, but early inhabitants cleared the mountaintop to graze sheep and cattle. The summit also has been used as a landing strip for small planes. In 1982, the USFS purchased the 392-acre grassy-top mountain for the A.T. and now uses mowing and controlled burns to maintain its bald appearance. The wide summit, at 4,629 feet, offers panoramic views of the Smokies to the south and a glimpse of Mt. Mitchell (at 6,684 feet, the highest peak east of the Mississippi) to the east.

Roaring Fork Shelter (2005)—Sleeps 8. Privy. Two water sources, both located on the A.T., 800 ft. north and south of side trail to shelter.

Caution: Recent reports indicate problem bears are frequently visiting both the Roaring Fork and Walnut Mountain shelters and grabbing food bags hung too close to the ground. Hikers at these sites should be extra cautious and diligently follow LNT practices.

Walnut Mountain Shelter (1938)—Sleeps 6. Privy. An old shelter, with a water source located down the blue-blazed trail to the left of Rattlesnake Trail; difficult to locate, may be seasonal.

Deer Park Mountain Shelter (1938)—Sleeps 5. Privy. A former farmstead; the water source is located on the trail to the shelter.

N.C. 209/Hot Springs, N.C. [P.O. ZIP 28743: M–F 8:30–11:30 & 1–4, Sa 8:30–10:30; (828) 622-3242]. The A.T., now marked by special diamonds in the sidewalk, passes through the center of Hot Springs on Bridge Street, and most services are located on the Trail. ■ *Lodging:* Duckett House B&B, (828) 622-7621, <www.duck-etthouseinn.com>, $50PP plus tax including B and laundry ($9.50 B for nonguests; make reservation); bunkhouse $15PP plus tax, limited to 4 people, includes shower; laundry $4, includes soap; Internet access when available; work-for-stay possible; will hold UPS and FedEx packages, for reserved guests only, sent to 433 Lance Ave., Hot Springs, NC 28743. The Sunnybank Inn, (828) 622-7206, owned by Elmer Hall, located at the white Victorian house across the street from the Dollar Store; thru-hiker rates $20PP, and organic vegetarian meals, $6 B, $10 D; work exchange is possible; no tents allowed; holds packages for guests mailed to 26 Walnut St., P.O. Box 233, Hot Springs, NC 28743. Creek Ridge Camping, (828) 622-9588, <www.creekridge-camping.com>; camping, chalets, and cabins from $20; dog-friendly, $5 per dog. Alpine Court Motel, (828) 622-3231, $44S, $66D, subject to change; credit cards not accepted; no dogs permitted in rooms. Hot Springs Resort and Spa, (828) 622-7267, <www.hotspringsnc.com>, short-term resupply; thru-hiker cabin rate $50–$72, $5EAP up to 5; tentsites $5PP up to 4; shower only, $2. ■ *Groceries:* Bluff Mountain Outfitters and Hillbilly Market (both long-term resupply); L&K's Deli (short-term resupply); Hot Springs Camp Store (short-term resupply), grill with pizza, BBQ,

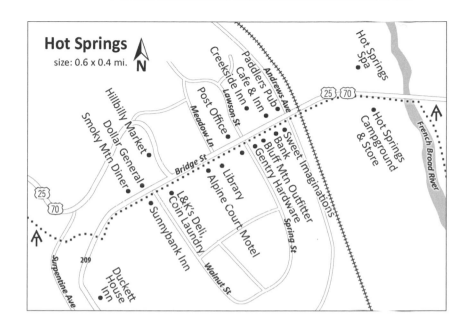

Hot Springs
size: 0.6 x 0.4 mi.

hoagies. ■ *Restaurants:* Smoky Mountain Diner, B/L/D; Rock Bottom Sports Grill, L/D, ask about lodging; Sweet Imaginations, W–Su, Mar–Nov, deli and ice cream. ■ *Outfitter:* Bluff Mountain Outfitters, (828) 622-7162, <www.bluffmountain.com>; owners, Dan Gallagher and Wayne Crosby; a full-service outfitter with fax service, ATM, Internet access, shuttle; packages can be sent to 152 Bridge St., P.O. Box 114, Hot Springs, NC 28743; ships UPS and FedEx packages. ■ *Internet access:* library, 88 Bridge St. (on A.T.), call (828) 622-3584 for hours. ■ *Other services:* coin laundry (L&K's Deli); bank; Dollar General; Gentry Hardware with Coleman fuel by the ounce; The Yellow Teapot book exchange.

Whitewater Rafting—Rafting companies offer guided trips on the French Broad River: Huck Finn River Adventures, (877) 520-4658; Nantahala Outdoor Center, (800) 232-7238; Blue Ridge Resort, (800) 303-7238.

Southbound permits for Smokies—Southbounders must have a backcountry permit before entering Great Smoky Mountains National Park (see page 33 for details). Permits can be obtained at Bluff Mountain Outfitters, (828) 622-7162, Sa–Su 9–5.

Hot Springs Spa—(828) 622-7676. At the northern end of town, on the southern bank of the French Broad River, the spa offers baths and massages at the famous therapeutic mineral baths for which the town was named. The springs were purchased in 1990 by Anne and Eugene Hicks, who developed the natural resource by adding Jacuzzi baths and piping in the 105-degree water. The springs have attracted people to the area since the late 1700s. During World War I, a detention center/prison was constructed on the spot to hold German prisoners of war, and many German-American prisoners enjoyed the springs so much that they stayed in the area after the war. During the 1800s, literature promoting the springs claimed the water could "bring vigor to a wasted frame"—just the remedy for worn-out hikers.

Spring Mountain Shelter (1938)—Sleeps 5. Privy. The shelter is located on the west side of the Trail. Water source is 75 yards down a blue-blazed trail on the east side of the A.T.

Allen Gap—Paint Creek is 350 yards west, but water quality is questionable.

Log Cabin Drive—**West** 0.7 mile to *Lodging:* Hemlock Hollow Farm Shoppe and Cabins, (423) 787-0917, <hemlockhiker@wildblue.net>, open all year. Go west for a few hundred yards on a dirt/rock road to Log Cabin Drive (gravel road). Turn left, and follow for 0.6 mile to paved Viking Mountain Rd. Shop is across the road on Chandler Circle. Free water and a.m. coffee for all hikers. Heated cabin $48D; heated bunkhouse with kitchenette $20; linens $3; tentsite $12 per tent; shower & towel and ride back to Trail included with all overnight stays; shower & towel only, $3. Campstore (short-term resupply); good variety of hiker foods, cold drinks, fresh fruit, hot soup or chili most days during spring; all types of fuel; first-aid and limited outfitter supplies. New in 2010: restaurant serving meals for guests. Hiker dogs, $2/day. Accepts mail drops at 645 Chandler Circle, Greenville, TN 37743. Will send out packages. Shuttles available. Free Internet access.

Little Laurel Shelter (1967)—Sleeps 5. Privy. Water source is 100 yards down a blue-blazed trail behind the shelter.

Jerry Cabin Shelter (1968)—Sleeps 6. Privy. Water source is on a small knoll, up a path found on the opposite side of the A.T. CMC member and honorary ALDHA life member Sam Waddle was the caretaker of this shelter and 2.9 miles of the Trail, from Round Knob to Big Butt, for 26 years until his death February 1, 2005. Sam had a good sense of humor and was responsible for a light bulb and telephone installed on the shelter wall. Sam's volunteer efforts transformed this shelter from "the dirtiest shelter on the entire Trail to one of the cleanest," according to Ed Garvey, by hauling out an estimated 20 bushels of litter. He was devoted to the A.T. and an inspiration to all volunteers who share the commitment it takes to make a difference. The electric outlet and telephone may be gone, but Sam's legacy will live forever.

Shelton Graves—North of Big Butt is the final resting place of William and David Shelton, who lived in Madison County, N.C., but enlisted in the Union army during the Civil War. While returning to a family gathering during the war, the uncle and nephew were ambushed near here and killed by Confederate troops.

Flint Mountain Shelter (1988)—Sleeps 8. Privy. Site of one of the more unusual animal encounters in Trail history. In 1994, a sleeping thru-hiker was bitten on the hand by a fox in the middle of the night, despite the presence of other hikers and two dogs. Water source is on the A.T. north of the shelter.

Hogback Ridge Shelter (1986)—Sleeps 6. Privy. Water source is a spring 0.3 mile on a side trail near the shelter.

Big Bald—True to its name, Big Bald offers 360-degree views at an elevation of 5,516 feet. From 1802 to 1834, the bald was inhabited by a cantankerous hermit named David Greer. Spurned by a woman, he retreated to the mountaintop where he lived in a small, cave-like structure (no longer visible). He declared himself sovereign of the mountain and eventually killed a man, only to be acquitted on grounds of insanity. The life of "Hog Greer," called so by the neighbors because he lived like one, ended when a local blacksmith shot him in the back; the blacksmith was never charged. Greer Bald eventually became known as Big Bald. A golf and ski resort, Wolf Laurel, is clearly visible from the summit of Big Bald. A spring and campsite can be found by following the A.T. 0.2 mile north of the summit to a dirt road and then walking west 0.3 mile down the dirt road.

Bald Mountain Shelter (1988)—Sleeps 10. Privy. This shelter is one of the highest on the A.T. (5,100 feet), and the area surrounding the shelter is too fragile for tenting. Water source is a spring located on the side trail to the shelter.

Tennessee Eastman Hiking Club—TEHC maintains the 134.8 miles between Spivey Gap and Damascus. Correspondence should be sent to TEHC, P.O. Box 511, Kingsport, TN 37662; <www.tehcc.org>.

No Business Knob Shelter (1963)—Sleeps 6. No privy. Surrounded by large Fraser magnolias and mammoth hemlocks, this concrete-block shelter was built by the Forest Service. Reliable water is found 0.2 mile south of the shelter on the A.T.

Chestoa Bridge/Erwin, Tenn. [P.O. ZIP 37650: M–F 8:30–4:45; Sa 10–12; (423) 743-9422]. *Hostel:* Nolichucky Hostel and Outfitters; owners, John and Charlotte Shores; (423) 735-0548; <www.unclejohnnys.net>, ; 151 River Road, Erwin, TN 37650; where A.T. crosses River Road. Hostel $15/night; private cabins $20–$45S, $40–$85D, group rates for 3 or more hikers; camping $8PP; showers with towel free with stay, shower without stay $3; laundry $4 load; dog-friendly; shuttles available; free Internet, WiFi, bicycles, and video library available. Outfitter store sells most normal fuel and gear. Shipments accepted addressed to 151 River Rd, Erwin, TN 37650.

West 1.3 miles to *Lodging:* 0.5 mile on River Road (best hitch), then 0.8 mile on Temple Hill Road to Holiday Inn Express, (423) 743-4100, $70D, $10EAP per night, no pets, hot B buffet, Internet in lobby, laundry, hot tub (seasonal), swimming pool, parking for section-hikers, mail drops accepted at 2002 Temple Hill Rd., Erwin, TN 37650.

West 3.8 miles on River Road (best hitch) to ■ *Lodging:* Clayton's Dogwood Inn, <www.claytonsdogwoodinn.com>, (423) 735-0093, $50S, $65D, reservations recommended, includes hot homestyle B, no pets, mail drops accepted at 430 Ohio Ave., Erwin, TN 37650; Best Southern Motel, (423) 743-6438, $35S, $39.95D, no pets, shuttles available, mail drops accepted, 1315 Jackson Love Hwy., Erwin, TN 37650; Super 8 Motel, (423) 743-0200, $49.95S, $54.95D includes B, shuttles, Internet, no pets, will accept mail drops at 1101 N. Buffalo St., Erwin, TN 37650. ■ *Camping:* Cherokee Adventures, (800) 445-7238, <www.cherokeeadventures.com>, tentsite $5PP, bunkhouse $8PP (call for availability), showers only $2, 1.4 miles west on Tenn. 81. ■ *Restaurants:* China Kitchen, Su buffet; Azteca Mexican Ristorante; El Corita Mexican Restaurant; Pizza Plus; Pizza Hut; Rocky's Pizza; Dairy Ace; Hardee's; Little Caesar's; Wendy's; McDonald's; Huddle House; Sonic Burger; River's Edge Café, L/D, Tu–Su (summer), seasonal (Nov–Mar), call (423) 743-3713 to check hours, live music on weekends, 5.5 miles from the A.T.; J.D.'s Market & Deli; Union Street Café, M–F, 11–2, 5–8 p.m. ■ *Groceries:* Food Lion, White's (2 locations), both long-

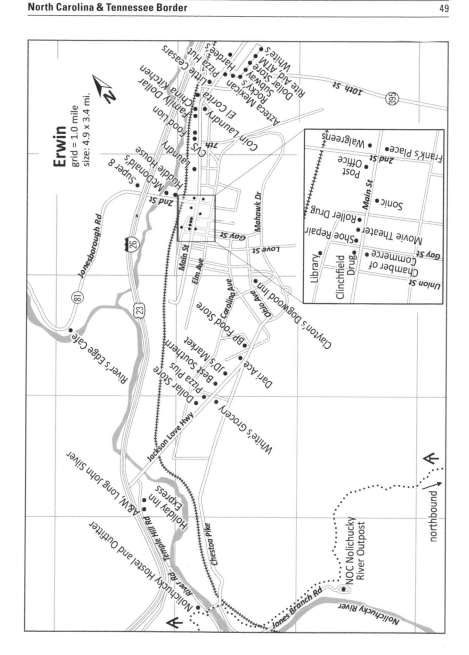

Erwin
grid = 1.0 mile
size: 4.9 x 3.4 mi.

term resupply; Dollar General (2 locations); and Family Dollar. ■ *Outfitter:* Mahoney's, (423) 282-8889, in Johnson City, 13 miles north. ■ *Internet access:* public library; Chamber of Commerce, (423) 743-3000, M–F 8–5, Sa 9–1, also has information on shuttles. ■ *Other services:* banks; ATM; barber; coin laundries; thrift stores; hardware; dentists; 24-hour emergency center; Walgreens; Walmart; shoe repair; movie theater; art gallery; veterinarian.

Whitewater Rafting—Rafting companies offer guided trips on the scenic, free-flowing Nolichucky River: NOC, (800) 232-7238; USA Raft, (800) USA-RAFT; Cherokee Adventure, (800) 445-7238; High Mountain Expeditions, (800) 262-9036; Wahoo's Adventures, (800) 444-RAFT, which also provides rafting on Watauga River near Hampton–Elizabethton.

Curley Maple Gap Shelter (1961, renovated 2009)—Sleeps 12. No privy. Water source is a spring south on the A.T.

Unaka Mountain—With a large stand of red spruce atop its 5,180-foot summit, Unaka will remind southbounders of the Maine woods. Unaka is the Cherokee word for "white." A series of 2008 relocations on the north side of Unaka Mountain, beginning 1 mile north of iron Mountain Gap and ending 0.75 mile north of the summit, added about a mile to the A.T. between Greasy Creek Gap and the summit of Unaka.

Cherry Gap Shelter (1962)—Sleeps 6. No privy. Water source is a spring found 80 yards on a blue-blazed trail from the shelter.

Tenn. 107, N.C. 226/Iron Mountain Gap—East 3 miles to *Groceries:* Buladean Shell Gas & Grocery (short-term resupply), (828) 628-4850, Su–Sa 7 a.m.–8 p.m., with made-to-order sandwiches, ice cream, and Coleman fuel.

West 10.3 miles to **Unicoi, Tenn. [P.O. ZIP 37692: M–F 8–11 & 12–4 Sa 8:30–10:30; (800) 275-8777]**, with Clarence's Restaurant B/L/D, Maple Grove Restaurant, mini-marts, and a doctor.

Greasy Creek Gap—East 0.6 mile to *Hostel:* Greasy Creek Friendly Hostel (short-term resupply), (828) 688-9948, <atrailagc@yahoo.com>; bunkhouse $10PP, one room (twin beds) $16PP, camping $7.50PP, includes shower/towel/soap for guests; nonguest shower $3; restricted kitchen privileges; shuttle, laundry, meals, ice cream, fuel, Internet; no dogs inside. Accepts mail drops sent to Greasy Creek Friendly (GCF),

1827 Greasy Creek Road, Bakerville, NC 28705. *Directions*: At sign, follow predominant old road descending to east of campsites, through service gate, to first house on right.

Clyde Smith Shelter (1976)—Sleeps 10. No privy. Water source is a spring 100 yards behind the shelter on a blue-blazed trail. Renovations include new roof and porch.

Roan Mountain—For northbounders, this will be the last time the A.T. climbs above 6,000 feet until Mt. Washington in New Hampshire. At the top is a parking area, with restroom and running water (May–Oct). Roan Mountain is arguably the coldest spot, year-round, on the southern A.T. Upon reaching the top of the main climb (for northbounders), enter a clearing, and pass the foundation of the former Cloudland Hotel. The Tennessee–North Carolina state line ran through the center of the hotel's ballroom when Cloudland was a thriving resort during the late 1800s and early 1900s. It was demolished in 1915, after loggers harvested the fir and spruce on the mountaintop. Much of the Catawba rhododendron was dug up and sold to ornamental nurseries. The remaining rhododendron flourished after the logging and quickly covered the slopes of Roan, hence the famous rhododendron gardens. The peak blooming time is usually around Jun 20. The gardens can be reached by following the Forest Service road (visible from the hotel foundation) west, uphill, along the top of the mountain, where an information station is located.

Roan High Knob Shelter (1980)—Sleeps 15. No privy. The highest shelter on the A.T. (6,275 feet). Originally an old firewarden's cabin, this shelter was rebuilt by Cherokee National Forest employees. The loft is known to leak. An unreliable water source can be found on a 100-yard, blue-blazed trail near the shelter. More reliable sources are south on the A.T. at the Roan Mountain restroom, when open, or a spring at Carvers Gap picnic area, 1.3 miles north.

Gray's lily—A protected, red, nodding lily can be found blooming on the slopes of Round Bald, Grassy Ridge, and Hump Mountain in late Jun–early Jul. The lily is named for botanist Asa Gray, who found the plant here during the 1840s. He called the Roan range, "without a doubt, the most beautiful mountain east of the Rockies."

Roan Mountain to Hump Mountain—Between Roan Mountain and Hump Mountain, the Trail crosses several balds. Round Bald (5,826 feet) is the site of a USFS experiment in which goats were used to keep briars and brambles from encroaching on the bald. Although the southern Appalachians do not rise above treeline, there are many balds, the origins of which remains a mystery to scientists. Some point to the harsh conditions at high elevations, while others claim Indians cleared the mountains for religious ceremonies. Many believe extensive grazing and cropping led to treeless summits, and still others say it's the work of spacemen. The 6,189-foot summit of Grassy Ridge is reached by following a side trail to the east before the A.T. begins its descent off the ridge to Stan Murray Shelter. It is the only natural 360-degree viewpoint above 6,000 feet near the Trail. (Clingmans Dome has its observation tower, and Mt. Washington's summit in New Hampshire is covered with numerous buildings.) To avoid potential damage to endangered species, please do *not* camp between the summit and the southern peak. For northbounders, the A.T. veers west from the North Carolina/Tennessee line into Tennessee at Doll Flats, where it remains until crossing into Virginia 3.5 miles south of Damascus.

N.C. 261/Carvers Gap—Picnic area and parking area with restrooms; piped spring beyond restrooms. North out of Carvers Gap, the Trail has been relocated with switchbacks to control erosion and heal the vivid scar of the old treadway. Please stay on the new treadway to allow this area to recover.

Stan Murray Shelter (1977)—Sleeps 6. No privy. Formerly the Roan Highlands Shelter, this shelter was renamed for the former chairman of the ATC and originator of the Appalachian Greenway concept. Water source is a spring on a blue-blazed trail opposite the shelter.

Overmountain Shelter (1983)—Sleeps 20. Privy. A large, red, converted barn once used as a backdrop for the movie "Winter People." Fires and cooking are permitted on the ground floor only. Water source is a spring found to the left once you reach the old road before the shelter. There are two separate water sources here, depending on the dryness of the year.

Apple House Shelter (1984)—Sleeps 6. No privy. Located near the road. This structure was first constructed in 1952 to store explosives for a quarry in the hollow and tools for a nearby orchard, before being rebuilt by TEHC and the Forest Service. Water source is behind the shelter.

Tennessee

Miles from Katahdin	Features	Services	Elev.	Miles from Springer
1,790.7	U.S. 19E **Elk Park, NC 08622;** **Roan Mtn, TN 37687**	R (E–0.5m M; 2.5m PO, G, M; 9m G, M, f, cl, @) (W–0.3m H, C, L, f, sh; 1m M; 3.4m PO, G, M, D, V; 7.5m C)	2,895	388.4
1,790.5	Bear Branch Rd	R	2,900	388.6
1,787.4	Buck Mtn Rd	R	3,340	391.7
1,787.1	Campbell Hollow Rd	R	3,330	392.0
1,784.3	Campsite	C, w	3,590	394.8
1,782.1	Campsite	C, w		397.0
1,781.9	**Mountaineer Shelter**... *9.3mS; 9.6mN*	S, w	3,470	397.2
1,781.1	Campsite	C, w		398.0
1,780.3	Walnut Mtn Rd	R	3,550	398.8
1,779.1	Stream		3,400	400.0
1,778.6	Viewpoint	W–0.2m H		400.5
1,778.1	Upper Laurel Fork	W–0.4m H, sh, @	3,290	401.0
1,774.2	Campsite	C, w	3,410	404.9
1,772.3	**Moreland Gap Shelter**... *9.6mS; 7.9mN*	S, w	3,815	406.8
1,771.0	White Rocks Mtn		4,206	408.1
1,770.2	Campsite	C, w		408.9
1,768.0	Trail to Coon Den Falls		2,660	411.1
1,766.3	Dennis Cove; USFS 50	R, w (E–0.3m C, G, L, cl, sh, f, @) (W–0.2m H, C, cl, sh, f)	2,550	412.8
1,765.1	Laurel Fork Falls	w	2,120	414.0
1,764.4	**Laurel Fork Shelter**... *7.9mS; 8.8mN*	S, w	2,450	414.7
1,764.1	Waycaster Spring	w		415.0
1,763.6	Side trail to U.S. 321	w (W–0.8m PO, G, M, L, D, f, @)	1,900	415.5
1,760.6	Pond Flats	C, w	3,780	418.5

Miles from Katahdin	Features	Services	Elev.	Miles from Springer
1,757.4	U.S. 321 **Hampton, TN 37658**	R (W–2m PO, G, M, L, D, f, @; 9m L, G, M, D, V, cl, @)	1,990	421.7
1,756.1	Griffith Branch	C, w	2,100	423.0
1,755.6	**Watauga Lake Shelter…** *8.8mS; 7.1mN*	S, w	2,130	423.5
1,754.5	Watauga Dam (north end)		1,915	424.6
1,753.2	Wilbur Dam Rd	R	2,250	425.9
1,750.2	Spring	w	3,400	428.9
1,748.5	**Vandeventer Shelter…** *7.1mS; 6.8mN*	S; W–0.3m w	3,620	430.6
1,744.7	Spring	w	3,900	434.4
1,743.3	Turkeypen Gap		3,840	435.8
1,741.9	Spring	w	4,000	437.2
1,741.7	**Iron Mtn Shelter…** *6.8mS; 7.6mN*	S, nw	4,125	437.4
1,740.4	Nick Grindstaff Monument		4,090	438.7
1,740.3	Spring	w		438.8
1,737.9	Stream	w		441.2
1,737.1	Tenn. 91	R	3,450	442.0
1,735.0	Campsite	C, w	3,990	444.1
1,734.1	Holston Mtn Trail, **Double Springs Shelter…** *7.6mS; 8.3mN*	S, w	4,060	445.0
1,730.6	U.S. 421, Low Gap **Shady Valley, TN 37688**	R, w (E–2.7m PO, C, G, M, f)	3,384	448.5
1,728.7	Double Spring Gap	w	3,650	450.4
1,727.3	McQueens Knob		3,900	451.8
1,726.9	McQueens Gap; USFS 69	R	3,680	452.2
1,725.8	**Abingdon Gap Shelter…** *8.3mS; 19.8mN*	S (E–0.2m w)	3,785	453.3
1,719.3	Tenn.–Va. State Line		3,302	459.8

In this 70-mile section, you will stroll along the Elk River, pass Jones and Mountaineer falls, see the impressive 50-foot Laurel Falls in the Pond Mountain Wilderness, look over the 16-mile-long Watauga Reservoir, and climb Iron Mountain.

U.S. 19E—Numerous incidents of vandalism have been reported at this parking area. Park at your own risk.

East 0.5 mile to *Restaurant:* King of the Road Restaurant and Steak House, L Su 11–3, D Th–Sa 4–9.

East 2.5 miles to **Elk Park, N.C. [P.O. ZIP 28622: M–F 7:30–12 & 1:30–4:15, Sa 7:30–11; (828) 733-5711].** ■ *Restaurant:* Times Square Diner, B/L/D, M–F L buffet 11–2 $5.90, Sa B buffet 7–12 $6.29, Su B/L 8–3; Hard Times Café and Coffee House, Tu–Sa 10–5; Betty & Carol's Place, take-out only, Tu, Th–Sa 11–8:30, W 11–6. ■ *Other services:* two small grocery stores (short-term resupply), hardware store with fuel.

East 9 miles to Newland, N.C. ■ *Restaurants:* San Dee's Restaurant; Fabio's; Papa's Pizza To Go; McDonald's; Hardee's; Subway Sandwiches & Salads. ■ *Groceries:* Ingles Food Store, Lowe's Food Store (both long-term resupply). ■ *Internet access:* library. ■ *Other services:* CVS pharmacy, Avery Hardware (sells fuel), coin laundry.

West 0.3 mile to *Lodging:* Mountain Harbour B&B and Hostel, 9151 Highway 19-E, Roan Mountain, TN 37687; (866) 772-9494; <www.mountainharbour.net>. Hostel overlooking creek above barn $18PP, semiprivate king bed $35, includes linens, shower, towels, full kitchen, wood burning stove, video library. Tenting with shower $8; shower only, with towels, $3; laundry $5, includes soap; phone available with calling card; fuel by ounce. B $9 during peak season, min. 4 person if not guests at B&B. Local town shuttle, $5 flat rate during stay. Slackpack & long-distance shuttles available; reservations suggested for long distance. Parking $2/day with shuttle or $5/day without. Mail drops free for guests, nonguest $5. USPS/UPS/FedEx. All B&B rooms include a/c, refrigerator, cable TV/DVD, and B; double bed $80, king $95; one suite with 4-poster California king, 2-person Jacuzzi tub, separate shower & fireplace, $135. Open year-round.

West to *Restaurants:* 1.0 mile to Highlander BBQ, W–F 11–2, 5–8, Sa 11–8, Su 11–6; 2.0 miles to Frank & Marty's, pizza/subs Tu W Sa 4–9, Th–F 11–9, closed Su–M. *Other services:* 2.4 miles, Dollar General.

West 3.4 miles to **Roan Mountain, Tenn. [P.O. ZIP 37687: M–F 8:15–11:30 & 12:30–4:15, Sa 8:15–11; (423) 772-3014].** ■ *Restaurants:* Mad Martha's Café, Tu–Sa 11–5; Bob's Dairyland, M–Sa 6 a.m.–8 p.m., Su 8–3; Snack Shack & Pizza, M–Sa 11–8; Subway, Su–Sa 10–10. ■ *Other services:* several small grocery stores (long-term resupply); bank with ATM; pharmacy; medical center, open M–F; veterinarian.

West 7.5 miles to *Camping:* Roan Mountain State Park on Tenn. 143, (423) 772-0190; campground with showers, $11 primitive campsite, $20–$25 for campsites with water and electricity, $95–$114 for cabins; visitors center and swimming pool.

Mountaineer Shelter (2006)—Sleeps 14. No privy. Water source 200 feet on blue-blaze. Constructed by the 6th annual Hard Core Trail Days volunteer crew led by Trail steward Bob Peoples and the TEHCC.

Trail to Abby's Place—On A.T. 2.0 miles north of gravel Walnut Mountain Road, look for bent-over tree bench beside tree with green/white A.T. sign, take path south 0.3 mile under powerline. Alternately, about 0.5 mile north on the A.T., just beyond signed Laurel Fork bridge, follow blue-blazed trail along creek 0.4 mile to Abby's Place, (423) 772-3450. Open Mar 15 for thru-hikers; donation $5 first night, $10/night afterward; heated bunkroom sleeps 8; misc. hiker-food resupply, beverages; Internet access; satellite TV; library; shower $3; wash $3, dryer $3, free clothesline; no deliveries, mail drops; pets allowed if leashed; secure parking, $1/day; quiet hours, 10 p.m.–8 a.m.

Moreland Gap Shelter (1960)—Sleeps 6. No privy. Water source is 0.2 mile down the hollow across from the shelter. Northwest exposure; wet during storms.

Dennis Cove Road/USFS 50—East 0.3 mile to *Lodging:* Laurel Fork Lodge, <lclodge@usit.net>, <www.laurelforklodge.com>, short-term resupply, (423) 725-5988; self-registration day or night; tentsite $5 two tents/site, bunkhouse $6, hostel cabin $12PP up to six people, private cabin $25PP up to three people; shower only without stay $2, laundry $2.50; fully equipped hiker kitchen area, frozen pizzas and burgers, cold sodas and ice cream, limited camping supplies, Coleman and denatured alcohol by the ounce, pay phone, free Internet, free coffee at 8 a.m., mail drops accepted addressed to Laurel Fork Lodge, 1511 Dennis Cove Rd., Hampton, TN 37658. No shuttles.

West 0.2 mile to *Hostel:* the never-closed Kincora Hiking Hostel, (423) 725-4409, with bunkroom, showers, tentsites, cooking facilities, laundry, Coleman and denatured alcohol by the ounce, phone, shuttles to Hampton (other shuttles need to be arranged), $4/night suggested donation; owner Bob Peoples holds packages for hikers mailed to 1278 Dennis Cove Rd., Hampton, TN 37658.

Laurel Fork Shelter (1977)—Sleeps 8. No privy. Constructed from native rocks, this shelter is located on the blue-blazed high-water route above the Laurel Fork. Water source is a stream found 50 yards behind the shelter.

U.S. 321—West 2 miles to **Hampton, Tenn. [P.O. ZIP 37658: M–F 7:30–11:30 & 12:30–4:30, Sa 8–10; (423) 725-2177].** ■ *Lodging:* Braemar Castle Hostel and Guest House, (423) 725-2411 or 725-2262. The Braemar Castle was constructed to house the offices and company store for the Pittsburgh Lumber Company, which operated in the Laurel Gorge area from 1909 until 1925. Sutton and Beverly Brown (Sutton's grandfather owned Braemar Castle) offer hiker space, kitchen, and showers for $15PP; private rooms, $20S $40D. Iron Mountain Inn B&B, (423) 768-2446 or (888) 781-2399, <www.ironmountaininn.com>; private room and bath $100, includes B. Lake House, <www.wataugalakecabin.com>, $100PP (hiker rate). Creekside Chalet, <www.creeksidechalet.net>, $75PP includes hot tub on deck, pet-friendly, call from Hampton for pick-up, packages held addressed c/o Woods, 138 Moreland Dr., Butler, TN 37640. ■ *Groceries:* Brown's Grocery, (423) 725-2411, long-term resupply, closed Su; check with Sutton at the grocery store for accommodations and shuttles; Coleman fuel and denatured alcohol; holds USPS and UPS packages addressed to Brown's Grocery, 613 Hwy. 321, Hampton, TN 37658. ■ *Other services:* TS Internet Café ($5 an hour, $3 half-hour), restaurants, market, convenience stores, health clinic, banks, and ATM. ■ *Shuttles:* Hampton Trails Bicycle Shop, (423) 725-5000, owner Brian White, <www.hamptontrails.com>, <hamptontrails@embarqmail. com>. *Note: The best access to Hampton from the A.T. is the 0.8-mile blue blazed trail in Laurel Gorge, two miles downstream from Laurel Falls.*

West 9 miles to Elizabethton, Tenn. ■ *Lodging:* Travelers Inn, (423) 543-3344, Su–Th $54.99D, F–Sa $59.99D includes continental B; Americourt Hotel, (423) 542-4466, <americourthotel@yahoo.com>, located on the U.S. 19E bypass, $59 hiker rate. ■ *Groceries:* Big G Supermarket (long-term resupply). ■ *Internet access:* library. ■ *Other services:* restaurants, convenience stores, doctor, bank, veterinarian, laundry, and ATM.

Shook Branch Recreation Area—This developed area on Watauga Lake offers picnic tables, restroom, water that is turned on after the last freeze of spring (usually by late Apr), and a beach for swimming.

Watauga Lake Shelter (1980)—Sleeps 6. No privy. A wooden structure on the shore of Watauga Lake. Water source is on A.T., south of the shelter.

Watauga Dam—The A.T. crosses the Watauga River on this dam at Watauga Lake. A visitors center with restroom, often closed during cold-weather months, can be reached by following Wilbur Lake Road 0.9 mile east. This TVA dam, completed in 1948, displaced about 700 people living along the river banks. All told, TVA dams in the South displaced nearly 75,000 people from their homes. The trade-off was flood control, electricity, jobs, and recreational opportunities.

Vandeventer Shelter (1961)—Sleeps 6. No privy. Water source is 0.3 mile down a steep, blue-blazed trail south of the shelter.

Iron Mountain Shelter (1960)—Sleeps 6. No privy. Water source is a spring 500 yards south on the A.T.

Nick Grindstaff Monument—Nick Grindstaff traveled west to win his fortune but was robbed of all his money during the journey. He then returned to Iron Mountain, where he lived for more than 40 years, becoming one of the region's most famous hermits. He died in 1923, and the plaque on the chimney was erected in 1925.

Double Springs Shelter (1960)—Sleeps 6. No privy. Water source is a spring located 100 yards in the draw beyond the shelter.

U.S. 421/Low Gap—A piped spring is located in the gap, on the A.T. **East** 2.7 miles to **Shady Valley, Tenn. [P.O. ZIP 37688: M–F 7:30–11 & 12–3:30, Sa 7:30–9:30; (423) 739-2173].** ■ *Groceries:* Shady Valley Country Store & Deli, (423) 739-2325, <www.shadyvalleycountrystore.com>, daily 6–9, short-term resupply, Coleman fuel, camping $10. Shady Valley General Store & Museum, (423) 739-2040, daily 6–9, short-term resupply, Coleman fuel. ■ *Restaurant:* Raceway, (423) 739-2499, B/L/D, open every day, call for hours.

Queens Knob Shelter (1934)—Sleeps 4. No privy. This shelter was the first on Holston Mountain on the A.T. and is one of the A.T.'s oldest shelters. Not up to current standards, it is intended *for emergency use only,* and, even then, the un-chinked walls allow for the weather to easily enter. No water at this site.

Abingdon Gap Shelter (1959)—Sleeps 5. No privy. Water source is a spring 0.2 mile east on a steep, blue-blazed side trail, downhill behind the shelter.

Tennessee/Virginia State Line—Although there is no official state-line marker, you'll know you're entering or leaving Virginia when you see the Mt. Rogers National Recreation Area sign.

Virginia—Part 1 (Southwest)

Miles from Katahdin	Features	Services	Elev.	Miles from Springer
1,719.3	Va.–Tenn. State Line		3,302	459.8
1,717.7	Spring	w	2,600	461.4
1,715.6	U.S. 58 **Damascus, VA 24236**	R, PO, H, G, L, M, O, D, cl, sh, f, @ (W–2m V; 12m G, L, M, O, V)	1,928	463.5
1,714.5	U.S. 58, Va. 91, Virginia Creeper Trail	R	1,928	464.6
1,712.1	Iron Mtn Trail, Feathercamp Ridge		2,850	467.0
1,710.7	Beech Grove Trail			468.4
1,710.0	U.S. 58, Straight Branch, Feathercamp Branch	R, w	2,200	469.1
1,708.7	Stream	w	2,490	470.4
1,708.0	Taylors Valley Side Trail		2,850	471.1
1,706.5	Straight Mtn		3,500	472.6
1,706.2	**Saunders Shelter**... *19.8mS; 6.6mN*	W–0.2m S, w	3,310	472.9
1,703.9	Beartree Gap Trail	W–0.6m C, w, sh	3,050	475.2
1,703.8	Campsite	C, w	3,020	475.3
1,702.0	Va. 728, Creek Jct	R	2,720	477.1
1,701.6	Virginia Creeper Trail, Whitetop Laurel Creek		2,690	477.5
1,701.0	Va. 859, Grassy Ridge Rd	R	2,900	478.1
1,700.8	Spring	w		478.3
1,699.8	**Lost Mtn Shelter**... *6.6mS; 12.2mN*	S, w	3,360	479.3
1,698.7	U.S. 58; Summit Cut, Va.	R	3,160	480.4
1,698.4	Campsites, stream	C, w		480.7
1,697.5	Va. 601 (Beech Mtn Rd)	R, w	3,600	481.6
1,695.0	Buzzard Rock, Whitetop Mtn		5,080	484.1
1,694.5	Spring	w	5,100	484.6
1,694.3	Whitetop Mtn Rd (USFS 89)	R, C, w	5,150	484.8
1,691.8	Va. 600, Elk Garden	R	4,434	487.3
1,689.8	Deep Gap	E–0.2m w	4,900	489.3

Miles from Katahdin	Features	Services	Elev.	Miles from Springer
1,688.0	Side trail to Mt. Rogers		5,490	491.1
1,687.6	**Thomas Knob Shelter**... *12.2mS; 5.1mN*	S, w	5,400	491.5
1,686.8	Rhododendron Gap		5,440	492.3
1,685.5	Wilburn Ridge		4,900	493.6
1,684.7	Service road to Massie Gap	E–2m C, G, sh	4,800	494.4
1,682.5	Grayson Highlands State Park, Wilson Creek Trail, **Wise Shelter**... *5.1mS; 5.9mN*	S, w (E–2m C, G, sh)	4,460	496.6
1,682.2	Big Wilson Creek	C, w	4,300	496.9
1,681.2	Spring	w	4,610	497.9
1,680.0	Stone Mtn		4,820	499.1
1,678.0	The Scales			499.4
1,678.3	Pine Mtn		5,000	500.8
1,676.6	**Old Orchard Shelter**... *5.9mS; 5.0mN*	S, w	4,050	502.5
1,674.9	Va. 603, Fox Creek	R, C, w on A.T.	3,480	504.2
1,672.9	Hurricane Mtn		4,320	506.2
1,672.6	Iron Mtn Trail, Chestnut Flats		4,240	506.5
1,671.6	**Hurricane Mtn Shelter**... *5.0mS; 9.1mN*	S, w	4,300	507.5
1,671.0	Barton Gap Trail			508.1
1,670.2	Stream	w	3,000	508.9
1,668.5	Hurricane Campground Trail	W–0.5m C, w, sh	3,090	510.6
1,667.6	Comers Creek, Comers Creek Falls Trail	w	3,100	511.5
1,666.4	Va. 650, Va. 16, Dickey Gap **Troutdale, VA 24378**	R (E–2.6m PO, H, G, M, D)	3,300	512.7
1,664.9	Campsite, spring	E–0.2m C, w	3,570	514.2
1,664.3	High Point		4,040	514.8
1,662.5	**Trimpi Shelter**... *9.1mS; 10.6mN*	S, w	2,900	516.6
1,661.0	Va. 672	R	2,700	518.1
1,659.7	Va. 670, South Fork Holston River	R	2,450	519.4

Miles from Katahdin	Features	Services	Elev.	Miles from Springer
1,655.9	Va. 601	R	3,250	523.2
1,651.9	**Partnership Shelter...** *10.6mS; 7.1mN*	S, w, sh	3,360	527.2
1,651.8	Va. 16, Mt. Rogers NRA Headquarters **Sugar Grove, VA 24375; Marion, VA 24354**	R (E–3.2m PO, G, L, M, f) (W–6m PO, G, M, L, cl)	3,220	527.3
1,651.1	Va. 622	R	3,270	528.0
1,650.6	Brushy Mtn		3,600	528.5
1,648.1	Locust Mtn		3,900	531.0
1,647.7	USFS 86	R, C, w	3,650	531.4
1,646.8	Glade Mtn		3,900	532.3
1,644.8	**Chatfield Shelter...** *7.1mS; 18.5mN*	S, w	3,150	534.3
1,644.5	USFS 644	R	3,100	534.6
1,643.0	Va. 615, Settlers Museum	R	2,650	536.1
1,642.5	Va. 729	R	2,700	536.6
1,640.3	Va. 683, U.S. 11, I-81 **Atkins, VA 24311; Marion, VA 24354**	R, G, M, L, sh, f, cl, H (E–6m H) (W– 3.2m PO, G, M, cl; 10.2m PO, G, M, L, cl)	2,420	538.8
1,639.2	Va. 617	R	2,580	539.9
1,638.5	Spring	E–50yds w	2,610	540.6
1,637.6	Davis Path Campsite	C, nw	2,840	541.5
1,635.1	Gullion (Little Brushy) Mtn		3,300	544.0
1,634.0	Crawfish Valley along Reed Creek	w on A.T. (E–0.3m C, w)	2,600	545.1
1,632.3	Tilson Gap, Big Walker Mtn		3,500	546.8
1,630.9	Va. 610	R	2,700	548.2
1,628.5	Va. 42	R (E–0.2m w)	2,650	550.6
1,627.6	Brushy Mtn		3,200	551.5
1,626.3	**Knot Maul Branch Shelter...** *18.5mS; 9mN*	S, nw	2,880	552.8
1,626.2	Spring	w	2,810	552.9
1,625.2	Lynn Camp Creek	w	2,400	553.9

Miles from Katahdin	Features	Services	Elev.	Miles from Springer
1,624.4	Lynn Camp Mtn		3,000	554.7
1,621.0	USFS 222	R	2,380	558.1
1,619.1	Spring–fed pond	w	3,800	560.0
1,617.3	**Chestnut Knob Shelter**... *9mS; 10mN*	S, nw	4,409	561.8
1,616.0	Walker Gap	R, w	3,520	563.1
1,611.1	Va. 623, Garden Mtn	R	3,880	568.0
1,610.3	Davis Farm Campsite	W–0.5m C, w	3,850	568.8
1,607.3	**Jenkins Shelter**... *10mS; 14.3mN*	S, w	2,500	571.8
1,603.1	Brushy Mtn		3,080	576.0
1,602.5	Va. 615, Laurel Creek	R, C, w	2,450	576.6
1,595.6	U.S. 21/52 **Bland, VA 24315; Bastian, VA 24314**	R (E–2.7m PO, G, L, M, D, @; 3.3m G, L, M) (W–2.5m PO; 3.5m D)	2,900	583.5
1,595.4	I-77 Crossing	R	2,750	583.7
1,594.8	Va. 612, Kimberling Creek	R, w	2,700	584.3
1,593.3	**Helveys Mill Shelter**... *14.3mS; 10.1mN*	E–0.3m S, w	3,090	585.8
1,586.6	Va. 611	R	2,820	592.5
1,585.2	Brushy Mtn		3,101	593.9
1,583.5	**Jenny Knob Shelter**... *10.1mS; 14.2mN*	S, w	2,800	595.6
1,582.3	Va. 608, Crandon	R	2,200	596.8
1,579.0	Brushy Mtn		2,900	600.1
1,577.1	Kimberling Creek suspension bridge		2,090	602.0
1,577.0	Va. 606	R (W–0.5m C, G, M, sh, f)	2,100	602.1
1,575.1	Dismal Creek Falls Trail	W–0.3m to falls	2,320	604.0
1,571.2	Ribble Trail, south jct; White Pine Horse Campground	W–0.5m C, w	2,400	607.9
1,570.8	Stream	w	2,500	608.3
1,569.3	**Wapiti Shelter**... *14.2mS; 8.4mN*	S, w	2,640	609.8
1,564.8	Ribble Trail, north jct	w	3,800	614.3

Miles from Katahdin	Features	Services	Elev.	Miles from Springer
1,564.7	USFS 103, Big Horse Gap	R	3,800	614.4
1,563.1	Sugar Run Gap, Sugar Run Gap Rd (Va. 663)	R (E–0.5m H)	3,450	616.0
1,560.9	**Doc's Knob Shelter**... *8.4mS; 15mN*	S, w	3,555	618.2
1,555.7	Campsite, spring	C, w	3,750	623.4
1,555.2	Angels Rest; Pearis Mtn		3,550	623.9
1,553.2	Va. 634	R	2,200	625.9

The state's highest mountain, Mt. Rogers, an area of spectacular highland meadows, routinely receives snowfall from October to May, making it considerably colder, wetter, and snowier than other areas of Virginia. Northbounders may be tempted to mail home their cold-weather gear, only to see spring flavored by winter.

Caution: According to Mt. Rogers National Recreation Area officials, more than 100 vehicle thefts have been reported in the area since 1999. Hikers should use caution when leaving vehicles at any local trailhead. Safer hiker parking is available at some locations in Damascus, as well as the Mt. Rogers NRA headquarters.

Mt. Rogers Appalachian Trail Club—MRATC maintains the 55.9 miles between Damascus and Va. 670 at the South Fork of the Holston River. Send correspondence to MRATC, P.O. Box 789, Damascus, VA 24236-0789; <www.mratc.org>.

U.S. 58/Damascus, Va. [P.O. ZIP 24236: M–F 8:30–1 & 2–4:30, Sa 9–11; (276) 475-3411]—Called "the friendliest town on the Trail" and the home of Trail Days (to be held May 13–16). First held in '87 as a commemorative event for the 50th anniversary of the A.T., the festival's activities and crowds have grown each year since. Activities include a hiker reunion and talent show, hiking-related exhibits, arts-and-crafts exhibits, a trout rodeo, street dances, live music, and the popular hiker parade through downtown. If you are unable to walk into Damascus for the weekend, rides are usually easy to find from all points along the Trail. Be aware that state open-container laws that restrict drinking in public places are enforced. Hiker camping during Trail Days is at the edge of town on Shady Lane. Camping is prohibited everywhere else, except on the grounds of The Place (see below). During your stay,

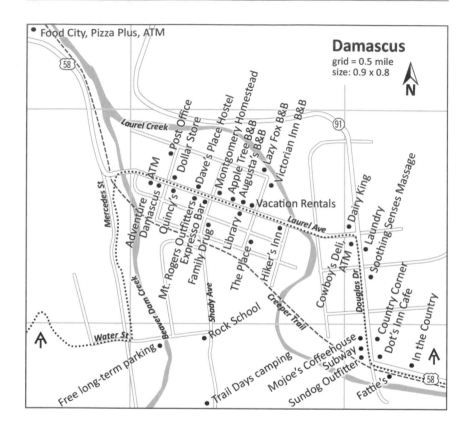

Food City, Pizza Plus, ATM

Damascus
grid = 0.5 mile
size: 0.9 x 0.8

keep in mind that most of the campsites are in residential areas. Please keep quiet in the late evening and early morning, and, upon departure, leave your campsite clean. Leave No Trace camping principles apply in town as well as on the Trail. You'll find all major services, except veterinary, in Damascus. ■ *Hostels:* The Place, provided by the Damascus First United Methodist Church, opens in late Mar and closes when the pipes are in danger of freezing. Stays and parking are limited to two days. A large house, with bunk space, showers, a back porch, and outside picnic tables. Four-dollar-per-night donation is requested, but larger donations are appreciated, in addition to cleaning chores. Smoking is not allowed on "The Place" property; absolutely no drinking is permitted on the property of the First United Methodist Church, its parking lot, and The Place. Dave's Place Hostel, run by Mt. Rogers Outfitters, 5 rooms with two bunks each, $10/person/night, shower without stay $3, ask about staying with dogs, daily parking $2/day, no alcohol on property. ■ *Lodging:* Apple Tree B&B, (276) 475-5261, across from the library; Augusta's Appalachian Inn B&B, (276) 475-3565, 125 Laurel Ave., P.O. Box 160 Damascus, VA 24236, free WiFi, long-distance phone, one load laundry/room for hikers, accepts mail drops for guests; The Hiker's Inn, (276) 475-3788, 216 East Laurel Ave.; Lazy Fox Inn, (276) 475-5838; Mountain Laurel Inn, (276) 475-5956, west of town; A Dancing Bear's Getaway, (276) 475-5900, 203 East Laurel Ave.; Montgomery Homestead B&B, (276) 475-5125 or cell (276) 492-6283, 103 Laurel Ave., mail drops accepted for guests sent to Susie Montgomery, P.O. Box 12, Damascus, VA 24236; The Victorian Inn B&B, (276) 475-5059, 203 N. Legion St.; The Rollin' Rock Inn B&B, (276) 475-6283, 761 Orchard Hill Rd. ■ *Groceries:* Food City (long-term resupply). ■ *Restaurants:* Quincey's Pizza; Dairy King; Subway; Dot's Inn; Cowboy's Deli and convenience store, with ATM; Country Corner; In the Country; Mojoe's Trailside Coffee House, B. ■ *Outfitters:* Mt. Rogers Outfitters (MRO), (276) 475-5416, owned and operated by 1990 thru-hiker and Damascus native Dave Patrick and son Jeff, backpacking gear and supplies, stove fuel, shuttles, accepts mail drops sent to 110 Laurel Ave. (P.O. Box 546), Damascus, VA 24236, open M–Sa 9–6, Su 12–6; Adventure Damascus Outdoor Company, (276) 475-6262 or (888) 595-2453, <info@adventuredamascus. com>, <www.adventuredamascus.com>, 128 W. Laurel Ave. (P.O. Box 1113), Damascus, VA 24236, backpacking gear and food, denatured alcohol and Coleman fuel by the ounce, other fuels, bike rentals, shuttles to area trailheads by arrangement, holds USPS and UPS mail drops, $2 shower ($4 with towel), open 7 days year-round; Sundog Outfitter, (276) 475-6252 or (866) 515-3441, <www.sundogoutfitter.com>, 331 Douglas Dr., Damascus, VA 24236, backpacking gear and clothing, repairs, hiker food, denatured alcohol and other fuels, will hold USPS and UPS mail drops, call ahead for shuttles, open 7 days a week. ■ *Internet access:* Damascus Public Library, WiFi, M–Th 11–7, F 11–5, Sa 9–1. ■ *Other services:* free long-term parking lot for hikers; coin laundry; medical clinic; pharmacy; hardware store; Dollar Store; two banks with ATM; Bunny Medeiros (Soothing Senses) massages, (276) 475-5140.

West 2 miles on U.S. 58 to Fisher Hollow Veterinary Clinic, (276) 475-5397.

West 12 miles on U.S. 58 to Abingdon, Va., a large town near I-81 with all major services, including a veterinarian, movie theater, and Highlands Ski & Outdoor Center, (276) 628-1329, open M–F 10–7, Sa 9–7, Su 12–6.

Virginia Creeper Trail—The Virginia Creeper stretches 33 miles along an old railroad bed from Abingdon to the Virginia–North Carolina state line. It began as a native-American footpath. Later, it was used by pioneers, including Daniel Boone, and, beginning in the early 1900s, by a quintessential mountain railroad, its namesake, with 100 trestles and bridges, as well as many steep grades and sharp curves. The A.T. shares the Creeper route north of Damascus for 300 yards and again 10 miles north.

Saunders Shelter (1987)—Sleeps 8. Privy. Shelter is located on a 0.2-mile blue-blazed trail. Water source is behind and to the right of the shelter, then down an old road to a reliable, seeping spring.

USFS Beartree Campground—*via* Bear Tree Gap Trail **West** 3 miles. Part of Mt. Rogers National Recreation Area, (276) 388-3642, with a lake and swimming area 1 mile from the A.T. Campground is 2 miles beyond swimming area, with tentsites $19S, $38D, and hot showers $4. Parking $5/day. Open mid-Apr–Oct.

Lost Mountain Shelter (1994)—Sleeps 8. Privy. Water source is on a trail to the left of the shelter.

Whitetop Mountain—At 5,520 feet, this is Virginia's second-highest peak, although the Trail does not go to the top. Nearby Whitetop is home to a ramp festival, held the weekend after Memorial Day. The celebration includes a ramp-eating contest thru-hikers have won in past years. Ramps emerge from the forest floor in early spring. The two-leafed greens sprout from an onion-like tuber that can be used to spice up Trail meals. Other plants have a similar look, but ramps are identified easily by their smell and taste, which are akin to onions and garlic. In years past, local residents held large music festivals on Whitetop Mountain.

Va. 600, Elk Garden—Elk Garden is named after the now-extinct eastern elk that once roamed throughout this area, along with timber wolves, mountain lions, and bison. Today, none of those exist here, but black bear, white-tailed deer, and wild turkey are common. Neotropical nesting birds of this area include such songbirds as Vesper's sparrow, common raven, various hawks, and several species of warblers.

Mt. Rogers—Virginia's highest peak, at 5,729 feet; the Trail does not go to the viewless summit, but it can be reached *via* a side trail, going west 0.5 mile. Camping is prohibited in the area from the A.T. to the summit due to fragile plant life and the endangered Wellers salamander. The Wellers, a dark blue-black salamander with gold splotches on its back, can be found only in coniferous forests above 5,000 feet. You may also see or hear northern birds, such as the hermit thrush and winter wren. Such species nest here because of the favorable altitude at the summit area.

Thomas Knob Shelter (1991)—Sleeps 16. Privy (moldering). This two-level shelter was built by the MRATC and Konnarock Crew. Water source is in an enclosed area in a pasture behind the shelter; lock the gate leading to the water source to keep the feral ponies in the area from polluting the water. Be aware those ponies like to chew on packs and other salty items.

Rhododendron Gap—Just below the highest point on the Virginia A.T. on Pine Mountain and Wilburn Ridge. In late Jun, rhododendron blooms here in full force. Panoramic views of the rhododendron thickets can be seen from a rock outcropping. Watch your step from Thomas Knob through the Grayson Highlands State Park area; cattle and feral ponies roam the area. In the spring, you will see mares tending their foals.

Grayson Highlands State Park—(276) 579-7092. At Massey Gap, a blue-blaze leads **East** 0.5 mile to a parking area, then 1.5 miles farther on roads to park's campground. Park is open year-round from dawn to 10 p.m. The campstore and showers are open May 1–Oct 31, closed in cold weather; Th–Su 10–5, Jul–Aug daily 10–5; may use phone at camp store with a calling card; tentsite with shower $21, shower only $5.

Wise Shelter (1996)—Sleeps 8. Privy. Water source is a reliable spring south of the shelter on a trail east of the A.T. No tenting around the shelter or in the state park. Tentsites are in the Mt. Rogers NRA, across Wilson Creek, 0.3 mile north. Follow the Wilson Creek Trail 2 miles east to Grayson Highlands State Park (see above).

Old Orchard Shelter (1970)—Sleeps 6. Privy. Water source is 100 yards on a blue-blazed trail to the right of the shelter.

Hurricane Mountain Shelter (2004)—Sleeps 8. Privy (moldering). Water source is a nearby stream.

USFS Hurricane Campground—**West** 0.5 mile *via* side trail to Hurricane Campground, (276) 783-5196, one of nine USFS campgrounds within the George Washington and Jefferson National Forests. The campground charges $16 per site; $2 shower 10-2. Open Apr 15–Oct 31, depending on weather.

Va. 650 & Va. 16/Dickey Gap—**East** 2.6 miles to **Troutdale, Va. [P.O. ZIP 24378: M–F 8:15–12 & 1–4:30, Sa 8:15–11:30; (276) 677-3221].** ■ *Groceries:* Jerry's Kitchen & Goods, 2.0 miles east on Va. 16, (276) 677-3010, <bartley16@hotmail.com>,

Su–Th 7–7, F-Sa 7–7, short-term resupply, fuel (white gas, alcohol, Heet, butane/pro-pane mix), dogs allowed, free Internet, WiFi, free shuttle to Fox Creek and Dickey Gap; also houses a restaurant serving B/L/D that closes around 7 p.m.; mail drops accepted (USPS, UPS) if sent to 10973 Troutdale Hwy., Troutdale, VA 24378; accepts all major credit cards and gives up to $20 cash back; cable TV in restaurant lounge. ■ *Hostel:* Troutdale Baptist Church, Pastor Ken Riggins, (276) 677-4092, located at 10148 Troutdale Hwy., offers a place to tent or use of a hiker bunkhouse, shower; pets welcome, donations accepted. ■ *Lodging:* Fox Hill Inn, 8568 Troutdale Hwy., Trout-dale, VA 24378, (276) 677-3313, (866) 943-7243; 4 miles south of Dickey Gap; call for shuttle. Thru-hiker rates April 1–July 15, $75S/D, $20EAP, includes B, phone with card, WiFi, kitchen; no smoking or pets inside. ■ *Other services:* ATM, bank, dentist, medical clinic.

East 3.2 miles to **USFS Raccoon Branch Campground** on the blue-blazed trail; tentsites $1 (subject to change: See <www.fs.fed.us/r8/gwj>), no showers, open Apr–Dec, no water after Oct 31.

Trimpi Shelter (1975)—Sleeps 8. Privy. A reliable spring is in front of the shelter.

Piedmont Appalachian Trail Hikers (PATH)—PATH maintains the 64.1 miles between Va. 670, South Fork of the Holston River, and U.S. 21/52 at Bland, Va. Correspondence can be sent to PATH, P.O. Box 4423, Greensboro, NC 27404; <www.path-at.org>.

Partnership Shelter (1998)—Sleeps 16. Privy and propane-powered warm-water shower (available during warmer months). No tenting around the shelter. Water source is a faucet behind the shelter. No alcoholic beverages allowed. For a week or more after Trail Days, expect law-enforcement officers to be checking in.

Mt. Rogers National Recreation Area Headquarters—(276) 783-5196 or (800) 628-7202, M–F 8–4:30 year-round, Sa 9–4 May–Oct (weather permitting). Only several hun-dred yards north of Partnership Shelter, the headquarters houses a bookshop and interpretive center with information about plants and animals found in the area. Water is available from a spigot outside (in nonfreezing weather). Restroom and soda machine inside. From the outside phone (free local calls, calling card needed for long distance), you can order pizza from several area pizzerias, including Pizza Hut, (276) 783-3104, to be delivered to gate. Do not sleep on the headquarters' covered porch. Obtain free permit to park overnight or weekly.

Va. 16—East 3.2 miles to **Sugar Grove, Va. [P.O. ZIP 24375: M–F 8:15–12 & 1:15–4:45, Sa 8:15–10:30; (276) 677-3200].** The town is home to the ATC Konnarock Volunteer Crew (see below). ■ *Groceries:* Mt. View Food Mart, (276) 677-3037, M–Sa 7–9:30, Su 8–9:30 (short-term resupply), has ATM, pizza, sandwiches, hamburgers, hotdogs, Coleman fuel by the gallon. ■ *Restaurant:* Sugar Grove Diner, (276) 677-3351, B/L/D, M–W 5–8, Th–Sa 5–8:30; may be closed, however. Possible shuttle to and from Trail and lodging may still be available; call (276) 677-3037 or (276) 667-3070.

West 6 miles to **Marion, Va. [P.O. ZIP 24354: M–F 8:30–5 Sa 9:30–12; (276) 783-5051],** a larger town near I-81 with all major services, including a Food Lion supermarket (long-term resupply), several restaurants, fast-food outlets, a coin laundry, and Greyhound bus service along the I-81 corridor, (276) 783-7114 (closed Sa, Su, and holidays). ■ *Lodging:* various motels, including the Virginia House Inn, (276) 783-5112, 1419 N. Main/U.S. 11, 0.25 mile beyond Walmart, hiker rate $35S, $45D (except during Bristol Raceway weekends), dogs $7, includes continental B, CATV, in-room phones, pool.

Konnarock Crew—Based 1 mile from Sugar Grove post office at USFS facility. If you want part of your experience to be a week on the crew that builds and rehabilitates the Trail, call the Blacksburg, Va., ATC regional office at (540) 953-3571 before your hike to make arrangements. Getting to base camp and back is your responsibility, but, once there, food and amenities are provided. Commitments include 5 days/4 nights along the Trail in the South. Be prepared to work and have a lot of fun.

Chatfield Shelter (1970s)—Sleeps 6. Privy. Named in honor of North Carolina conservationist and PATH founder Louise Meroney Chatfield. A creek is in front.

Va. 615, Settlers Museum—On USFS lands adjacent to the Trail, the farmstead and visitors center include exhibits of rural life at the time the valley was settled. Admission free to hikers.

Va. 683, U.S. 11, I-81—At Groseclose, Va. (no post office), this is the southernmost crossing of I-81. ■ *Restaurant:* The Barn Restaurant, B/L/D, M–Sa 7–8, Su 7–3 buffet; ask permission for long-term parking, (276) 686-6222, mail drops accepted (no fee), 7412 Lee Hwy, Rural Retreat, VA 24368. ■ *Groceries:* Exxon Truckstop (Shell), short-term resupply, deli, ATM, fuel available; (276) 783-5454. ■ *Hostel:* Happy Hiker Hollow, 484 Phillipi Hollow Rd., Atkins, VA 24311, (276) 783-3754. Rambunny and Aqua, proprietor, have more than 10,000 combined miles of hiking experience. Call from Settler's Museum, Partnership Shelter, or U.S. 11 for slackpack to hostel. Shower; accepts mail drops; long-term parking; shuttles; Internet access; unlimited long-distance calls; 2 indoor rooms plus barn; camping; special treatment for Trail maintainers. Call for reservations. ■ *Lodging:* The Relax Inn, 7253 Lee Hwy, Rural Retreat, VA 24368, (276) 783-5811, $40S, $45D, $5EAP, $10 per pet; long-term hiker parking $3/day; coin laundry; call for info on shuttle to Trailhead; holds USPS, UPS, FedEx packages (nonguests $5); please provide your ETA.

West 3.2 miles (on U.S. 11 south) to **Atkins, Va. [P.O. ZIP 24311: M–F 9–1 & 2:30–4, Sa 9:30–11; (276) 783-5551]**, with restaurants. ■ *Groceries:* Atkins Grocery & Deli (long-term resupply), M–F 6–10, Sa 9:30–11. ■ *Other services:* laundromat near grocery store, at opposite end of building (no sign), M–F 7–8, Sa 7-7.

West 10.2 miles (on U.S. 11 south) to **Marion, Va.** (see above), a larger town.

Davis Path Campsite—The shelter roof and walls were removed in 2008, but tent platform, table, and privy remain. Located near an eighteenth-century settlers' route through Davis Valley. Water source is a spring 0.9 mile south of the shelter. South-bounders can carry water from Crawfish Valley, 3.5 miles north. Once sidehill campsites are built from the shelter logs, the platform will be removed as well.

Knot Maul Branch Shelter (1980s)—Sleeps 8. Privy. Named for the knotty wood settlers used as mauls for their farm work. Water source is 0.2 mile north on the A.T.

Chestnut Knob Shelter (renovated 1994)—Sleeps 8. Privy. A former firewarden's cabin, the shelter was once called "the cave" but now includes plexiglass windows to let in some light. No water is available at this shelter, but water is sometimes found 0.2 mile south on the A.T., then 50 yards east on an old Jeep road. Otherwise, south-bounders can find water 1.3 miles north in Walker Gap, and northbounders can find water at a spring-fed pond 1.8 miles south.

Burkes Garden—Chestnut Knob Shelter, elevation 4,410 feet, overlooks this unusual geologic feature, which was the Vanderbilts' first choice for their Biltmore estate, later constructed near Asheville, N.C. It is a large, crater-shaped depression surrounded on all sides by a high ridge that the A.T. follows for nearly 8 miles. From Chestnut Knob, you can see how it got its nickname, "God's Thumbprint."

Jenkins Shelter (1960s)—Sleeps 8. Privy. Formerly the Monster Rock Shelter, built when the A.T. followed the ridge of Walker Mountain. It was moved in the early 1980s, when the Trail was. Water source is a stream 100 yards north on a blue-blazed trail.

Laurel Creek footbridge closure: Located at Va. 615, 6.9 miles south of U.S. 21/52 near Bastian, Va., the A.T. footbridge across Laurel Creek is closed for repairs. Hikers may ford the creek or follow a blue-blazed trail that leads to/from an alternate crossing on Va. 615. Signs have been posted to direct hikers onto the temporary route. Note that the formerly blue-blazed high-water route just south of Va. 615 has been changed to white-blazed. The formerly white-blazed route along Little Wolf Creek has been repainted blue. This route change may be temporary.

U.S. 52—**East** 2.7 miles to **Bland, Va.** [**P.O. ZIP 24315: M–F 8–11:30 & 12–4, Sa 9–11; (276) 688-3751**]. Larger than Bastian, with more services. ■ *Restaurants*: Bland Square Grill (in Bland Square Citgo, 8870 South Scenic Hwy, first block west of Main on U.S. 52 in downtown Bland, B/L/D, 7 days. ■ *Groceries:* Bruce's IGA Supermarket (long-term resupply), (276) 688-4461, M–Sa 7–10, Su 8–9, credit cards accepted. ■ *Internet access:* library, (276) 688-3737, MWF 9:30–4:30, Tu, Th 9:30–8. ■ *Other services:* hardware store; medical clinic, (276) 688-4800, MTW 9–5, Th 9–12; two banks with ATM.

East 3.3 miles to ■ *Lodging:* Big Walker Motel, 70 Skyview Lane, Bland, VA 24315, (276) 688 3331, $57.73 1-2 persons, $62.01 3 or more, pets OK, WiFi, will hold packages only for guests. Call for shuttle possibilities. ■ *Other services:* Dairy Queen with ATM, Subway, Dollar General. There is no place to camp in Bland.

West 2.5 miles to **Bastian, Va.** [**P.O. ZIP 24314: M–F 8–12 & 12:30–4, Sa 8–10:30; (276) 688-4631**]. P.O. is **West** 1.9 miles, left on Railroad Trail, right on Walnut Drive. Two miles farther down U.S. 52 to *Other services:* medical clinic, (276) 688-4331, M, W 8:30–6, Tu 8:30–8, Th 8:30–8, F 8:30–5; pharmacy next door, (276) 688-4204, M–F 9–5, Tu 9–8, Sa 9–12; Greyhound bus service, (304) 325-9442, available for the I-77 corridor in Bluefield, W.Va., about 10 miles beyond Bastian on U.S. 52 (closed Su and holidays); Pizza Plus, (276) 688-3332, will deliver to U.S. 52 Trailhead and Bland.

Outdoor Club at Virginia Tech—OCVT maintains the 9 miles between U.S. 21/52 and Va. 611 and 18.8 miles in central Virginia between U.S. 460 and Pine Swamp Branch Shelter. Correspondence should be sent to OCVT, P.O. Box 538, Blacksburg, VA 24060; <www.outdoor.org.vt.edu>.

Helveys Mill Shelter (1960s)—Sleeps 6. Privy. Relocated here when the A.T. was moved off Walker Mountain in the 1980s. Water source is down a switch-backed trail in front of the shelter.

Jenny Knob Shelter (1960s)—Sleeps 6. Privy. Also relocated here when the A.T. was moved off Walker Mountain. Water source is a spring near the shelter.

 Va. 608, Va. 42—East 0.8 mile to the community of Crandon. Bruce's General Store, (276) 688-3132, M–Sa 7–7, Su 10–6; fuel by the ounce.

Roanoke Appalachian Trail Club—RATC maintains the 34.4 miles between Va. 611 and U.S. 460 and 87.0 miles in the next section between Pine Swamp Branch Shelter and Black Horse Gap. Correspondence should be sent to RATC, P.O. Box 12282, Roanoke, VA 24024; <www.ratc.org>.

 Va. 606—West 0.5 mile to *Groceries:* Trent's Grocery with deli and pizza. Open daily M–Sa 7–9, Su 9–9, Coleman and denatured alcohol by the ounce, pay phone, and soda machines. Camping, shower, and laundry $6, or warm shower and laundry only $3.

Wapiti Shelter (1980)—Sleeps 8. Privy. Water source is Dismal Creek, just south of the turn-off to the shelter.

 Sugar Run Road/Sugar Run Gap—East 0.5 mile to *Hostel:* Woodshole Hostel, (540) 921-3444, <www.woodsholehostel.com>. An old homestead discovered by Roy and Tillie Wood while Roy was studying elk (wapiti) in the early 1940s. They opened the hostel in 1986. After Roy passed away in 1987, Tillie and volunteers continued hosting thru-hikers for 21 years. She passed away in 2007. Her granddaughter, Neville, and partner, Michael, and volunteers continue her hospitality. Woodshole is an 1880s chestnut-log cabin (recently renovated) and hikers' bunkhouse surrounded by the Jefferson National Forest. The bunkhouse, with mattresses in the loft for sleeping, and nearby solar shower are free. Donations appreciated. Sodas, candy bars, pizza, smoothies, Coleman fuel and denatured alcohol for sale. A family-style breakfast served in the cabin at 7:30 a.m. is available for limited number of guests, $6. No reservations, please. A telephone is available for making credit-card or collect calls before 8 p.m. Foot massage/massage therapy available from Neville and Michael. *Directions:* Going north, at Sugar Run Gap, turn right on dirt road, bear left at the fork, and go 0.5 mile down the road to Woods-hole on right; watch for signs. Long-distance hikers welcome beginning May 1.

Doc's Knob Shelter (1971)—Sleeps 8. Privy. A reliable spring is to left of the shelter.

Virginia—Part 2 (Central)

Miles from Katahdin	Features	Services	Elev.	Miles from Springer
1,553.2	Va. 634	R	2,200	625.9
1,552.7	Lane Street **Pearisburg, VA 24134**	R, L, G, sh, f (E–1m PO, G, L, M, D, V, f, cl, @; 2.9m H; 6m O; 20m G, L, M, O) (W–3m L, M, G)	1,650	626.4
1,552.2	U.S. 460, Senator Shumate Bridge (east end), New River	R	1,600	626.9
1,550.7	Clendennin Rd (Va. 641)	R	1,750	628.4
1,548.5	Springs	C, w	3,250	630.6
1,545.9	**Rice Field Shelter**... *15mS; 12.5mN*	S (E–0.3m w)	3,375	633.2
1,544.3	Campsite, water	C, w	3,300	634.8
1,540.8	Symms Gap Meadow	C, w	3,320	638.3
1,539.8	Groundhog Trail		3,400	639.3
1,538.3	Dickinson Gap		3,300	640.8
1,536.1	Peters Mtn		3,500	643.0
1,535.9	Allegheny Trail			643.2
1,533.4	**Pine Swamp Branch Shelter**... *12.5mS; 3.9mN*	S, w	2,530	645.7
1,533.1	Va. 635, Stony Creek Valley	R	2,370	646.0
1,532.0	Dismal Branch	w	2,480	647.1
1,531.0	Va. 635, Stony Creek	R, w	2,450	648.1
1,529.7	Spring	w	3,490	649.4
1,529.5	**Bailey Gap Shelter**... *3.9mS; 8.8mN*	S, w	3,525	649.6
1,525.8	Va. 613, Salt Sulphur Tpk	R	3,950	653.3
1,525.6	Wind Rock		4,100	653.5
1,524.4	Campsites, spring	C, w	4,000	654.7
1,520.7	**War Spur Shelter**... *8.8mS; 5.8mN*	S, w	2,340	658.4
1,519.9	USFS 156, Johns Creek Valley	R, w	2,080	659.2
1,518.9	Stream	w	2,700	660.2
1,517.9	Va. 601, Rocky Gap	R	3,250	661.2

Miles from Katahdin	Features	Services	Elev.	Miles from Springer
1,514.9	**Laurel Creek Shelter...** *5.8mS; 6.7mN*	S, w	2,720	664.2
1,513.9	Spring	w	2,400	665.2
1,512.5	Va. 42, Sinking Creek Valley	R (E–0.5m L)	2,200	666.6
1,511.6	Va. 630, Sinking Creek	R, w (W–0.5m L)	2,100	667.5
1,511.2	Keffer Oak		2,240	667.9
1,508.5	**Sarver Hollow Shelter...** *6.7mS; 6.3mN*	E–0.3m S, w	3,000	670.6
1,504.9	Sinking Creek Mtn		3,450	674.2
1,503.2	Cabin Branch	C, w	2,490	675.9
1,502.5	**Niday Shelter...** *6.3mS; 10.4mN*	S, w	1,800	676.6
1,501.2	Va. 621, Craig Creek Valley	R	1,540	677.9
1,497.4	Audie Murphy Monument		3,100	681.7
1,493.6	Va. 620, Trout Creek	R, w	1,525	685.5
1,492.4	**Pickle Branch Shelter...** *10.4mS; 13.9mN*	E–0.3m S, w	1,845	686.7
1,488.2	Cove Mtn, Dragons Tooth		3,020	690.9
1,487.2	Lost Spectacles Gap		2,550	691.9
1,486.7	Rawies Rest		2,350	692.4
1,485.7	Va. 624, North Mtn Trail	R (W–0.4m G, M)	1,810	693.4
1,484.1	Va. 785	R	1,790	695.0
1,479.8	Va. 311 **Catawba, VA 24070**	R (W–1m PO, C, G; 1.3m M)	1,990	699.3
1,478.8	**Johns Spring Shelter...** *13.9mS; 1mN*	S, w	1,980	700.3
1,477.8	**Catawba Mtn Shelter...** *1mS; 2.4mN*	S, w	2,580	701.3
1,476.1	McAfee Knob		3,197	703.0
1,475.5	Pig Farm Campsite	C, w	3,000	703.6
1,475.4	**Campbell Shelter...** *2.4mS; 6mN*	S, w	2,580	703.7
1,472.3	Brickey's Gap		2,250	706.8
1,470.5	Tinker Cliffs		3,000	708.6
1,470.0	Scorched Earth Gap, Andy Layne Trail		2,600	709.1

Miles from Katahdin	Features	Services	Elev.	Miles from Springer
1,469.4	**Lamberts Meadow Shelter...** *6mS; 14.4mN*	S, w	2,080	709.7
1,469.1	Lamberts Meadow Campsite, Sawmill Run	C, w	2,000	710.0
1,465.1	Angels Gap		1,800	714.0
1,464.0	Hay Rock, Tinker Ridge		1,900	715.1
1,460.5	Tinker Creek		1,165	718.6
1,460.0	U.S. 220, Va. 816 **Cloverdale, VA 24077; Daleville, VA 24083**	R; G, L, M, cl (E– 0.8m G, M, L, cl, sh; 2.3m PO G, L, M; 12m G, M, O, D, V) (W–0.3m G, M O, f; 1m PO)	1,350	719.1
1,458.8	Va. 779, I-81	R	1,400	720.3
1,458.5	U.S. 11, Norfolk & Western Railway **Troutville, VA 24175**	R (W–1.3m PO, C, G, M)	1,300	720.6
1,457.9	Va. 652	R	1,450	721.2
1,455.0	**Fullhardt Knob Shelter...** *14.4mS; 6.2mN*	S, w	2,670	724.1
1,452.2	USFS 191, Salt Pond Rd	R	2,260	726.9
1,451.4	Curry Creek	w	1,680	727.7
1,449.5	Wilson Creek	w	1,690	729.6
1,448.8	**Wilson Creek Shelter...** *6.2mS; 7.5mN*	S, w	1,830	730.3
1,448.4	Spring	w	2,050	730.7
1,446.4	USFS 186; BRP mp 97.7; Old Fincastle Rd; Black Horse Gap	R	2,402	732.7
1,445.6	BRP mp 97.0; Taylors Mtn Overlook	R	2,350	733.5
1,444.5	BRP mp 95.9; Montvale Overlook	R	2,400	734.6
1,443.9	BRP mp 95.3;Harveys Knob Overlook	R	2,550	735.2
1,441.5	**Bobblets Gap Shelter...** *7.5mS; 6.7mN*	W–0.2m S, w	1,920	737.6
1,440.8	BRP mp 92.5; Sharp Top Overlook	R	2,350	738.3
1,440.1	BRP mp 91.8; Mills Gap Overlook	R	2,450	739.0

Miles from Katahdin	Features	Services	Elev.	Miles from Springer
1,438.4	Va. 43, Bearwallow Gap; BRP mp 90.9 **Buchanan, VA 24066**	R (E–4.4m C, L, M) (W–5m PO, G, M, @; 7m L, M)	2,228	740.7
1,436.8	Cove Mtn		2,720	742.3
1,436.4	Little Cove Mtn Trail		2,600	742.7
1,435.0	**Cove Mtn Shelter**... *6.7mS; 7mN*	S, nw	1,925	744.1
1,433.3	Buchanan Trail		1,790	745.8
1,431.8	Va. 614, Jennings Creek	R, C, w (E–0.3m w; 1.4m C, G, cl, sh, f) (W–4.5m L, M)	951	747.3
1,430.2	Fork Mtn		2,042	748.9
1,428.0	**Bryant Ridge Shelter**... *7mS; 4.9mN*	S, w	1,320	751.1
1,423.7	Floyd Mtn		3,560	755.4
1,423.1	**Cornelius Creek Shelter**... *4.9mS; 5.3mN*	S, w	3,145	756.0
1,422.2	Black Rock		3,450	756.9
1,420.5	Apple Orchard Falls Trail		3,250	758.6
1,420.4	USFS 812, Parkers Gap Rd; BRP mp 78.4	R	3,430	758.7
1,419.0	Apple Orchard Mtn		4,225	760.1
1,418.7	The Guillotine		4,090	760.4
1,418.1	Upper BRP mp 76.3	R	3,900	761.0
1,417.8	**Thunder Hill Shelter**... *5.3mS; 12.4mN*	S, w	3,960	761.3
1,416.8	Lower BRP mp 74.9	R	3,650	762.3
1,416.4	Thunder Ridge Overlook; BRP mp 74.7	R	3,501	762.7
1,414.5	Harrison Ground Spring	w	3,200	764.6
1,413.1	USFS 35, Petites Gap; BRP mp 71.0	R	2,369	766.0
1,411.9	High Cock Knob		3,073	767.2
1,410.9	Marble Spring	C, w	2,290	768.2
1,410.4	Sulphur Spring Trail (south crossing)		2,400	768.7
1,408.6	Belfast Trail, Hickory Stand		2,650	770.5

Miles from Katahdin	Features	Services	Elev.	Miles from Springer
1,408.1	Sulphur Spring Trail (north crossing)		2,588	771.0
1,407.3	Big Cove Branch	w	1,890	771.8
1,405.4	**Matts Creek Shelter**... *12.4mS; 3.9mN*	S, w	835	773.7
1,404.6	Campsite	C, w	700	774.5
1,403.4	James River Foot Bridge		678	775.7
1,403.2	U.S. 501, Va. 130, James River **Big Island, VA 24526; Glasgow, VA 24555**	R (F—4.7m C, G, L, cl, sh; 5.1m PO, G, M, D) (W—5.9m PO, G, L, M, cl, f, @)	680	775.9
1,403.1	Lower Rocky Row Run Bridge	w	670	776.0
1,402.2	Rocky Row Run	C, w	760	776.9
1,402.1	Va. 812, USFS 36	R	825	777.0
1,401.5	**Johns Hollow Shelter**... *3.9mS; 9mN*	S, w	1,020	777.6
1,399.5	Rocky Row Trail		2,400	779.6
1,399.4	Fullers Rocks, Little Rocky Row		2,472	779.7
1,398.4	Big Rocky Row		2,992	780.7
1,396.9	Saddle Gap, Saddle Gap Trail		2,600	782.2
1,395.8	Saltlog Gap (south)		2,573	783.3
1,394.3	Bluff Mtn		3,372	784.8
1,393.2	Punchbowl Mtn		2,850	785.9
1,392.7	**Punchbowl Shelter**... *9mS; 9.7mN*	W—0.2m S, w	2,500	786.4
1,392.3	Punchbowl Mtn Crossing; BRP mp 51.7	R, w	2,170	786.8
1,392.0	Va. 607, Robinson Gap Rd	R	2,100	787.1
1,390.1	Rice Mtn		2,228	789.0
1,388.2	USFS 39, Pedlar River	R	990	790.9
1,385.2	Pedlar Lake Rd (USFS 38)	R	1,000	793.9
1,383.2	**Brown Mtn Creek Shelter**... *9.7mS; 6.2mN*	S, w	1,395	795.9

Miles from Katahdin	Features	Services	Elev.	Miles from Springer
1,381.4	U.S. 60 **Buena Vista, VA 24416;** **Lexington, VA 24450**	R (W–9.3m PO, C, G, L, M, D, V, cl, sh; 15m PO, G, L, M, D, V, O, f)	2,065	797.7
1,378.6	Bald Knob		4,059	800.5
1,377.6	Old Hotel Trail, **Cow Camp Gap Shelter**... *6.2mS; 10.8mN*	E–0.6m S, w	3,160	801.5
1,376.4	Cold Mtn		4,022	802.7
1,375.1	USFS 48, Hog Camp Gap	R, C, w	3,485	804.0
1,374.2	Tar Jacket Ridge		3,847	804.9
1,372.9	USFS 63, Salt Log Gap (north)	R	3,257	806.2
1,371.7	USFS 246	R	3,500	807.4
1,371.2	Greasy Spring Rd	R	3,600	807.9
1,369.3	N Fork of Piney River	C, w	3,500	809.8
1,368.1	Elk Pond Branch	C, w	3,750	811.0
1,367.4	**Seeley-Woodworth Shelter**... *10.8mS; 6.9mN*	S, w	3,770	811.7
1,366.3	Porters Field	C, w	3,650	812.8
1,365.1	Spy Rock Rd **Montebello, VA 24464**	R (W–2.5m PO; 2.2m C, G, L, M, cl, sh, f)	3,454	814.0
1,364.6	Spy Rock		3,680	814.5
1,364.3	Main Top Mtn		4,040	814.8
1,363.5	Cash Hollow Rock		3,550	815.6
1,362.2	Cash Hollow Rd	R	3,280	816.9
1,361.4	Va. 826, Crabtree Farm Rd, Crabtree Falls Trail	W–0.5m C, w	3,350	817.7
1,360.5	**The Priest Shelter**... *6.9mS; 7.5mN*	S, w	3,840	818.6
1,360.0	The Priest		4,063	819.1
1,357.0	Cripple Creek	w	1,800	822.1
1,355.7	Va. 56, Tye River	R, C, w (W–4m C, G, sh)	970	823.4
1,354.0	Mau-Har Trail		2,090	825.1
1,353.0	**Harpers Creek Shelter**... *7.5mS; 6.2mN*	S, w	1,800	826.1
1,351.0	Chimney Rocks		3,190	828.1

Miles from Katahdin	Features	Services	Elev.	Miles from Springer
1,349.7	Three Ridges		3,870	829.4
1,348.8	Hanging Rock Vista		3,750	830.3
1,346.8	**Maupin Field Shelter**... *6.2mS; 15.8mN*	S, w (W–2m G, L) (W–2.8m H)	2,720	832.3
1,345.1	Va. 664, Reeds Gap; BRP mp 13.6	R	2,650	834.0
1,344.6	BRP mp 13.1; Three Ridges Parking Overlook	R	2,700	834.5
1,340.8	Cedar Cliffs		2,800	838.3
1,340.3	BRP mp 9.6; Dripping Rock Parking Area	R, w	2,950	838.8
1,337.5	Humpback Mtn; trail to Humpback Rocks		3,250	841.6
1,336.5	Trail to Humpback Rocks			842.6
1,335.0	Bear Spring	w	3,200	844.1
1,332.8	Glass Hollow Overlook		2,750	846.3
1,332.5	Trail to Humpback Visitors Center	W–1.3m w	2,150	846.6
1,331.0	Mill Creek, **Paul C. Wolfe Shelter**... *15.8mS; 12.3mN*	S, w	1,700	848.1
1,326.0	U.S. 250, I-64, Rockfish Gap **Waynesboro, VA 22980**	R, G, L, M (W–1m L; 4.5m PO, H, C, G, L, M, O, D, V, cl, sh, f, @)	1,902	853.1

BRP=Blue Ridge Parkway, mp=milepost

Central Virginia's treadway is well-graded and includes several 2,000- to 3,000-foot climbs. You will traverse some of the northernmost balds on the Trail. Unusual rock formations offer up views to the valley below from the peaks of Humpback Rocks, Three Ridges, The Priest, McAfee Knob, and Dragons Tooth. This section is more rugged and remote than Shenandoah to the north and parallels the Blue Ridge Parkway for 90 miles.

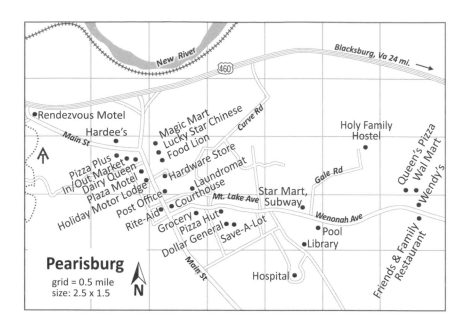

U.S.460/Pearisburg, Va. On A.T. ■ *Lodging:* Rendezvous Motel, (540) 921-2636, $41.04S, $49.68D up to 4, dogs permitted, long-distance phone, laundry, denatured alcohol, Coleman and canister fuel, possible shuttle, shower without stay $8, holds mail and packages for guests addressed to 795 North Main St., Pearisburg, VA 24134. If you leave on a Sunday, they will mail your packages for you.

East 1 mile to **Pearisburg, Va. [P.O. ZIP 24134: M–F 9–4:30, Sa 10–12: (540) 921-1100].**
■ *Lodging:* Plaza Motel, (540) 921-2591, $35S, $45D, $50T, $5EAP, laundry, no pets, will hold packages whether guest or not, 415 North Main St., e-mail available in office; Holiday Motor Lodge, (540) 921-1551, $35.95S, $42.60D, $4EAP, Internet access, swimming pool during the season, pet-friendly, restaurant closed on premises, accepts packages for guests only, 401 North Main St. ■ *Groceries:* Food Lion, Sav-a-Lot, and 7-Day Market (all long-term resupply). ■ *Restaurants:* Courthouse Café, 414 Wenonah Ave., one block from P.O., gourmet coffee, tea, specialty drinks, pastry, Internet access, live music Friday nights; Subway; Hardee's; Pizza Plus, buy one pizza, get one free, AYCE salad/pizza buffet, and free delivery; Dairy Queen; Papa's Pizza Inn with subs, salads; Pizza Hut with AYCE L buffet; Queens Subs; Lucky Star Chinese; Friends & Family. ■ *Internet access:* Courthouse Café, Pearisburg Public Library. ■ *Other services:* Rite Aid with one-hour photo service;

automotive and hardware stores; hair salon and barber; Walmart; coin laundry; ATM; hospital; dentist; veterinarian; municipal swimming pool open to the public Memorial Day to Labor Day for small fee. ■ *Shuttle:* Tom Hoffman, (840) 921-1184, <gopullman@aol.com>.

East 2.9 miles, follow blue-blaze to *Hostel:* Holy Family Church Hostel, located in a peaceful setting on a hill, is hidden by trees beyond the church parking lot. Members of the church dismantled an old barn and reconstructed it as a hostel expressly for backpackers. Refrigerator, stove, microwave, shower, and loft with sleeping pads. Camping permitted on lawn and in gazebo. Stays are limited to two nights. Closed Oct 15–Apr 15. Donations are appreciated, as is cleaning the hostel. Alcoholic beverages, drugs, and pets prohibited. Side trail from hostel to Walmart, 0.25 mile. Mail drops no longer accepted. No pay phone. Contact church office, (540) 921-3457.

East 6 miles on U.S. 460 to *Outfitter:* Tangent Outfitters, 201 Cascade Dr., Pembroke, VA 24136, <www.newrivertrail.com>, primarily oriented to rafters.

East 20 miles *via* U.S. 460 to Blacksburg, Va., home of Virginia Tech, with all services. ATC's Virginia regional office, (540) 953-3571, is located at 110 Southpark Dr. in a USFS facility. *Outfitter:* Back Country Ski & Sports, (800) 560-6401 or (540) 552-6400, open M–Sa 10–8, Su 1–5.

West 3 miles *via* U.S. 460 to Rt. 61/MacArthur Lane and *Lodging:* MacArthur Inn, 117 MacArthur Lane, Narrows, VA 24124, (540) 726-7510; renovated hotel, 26 rooms, $70S, $82D, includes full B for 2, laundry; no pets; WiFi; long-distance phone (no charge); shuttle to and from Trail (call from Pearisburg); accepts mail drops; restaurant; deli; groceries across road.

Senator Shumate (U.S. 460) Bridge—The large manufacturing facility in Narrows seen from the bridge over the New River is the Celco (Celanese Acetate) Plant, a major employer in the area that has been working with ATC and the Forest Service to significantly relocate the Trail north of the river.

Rice Field Shelter (1995)—Sleeps 7. Privy. This shelter has an excellent viewing area for sunsets and clouded valleys in the morning. Water is on a steep, 0.3-mile downhill hike behind and to the left of the shelter.

Symms Gap Meadow—The traverse of Peters Mountain along the Virginia–West Virginia state line is a dry one. At this mountain meadow, with views into West Virginia, a small pond is located downhill from the A.T. on the West Virginia side of the ridge, with spots for camping nearby.

Allegheny Trail—2.5 miles south of Pine Swamp Branch Shelter is the A.T.'s junction with the southern terminus of the Allegheny Trail, which extends about 300 miles across West Virginia to the Pennsylvania border. The trail is maintained by the West Virginia Scenic Trails Association, P.O. Box 4042, Charleston, WV 25364; <www. wvscenictrails.org>.

Pine Swamp Branch Shelter (1980s)—Sleeps 8. Privy. Stone shelter. Water is from the stream 75 yards down a blue-blazed trail west of the side trail to the shelter. The shelter was damaged in 2007 by a tree falling on the roof, but many hours of volunteer labor have repaired it.

Bailey Gap Shelter (1960s)—Sleeps 6. Privy. Water is 0.2 mile south on the A.T., then east down a blue-blazed trail.

Va. 613, Salt Sulfur Turnpike— **East** 5 miles to *Lodging:* Mountain Lake Conservancy and Hotel, (800) 346-3334, <www.mountainlakehotel.com>, site of one of only two natural lakes in Virginia; rates begin at $125S/$175D, includes B & D, access to resort amenities, shuttle from and to A.T.; reservations required. Will hold packages for registered guests mailed to 115 Hotel Circle, Pembroke, VA 24136.

War Spur Shelter (1960s)—Sleeps 6. Privy. Water source is a stream 80 yards north of the shelter on the A.T.

Laurel Creek Shelter (1988)—Sleeps 6. Privy. Water is west on the A.T., 45 yards south of the shelter-trail junction.

Va. 42, Sinking Creek Valley—**East** 0.5 mile to *Lodging:* The Huffman House B&B at Creekside Farm, <www.thehuffmanhousebandb.com>, owned by 1999 thru-hikers Ron and Carol Baker (Leafhopper & Snowy Egret), (540) 544-6942, $120–$159D, $20EAP, reservations required, will hold packages for registered guests sent to 16 Old Huffman Store Rd., Newport, VA 24128.

Keffer Oak—Located about 0.2 mile north of Va. 630, this is the largest oak tree on the A.T. in the South. Last measured, the girth was 18 feet, 3 inches; it is estimated to be 300 years old. The Dover Oak along the A.T. in New York is slightly larger.

Sarver Hollow Shelter (2001)—Sleeps 6. Privy. Water source is a spring located on a blue-blazed trail near the shelter.

Sinking Creek Mountain—This is the northernmost spot on the Trail where the route crosses a significant "continental divide." Waters flowing down the western side of the ridge drain into Sinking Creek Valley and the Mississippi River to the Gulf of Mexico. Waters flowing on the eastern side empty into Craig Creek Valley, the James River, and eventually the Atlantic Ocean. Between here and mid-Pennsylvania, except for a short section near Roanoke, the Trail is in the Chesapeake Bay watershed.

Niday Shelter (1980)—Sleeps 6. Privy. Water source is 75 yards down a blue-blazed trail west of the A.T.

Audie Murphy Monument—located on a blue-blazed trail to the west on Brushy Mountain. Murphy was the most decorated American soldier of World War II, and his single-handed capture of a large number of German soldiers made him a legend. After the war, he starred in many Hollywood war and B-grade western movies. He died in a 1971 plane crash near this site. A trail leads beyond the monument to a view from a rock outcropping.

Pickle Branch Shelter (1980)—Sleeps 6. Privy. Water is from the stream below the shelter.

Dragons Tooth—Named by Tom Campbell, an early member of RATC and prime mover in the 1930s–1950s in locating the A.T. on its current route. He also named Lost Spectacles Gap, north of Dragons Tooth, after his glasses disappeared on a scouting/work hike.

Camping Restrictions—Between Va. 624 and U.S. 220, camping and fires are allowed only at the following designated sites of this heavily used section: Johns Spring, Catawba Mountain, Campbell, and Lamberts Meadow shelters and Pig Farm and Lamberts Meadow campsites.

Va. 624/North Mountain Trail—West 0.3 mile to Va. 311, then left 0.1 mile to Catawba Grocery (short-term resupply), open M–Th 5–10, F–Sa 5–11, Su 6–10. Pay phone outside. Nearby North Mountain Trail was once the A.T. route. A 30-mile loop is possible.

Va. 311—West 1 mile to **Catawba, Va. [P.O.** ZIP 24070: M–F 7:30–12 & 1–5, Sᴀ 8–
10:30; (540) 384-6011], and Catawba Valley General Store *(for sale in fall 2009)*,
M–F 6–8, Sa 7–8, closed Su; sandwiches and pizzas; accepts UPS mail drops to 4905
Catawba Valley Dr., Catawba, VA 24070; camping (one night, $3PP) and portable
toilet behind store.

West 1.3 miles to the Homeplace Restaurant with AYCE meals $13 for two meats,
$14 for three meats, less if you're a vegetarian. Open Th–F 4–8, Sa 3–8, Su 11–6 (closed
the week of Jul 4 and two weeks in late Dec); Th is Southern-barbeque night. No
public restroom.

Plans are in the works for a blue-blazed trail from the Va. 311 parking lot to Catawba through a 400-acre Virginia Tech farm; watch for updates along the Trail and
in the Trail-conditions section of <www.appalachiantrail.org>.

Johns Spring Shelter (2003)—Sleeps 6. Privy. Site of the former Boy Scout Shelter.
Unreliable water in front of the shelter; follow blue-blazed trail 0.25 mile to a
slightly more reliable spring.

Catawba Mountain Shelter (1984)—Sleeps 6. Privy. Two water sources for this shelter:
One is a piped spring 50 yards south on the A.T., and the other is crossed a few feet
north of the piped spring, but often goes dry in summer. Tentsites available north
on the A.T.

McAfee Knob—Considered by many to have the best view in Virginia, McAfee Knob
is a tempting campsite. However, it is absolutely *verboten* to camp here; the knob
already sustains tremendous impact. Campbell Shelter or Pig Farm Campsite are
good alternatives if you want to climb back up to catch the sunset or sunrise from
the cliff.

Campbell Shelter (1989)—Sleeps 6. Privy. Water can be found by following the blue-
blazed trail left and behind the shelter. Follow the trail through the "electric meadow"
to the spring.

Tinker Cliffs—A cliff-walk half a mile long, with views back to McAfee Knob. Folk-
lore says the name comes from Revolutionary War deserters who hid near here and
repaired pots and pans ("tinkers").

Lamberts Meadow Shelter (1974)—Sleeps 6. Privy. Tentsites are 0.3 mile farther north on the A.T. Water is 50 yards down the trail in front of the shelter; reported dry in Aug 2007.

 U.S. 220/I-81 Interchange Area—The interchange area offers all the comforts of interstate vehicular travel, with most services near the A.T.

On U.S. 220. ▪ *Lodging:* Super 8, (540) 992-3000, hiker rates subject to availability, $36S/D, $6EAP, coin laundry, pool, no pets; Howard Johnson Express Inn, (540) 992-1234, hiker rate $55S/D, $5EAP, includes full B, holds UPS and USPS packages for registered guests sent to 437 Roanoke Road, Daleville, VA 24083, microwave & refrigerator, coin laundry, dogs permitted, $15 per pet. Both motels fill up quickly, particularly on the weekends. If you wish to stay there, make reservations during an earlier town stop. ▪ *Restaurants:* Pizza Hut with AYCE salad bar; Rancho Viejo Mexican. ▪ *Other services:* Several convenience stores.

West 0.3 mile to Botetourt Commons Shopping Plaza. ▪ *Restaurants:* Mill Mountain Coffee House, 3 Little Pigs BBQ, Wendy's, Bojangles. ▪ *Groceries:* Kroger Super Store, with pharmacy (long-term resupply). ▪ *Outfitter:* Outdoor Trails, (540) 992-5850, (M–F 10–8, Sa 9–6, closed Su), a full-service outfitter, sells fuel by the ounce and holds packages mailed to it at Botetourt Commons, 28 Kingston Dr., Daleville, VA 24083; make reservation for shuttle or slackpacking. ▪ *Internet access:* Outdoor Trails, if computer is not needed for the business. ▪ *Other services:* UPS Store, (540) 966-0220, M–F 8–6, Sa 9–5; bank with ATM.

West 1 mile to **Daleville, Va. [P.O. ZIP 24083: M–F 8–5, Sa 8–12 (540) 992-4422]**. Convenience stores and bank are nearby.

East 0.8 mile to U.S. 11. ▪ *Lodging:* Travelodge, (540) 992-6700, 2619 Lee Hwy., Troutville, VA 24175, $35D, $6EAP (total of 4 per room), pool, dogs $6, continental B; Comfort Inn, (540) 992-5600, 2545 Lee Hwy, Troutville, VA 24175, will hold UPS/USPS packages for incoming guests, ask for the "hiker-corporate" rates of $49.99S/D, $5EAP, includes continental B, pets $25, pool, and Internet access; Day Stop Inn (Travel Centers of America), (540) 992-3100, $50S/D, $6EAP up to 4 people, no pets allowed, 24-hour restaurant, coin laundry, showers available to nonguests $10; Red Roof Inn, (540) 992-5055, $46S/D, $5EAP, limited continental B, pets permitted, pool, hot tub, exercise room; Quality Inn, (540) 992-5335, $70S/D, pets permitted with one-time $25 fee, hot and cold continental B, pool, exercise room, microwave and refrigerator, will hold packages sent to 3139 Lee Hwy. South, Troutville, VA 24175; Holiday Inn Express, (540) 966-4444, $109S/D, weekends add $10, microwave and refrigerator in rooms, pool, continental B, holds UPS and USPS packages for registered guests mailed to 3200 Lee Hwy. South, Troutville, VA 24175. ▪ *Restaurants:*

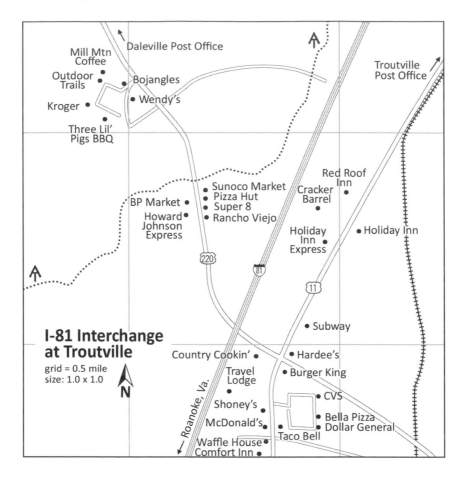

I-81 Interchange at Troutville

grid = 0.5 mile
size: 1.0 x 1.0

N

Mill Mtn Coffee
Daleville Post Office
Outdoor Trails
Bojangles
Kroger
Wendy's
Three Lil' Pigs BBQ
Troutville Post Office

BP Market
Sunoco Market
Pizza Hut
Super 8
Rancho Viejo
Howard Johnson Express
Cracker Barrel
Red Roof Inn
Holiday Inn Express
Holiday Inn

220
81
11

Subway
Country Cookin'
Hardee's
Burger King
Travel Lodge
CVS
Shoney's
McDonald's
Bella Pizza
Dollar General
Waffle House
Taco Bell
Comfort Inn
Roanoke, Va.

Cracker Barrel; Country Cookin', with $4.99 L and $5.99 D; Shoney's with $6.49 ($7.49 weekends and holidays) B bar; Italian Bella with AYCE L $5.49 Tu–F; Taco Bell; Waffle House; Best Wok; Subway inside Pilot Truck Stop, which also has $10 pay shower.

East 2.3 miles to **Cloverdale, Va. [P.O. ZIP 24077: M–F 8:30–11 & 11:30–4, Sa 9–12; (540) 992-2334]**, *via* U.S. 220 and U.S. 11 from the interchange area. ■ *Lodging:* Hollins Motel, (540) 992-2971, $35S, $40D, $45T, $48 for 4. ■ *Groceries:* Greenway Market (short-term resupply), open till 11. ■ *Restaurant:* Cloverdale Grill, M–F 8:30–3:30.

East 12 miles to Roanoke. ■ *Outfitters:* In downtown Roanoke, Walkabout Outfitters, (540) 777-2727, owned by 1999 thru-hiker Kirk Miller (Flying Money). Nearby in Salem, Va.: Backcountry Ski and Sports, (540) 389-8602. ■ *Other services:* Medical center that fits in hikers as schedule permits; veterinarian; CVS drug store; and several convenience stores.

U.S. 11—West 1.3 mile (1.5 miles north of the interchange area) to **Troutville, Va. [P.O. ZIP 24175: M–F 9–12 & 1–5, Sa 9–11; (540) 992-1472]**. Town hall, (540) 992-4401, M–F 9–5, sometimes allows hikers to camp at the city park, must check with town hall or find park manager; bathrooms and water available. ■ *Groceries:* Thriftway Market (long-term resupply), M–Sa 8–8, closed Su. ■ *Other services:* banks with ATMs. ■ *Shuttles:* Del Schechterly, (540) 529-6028, <dschecht1@juno. com>, helps hikers in need and shuttles from Pearisburg to Waynesboro.

Fullhardt Knob Shelter (1960s)—Sleeps 6. Privy. The water source for this shelter is an elaborate cistern system of water run-off hooked to the shelter's roof. Give the water enough time to flow through the freeze-proof valve, which is a few feet up the pipe toward the cistern. Please make sure spigot is off when you have finished getting water.

Wilson Creek Shelter (1986)—Sleeps 6. Privy. Water source is a reliable stream 200 yards in front of the shelter.

Blue Ridge Parkway—Black Horse Gap is the A.T.'s southernmost encounter with the Blue Ridge Parkway (BRP). The A.T. parallels BRP, and later Skyline Drive, for approximately 200 miles. Much of the original A.T. route along the Blue Ridge south of Roanoke was displaced by the parkway when it was built. Hitchhiking is not permitted on the BRP.

Natural Bridge Appalachian Trail Club—NBATC maintains the 90.7 miles between Black Horse Gap and the Tye River. Correspondence should be sent to NBATC, P.O. Box 3012, Lynchburg, VA 24503; <happifeet@msn.com>.

Bobblets Gap Shelter (1961)—Sleeps 6. Privy. Built by the USFS; the water source is a spring to the left of the shelter that is prone to go dry after prolonged rainless periods. Look farther downstream if the first source is dry.

Va. 43/Bearwallow Gap—**East,** then north 4.4 miles on the BRP to Peaks of Otter Area, (540) 586-1081, with lodge, restaurant, campground (no showers). Lodge rates vary, $80 and up, depending on day and time of year; reservations suggested. Restaurant serves a B buffet Sa and Su (only Su in winter), B/L/D daily. Campsites open May–Oct, $16, (540) 586-7321.

West 5 miles on Va. 43 to **Buchanan, Va. [P.O. ZIP 24066: M–F 8:30–1 & 1:30–4:30, Sa 10–12; (540) 254-2178].** ▪ *Lodging:* Wattstull Motel & Restaurant, (540) 254-1551, is 2 miles north of town on I-81, rates $65–$75, Internet access in some rooms. ▪ *Internet access:* Buchanan Library. ▪ *Other services:* grocery store, bank with ATM, restaurants.

Cove Mountain Shelter (1981)—Sleeps 6. Privy. No convenient water source at this shelter. A steep, unmarked trail to the left of the shelter leads 0.5 mile downhill to a stream.

Va. 614/Jennings Creek—Jennings Creek is a popular swimming hole for both hikers and local residents, with good tentsites in the woods beyond the bridge.

East 0.2 mile to Va. 618, then 0.1 mile to the USFS Middle Creek Picnic Area with covered picnic pavilions and well water; 1.1 miles farther on Va. 618 to *Camping:* Middle Creek Campground, (540) 254-2550, tentsites for 4 with shower $26; cabins sleep 4–6, $65 for 4, $75 for 6; showers $5. Campstore (short-term resupply), Coleman fuel and denatured alcohol by the ounce, Esbit, and coin laundry; accepts packages sent to 1164 Middle Creek Rd., Buchanan, VA 24066; when available, shuttle to the A.T.

West 4.5 miles to Wattstull Motel & Restaurant (see Buchanan entry above).

Bryant Ridge Shelter (1992)—Sleeps 20. Privy. This trilevel, timber-frame shelter is one of the A.T.'s largest. Water source is a stream 25 yards in front of the shelter, also crossed on the trail to the shelter.

Cornelius Creek Shelter (1960)—Sleeps 6. Privy. A blue-blazed trail leads to the shelter, but just north of the turn-off is a branch of Cornelius Creek where you can find water. Water can also be found on the trail to the shelter. An unmarked trail behind the shelter leads 0.1 mile to a fire road and then left 0.2 mile to the BRP, where it is then 6 miles south to the Peaks of Otter Area.

Apple Orchard Falls Trail—Located 2.6 miles north of Cornelius Creek Shelter. When the water is high, these falls are impressive, making the 3-mile round-trip worth the effort.

Apple Orchard Mountain—When you reach the top, you will be at 4,225 feet. Once an Air Force radar base, the meadows were covered with barracks and support-service buildings for 250 people. On the northern side of the mountain, the A.T. leads you under The Guillotine—an impressively large boulder stuck over the Trail between rock formations. No camping is permitted on top of the mountain, the highest point on the A.T. between Chestnut Knob and Mt. Moosilauke in New Hampshire.

Thunder Hill Shelter (1962)—Sleeps 6. Privy. Water source is a walled-in spring south of the shelter, prone to go dry by late summer. A larger, reliable spring can be found by going south on the A.T. to the BRP. At the BRP, turn left, walk 0.3 mile to a gated road on the left; 500 feet down the gated road, where the road turns left, angle right to a spring basin.

Matts Creek Shelter (1961)—Sleeps 6. Privy. Several small swimming holes are nearby. The rocks you will find in this area are 500 million years old. Tentsites can be found north 1.0 mile, where Matts Creek flows into the James River, with river views and the sound of trains across the river. Water source is Matts Creek, in front of the shelter.

James River Foot Bridge—This bridge, the longest foot-use-only bridge on the A.T., is dedicated to the memory of Bill Foot, a 1987 thru-hiker and ALDHA honorary life member (Trail-named "The Happy Feet" with his wife, Laurie) whose efforts in securing the existing piers, applying for grants, and gaining numerous agencies' cooperation made the bridge a reality.

U.S. 501 & Va. 130/James River—The two roads diverge at a fork east of the Trail crossing. On Va. 130, **East** 4.8 miles to *Camping:* Wildwood Campground, (434) 299-5228. Owners Terry and Dona Farmer provide tentsites $20 per tent, cabins $55–$75 for 4 adults, $3EAP; camp store, showers for registered guests, laundry facilities, pool, and snack bar.

On U.S. 501, **East** 5.3 miles to **Big Island, Va. [P.O. ZIP 24526: M–F 8:30–12:30 & 1:30–4:30, Sa 8–10; (434) 299-5072].** ■ *Groceries:* H&H Market, (434) 299-5153, open daily 5:15–9 (long-term resupply), short-order restaurant, B/L/D, and phone. *Restaurants:* Sharon's Pizza and More, (434) 299-7111, Tu–Sa 10:30–8, pizza, pasta, subs, desserts. ■ *Other services:* bank with ATM and medical center, (434) 299-5951.

   West 6.0 miles to **Glasgow, Va.** [**P.O. ZIP 24555: M–F 8–11:30, 12:30–4:30, Sa 8:30–10:30; (540) 258-2852**]. ■ *Lodging and Restaurant:* Howard's Family Restaurant & Motel, (540) 258-1300, 853 Rockbridge Rd.; home-cooked meals, daily buffet, F seafood buffet, Su fried chicken, home-made desserts and soups daily, B/L/D, M–Sa 6 a.m.–7 p.m., Su 7–6; rooms $42D, pets $20 unless service; short-term hiker box. ■ *Groceries:* Glasgow Grocery Express, open 6–11:30, has Coleman fuel by the ounce, denatured alcohol, and Heet. ■ *Restaurants:* Howard's (above); CC's Stop & Go, (540) 258-1900, deli and convenience store, M–Sa 6–11:30, Su 8–9, deli open M–Sa 10–7, Su 8–7. ■ *Internet access:* library, (540) 258-2509; M, Th 10–7; T, W 10–5:30. ■ *Other services:* Dollar General, coin laundry, bank with ATM. ■ *Shuttles:* Ken Wallace, (800) 918-6612, (434) 609-2704, between Black Horse Gap and Tye River (May–mid-Oct), sometimes farther.

Johns Hollow Shelter (1961)—Sleeps 6. Privy. Water source is a spring to the left of the shelter or a stream to right 25 yards from the shelter.

Bluff Mountain—Site of a monument to four-year-old Ottie Cline Powell. In the fall of 1890, Ottie went into the woods to gather firewood for his schoolhouse and never returned. His body was found five months later on top of this mountain. Some NBATC members erected a permanent gravestone for his final resting place, seven miles from the monument.

Punchbowl Shelter (1961)—Sleeps 6. Privy. Some believe this shelter is haunted by the ghost of Little Ottie. Tentsites nearby if the shelter is full, which it often is. Water source is a spring by a tree next to the pond drainage in front and to the left of the shelter. An alternative water source is a spring in the ravine north 0.4 mile, shortly after crossing the BRP.

Brown Mountain Creek Valley—Community of freed slaves lived here from the Civil War until about 1918; remains of cabins and interpretive signs tell of life in the valley then. ATC-involved archaeological studies are underway.

Brown Mountain Creek Shelter (1961)—Sleeps 6. Privy. Water source is a spring in front of, and uphill from, the shelter. In dry conditions, get water from Brown Mountain Creek, crossed on the side trail to the shelter.

U.S. 60—West 9.3 miles to **Buena Vista [P.O. ZIP 24416: M–F 8:30–4:30, closed Sa; (540) 261-8959].** ■ *Lodging:* Buena Vista Motel, (540) 261-2138, $49–$79; Budget Inn, (540) 261-2156, $44.95S, $59.95D, $10EAP, pet fee (allowed in smoking rooms only), laundry, Subway restaurant in motel, WiFi, continental B on weekends, possible shuttle to and from the Trail. ■ *Camping:* Glen Maury Campground, (540) 261-7321, tentsites with shower, $20 + 9% tax per tent, $2 shower without stay, pool $2 for guests. Pool closes mid-Aug. ■ *Groceries:* Food Lion (long-term resupply). ■ *Restaurants:* Todd's Barbeque and several fast-food options. ■ *Shuttles:* Rockbridge Taxi Service, (540) 261-7733, provides local shuttles, $2 per mile, farther distances with advance notice. ■ *Other services:* coin laundry, banks with ATM, hardware store, doctor, dentist, pharmacy, and veterinarian. ■ *Other attractions:* The annual Maury River Fiddlers Convention, popular with hikers, will be held at Glen Maury Park, the third weekend (Th, F, Sa) in Jun; Bluegrass Festival, the 4th weekend (Th, F, Sa) in Sep.

West 15 miles to **Lexington [P.O. ZIP 24450: M–F 9–5, Sa 10–12; (540) 463-6449].** A large town with groceries, motels, doctors, vets. *Outfitter:* Walkabout Outfitter, (540) 464-HIKE, 15 W. Washington St., M–Sa 10–5, owned by Kirk Miller (Flying Monkey '99), full-service outfitter, white gas by ounce, MSR canisters.

Cow Camp Gap Shelter (1986)—Sleeps 8. Privy. Water source is on blue-blazed trail to the left of the shelter; if you have crossed a small stream, you missed the spring.

Cold Mountain—Bald Knob, south of Cold Mountain, isn't a bald, but Cold Mountain and Tar Jacket Ridge are. A mowing project was undertaken by NBATC and the Forest Service to preserve the open views and habitat for northern cottontail rabbits, various raptors, turkey, and grouse. A 1994 law created the Mt. Pleasant National Scenic Area, including Cold Mountain and areas east.

Seeley–Woodworth Shelter (1984)—Sleeps 8. Privy. Continue 0.1 mile farther on blue-blaze to a piped spring.

Porters Field—West to a spring and campsite 300 feet down the second of two dirt roads.

 Spy Rock Road—This "road"—formerly known as Fish Hatchery Road—is a gated, one-lane dirt road with no traffic.

West 1.5 miles to the fish hatchery, 0.7 mile farther to **Montebello, Va. [P.O. ZIP 24464: M–F 8–12 & 12:30–4:30, Sa 9–11; (540) 377-9218]**, on Va. 56. Turn left, and reach town in 0.3 mile, with post office, grocery store, and campground. *Lodging:* Montebello Camping and Fishing (long-term resupply), (540) 377-2650, special thruhiker-rate tentsites with shower $10S, $3EAP, furnished efficiency cabin $80–$115, bed-only camping cabin $45–$55, shower only (without stay) $3.50 (pay at store first), denatured alcohol, propane fuel, laundry; Dutch Haus B&B, owners Earl and Lois Arnold, (800) 341-9777, $30PP, free L to thru-hikers May–Jun (SOBOs, call ahead), D extra, fuel by the ounce, credit cards accepted, laundry, shuttle, Internet access, holds mail drops sent to 655 Fork Mountain Ln., Montebello, VA 24464, call from top of Spy Rock Road for pick-up at bottom gate.

Crabtree Farm Road—West 0.5 mile to campsite and spring; 2 miles farther on the Crabtree Falls Trail to Crabtree Falls, one of the highest cascades in the East.

The Priest Shelter (1960)—Sleeps 8. Privy. Named for the massif dominating the area, this shelter is near a busy access for backpackers and is often full. Water source is a spring to the left of the shelter.

Va. 56/Tye River—West 3.9 miles to *Camping:* Crabtree Falls Campground (shortterm resupply), (540) 377-2066, <www.crabtreefallscampground.com>, <cfcg@ceva. net>. Go west 0.5 mile on Crabtree Farm Road to Crabtree Meadows parking area, then down Crabtree Falls Trail 2.9 miles to Va. 56, then east 0.5 mile to the campground. The campground offers tentsites with shower $23D, cabins $55D w/tax; M–Th 9–6, F–Sa 9–10, Su 9–2, no charge for shower without stay. Campground accepts packages for guests mailed to 11039 Crabtree Falls Hwy., Tyro, VA 22976; packages accepted are limited to shoebox size.

A 2008 relocation begins 0.5 mile north of the Tye River footbridge and ends at the southern Mau-Har Trail junction (reflected in the table at the beginning of this chapter). The new section passes through two mountain-laurel thickets and the remnants of a long-abandoned farm.

Tidewater Appalachian Trail Club—TATC maintains the 10.6 miles between the Tye River and Reeds Gap. Correspondence should be sent to P.O. Box 8246, Norfolk, VA 23503; <president@tidewateratc.org>; <www.tidewateratc.org>.

Mau-Har Trail—Traversing an area rich in waterfalls and good swimming holes, this steep, 3-mile blue-blaze connects with the A.T. at Maupin Field Shelter. It's shorter, but harder, than the white-blazed route.

Harpers Creek Shelter (1960)—Sleeps 6. Privy. Designated low-impact tentsites, which campers are requested to use. Water source is Harpers Creek, in front of the shelter. In extreme droughts, go upstream, and find water in the spring-fed ponds.

Maupin Field Shelter (1960)—Sleeps 6. Privy. Designated low-impact tentsites, which campers are requested to use. The Mau-Har Trail begins behind the shelter and rejoins the A.T. 3 miles south. Water source is a dependable spring behind the shelter.

Fire Road to Blue Ridge Parkway— From Maupin Field Shelter, turn left on fire road (just north of shelter), 1.2 miles to BRP. **South** on BRP 1.3 miles to *Hostel:* Rusty's Hard Time Hollow—Rusty Nesbitt's gravel driveway with gray pipe gate is on the left at BRP mile 16.7. Open 365/24/7. Section-hikers, thru-hikers, long-distance cyclists, and weekenders are welcome (no groups). Since 1982, Rusty has hosted more than 14,000 hikers and cyclists. The Hollow is a primitive, 19-acre, back-to-basics, Appalachian mountain farm and includes bunkhouses, springhouse, outhouse, and rainwater shower. No tenting allowed during peak season. Limited stay; exceptions for medical conditions. No dogs (because of free-ranging farm animals). Trips to nearby Sherando Lake for swimming on hot days. Rides back to the Trail. Keep in mind that the Hollow is Rusty's home. Donations are needed and appreciated, since Rusty has no other means to keep the Hollow going. No illegal drugs allowed. Mail drops not accepted.

Old Dominion Appalachian Trail Club—ODATC maintains the 19.1 miles between Reeds Gap and Rockfish Gap. Correspondence should be sent to P.O. Box 25283, Richmond, VA 23260; <dolli@smv.org>; <www.odatc.net>.

Humpback Rocks—The Trail circumvents the rocks, but, if you are seeking a bouldering opportunity, they may still be reached by a short, blue-blazed side trail.

Paul C. Wolfe Shelter (1991)—Sleeps 10. Privy. Built by ODATC and the Konnarock Crew, this shelter has windows and a porch cooking area. Tentsites available. Water source is Mill Creek, located 50 yards in front of the shelter.

Paul Wolfe Shelter to Rockfish Gap—The Trail passes through an old settlement, including home sites, terraced gardens, and a cemetery, all reputedly haunted.

Virginia—Part 3
(Shenandoah National Park)

Miles from Katahdin	Features	Services	Elev.	Miles from Springer
1,326.0	U.S. 250, I-64, Rockfish Gap **Waynesboro, VA 22980**	R, L, M (W–1m L; 4.5m PO, H, C, G, L, M, O, D, V, cl, sh, f, @)	1,902	853.1
1,326.6	I-64 overpass	R	1,902	852.5
1,326.4	Skyline Drive mp 105.2	R	1,902	852.7
1,325.9	SNP kiosk for camping permits self-registration; park entrance station	Kiosk on trail (W– 0.2m R)	2,200	853.2
1,323.0	Skyline Drive mp 102.1; McCormick Gap	R	2,450	856.1
1,321.7	Bear Den Mtn		2,885	857.4
1,321.2	Skyline Drive mp 99.5; Beagle Gap	R	2,550	857.9
1,319.7	**Calf Mtn Shelter...** *12.3mS; 13.5mN*	W–0.3m S, w	2,700	859.4
1,319.1	Spring	w	2,200	860.0
1,318.7	Skyline Drive mp 96.9; SNP southern boundary; Jarman Gap	R	2,250	860.4
1,318.5	Spring	w	2,150	860.6
1,316.9	Skyline Drive mp 95.3; Sawmill Run Overlook	R	2,200	862.2
1,315.3	Skyline Drive mp 94.1; Turk Gap	R	2,600	863.8
1,313.3	Skyline Drive mp 92.4	R	3,100	865.8
1,309.2	Skyline Drive mp 88.9	R	2,350	869.9
1,307.4	Skyline Drive mp 87.4; Blackrock Gap	R	2,321	871.7
1,307.2	Skyline Drive mp 87.2	R	2,700	871.9
1,306.7	**Blackrock Hut...** *13.5mS; 13.5mN*	E–0.2m S, w	2,645	872.4
1,306.1	Blackrock		3,100	873.0
1,305.1	Skyline Drive mp 84.3	R	2,800	874.0

Miles from Katahdin	Features	Services	Elev.	Miles from Springer
1,303.6	Skyline Drive mp 82.9; Browns Gap	R	2,600	875.5
1,302.7	Skyline Drive mp 82.2	R	2,800	876.4
1,302.3	Skyline Drive mp 81.9; Doyles River Parking Overlook	R	2,800	876.8
1,301.4	Skyline Drive mp 81.1; Doyles River Cabin (locked)	R (E–0.3m w)	2,900	877.7
1,299.3	+Loft Mtn Campground	W–0.2m C, G, cl, sh; 1.2m M	3,300	879.8
1,298.2	Frazier Discovery Trail to Loft Mtn Wayside	W–0.6m R, M	2,950	880.9
1,297.5	Loft Mtn		3,200	881.6
1,297.2	Spring	W–0.1m w	2,950	881.9
1,295.1	Skyline Drive mp 77.5; Ivy Creek Overlook	R	2,800	884.0
1,293.5	**Pinefield Hut**... *13.5mS; 8.4mN*	E–0.1m S, C, w	2,430	885.6
1,293.3	Skyline Drive mp 75.2; Pinefield Gap	R	2,590	885.8
1,291.4	Skyline Drive mp 73.2; Simmons Gap	R (E–0.2m w)	2,250	887.7
1,288.1	Skyline Drive mp 69.9; Powell Gap	R	2,294	891.0
1,287.7	Little Roundtop Mtn		2,700	891.4
1,286.5	Skyline Drive mp 68.6; Smith Roach Gap	R	2,600	892.6
1,285.3	**Hightop Hut**... *8.4mS; 12.6mN*	W–0.1m S; 0.2m C, w	3,175	893.8
1,284.8	Spring	w	3,450	894.3
1,284.7	Hightop Mtn		3,587	894.4
1,283.2	Skyline Drive mp 66.7	R	2,650	895.9
1,281.9	Skyline Drive mp 65.5; Swift Run Gap, U.S.33 **Elkton, VA 22827**	R (W–2.9m L; 3.2m C, L, G, M, cl; 7.5m PO, G, M)	2,367	897.2
1,278.9	South River Picnic Grounds	W–0.1m w	3,200	900.2
1,275.5	Pocosin Cabin (locked)	W–0.1m w	3,150	903.6
1,275.4	Spring	w	3,100	903.7
1,273.6	Skyline Drive mp 57.6; +Lewis Mtn Campground/Cabins	R (W–0.1m C, L, G, cl, sh)	3,500	905.5

Miles from Katahdin	Features	Services	Elev.	Miles from Springer
1,272.9	**Bearfence Mtn Hut**... *12.6mS; 11.8mN*	E–0.1m S, C, w	3,110	906.2
1,270.3	Skyline Drive mp 55.1; Bootens Gap	R	3,243	908.8
1,269.4	Hazeltop		3,812	909.7
1,267.5	Skyline Drive mp 52.8; Milam Gap	R	3,300	911.6
1,266.6	Spring	w	3,380	912.5
1,265.8	Big Meadows Wayside; Harry F. Bird, Sr., Visitor Ctr	R, w (E–0.4m G, M)	3,390	913.3
1,264.9	Big Meadows Lodge; +Big Meadows Campground	E–0.1m C, L, M, cl, sh, @; 0.9m G, M	3,500	914.2
1,264.3	David Spring	w	3,490	914.8
1,263.3	Skyline Drive mp 49.3; Fishers Gap	R	3,050	915.8
1,261.4	**Rock Spring Hut** and (locked) Cabin... *11.8mS; 11.1mN*	W–0.2m S, C, w	3,465	917.7
1,261.1	Trail to Hawksbill Mtn, Byrd's Nest #2 Picnic Shelter	E– 0.9m	3,600	918.0
1,260.1	Skyline Drive mp 45.6; Hawksbill Gap	R	3,361	919.0
1,259.7	Skyline Drive mp 44.4; trail to Crescent Rock Overlook		3,450	919.4
1,257.6	Skyland Service Rd (south— horse stables)	R	3,550	921.5
1,256.8	Skyland Service Rd (north— best access to Skyland)	R (W–0.2m M, L)	3,790	922.3
1,256.4	Trail to Stony Man Summit		3,837	922.7
1,254.8	Skyline Drive mp 38.6; Hughes River Gap; trail to Stony Man Mtn Overlook	R, w	3,097	924.3
1,252.6	Skyline Drive mp 36.7; Pinnacles Picnic Ground	R, w	3,390	926.5
1,252.5	Skyline Drive mp 36.4; Trail to Jewell Hollow Overlook	R	3,350	926.6
1,251.5	The Pinnacle		3,730	927.6
1,250.5	**Byrds Nest #3 Hut**... *11.1mS; 4.6mN*	E–0.3m w, C, S	3,290	928.6
1,249.8	Meadow Spring	E–0.3m w	3,100	929.3
1,249.2	Marys Rock		3,514	929.9

Miles from Katahdin	Features	Services	Elev.	Miles from Springer
1,247.3	Skyline Drive mp 31.5; Thornton Gap, U.S. 211 **Luray, VA 22835**	R (W–0.1m w; 4.6m L, M; 5.6m C, G, cl; 8m PO, L, M, G, O, D, V, cl, @)	2,307	931.8
1,246.1	**Pass Mtn Hut...** *4.6mS; 13.5mN*	E–0.2m S, w	2,690	933.0
1,245.3	Pass Mtn		3,052	933.8
1,244.0	Skyline Drive mp 28.6; Beahms Gap	R	2,490	935.1
1,243.9	Skyline Drive mp 28.5	R	2,490	935.2
1,243.8	Byrds Nest #4 Picnic Shelter	E–0.5m	2,600	935.3
1,239.2	Spring	w	2,600	939.9
1,238.7	Skyline Drive mp 23.9; Elkwallow Gap; Elkwallow Wayside	R (E–0.1m G, M)	2,480	940.4
1,237.9	Range View Cabin (locked)	E–0.1m w	2,950	941.2
1,237.2	Skyline Drive mp 21.9; Rattlesnake Point Overlook	R	3,100	941.9
1,236.6	Tuscarora Trail (southern terminus) to +Matthews Arm Campground	W–0.7m C	3,400	942.5
1,236.2	Skyline Drive mp 21.1	R	3,350	942.9
1,236.0	Hogback Third Peak		3,400	943.1
1,235.9	Skyline Drive mp 20.8	R	3,350	943.2
1,235.7	Hogback Second Peak		3,475	943.4
1,235.5	Spring	E–0.2m w	3,250	943.6
1,235.4	Hogback First Peak		3,390	943.7
1,234.8	Skyline Drive mp 19.7; Little Hogback Overlook	R	3,000	944.3
1,234.6	Little Hogback Mtn		3,050	944.5
1,234.1	Skyline Drive mp 18.9	R	2,850	945.0
1,233.0	**Gravel Springs Hut...** *13.5mS; 10.7mN*	E–0.2m S, C, w	2,480	946.1
1,232.8	Skyline Drive mp 17.7; Gravel Springs Gap	R	2,666	946.3
1,231.7	South Marshall Mtn		3,212	947.4
1,231.2	Skyline Drive mp 15.9	R	3,050	947.9
1,230.5	North Marshall Mtn		3,368	948.6
1,229.6	Hogwallow Spring	w	2,950	949.5

Miles from Katahdin	Features	Services	Elev.	Miles from Springer
1,229.0	Skyline Drive mp 14.2; Hogwallow Gap	R	2,739	950.1
1,227.3	Skyline Drive mp 12.3; Jenkins Gap	R	2,400	951.8
1,226.4	Compton Springs	w	2,700	952.7
1,226.0	Compton Peak		2,909	953.1
1,225.2	Skyline Drive mp 10.4; Compton Gap	R	2,550	953.9
1,225.0	Indian Run Spring	E–0.3m w	2,350	954.1
1,223.5	SNP kiosk for camping permits self-registration; Compton Gap Rd, Compton Gap Trail	N–0.5m H, sh, f, M	2,350	955.6
1,223.3	SNP northern boundary, Possums Rest Overlook		2,300	955.8
1,222.5	**Tom Floyd Wayside...** *10.7mS; 8.1mN*	S	1,900	956.6
1,221.5	Northern Virginia 4-H Swimming Pool	W–0.3m	1,350	957.6
1,221.0	Va. 602	R	1,150	958.1
1,219.6	U.S. 522 **Front Royal, VA 22630**	R (W 3.2m G, L, M, O, cl, f, @; 4.2m PO, M, D, @)	950	959.5

+Fee charged, mp=milepost

Shenandoah National Park, with 103 miles of well-graded Appalachian Trail, is memorable for its many vistas and abundant wildlife. Skyline Drive, which you will cross 28 times, has many waysides and concessions for resupply stops. *Backcountry permits are required when camping in the park.*

U.S. 250, I-64/Rockfish Gap—Where the A.T. crosses U.S. 250, it is **West** 500 yards to the new Rockfish Gap Visitors Center (on the hill next to the Inn at Afton), (540) 943-5187. Open daily 9–5, it offers an information packet on the area, created specifically for hikers, that notes all services and includes a list of people who provide free shuttles to town. If closed, packets are in box near door and a pay phone. ∎ *Lodging:* Inn at Afton, (540) 942-5201, above and behind the visitors' center, $60–$100, B/L/D, pool, pets allowed, vehicles may be parked in lot; leave name, vehicle information, and date of return with desk staff.

West 1 mile to *Lodging:* Colony House Motel, (540) 942-4156, hiker rate $48.80 incl. tax., pets $10, pool, laundry, can shuttle back to Trail if asked and available. **West** 4.5 miles to **Waynesboro, Va. [P.O. ZIP 22980: M–F 9–5, closed Sa; (540) 942-7320]**, a large, hiker-friendly town with most services. The tourism office and the Waynesboro "Trail angels" are holding their sixth annual Hiker Fest on June 5 at Grace Evangelical Lutheran Church, 500 South Wayne Ave. The fest will include dinner, a movie, and much more for a nominal fee. All hikers are welcome! ■ *Hostel:* Grace Evangelical Lutheran Church, 500 South Wayne Ave., open May 17–Jun 27, closed Su nights, check-in 5–9 p.m., check-out 9 a.m, but will store packs for those staying over another night. Lounge with big-screen TV, a/c, Internet, showers, cots, kitchen, snacks, and continental breakfast. Members of the congregation host a W night supper for hikers (max. 15) followed by an optional vespers service. No pets, drugs, smoking, alcohol, firearms, foul language. Maximum 15 hikers; 2-night limit. Donations accepted. ■ *Camping:* Waynesboro Family YMCA, (540) 942-5107, on South Wayne Ave., offers tentsites on a grassy area near the South River. Check-in at desk M–F 5:15 a.m.–10 p.m., Sa 8–5, Su 1–5. Although not officially a hostel, the YMCA offers showers, restroom, gym, and pay phone; donations appreciated. ■ *Lodging:* Quality Inn, (540) 942-1171, new owners may not give hiker rate, $52–$75, pets in smoking rooms only $10; Tree Streets Inn B&B, (540) 949-4484, $65S/D includes B, shuttle, mail drops accepted for guests sent to 421 Walnut Ave. ■ *Groceries:* Kroger (long-term resupply). ■ *Restaurants:* Ming Garden, AYCE L/D; Gavid's Steaks; Scottos Italian; Ciros Pizza; Pizza Hut, AYCE L/D; Chickpeas; Shukis BBQ, Weasie's Kitchen, B/L/D with AYCE pancake B anytime, open M–Sa 5:30–8, Su 7–2; many fast-food outlets. ■ *Outfitter:* Rockfish Gap Outfitters, (540) 943-1461, located on U.S. 250 on the way to town; fuel by the ounce, backpacking gear, large footwear selection, minor gear repairs, and warranty assistance. ■ *Internet access:* Waynesboro Public Library, M–F 9–9, Sa 9–5; Grace Church during times of hostel operation (see above). ■ *Other services:* cobbler, coin laundry, pharmacy, ATM, doctor, dentist, veterinarian, barber, massages, Western Union, and one-hour photo service. More motels, restaurants, and groceries are 2 miles south on U.S. 340 (Rosser Ave.) at I-64.

Potomac Appalachian Trail Club—PATC maintains the 239.7 miles between Rockfish Gap and Pine Grove Furnace State Park in Pennsylvania. Send correspondence to PATC, 118 Park St. SE, Vienna, VA 22180; (703) 242-0693; <www.potomacappalachian.org>; <info@patc.net>.

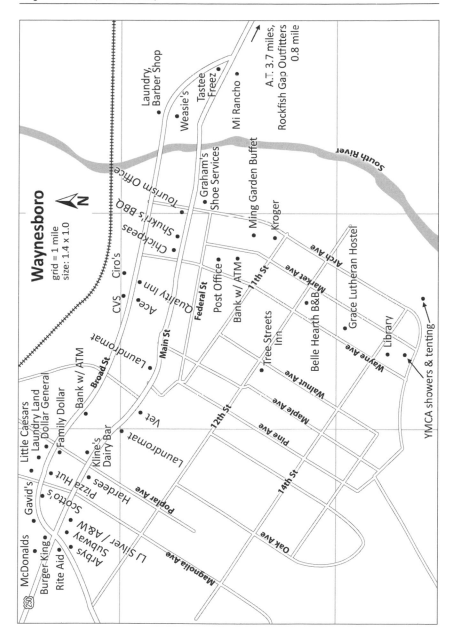

Waynesboro

grid = 1 mile
size: 1.4 x 1.0

N

A.T. 3.7 miles,
Rockfish Gap Outfitters
0.8 mile

Laundry,
Barber Shop

Weasie's

Tastee
Freez

Mi Rancho

South River

Graham's
Shoe Services

Tourism Office

Ming Garden Buffet

Kroger

Shukri's BBQ

Chickpeas

Ciro's

CVS

Ace

Quality Inn

Federal St

Post Office

Bank w/ ATM

11th St

Market Ave

Arch Ave

Grace Lutheran Hostel

Belle Hearth B&B

Library

Wayne Ave

Tree Streets
Inn

Main St

Laundromat

Broad St

Bank w/ ATM

Walnut Ave

Maple Ave

YMCA showers & tenting

Little Caesars

Laundry Land

Dollar General

Family Dollar

Vet

12th St

Pine Ave

Laundromat

14th St

Kline's
Dairy Bar

Hardees

Poplar Ave

Pizza Hut

Scotto's

Gavid's

Oak Ave

Magnolia Ave

McDonalds

Burger King

Arbys

Subway

LJ Silver / A&W

Rite Aid

250

Shenandoah National Park—Although the SNP presents some significant ascents and descents, hikers generally will find the Trail within the park well-graded.

Park history—In 1926, Congress authorized the creation of the Shenandoah and Great Smoky Mountains national parks. Unlike western parks, most of today's Shenandoah parkland was privately owned; the Blue Ridge here had been dotted with communities and isolated groups of settlers since the 1750s. Areas had long been farmed and grazed. Out-of-state corporations had exploited some areas for timber products and mineral ores. Three resorts provided Victorian-era vacationers with cool mountain breezes and recreation.

By the 1910s, conditions were changing. A blight killing American chestnut trees, some 30–40 percent of the Appalachian forest, had destroyed not only large swaths of the forest but a way of life for many. Those trees provided nuts that were shipped by railroad to cities, providing mountain families with cash income. The chestnut was strong, straight, and rot-resistant, and its wood was valuable for fence posts, railroad ties, roof shingles, siding boards, and general lumber that residents used and sold in the Shenandoah Valley and the Piedmont.

In 1927, Virginia authorized condemnation of all private property within the boundary of the proposed park. More than 4,000 tracts were surveyed, and 1,081 were purchased and given to the federal government, uprooting most of the 465 families who lived on the land. Virginia resettled the majority and evicted those unwilling to move. Approximately 45 elderly residents were allowed to spend the remainder of their years in their homes.

In 1931, four years before Shenandoah was established, construction of Skyline Drive began. First built as a second entrance to President Herbert Hoover's summer White House, Rapidan Camp, the road was only to go from the camp to Skyland. State leaders successfully lobbied for congressional appropriations to extend the highway north to Thornton Gap (U.S. 211), on to Front Royal, and then south to Rockfish Gap. But, until the park was established in December 1935, Skyline Drive existed only as a 100-foot right-of-way within privately held land that basically co-incided with the route of the A.T. In 1933, President Franklin D. Roosevelt's CCC "boys" established camps along the route and built many of the facilities, overlooks, rock walls, and gutters seen there today. They planted hundreds of thousands of trees and shrubs, creating the landscape that draws millions of visitors to the park, and built a new route for the A.T. ATC Chair Myron Avery's acceptance of this disruption produced an open schism between the organization's leadership and founder Benton MacKaye and his allies in New York and New England.

Today, 95 percent reforested, the park is home to wild turkey, white-tailed deer, black bears, and shelter mice. Hundreds of migrating birds and butterflies summer or stop over in this central Appalachian biome. Nearly one million visitors a year come to watch wildlife, get back to nature, view the Shenandoah Valley to the west and the foothills to the east, or visit land on which their ancestors lived.

Ranger Programs—From Memorial Day through Oct, rangers present a variety of organized hikes, programs, and participatory events highlighting the natural and human history of the park. The SNP visitors' guide, available at entrance stations and visitors centers, outlines the seasonal schedule.

Forest Damage—Hurricane Isabel (2003) and fires before it damaged thousands of acres. Coupled with the floods, Tropical Storm Fran in 1996, a severe ice storm in 1998 and 2006, and gypsy-moth and woolly adelgid infestations, the park has been hit hard in recent years. Be mindful of trees and branches that have been weakened by those events and could still fall.

Fee—Hikers entering the park *via* the A.T. are not charged a fee; hikers entering at other trailheads in SNP may incur one. During the spring (mid-Feb to mid-Apr), the park occasionally conducts prescribed burns along the A.T. to manage vegetation. During burns, a hut may be closed up to 3 days. Check the ATC or park Web sites or ask at any NPS station for current information.

Backcountry Permits—While there is no charge for permits, they are required of all thru-hikers and overnight backcountry travelers. Backcountry self-registration kiosks are located on the A.T. near the north and south boundaries of SNP. If you fail to register or can't show proof of registration when rangers ask for it, they may issue a citation or fine. Permits may also be obtained at Skyline Drive entrance stations and park visitors centers when they are open. A permit can be acquired in advance by calling (540) 999-3500, M–F 8–4. Be familiar with the regulations, have your exact itinerary ready, and allow 5–7 business days for the permit to be mailed. Write to: Superintendent, ATTN: Backcountry Camping Permit, 3655 U.S. Hwy. 211 East, Luray, VA 22835. See also <www.nps.gov/shen/planyourvisit/cambc_regs.htm>.

Backcountry Accommodations—Two types of three-sided structures are near the A.T.—day-use (called "shelters") and overnight-use (called "huts"). Camping at or near the day-use shelters is prohibited. Huts are available to long-distance hikers (those having an itinerary of at least three consecutive nights) on a first-come, first-served basis. Tenting at huts is permitted in designated campsites marked with a post and a tenting symbol; all huts within the park have campsites available. The PATC also operates several locked cabins within the park that require advance reservations and other arrangements. Contact PATC for details.

Backcountry Regulations

- Campfires are prohibited in SNP, except at the commercial campgrounds and established fireplaces at shelters, huts, and cabins. Use a backpacking stove.

- Camping is prohibited within 10 yards of a stream or other natural water source; within 20 yards of a park trail or unpaved fire road; within 50 yards of culturally historic sites, other campers, or no-camping signs; within 100 yards of a hut, cabin, or day-use shelter (except designated sites); within 0.25 mile of a paved road, park boundary, picnic area, visitors center, or commercial facility. Several zones have been designated "noncamping areas," including Limberlost, Hawksbill Summit, Whiteoak Canyon, Old Rag summit, Big Meadows clearing, and Rapidan Camp.

- Camping is permitted almost everywhere else. New regulations encourage hikers to seek "preexisting campsites" in legal locations that show signs of use and are not posted with no-camping signs. Camping at those sites is limited to two consecutive nights. If necessary, dispersed camping at undisturbed sites is permissible, but they must be left in pristine condition; use such sites only one night.

- Maximum group size is 10 people.

- Food must be stored so that wildlife cannot get it—hang food from a tree branch at least ten feet from the ground and four feet away from a tree's trunk. Alternatively, overnight huts feature food-storage poles, which are to be used instead of the familiar "mouse hangers." Park-approved, bear-resistant food-storage canisters are also permissible.

- Solid human waste should be buried in accordance with Leave No Trace ethics, under 6 inches of soil, more than 200 feet from trails, water sources, or roads.

- Carry out all trash from the backcountry, and dispose of it properly.

- Glass containers are discouraged.

- Pets must be leashed at all times and are prohibited on certain side trails.

Commercial Facilities—Campgrounds, restaurants, lodges, waysides, and small stores are normally open spring through fall and are located strategically near the A.T. and Skyline Drive. Long-distance hikers may be able to save pack weight by resupplying or taking meals at these facilities. Call the park for the precise dates and times of operation. Most operate weekends-only Apr through mid-May and daily thereafter through Oct. More details can be found at <www.visitshenandoah. com>. Campground reservations: (877) 444-6777 or <www.recreation.gov>. Site rates range from $17 to $20.

Calf Mountain Shelter (1984)—Sleeps 6. Privy. Featuring two skylights, this shelter is not a part of the SNP hut system, so SNP rules don't apply here. Water source is a piped spring on the access trail to the shelter.

Blackrock Hut (1941)—Sleeps 6. Privy. Designated tentsites nearby. Water source is a piped spring 10 yards in front of the shelter.

Loft Mountain Campground—Open mid-May to late Oct. The A.T. skirts the campground, but several short side trails lead to campsites and the camp store (short-term resupply). Campsites $16, subject to change; showers $1, laundry, restroom, soda machine, and pay phone at entrance station. Loft Mountain Wayside and Grill serves B/L/D, short-order menu, soda machine. From the camp store, follow the paved road 1.0 mile downhill to Skyline Drive or continue north on the A.T. 0.9 mile and take the Frazier Discovery Trail 0.5 mile west (steep descent) to Skyline Drive.

Pinefield Hut (1940)—Sleeps 6. Privy. Designated tentsites nearby. Water source is a spring behind the shelter 50 yards. It tends to fail during dry seasons, in which case you can get water from Ivy Creek or Loft Mountain Campground, for northbounders, and an outdoor spigot at the Simmons Gap ranger station, for southbounders.

Simmons Gap—Simmons Gap ranger station is down the paved road 0.2 mile east from where the A.T. crosses Skyline Drive. Frost-free pump.

Hightop Hut (1939)—Sleeps 6. Privy. Designated campsites nearby. Water source is a usually reliable piped spring 0.1 mile from the shelter on a side trail. An alternative water source is a boxed spring 0.5 mile north on the Trail.

U.S.33/Swift Run Gap/Spotswood Trail—West from Skyline Drive to pay phone, water. Backcountry self-registration station located at SNP entrance station, north of U.S. 33 bridge.

On U.S. 33—West 2.9 miles to *Lodging:* Country View Motel, (540) 298-0025, $40, no pet fee, shuttle possible back to Trail and Elkton, mail drops accepted for guests sent to 19974 Spotswood Trail, Elkton, VA 22827; Misty Mountain Motel, (540) 298-9771, $43–$53 1–4 people, no pets, all rooms nonsmoking.

West 3.2 miles to *Lodging:* Elkton Motel, (540) 298-1463, $39–$54D (one bed), no pets, CATV, refrigerator, microwave. ▪ *Camping:* Swift Run Camping, (540) 298-8086, $20 campsite, laundry, pool, and snack bar. ▪ *Groceries:* Bear Mountain Grocery, with a deli, daily 6–9.

West 7.5 miles to **Elkton, Va. [P.O. ZIP 22827: M–F 8:30–4:30, Sa 9–11; (540) 298-7772].**
▪ *Groceries:* Food Lion, O'Dell's Grocery (both long-term resupply). ▪ *Restaurants:* several fast-food places. ▪ *Other services:* pharmacy, bank, and ATM.

South River Parking Area—Water, picnic benches, restrooms with sinks.

Lewis Mountain Campground and Cabins—(540) 999-2255. Open Apr 9–Nov 7; reservations, (800) 999-4714. The A.T. passes in sight of the campground, and several short side trails lead to campsites and the camp store. Campsites $16; hiker special only for cabins available *via* <www.visitshenandoah.com/mvs> or by calling (877) 778-2871 (press option 2, and ask for code SHMVS). *Campground sites are not on the reservation system.* Lewis Mountain Camp Store (short-term resupply), open 9–7 in summer. Showers $1, laundry, restroom, soda machine, and pay phone.

Bearfence Mountain Hut (1940)—Sleeps 6. Privy. Designated tentsites nearby. Located on a blue-blazed trail. Water source is a piped spring in front of the shelter; prone to fail during even moderately dry spells.

Big Meadows Lodge, Campground, and Wayside—The A.T. passes within sight of the campground, and short side trails lead to the lodge, which also houses a restaurant and tap room and has Internet access. ▪ *Lodging:* hiker special (includes B, taxes, B gratuity) available available *via* <www.visitshenandoah.com/mvs> or by calling (877) 778-2871 (press option 2, and ask for code SHMVS); rooms available in main lodge; also cabins, suites, and motel-type accommodations. A few pet-friendly rooms. Reservations required. Lodging and restaurant open May 20–Nov 7. ▪ *Camping:* Open Apr 1–Nov 28, reservations recommended. Walk-ins are possible, but the campground is often full; (800) 365-CAMP (use SHEN designator); showers $1, laundry. ■ *Restaurant:* Dining room open daily for L/D; tap room, with nightly entertainment and light fare, open daily from late afternoon to late evening. From the lodge, follow the paved entrance road 0.9 mile to Big Meadows Wayside and Grill, B/L/D, open Apr 1–Nov 28, with short-order menu. ■ *Groceries:* Wayside has a good selection (short-term resupply) and camping supplies, pay phone, and soda machine. Next door is the Harry F. Byrd, Sr., Visitors Center, with exhibits and videos on the history of the area.

Rock Spring Hut (1940, updated 1980)—former Shaver Hollow Shelter, moved and rebuilt by PATC with chestnut logs from original CCC shelters. Sleeps 8. Privy. Designated tentsites nearby. Located on 0.2-mile blue-blazed trail. Water source, down a steep trail in front of the hut, flows from beneath a rock.

Skyland Service Road/Skyland—Skyland was originally a 19th-century mountain summer resort owned by George Freeman Pollack, who pushed hard to evict surrounding small landholders and create a national park and then, ironically, was forced to sell and give up management of the resort. Cross the road at the stables, and follow the A.T. north, passing a water tank on your right and the junction marked by a concrete post, which points to Skyland and dining room.

   West 0.2 mile to *Lodging:* Skyland, (800) 999-4714, open Apr 1–Nov 28; hiker special (includes B, taxes, B gratuity) available available *via* <www.visitshenandoah.com/mvs> or by calling (877) 778-2871 (press option 2, and ask for code SHMVS); also motel-type accommodations and suites, reservations required. A few pet-friendly rooms. ■ *Restaurant:* Pollack Dining Room serves B/L/D; limited hours. Tap room, light fare, nightly entertainment.

Pinnacles Picnic Area—Restrooms, covered area, picnic tables, fireplaces. Uphill from picinic pavilion is a frost-free pump for year-round water.

Byrds Nest #3 Hut—A picnic shelter converted to overnight use in the fall of 2008; sleeps 8. Privy. A spring is 0.3 mile east, down the fire road.

U.S. 211/Thornton Gap/Panorama—A short side trail, on the southern side of Thornton Gap, leads to Panorama area. The restaurant and backcountry-permit office were torn down in 2008; new restrooms, water source, pay phone, and a parking area have been installed at "east" end of lot. Park entrance station is north of U.S. 211, east of where the Trail crosses Skyline Drive, with water.

   On U.S. 211—West 4.6 miles to *Lodging:* Brookside Cabins, (540) 743-5698, luxury cabins $85–$195; full-menu restaurant featuring home-style foods and daily AYCE L/D buffet, weekend B buffet, open 8–8 (summer until 9). Closed early Dec–Jan 1.

West 5.6 miles to ■ *Lodging:* Days Inn, (540) 743-4521, $50–$200, pets $10.

■ *Camping:* Yogi Bear's Jellystone Park, (540) 743-4002, <www.campwray.com>, tentsites $25–$45, cabins $45–$149, two-night minimum on weekends, campstore (short-term resupply), pool, pay phone, laundry.

West 8.0 miles to the town of **Luray, Va. [P.O. ZIP 22835: M–F 8:30–4:30, closed Sa; (540) 743-2100]**. Page County Chamber of Commerce, <www.luraypage.com>, 18 Campbell St., (540) 743-3915, M–Sa 9–5, Su 12–4. ■ *Lodging:* Best Value Cardinal Inn, (888) 648-4633, $59 and up, no pets; Best Western Motel, (540) 743-6511, $70–$160, pets $20; Budget Inn, (540) 743-5176, $49s and up, pets $5. ■ *Groceries:* Farmer's Foods, Food Lion, Walmart (all long-term resupply). ■ *Restaurants:* Anthony's Pizza XII, L/D; Southern Station Diner, B/L/D; East Wok, L/D and AYCE L; Mindi's Mexican, L/D; Moment to Remember, espresso, sandwiches, desserts; Artisan's Grill, deli sandwiches and full meals; Uncle Buck's; The Speakeasy at the Mimslyn Inn, sandwiches and D 4–10 p.m., full bar; and several fast-food restaurants. ■ *Internet access:* Page County Library. ■ *Outfitters:* Appalachian Outdoors Adventures, 18 E. Main St., (540) 743-7400, full-service outfitter, fuel by the ounce, M–Sa 10–6, Su 1–5. ■ *Other services:* veterinarian, Blue Mountain Animal Clinic, (540) 743-PETS; 3 laundromats; hospital; ATM; and 5-screen Page Theater. ■ *Shuttles:* Mountain & Valley Shuttle Service, Rodney Ketterman and Jim "Skyline" Austin, Luray, Va., (877) 789-3210, <www.mvshuttle.com>, offers shuttles between Duncannon, Pa., and Daleville, Va. Also serves nearby airports, Amtrak, Greyhound. Offers trail logistics, town assistance (one-day notice appreciated). Free limited rustic camping for shuttle clients night before or upon conclusion of hike, on-site parking at base camp (shelter, picnic table, grill, fire pit, hot shower, flush toilet). Accepts Visa, MC, Discover.

Pass Mountain Hut (1939)—Sleeps 8. Privy. Known for the "kissing trees," the shelter is located on a blue-blazed trail. Designated campsites nearby. Water source is a piped spring 15 yards behind the shelter.

Elkwallow Wayside and Grill—Open 9–7 early Apr–early Oct. Visible from where the A.T. crosses Skyline Drive in Elkwallow Gap, the wayside includes a grill, gift shop, and restroom. Grill, B/L/D. Last chance in SNP for northbounders to get a blackberry milkshake. Gift shop offers limited groceries and camping supplies. Pay phone, soda machine outside. Frost-free pump at picnic area.

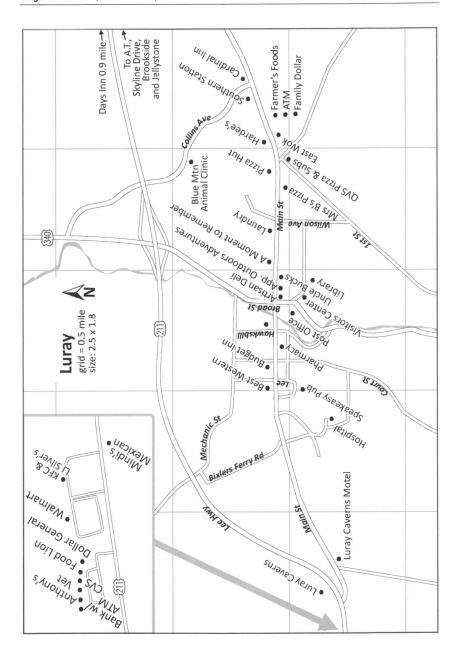

Mathews Arm Campground—West 1.2 miles from the A.T., 0.3 mile south of the Hogback Parking Area *via* the Tuscarora and Traces trails. Signs lead to nearby primitive (*i.e.,* no services) campground, open mid-May–late Oct, campsites $16 per night, rate subject to change. This junction is the southern end of the 260-mile Tuscarora Trail. The northern is on the A.T. south of Darlington Shelter in Pennsylvania.

Gravel Springs Hut (1940)—Sleeps 8. Privy. Designated tentsites nearby. On a blue-blazed trail. The water source is a boxed spring found on side trail near the shelter.

Compton Gap Trail—At the last SNP concrete post on the Trail, labeled Va. 610/Chester Gap, the A.T. will turn left. Go straight, following the Compton Gap Trail 0.5 mile ahead to road. ■ *Hostel:* Front Royal Terrapin Station Hostel, 304 Chester Gap Rd., Chester Gap, VA 22623, (540) 539-0509, (540) 631-0777, is the first house on left side of the paved road. Enter around back through marked gate (residential neighborhood; please respect noise level). Open May 2–Jul 10, includes bunk with mattress and sheets, shower, soap, shampoo, towels, shower clothes, toaster oven, laundry, free computer, free shuttle to town; mail drops for guests only; fuel, snacks, soda, ice cream, and oven pizza on site. Shuttles and slackpacking available. Cost: 1 hiker, $19 one day; couple, $34 one day; hiking groups, $17 PP one day; each extra night, $16/hiker, $30/couple, $15PP/groups. Owned by Mike Evans, (AT'95, PCT'98), <gratefulgg@hotmail.com>.

Southbound Registration Station—1.0 mile south of Tom Floyd Wayside.

Tom Floyd Wayside (1980s)—Sleeps 6. Privy. Shelter has an overhanging front deck with storage space above, a railed deck with benches, and several designated tentsites. Outside the SNP boundary, so SNP rules don't apply. Water source 0.2 mile on a blue-blazed trail to the right of the shelter often stops flowing. Next closest water source is a stream crossed about 1.5 miles north on the A.T. near Va. 602.

Northern Virginia 4-H Swimming Pool—Blue-blazed side trail 0.9 mile north of Tom Floyd Wayside leads 0.3 mile **West** to the swimming pool. It is open to the public, including hikers, 12–6 daily (Memorial Day–Labor Day), $5 admission, swimsuits required. Inquire at 4-H office about multiday parking availability (advance arrangements required). Mountain & Valley Shuttle Service (above) can facilitate parking here for clients unable to visit 4-H during office hours.

Virginia—Part 4 (Northern Virginia)

Miles from Katahdin	Features	Services	Elev.	Miles from Springer
1,219.6	U.S. 522 **Front Royal, VA 22630**	R (W–3.2m G, L, M, O, cl, f, @; 4.2m PO, M, D, @)	950	959.5
1,218.8	Nat'l Zoological Park Research Center		990	960.3
1,215.6	Mosby Campsite, Tom Sealock Spring	C, w	1,800	963.5
1,213.7	**Jim and Molly Denton Shelter**... *8.1mS; 5.5mN*	S, w	1,310	965.4
1,212.6	Va. 638 **Linden, VA 22642**	R (W–1m PO, G; 2.5m G, M; 7m G, L, M, O, cl, f, @)	1,150	966.5
1,210.7	Va. 55, Manassas Gap **Linden, VA 22642**	R (W–1.1m PO, G, M; 2.6m G, M)	800	968.4
1,208.2	**Manassas Gap Shelter**... *5.5mS; 4.7mN*	S, w	1,655	970.9
1,206.3	Trillium Trail		1,900	972.8
1,203.7	**Dick's Dome Shelter**... *4.7mS; 8.8mN*	E–0.2m S, w	1,230	975.4
1,202.7	Spring	C, w	1,850	976.4
1,201.5	+Sky Meadows State Park Side Trail	E–1.7m C, w	1,780	977.6
1,198.9	U.S. 50, Ashby Gap	R (E–1.1m L, M) (W–0.9m M)	900	980.2
1,195.3	**Rod Hollow Shelter**... *8.8mS; 7.1mN*	W–0.2m S, w	840	983.8
1,191.6	Morgans Mill Road (Va. 605)	R	1,140	987.5
1,190.4	Spring	w	1,150	988.7
1,188.4	Sawmill Spring, **Sam Moore Shelter**... *7.1mS; 11.2mN*	S, w	990	990.7
1,185.4	Bears Den Rocks, Bears Den Hostel	E–0.2m w, H, C, G, L, cl, sh, f, @	1,350	993.7
1,184.8	Va. 7, Va. 679, Snickers Gap **Bluemont, VA 20135**	R (E–1.6m G; 1.7m PO) (W–0.3m M; 0.9m M; 1.0m G)	1,000	994.3
1,182.6	Spring	w	1,083	996.5
1,182.3	Va.–W.Va. State Line		1,140	996.8

Miles from Katahdin	Features	Services	Elev.	Miles from Springer
1,182.2	Crescent Rock		1,312	996.9
1,181.6	Sand Spring	w	1,150	997.5
1,181.5	Devils Racecourse		1,200	997.6
1,178.7	Wilson Gap		1,380	1,000.4
1,177.5	**Blackburn Trail Center**... *11.2mS; 3.6mN*	E–0.1m C; 0.3m S, w	1,650	1,001.6
1,174.3	**David Lesser Memorial Shelter**... *3.6mS; 15.8mN*	E–0.1m S; 0.3m C, w	1,430	1,004.8
1,171.3	Keys Gap, W.Va. 9	R (E–0.3m G) (W– 0.3m G, M, w)	935	1,007.8

+ Fee charged

Higher rates of Lyme disease occur from northern Virginia into New England. Take precautions to prevent infection.

This 52-mile section follows a long, low ridge rich in American history and home to the infamous "roller-coaster" south of Snickers Gap.

U.S. 522—West 3.2 miles to **Front Royal, Va. [P.O. ZIP 22630: M–F 8:30–5, Sa 8:30–1; (540) 635-7983].** The post office is 1.0 mile farther. The large town offers all major services, but they are spread out over a wide area. Except for the post office, most services are located near the U.S. 522 and Va. 55 intersection as you come into town from the A.T. Weasel Creek Outfitters is a hiker's best source for help and information in town. ■ *Lodging:* Front Royal is the gateway to Shenandoah National Park, with motel rates that vary considerably according to season; be sure to specify you are a hiker, as most have special rates. Skyline Resort Motel, (540) 635-5354, no dogs; Pioneer Motel, (540) 635-4784, pool, CATV, dogs sometimes allowed for a fee; Scottish Inns, (540) 636-6168; Center City Motel, (540) 635-4050; Super 8 Motel, (540) 636-4888, dogs $8; Quality Inn, (540) 635-3161, no dogs; Woodward House B&B, (540) 635-7010 or (800) 635-7011, no dogs, includes full B, shuttle to and from Trail, other area shuttles for a fee, no smoking in house; Blue Ridge Motel, (540) 636-7200, no dogs, free shuttle back to the Trail. ■ *Groceries:* Food Lion, Martin's, Better Thymes natural foods (all long-term resupply). ■ *Restaurants:* Victoria's, AYCE L/D; South Street Grill; Dean's Steak House; Pirate Pizza; Jalisco

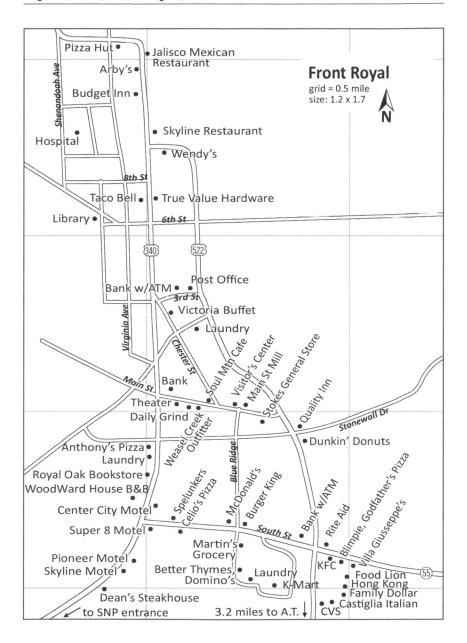

Pizza Hut •   • Jalisco Mexican
Arby's •   Restaurant
Budget Inn •

Front Royal
grid = 0.5 mile
size: 1.2 x 1.7
N

Shenandoah Ave

Hospital •

• Skyline Restaurant

• Wendy's

8th St

Taco Bell • • True Value Hardware

Library •   *6th St*

340   522

Bank w/ATM • • Post Office
               3rd St
            • Victoria Buffet

Virginia Ave

            • Laundry

Chester St

Soul Mtn Cafe
Visitor's Center
Main St Mill
Stokes General Store

Main St   Bank •

Theater •
Daily Grind •

Quality Inn

Stonewall Dr

Anthony's Pizza •
Laundry •
Royal Oak Bookstore •
WoodWard House B&B •

Weasel Creek Outfitter

Blue Ridge

• Dunkin' Donuts

Center City Motel •
Super 8 Motel •

Spelunkers
Celio's Pizza

McDonald's
Burger King

Bank w/ATM

Rite Aid

Blimpie, Godfather's Pizza

Villa Giusseppe's

Pioneer Motel •
Skyline Motel •

Martin's •
Grocery

South St

Better Thymes, •
Domino's •

• Laundry

KFC •

• K-Mart

• Food Lion   55
• Hong Kong
• Family Dollar
• Castiglia Italian

Dean's Steakhouse
◄— to SNP entrance   3.2 miles to A.T. ↓   CVS

Mexican; Anthony's Pizza and Son's; Soul Mountain Café; Pizza Hut, AYCE; Royal Dairy, open 7–9; Villa Guissepies Italian, with N.Y. Pizza; China Jade, AYCE L buffet; and many fast-food outlets. ■ *Outfitter:* Weasel Creek Outfitters, (540) 622-6909, closed M. Brandon, Wendy, and their team provide minor repairs, warranty work, hiker box, pack lock-up, Internet access, possible shuttles, pack fitting, all stove fuels, Coleman and alcohol by the ounce. ■ *Internet access:* Samuels Public Library and Weasel Creek Outfitters. ■ *Other services:* coin laundry, daily 7–10; banks with ATM; hospital; doctors, dentists; veterinarian; pharmacies; Stokes General; Ramsey's Hardware, (540) 635-2547, Coleman fuel and alcohol by the ounce; Royal Oak Bookstore; movie theater; Royal Taxi, (540) 635-3214; Ace Taxi, (540) 635-6100 for local and D.C. airports; flea market on Sa on U.S. 522, spring and summer.

National Zoological Park—Adjacent to U.S. 522 is the National Zoological Park Conservation and Research Center. On the northern side of the highway, the Trail follows along one of the center's fences. Exotic animals are sometimes visible.

Jim and Molly Denton Shelter (1991)—Sleeps 8. Privy. Enlarged front porch for extra sleepers. Water source is a spring on the A.T. near the solar shower (reported broken in 2007; spring reported dry).

 Va. 638—West 1.1 mile to **Linden, Va. [P.O. ZIP 22642: M–F 8–12 & 1–5, Sa 8–12; (540) 636-9936].** A small outpost on Va. 55, Linden offers only a post office and convenience store, but it's an alternative to hitching into Front Royal to pick up a mail drop. ■ *Groceries:* Monterey Service Station (good short-term resupply), M–F 4:30–9, Sa 6–9, Su 7–8, hiker-friendly.

West 1.5 miles to ■ *Restaurant:* Apple House, fresh-baked pies, doughnuts, sandwiches, BBQ, buffalo(!) burgers, B, deli foods; M 7–5, Tu–Su 7–8; credit cards accepted. ■ *Groceries:* Quarles Shell, (540) 635-1899, open 24 hrs., deli sandwiches, ice cream, short-term resupply, pay phone; Apple Mountain Exxon, (540) 636-2960, large store, open 24 hrs., ATM, a must stop for hungry hikers, fresh pies, deli sandwiches, hand-dipped ice cream, pay phone outside.

West 7 miles to Front Royal on Va. 55 (see above).

 Va. 55, Manassas Gap—West 1.1 miles into Linden (see previous entry). This is a busier road, parallel to I-66, which leads east to Washington, D.C.

Manassas Gap Shelter (1940s/2002)—Sleeps 6. Privy. Food-hoist cables available. Water source is a reliable spring near the shelter on a side trail.

Dick's Dome Shelter (1985)—Slccps 4. Privy. This unusually shaped shelter was built on private land by PATC member Dick George. Food-hoist cables available. Water source (which hikers should treat) is Whiskey Hollow Creek in front of the shelter. Scheduled for rebuilding.

Sky Meadows State Park Side Trail—Look for the resting bench at path that leads **East** 1.7 miles to the park's visitors center in Mt. Bleak Mansion, built in the 1820s. Now one of Virginia's finest parks, open daily 8–8:30/dusk. Cultural events are scheduled on summer weekends. Telephone, water fountain, and soda machine available at the visitors center. Hike-in primitive camping (12 sites) 1.25 mi from A.T. and primitive group-camping area, $13PP, on the way to the visitors center. Reservations required, (540) 592-3556 or (800) 933-7275, and campers must arrive before dusk, when the park closes.

U.S. 50, U.S. 17/Ashby Gap—**East** 0.8 mile on U.S. 50/17, then 0.3 mile south past barrier on Va. 759 to community of Paris. ■ *Lodging:* The Ashby Inn, (540) 592-3900, restaurant serves L 12–2:30, D W–Sa 5–10, Su 5–9, Su brunch $35; rooms $195 and up, includes B; restaurant closed M–Tu; reservations recommended. **West** 0.9 mile to ■ *Restaurant:* The Blue Skillet, (540) 837-1726, open Tu–Th 6:30–9, F 6:30–10, Sa 8–10, Su 8–8, credit cards accepted.

Rod Hollow Shelter (1986)—Sleeps 8. Privy. Located on a blue-blazed trail. Water source is a spring or the streams just south of the shelter.

The "Roller Coaster"—Northbounders leaving the Rod Hollow Shelter will enter the "roller coaster," a 13.5-mile section with ten ascents and descents. Southbounders have just completed their ride. The Virginia corridor is narrow here, leaving Trail crews very little choice other than to route the path up and over each of these viewless and rocky ridges. (Switchbacks coming!)

Sam Moore Shelter (1990)—Sleeps 6. Privy. Constructed of materials salvaged from the old Keys Gap Shelter. Named for maintainer Sam Moore, who gave 55 years of volunteer service to the A.T. Water source is Sawmill Spring in front of shelter or spring to left of shelter.

Bears Den—A stop at Bears Den Rocks provides a fine view of the Shenandoah Valley to the west. Nearby Bears Den Hostel, 0.1 mile off the Trail, is owned by ATC and operated by PATC; (540) 554-8708, <info@bearsdencenter.org>. Hiker Special includes bunk, shower, laundry, pizza, soda, and pint of Ben & Jerry's ice cream for $27.50 plus tax; bunk & shower, $15; camping $10 (with privileges); shower only $3; laundry $3; short-term resupply; fuel by the ounce; cooking privileges; and water. Store office and check-in 5–9:30 p.m. Hiker room is accessible all day. Free Internet and phone in hiker room. Mail drops can be sent to Bears Den Hostel, 18393 Blue Ridge Mountain Rd., Bluemont, VA 20135.

Va. 7, Va. 679/Snickers Gap—East 1.7 miles to **Bluemont, Va. [P.O. ZIP 20135: M–F 8:30–12 & 1–5, Sa 8:30–12; (540) 554-4537].** Follow Va. 7 **East** 0.9 mile over Snickers Gap to the Snickersville Turnpike sign, turn right, and continue 0.8 mile to the post office on Va. 670.

East 1.6 mi to Bluemont General Store, open M–F 6:30–7, Sa–Su 7–7; (540) 554-2054, short-term resupply, pizza by the slice, sandwiches, ice cream, pies.

On Va. 679, **West** 0.3 mile to *Restaurant:* Horseshoe Curve Restaurant, (540) 554-8291, open Tu–Sa 12–11 (or later), Su 12–7. Excellent hiker portions.

West 0.9 mile to *Restaurant:* Pine Grove Restaurant, (540) 554-8126, open M–Sa 6:30 a.m.–8 p.m., Su 7 a.m.–1 p.m.

West 1.0 mile to *Groceries:* Village Market, (540) 554-8422, open M–Sa 7–7; short-term resupply, ice cream, may give ride back to Trail if not busy.

Blackburn Trail Center—**East** 0.2 mile *via* either of two blue-blazed trails. This PATC facility, (540) 338-9028, is staffed during the summer months by a PATC caretaker. From the porch, on clear days, you may be able to glimpse the Washington Monument and National Cathedral in the distance to the east. The center has a free bunkhouse that sleeps 8 with a wood-burning stove, a picnic pavilion with table and benches built in 2002 with ALDHA donations in memory of Edward B. Garvey. Six tentsites and a tent platform are nearby, and a camping area with privy is 0.1 mile north of the main building on the blue-blazed trail. Water available year-round from an outside spigot, pay phone located on the porch, and solar-heated shower on front lawn. Donations appreciated. During the summer months, PATC work and hiking groups are often here. ALDHA member "Weathercarrot" has done a tremendous amount of rockwork to rebuild the stone retaining walls.

David Lesser Shelter (1994)—Sleeps 6. Privy. A shelter-engineering feat. Water source is a spring located 0.4 mile downhill from the shelter.

West Virginia

Miles from Katahdin	Features	Services	Elev.	Miles from Springer
1,171.3	Keys Gap, W.Va. 9	R (E–0.3m G) (W–0.3m G, M, w)	935	1,007.2
1,167.4	Loudoun Heights Trail, Va.–W.Va. State Line		1,279	1,011.1
1,166.7	W. Va. 32 (Chestnut Hill Rd)	R	820	1,011.8
1,166.0	U.S. 340, Shenandoah River Bridge (north end)	R (W–0.1m L; 1.2m C, cl, sh) (E–3.7m H, sh, cl, @)	312	1,012.5
1,165.7	ATC side trail **Harpers Ferry, WV 25425**	W–0.2m ATC, f, @; 0.4m M; 0.5m PO; 0.6m L; 0.7m O; 1.1m G, G, D, @; 1.7m C, cl, sh	394	1,012.8
1,165.1	Shenandoah Street; Harpers Ferry Nat'l Historical Park	R (W–0.1m M, O, f)	315	1,013.4
1,165.0	Potomac River, Goodloe Byron Memorial Footbridge, W.Va.–Md. State Line		263	1,013.5

 W.Va. 9/Keys Gap—East 0.3 mile to *Groceries:* Sweet Springs Country Store (short-term resupply), (540) 668-7200, M–Sa 4–11, Su 7–11, Ben & Jerry's, deli, ATM.

West 0.3 mile to ■ *Groceries:* Torlone Mini-Mart (short-term resupply), M–Su 8–9. ■ *Restaurant:* Torlone Pizza, Pasta & Subs, (304) 725-0916, ATM and pay phone, open M–Sa 8–9, Su 8–8.

Camping and fires are prohibited a half-mile on either side of Keys Gap.

Harpers Ferry National Historical Park—Nearly half the town of Harpers Ferry and surrounding ridges (including those south of the Shenandoah River crossing) have been a historical park since 1963, with gradual land acquisition outside the town proper ever since. Part of the town was a national monument from June 30, 1944, when President Franklin D. Roosevelt signed legislation designating it, until 1963. It saw extensive Civil War action, especially before the slaughter at nearby Antietam, Md., but is probably best known for the raid of John Brown, an abolitionist from Kansas who attempted to capture the federal arsenal here in 1859. The arsenal was to be the staging point for a slave uprising. A U.S. colonel named Robert E. Lee crushed the raid in less than 36 hours, and historians point to the event as a step-pingstone to the war, which began 16 months after Brown was hanged for treason in nearby Charles Town. But, the history of Harpers Ferry is more than one event, one date, or one individual. It is multilayered, involving a diverse number of people and events that influenced the course of American history. Harpers Ferry also wit-nessed the first successful application of interchangeable manufacture, the arrival of the first successful American railroad, the largest surrender of federal troops during the Civil War, the education of former slaves in one of the earliest integrated schools in the United States, and the first organized civil rights movement in the country. The park's visitors center (west of town along U.S. 340) offers parking and a free shuttle to the historic district. *Note: Hikers parking in lot must register at the visitors center, open 8–5.* Parking-lot gates open at 8, close at dusk. Entrance fee is $6 per vehicle for up to 2 weeks. Today, the Park Service runs many interpretive exhibits in renovated buildings dating back to the mid-19th century. More informa-tion on the historic town is available at ATC headquarters, (304) 535-6331, as well as the park's visitors center.

U.S. 340/Shenandoah River—East 20 miles to Frederick, Md., with all services, including Quality Shoe Service, 319 North Market St., (301) 695-9255, for boot repair, and The Trail House, an outfitter, 17 South Market St., (301) 694-8448. *Traffic can be extremely heavy at this Trailhead, and it is neither safe nor legal to hitchhike here; local police often are nearby, watching for speeders.*

West 0.1 mile to *Lodging:* Comfort Inn, (304) 535-6391, $77–85S/D weekdays, $96–$120S/D weekends, no pets, expanded continental B, pay phone outside, laundry $6 per load, refrigerator and microwave in rooms, no pool. Signs on U.S. 340 say "Appalachian Trail Visitor Center"—that's the ATC visitors center.

West 1.2 miles to *Camping:* Harpers Ferry KOA (short-term resupply), (304) 535-6895, cabins $53.95 and up, tentsites M–F $35.95, Sa–Su $37.95, lodges available, shower only $5, coin laundry, campstore, snack bar, pizzeria, pool, leashed pets welcome except Rottweillers, pit bulls, or Dobermans. ■ *Lodging and Restaurant:* Quality Hotel Conference Center, (304) 535-6302, 4328 William L. Wilson Freeway, Harpers Ferry, WV 25425, bar and grill, call for current rates, microwave and re-frigerator in rooms, some rooms with Jacuzzi, WiFi with computer access for hikers, pets allowed for $50 nonrefundable fee per stay), coin laundry, indoor pool, fitness center, FedEx and postal services available, will hold and mail out packages for guests, long-term parking for guests. Vista Gourmet Dining Room, D 5–9. Vista Tavern, L/D, open 11–9.

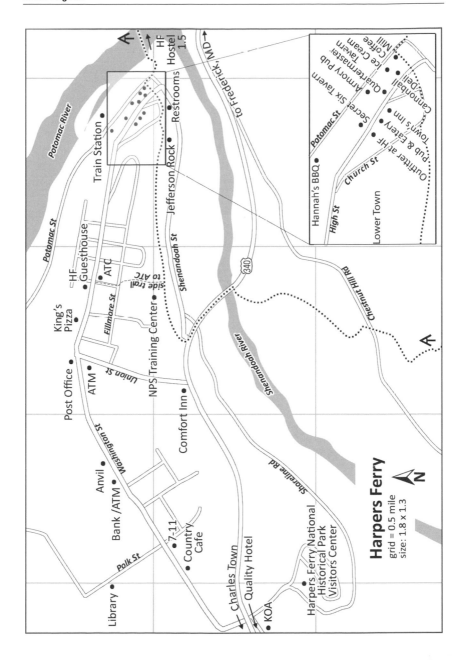

Harpers Ferry
grid = 0.5 mile
size: 1.8 x 1.3

East 3.7 miles to *Hostel:* Harpers Ferry Hostel, Keep Tryst Rd., Sandy Hook/Knoxville, Md. (see next chapter for details).

West 6 miles to Charles Town, W.Va., with all services, including Walmart, Jefferson Urgent Care Medical Facility, and a hospital.

West 20 miles (U.S. 340 to W.Va. 9 before Charles Town) to Martinsburg, W.Va., with all services, including movie theaters, malls, as well as many restaurants. For bus service to those towns, see Harpers Ferry entry below.

Note: Hitchhiking is illegal on state-maintained roads in West Virginia. That includes U.S. 340 and the main street through Harpers Ferry and adjacent Bolivar. Hikers hitchhiking in the area in '09 received hefty fines.

Harpers Ferry, W.Va. [P.O. ZIP 25425: M–F 9–4 , Sa 9–12; (304) 535-2479]. The post office and most services are available above the old town *via* the 0.2-mile blue-blazed trail to ATC headquarters (see below). The A.T. itself leads through the historic district at the bottom of the hill along the riverfronts, with museums, stores, and restaurants. Many businesses in the historic district are closed in the winter or open only on weekends then. The national historical park is open 7 days a week year-round, but its visitors center closes Thanksgiving, Christmas, and New Year's Day. ■ *Hostels:* The Town's Inn, 175–179 High St., right in historic lower town, (877) 489-2447, <info@TheTownsInn.com>, beds available at $30, semiprivate rooms $35–$40PP. ■ *Lodging:* Hilltop House Hotel is closed indefinitely for renovations. Several B&Bs are located in town: Check at ATC for further information. ■ *Groceries:* 7-11 convenience store (short-term resupply), 1 mile **west** of ATC; outfitter 0.5 mile **east** of ATC (short-term resupply); Press on the Potomac General Store 0.4 mile **west** of ATC, with WiFi, printer, occasional after-hours events, W–Su 7 a.m.–8 p.m.; supermarkets and Walmart (long-term resupply) in Charles Town, 6 miles **west**. ■ *Restaurants.* **West** of ATC: 0.1 mile, Ariano's King's Pizza, L/D, closed M; 0.3 mile, Canal House Café; 0.5 mile, Anvil Restaurant, W–Su 11–9; 0.9 mile, The Pub, L/D M–F 11–11, Sa 3–11, Su 1–11, sometimes open later on weekends; 1 mile, Country Café, B/L. **East** of ATC in lower town: The Town's Inn Pub & Eatery, B/L/D; Hannah's Train Depot Seafood & BBQ, expected to open in 2010; Secret Six Tavern, Su–Th 11–8, F–Sa 11–9; Armory Pub; Coffee Mill; Family Tavern; Swiss Miss Restaurant; Cannonball Restaurant; Scoops Ice Cream Café. ■ *Outfitter:* The Outfitter at Harpers Ferry, 189 High St., (304) 535-2087 or (888) 535-2087, full-service outfitter (short-term resupply), open daily 10–6, Jan–Feb weekends only, <www.theoutfitteratharpersferry.com>. ■ *Internet access:* Harpers Ferry/Bolivar Library, (304) 535-2301, M, Tu, F, Sa 10–5:30, W, Th 10–8; ATC. ■ *Other services:* banks with ATM; pay phone at library; dentist, Dr. John Mayhew, M–Th, (304) 535-2409; Caring Hands

Chiropractic and Advanced Massage Therapy, Dr. Jenny Foster, a hiker (located near Middletown, Md.), (301) 371-3922, call ahead for possible pick-up (schedule permitting) at Harpers Ferry Hostel or Old South Mountain Inn; Foot and Ankle Care Office, Drs. Warren BeVards and David Grace, (304) 535-3040, W 8:30–11:30, F 1:30–4:30; bicycle rental at The Outfitter's General Store, 129 Potomac St., (304) 535-2296. ■ *Bus service:* Pan Tran bus to Charles Town or Martinsburg operates M–F; limited Sa service; flag the bus across the street from the ATC office. The charge is $2.50 one-way. Bus leaves town at 6:45 a.m., 9:05 a.m., 10:40 a.m., 1:35 p.m., 3:05 p.m., 4:45 p.m., 7:30 p.m.; Sa 10:25 a.m., 4:20 p.m. Leaves Walmart in Charles Town for Harpers Ferry at 8:50 a.m., 10:25 a.m., 1:20 p.m., 2:50 p.m., 4:30 p.m. and 7:15 p.m.; Sa 10:10 a.m., 4:05 p.m. No dogs; packs OK unless driver believes one may be suspicious. Times are subject to change.

Appalachian Trail Conservancy (ATC)—Reached *via* 0.2-mile blue-blazed trail 0.3 mile north of the junction of U.S. 340 and Shenandoah Street, before northbounders reach the historic section of Harpers Ferry; at the corner of Washington Street and Storer College Place.

ATC was formed in 1925 by private citizens to make the dream of an Appalachian Trail a reality. After the initial Trail route was pieced together in 1937 (much of it on roads and across private land), ATC continued to work to identify better routes for the Trail and worked with Congress, the National Park Service, the U.S. Forest Service, states, and others to ensure a continuously protected corridor. Today, ATC is the primary organization responsible for the stewardship of the footpath and 250,000 acres of public land surrounding it. Working with more than 6,000 volunteers (mostly in 30 affiliated local clubs) and multiple public agencies, ATC leads the efforts to improve the footpath, protect the plants and animals along the Trail (and the experience of hiking it), engage communities along the A.T. to support it, and guard against encroachments. Much of the behind-the-scenes work that continues to makes the A.T. experience possible takes place out of sight in offices upstairs and the connected annex. As you know, no dues or fees are required to enjoy the Trail, even if you spend six months hiking it. The single largest source of ATC's funding is individual membership dues and small contributions. If you're not already an ATC member, consider joining here to help support continued protection of the Trail.

ATC publications and products are for sale at the information/visitors center. Benton MacKaye's typewriter and Myron Avery's measuring wheel are on display as part of the A.T. Museum Society's first exhibit, sharing a room with a 10-foot-long raised-relief map of the A.T. Volunteers or staffers John Fletcher and Laurie Pot-teiger (Mountain Laurel of 1987) can answer your Trail questions. The office accepts donations for Coleman fuel and denatured alcohol and holds packages sent to P.O. Box 807 or 799 Washington St., Harpers Ferry, WV 25425. Thru- and section-hikers are encouraged to stop at ATC headquarters to sign the register and have their picture taken to be counted among the class of 2010. The same photo can be pur-chased as a postcard for $1 (postage included). Volunteers are needed periodically at headquarters and almost always at the sales-distribution center 11 miles away.

The ATC Visitors Center, (304) 535-6331, is open daily 9–5 except Thanksgiving, Christmas, and New Year's Day. Drinks for sale. Bench and picnic tables in side yard. Phone and Internet access for hikers. Ask there for ATC's often-updated "Guide to Harpers Ferry Hiker Services," with more details on area services. Driving directions are available at <www.appalachiantrail.org> under offices under About ATC.

Jefferson Rock—The white blazes take you past this Harpers Ferry viewpoint that overlooks the confluence of the Potomac and Shenandoah rivers. Named in honor of Thomas Jefferson, who was inspired by the beautiful view in 1783. Several large slabs of shale originally rested naturally but not securely atop each other. "Jefferson Rock" now rests securely on a set of short pillars erected in the 1850s.

Trains to Washington, D.C.—Amtrak, (800) USA-RAIL, <www.amtrak.com>: Train No. 30 (Capitol Limited) is scheduled to depart Harpers Ferry at 11:30 a.m. (although it is often 2 or more hours late) and to arrive at D.C.'s Union Station at 1:15 p.m. Train No. 29 is scheduled to leave D.C. at 4:05 p.m., arriving in Harpers Ferry at 5:16 p.m. Coach fares are $11–$20 one way (cost may be more if coach is not available). Fares and schedules subject to change. Harpers Ferry station is not staffed. Reservations are required; backpacks allowed, but not bikes. Maryland Rail Commuter Service (MARC), [(800) 325-7245 outside local calling area; others call (301) 834-8360; <www. mtamaryland.com>]: Two scheduled commuter trains on the Brunswick line leave Harpers Ferry for D.C. on weekdays. They depart at 5:51 a.m. and 6:56 a.m., arriving at 7:28 a.m. and 8:30 a.m. Three trains leave D.C. for Harpers Ferry on weekdays. They depart at 4:55 p.m., 5:35 p.m., and 7:15 p.m. and arrive at 6:16 p.m., 7:09 p.m., and 8:42 p.m. Fares are $11 one way.

Maryland

Miles from Katahdin	Features	Services	Elev.	Miles from Springer
1,165.0	Potomac River, Goodloe Byron Memorial Footbridge, Md.–W.Va. State Line		263	1,014.1
1,164.8	C&O Canal Towpath (west jct)		290	1,014.3
1,163.7	U.S. 340, Sandy Hook Bridge	R	290	1,015.4
1,162.2	C&O Canal Towpath (east jct)	W–G	290	1,016.9
1,162.1	Keep Tryst Rd; RR tracks	R (E–2.5m L, M) (W–1.1m H, L, G, M, cl, sh, f)	320	1,017.0
1,161.9	U.S. 340 Underpass		400	1,017.2
1,161.7	Weverton Rd	R (W–1.4m G)	420	1,017.4
1,160.8	Weverton Cliffs Trail		780	1,018.3
1,158.7	**Ed Garvey Shelter**... *15.8mS; 4.5mN*	E–0.1m S; 0.5m w	1,100	1,020.4
1,156.7	Brownsville Gap		1,140	1,022.4
1,155.0	Crampton Gap, Gathland State Park, Gapland Rd (Md. 572)	R, w (W–0.4m C, G, f, @)	950	1,024.1
1,154.6	**Crampton Gap Shelter**... *4.5mS; 5.5mN*	E–0.3m S, w	1,000	1,024.5
1,152.0	Trail to Bear Spring Cabin (locked)	W–0.5m w	1,480	1,027.1
1,151.4	White Rocks Cliff		1,500	1,027.7
1,151.2	Lamb's Knoll		1,600	1,027.9
1,149.6	**Rocky Run Shelters**... *5.5mS; 7.8mN*	W–0.2m S, C, w	970	1,029.5
1,148.6	Reno Monument Rd	R	91,0	1,030.5
1,147.8	Dahlgren Back Pack Campground	C, M, sh, w	980	1,031.3
1,147.6	Turners Gap, U.S. Alt. 40 **Boonsboro, MD 21713**	R, M (W–2.4m PO, M, D, V, cl, @; 3.8m G)	1,000	1,031.5
1,146.2	Monument Rd	R	1,350	1,032.9
1,146.0	Washington Monument Rd	R, w	1,400	1,033.1
1,145.6	Washington Monument		1,550	1,033.5
1,143.5	Boonsboro Mtn Rd	R	1,300	1,035.6

Miles from Katahdin	Features	Services	Elev.	Miles from Springer
1,143.2	Bartman Hill Trail to Greenbrier State Park	W–0.6m C, f		1,035.9
1,142.7	I-70 Footbridge, U.S. 40, Greenbrier State Park	R (W–0.5m M, w; 1.4m C, f)	1,200	1,036.4
1,142.1	**Pine Knob Shelter**... *7.8mS; 8.2mN*	W–0.1m S, C, w	1,360	1,037.0
1,140.5	Trail to Annapolis Rock	W–0.2m C, 0.4m w	1,820	1,038.6
1,139.5	Black Rock Cliffs		1,800	1,039.6
1,138.9	Pogo Memorial Campsite	C, w	1,500	1,040.2
1,134.1	Md. 17, Wolfsville Rd **Smithsburg, MD 21783**	R (W–0.3m H, M, sh, cl, @; 1.8m G, D, V; 2.4m PO, G, M, D, cl, @)	1,400	1,045.0
1,133.9	**Ensign Cowall Shelter**... *8.2mS; 5mN*	S, w	1,430	1,045.2
1,132.6	Md. 77, Foxville Rd	R	1,450	1,046.5
1,130.8	Warner Gap Rd	R, w	1,150	1,048.3
1,130.0	Md. 491, Raven Rock Hollow	R	1,190	1,049.1
1,129.0	**Devils Racecourse Shelter**... *5mS; 9.9mN*	W–0.3m C, S, w	1,480	1,050.1
1,127.2	Trail to High Rock	R	1,950	1,051.9
1,124.3	Pen Mar County Park **Cascade, MD 21719**	R, w (E–1.7m PO, G, L, cl)	1,330	1,054.8
1,124.1	Mason–Dixon Line, Md.–Pa. State Line	R	1,250	1,055.0

Overnight camping in Maryland is allowed only at designated campsites. Please obey camping regulations in this heavily used section.

This section boasts easy terrain, the C & O Canal towpath along the Potomac River, a free on-trail hot-water shower, Civil War history, the War Correspondents Monument, the first monument to George Washington, and the Mason-Dixon line.

The "four-state challenge"—hiking in Virginia, West Virginia, Maryland, and Pennsylvania all in one day—is an A.T. tradition that begins just south of here, up where you (northbounders) left the Virginia line to head down to the Shenandoah River at Harpers Ferry. You can also hike Maryland all in one day during a Mountain Club of Maryland event held every other year; the next will be in 2011.

C&O Canal Towpath—The southernmost 2.8 miles of the Trail in Maryland follow this path from which mules towed barges, between what's left of the canal on one side and the Potomac River on the other, until 1924. Stretching 185 miles from Washington, D.C., to Cumberland, Md., it was rescued from highway development by a protest hike led by Supreme Court Justice William O. Douglas, an A.T. 2,000-miler. Now, it is part of a national historical park, accessible to both hikers and bicyclists. Blazes are scarce, but the points at which the Trail enters and leaves it are hard to miss.

Keep Tryst Road—East 2.5 mile to Brunswick, Md., *via* U.S. 340 and Md. 478 at Knoxville exit. *Lodging:* Green Country Inn, (301) 834-9151, 620 Souder Rd., B/L/D, open 24/7, rates from $49, weekends higher, pets $15 deposit.

West 0.9 mile to Sandy Hook Road and *Groceries:* Shady Hook Grocery, (301) 843-8353, 18806 Sandy Hook Road (short-term resupply), ice cream, outside soda machine, open 7 days 3–10 p.m.

West 1.1 mile to (left on Sandy Hook Road) ■ *Hostel:* Harpers Ferry Hostel (Hostelling International), (301) 834-7652, <www.harpersferryhostel.org>, <mail@harpersferryhostel.org>, bunk $18PP for thru-hikers or HI members, $21PP for non-members, includes shower, kitchen privileges, a/c, Internet access; tenting $10PP; groups of more than 10 $6 PP. Laundry $4, nonguest shower $5, parking $5 per day. Vending machine on porch with refrigerator. Building open 7 a.m.–10 p.m. Dogs allowed if camping. No alcohol. Closed Nov 15–Apr 14. Mail drops for hikers, send to 19123 Sandy Hook Rd., Knoxville, MD 21758-1330 (mark "Hold for A.T. Hiker" with hiker's real name). ■ *Lodging:* Hillside Motel, (301) 834-8144, Su–Th $45S $55D, F–Sa $50S $60D, no pets. ■ *Groceries:* Hillside Station, (301) 834-5300; deli hot food, pizza, ice cream, hot wings; ATM; M–F 5 a.m–10 p.m., Sa 6–9, Su 7–9. ■ *Restaurant:* Cindy Dee's, (301) 695-8181, B/L/D, Su–Th 6 a.m–10 p.m., F–Sa 7–10; fried chicken, pay phone.

Ed Garvey Shelter (2001)—Sleeps 12. New composting privy may be ready in 2010. Two tentsites north and south of shelter. Water source is found at the end of a 0.5-mile, steep side trail in front of the shelter.

Gathland State Park—Located in Crampton Gap, the state-run facility has water (frost-free faucet), soda and juice vending machines, restroom, covered picnic pavilion, and telephone. No camping here. Two museums—Civil War and War Correspondent—are open 7 days a week, Apr–Oct, 8 a.m–4 p.m. The monument to war correspondents is the only one of its kind in the country. Southbounders may want to pick up water here before heading to Ed Garvey Shelter.

Gapland Road—West 0.4 mile on Gapland Rd., right on Townsend Rd. to *Camping:* Maple Tree Campground, 20716 Townsend Rd., Gapland, MD 21779, (301) 432-5585, <thetreehousecamp2@aol.com>; tentsites, ask for rate; rustic tree house $40/night; cottages $56/night; new cottages with woodstove $66/night, 4-hiker maximum. All with picnic table, fire ring, grill. Short-term resupply; white gas, denatured alcohol, canisters; mail drops accepted; dogs on leashes okay, no extra fee; Internet access.

Crampton Gap Shelter (1941)—Sleeps 6. Privy. Built by the CCC. Water source is an intermittent spring 0.1 mile south on the A.T. that may go dry in June. Northbounders may want to get water from faucet at Gathland State Park, 0.25 mile south on the A.T.

Rocky Run Shelters (CCC–1941, PATC–2008)—New shelter opened in 2008 on blueblaze just north of old-road/blue-blaze to old CCC shelter; sleeps 16. Composting privy. Water is Rocky Run Spring at site of old shelter a few hundred yards on blueblaze; old shelter sleeps 6. Tent and hammock sites at both locations.

Reno Monument marks the spot where Maj. Gen Jesee Lee Reno was killed in the Civil War Battle of South Mountain, the antecedent to bloody Antietam to the west a few miles.

Dahlgren Backpack Campground—No, it's not a mirage; that really is a bathhouse with hot showers and flush toilets. Operated by the state at no charge, the bathhouse, campsites with gravel tentpads, hammock sites, fire rings, utility sink behind bathhouse, frost-free faucet 100 ft. up gravel road to Old South Mountain Inn, and picnic areas are open Apr–Nov.

Rocky Run Shelter by Laurie Potteiger

U.S. 40-A/Turners Gap—*Restaurant:* Old South Mountain Inn, (301) 371-5400, D Tu–Fr 5–9 Sa 4–10, L Sa 11:30–2:30, Su brunch 10:30–2. Hikers staying at Dahlgren Campground can literally shower and shave before an elegant dining experience, then walk back to camp in minutes. (Take your pack with you.) ■ *Other services:* chiropractic and therapeutic massage, Dr. Jenny Foster, (301) 371-3922, can pick up at Old South Mountain Inn, schedule permitting.

West 2.4 miles to **Boonsboro, Md. [P.O. ZIP 21713: M–F 9–1 & 2–5, Sa 9–12; (301) 432-6861].** ■ *Restaurants:* Crawford Confectionery (candy & sweets); Subway; Palettie Restaurant; Vesta Pizzera & Restaurant; Potomac Street Creamery ice-cream shop; Mountainside Deli. ■ *Internet access:* library; Bruce Wilder's Turn the Page Bookstore Café (featuring supernovelist Nora Roberts, wife of Bruce), with A.T. books and maps. ■ *Other services:* Marcy's Laundry, (301) 491-5849, 6 a.m–9:30 p.m. daily; banks with ATM; doctor; dentist; veterinarian; hardware store; and pharmacy.

West 3.8 miles to *Groceries:* Cronise Market Place, Boonsboro Produce Market (both short-term resupply); Weis Supermarket & Pharmacy (long-term resupply).

Washington Monument State Park—A state park built around the first monument to George Washington. The bottle-shaped structure is more modest than the big one in Washington, D.C., but impressive for small-town Marylanders in 1827. When open, the observation deck on top provides views of the surrounding countryside. South of the monument, on the A.T., are park facilities with picnic shelters, restroom, soda machine, and pay phone by the restroom near the museum. Museum is open 9 a.m–5 p.m. daily May–Sept, weekends only Apr and Oct. No camping permitted in the park; the campsite near the southern entrance is for youth groups with permits. Frost-free faucet on trail above main parking lot. Overnight parking permitted after registration at kiosk.

U.S. 40/Greenbrier State Park—North of the I-70 footbridge, the A.T. crosses U.S. 40. **West** 0.4 mile to the park entrance, across the road from *Restaurant:* Dogpatch Tavern, ATM.

West 1.4 miles to *Camping:* Greenbrier State Park, (301) 791-4767, open May–Oct, no pets allowed. Visitors center, restroom, concession stand, campstore with snacks, Coleman fuel by the gallon, and swimming in Greenbrier Lake. Tentsites with hot showers $25. Reservations recommended on the weekends; two-night minimum, but walk-in hikers may be allowed a one-night stay if a site is available.

Pine Knob Shelter (1939)—Sleeps 5. Privy. Shelter is located on a blue-blazed trail. Tent and hammock sites. Water source is a piped spring beside the shelter.

Annapolis Rock Campsite—13 tentsites and two privies at this popular area; caretaker on site. Tentsites are near an outstanding overlook popular with climbers. Spring location is marked.

Pogo Memorial Campsite—The campsite is immediately to the east of the Trail, with a spring 30 yards on a blue-blazed trail to the west.

Md. 17/Wolfsville Road—**West** 0.3 mile to *Hostel:* The Free State Hiker Hostel, owned by '06 thru-hiker Ken "Bone Pac" and Jennel Berry, (301) 824-2407, 11626 Wolfsville Road, Smithsburg, MD 21783. Open Mar 15–Nov 15; $32 includes bunk room, all linens, shower, laundry, Internet, phone. Credit cards accepted. Pizza and Mexican delivery available. Snacks, sodas, ice cream on site. Water available from spigot in front. No alcohol and no pets. Two-night maximum. Mail drops accepted for $2 handling fee (fee waived for overnight stay).

West 1.7 miles on Wolfsville Road and then left 0.1 mile on Md. 64 to a small shopping center. ■ *Groceries:* Phil & Jerry's Meats & More, (301) 824-3750 (short-term resupply); Dollar General Store. ■ *Other services:* veterinarian; medical clinics; pharmacy; pay phone; two banks with ATM, near shopping center.
West 2.4 miles *via* Wolfsville Road and Md. 77 to **Smithsburg, Md. [P.O. ZIP 21783: M–F 8:30–1 & 2–4:30, Sa 8:30–12; (301) 824-2828].** ■ *Groceries:* Smithsburg Market, Food Lion, Lewis Farm Market, and Mountain Valley Orchard. ■ *Restaurants:* Vince's Pizza; South of the Border; Dixie Eatery; Subway. ■ *Internet access:* library, M–F 10–7, Sa 10–2. ■ *Other services:* Ace Hardware, fuel; coin laundry; dentist; Rite-Aid pharmacy; and banks with ATM.

Ensign Cowall Shelter (1999)—Sleeps 8. Privy. Named for Ensign Phillip Cowall, who passed away in 1998. Built by the PATC and volunteers and students from Gallaudet University and its Model Secondary School for the Deaf (MSSD), located in Washington, D.C. Five tent pads, picnic table, fire ring with grill. Water source is a boxed spring south of the shelter 0.2 mile on the A.T.

Devils Racecourse Shelter (1950s)—**East** 0.3 mile downhill, with pit privy, picnic table, spring, campsites. The actual Devils Racecourse is 0.2 mile east of the shelter. Road is 0.3 mile east of the shelter. Sleeps 7. Will remain open until new Raven Rocks Shelter is completed.

Raven Rock Shelter (2010)—Will replace Devils Racecourse Shelter to **east** sometime in 2010. Privy. Water source is a spring 200 feet east from the A.T. (on the trail to the old shelter).

Pen Mar County Park—Open from the first Su in May to the last Su in Oct. No camping in the park. The pavilion provides views of the countryside to the west. Snack bar, soda machine. Museum (pay phone inside) open Sa and Su. Restroom locked in the evening. No alcohol permitted in the park. Bobby D's, (717) 762-0388, will deliver food from menu to the park Su–Th 11–9, F–Sa 'til 10.
East 1.4 miles to the small community of **Cascade, Md. [P.O. ZIP 21719: M–F 8–1 & 2–5, Sa 8–12; (301) 241-3403].** To reach town from the park entrance, turn left on High Rock Road to Pen-Mar Road, go straight at intersection, pass under a railroad trestle, turn right at the stop sign onto Md. 550. To reach the post office, continue 0.1 mile, and turn left on Ft. Ritchie Road across from the entrance to decommissioned Ft. Ritchie. ■ *Lodging:* The Cascade Inn, 14700 Eyler Ave., Cascade, MD 21719; call for rates, hiker discounts, (800) 362-9526 or (301) 241-4161, <thecasca-

deinn@comcast.net>; shuttles and mail drops for guests; dogs okay. ■ *Restaurant:* Vince's Pizza, (301) 241-4331, closed Tu. ■ *Groceries:* GT's Handimart (short-term resupply), (301) 241-3434, 5 a.m–11 p.m. daily, outside pay phone, ice cream, sandwiches, hot bar, ATM; Sanders Market (long-term resupply), (301) 241-3612, open M, W–Sa. ■ *Other services:* Cascade Coin Laundry.

Mason-Dixon Line—A marker was once on the Trail to signify the historical survey line and the Pennsylvania–Maryland state line. The marker has not been seen for several years. Incidentally, the moniker "Dixie" was not derived from Dixon. Prior to the Civil War, a Louisiana bank began printing $10 bills. In French, the word for 10 is *dix.* The bills were so widely distributed that the South soon became known as Dixie. The song "Dixie" was written by a minstrel-show musician from Ohio and was one of President Lincoln's favorite tunes.

Pennsylvania

Miles from Katahdin	Features	Services	Elev.	Miles from Springer
1,124.1	Mason–Dixon Line, Pa.–Md. State Line	R	1,250	1,055.0
1,124.0	Pen Mar Rd	R	1,240	1,055.1
1,123.0	Buena Vista Rd	R, w	1,290	1,056.1
1,121.8	Old Pa. 16	R	1,350	1,057.3
1,121.5	Pa. 16 **Blue Ridge Summit, PA 17214; Waynesboro, PA 17268**	R (E–1.2m PO, G, M, D, cl, f, @) (W–2m G, M; 2.3m G; 5m PO, G, M, L, V, cl, f, @)	1,200	1,057.6
1,121.3	Mackie Run, Mentzer Gap Rd	R	1,250	1,057.8
1,120.7	Bailey Spring	w	1,300	1,058.4
1,119.4	**Deer Lick Shelters...** *9.9mS; 2.6mN*	S (E–0.2m w)	1,420	1,059.7
1,117.0	**Old Forge Park, Antietam Shelter...** *2.6mS; 1.2mN*	R, S (w 0.2m N on A.T.)	890	1,062.1
1,116.6	Rattlesnake Run Rd	R	900	1,062.5
1,116.0	Old Forge Rd	R	1,000	1,063.1
1,115.8	**Tumbling Run Shelters...** *1.2mS; 6.8mN*	S, w	1,120	1,063.3
1,114.5	Chimney Rocks		1,900	1,064.6
1,111.2	Swamp Rd	R	1,560	1,067.9
1,110.9	Pa. 233 **South Mountain, PA 17261**	R (E–1.2m PO, L, M)	1,600	1,068.2
1,109.2	**Rocky Mtn Shelters...** *6.8mS; 5.8mN*	E–0.2m S; 0.5m w	1,520	1,069.9
1,106.2	U.S. 30, Caledonia State Park **Fayetteville, PA 17222**	R, C, M, sh, w (W–0.3m M; 0.7m G; 3.5m PO, G, M, L, D, cl)	960	1,072.9
1,104.3	Quarry Gap Rd	R	1,250	1,074.8
1,103.6	**Quarry Gap Shelters...** *5.8mS; 7.4mN*	S, w	1,455	1,075.5
1,102.1	Sandy Sod Jct	R	1,980	1,077.0
1,099.5	Middle Ridge Rd	R	2,050	1,079.6
1,099.0	Ridge Rd, Means Hollow Rd	R	1,800	1,080.1

Miles from Katahdin	Features	Services	Elev.	Miles from Springer
1,098.6	Milesburn Rd, Milesburn Cabin (locked)	R, w	1,600	1,080.5
1,096.2	**Birch Run Shelter...** *7.4mS; 6.2mN*	S, w	1,795	1,082.9
1,094.9	Shippensburg Rd, Big Flat Fire Tower	R	2,040	1,084.2
1,093.0	Michener Cabin (locked)	E–0.3m w	1,850	1,086.1
1,091.1	Woodrow Rd	R	1,850	1,088.0
1,090.0	**Toms Run Shelters...** *6.2mS; 11.1mN*	S, w	1,300	1,089.1
1,086.6	Pa. 233	R	900	1,092.5
1,086.3	Pine Grove Furnace State Park	R, H, C, G, w, sh	850	1,092.8
1,085.3	Midpoint Marker **(4.25mi N of midpoint)**		1,000	1,093.8
1,083.8	Pole Steeple side trail		1,300	1,095.3
1,080.3	Trail to Mtn Creek Campground	W–0.7m C, G	1,050	1,098.8
1,079.1	**James Fry (Tagg Run) Shelter...** *11.1mS; 8.5mN*	E–0.2m S, w	805	1,100.0
1,078.6	Pine Grove Rd	R (W–0.4m C, M)	750	1,100.5
1,077.7	Hunters Run Rd, Pa. 34	R (E–0.2m G, f)	670	1,101.4
1,075.9	Pa. 94 **Mt. Holly Springs, PA 17065**	R (W–2.5m PO, G, M, L, D, cl, @)	880	1,103.2
1,073.1	Whiskey Spring, Whiskey Spring Rd	R, w	830	1,106.0
1,071.0	**Alec Kennedy Shelter...** *8.5mS; 18.4mN*	E–0.2m S, w	850	1,108.1
1,070.1	Center Point Knob		1,060	1,109.0
1,067.6	Backpackers' Campsite	C, w		1,111.5
1,067.4	Yellow Breeches Creek	R, C	500	1,111.7
1,067.1	Pa. 174, ATC Mid-Atlantic Office **Boiling Springs, PA 17007**	R, w, PO, sh, f (W–0.1m G, M, L; 1m G, D, V)	500	1,112.0
1,065.1	Pa. 74	R	580	1,114.0
1,063.0	Pa. 641, Trindle Rd	R	540	1,116.1
1,060.3	Pennsylvania Turnpike	R	495	1,118.8

Miles from Katahdin	Features	Services	Elev.	Miles from Springer
1,059.1	U.S. 11 Footbridge	R (E−7m O) (W−0.5m M, L, sh; 5m G, L, M)	490	1,120.0
1,058.2	I-81 Overpass	R	485	1,120.9
1,056.8	Conodoguinet Creek Bridge, ATC Scott Farm Trail Work Center	R, w	480	1,122.3
1,054.8	Pa. 944	R	480	1,124.3
1,053.8	Spring	w	650	1,125.3
1,052.9	Tuscarora Trail (northern terminus), Darlington Trail		1,390	1,126.2
1,052.8	**Darlington Shelter...** *18.4mS; 7.3mN*	S, w	1,170	1,126.3
1,050.5	Pa. 850	R	650	1,128.6
1,045.5	**Cove Mtn Shelter...** *7.3mS; 8.6mN*	S, w	1,120	1,133.6
1,043.6	Hawk Rock		1,140	1,135.5
1,041.9	U.S. 11 & 15, Pa. 274	R (W−0.5m G; 2m L)	385	1,137.2
1,041.4	Market St **Duncannon, PA 17020**	R, PO, G, L, M, cl, f, @	385	1,137.7
1,040.4	Pa. 849, Juniata River	R, C, sh	380	1,138.7
1,040.2	Clarks Ferry Bridge, Susquehanna River (west end)	R (W−0.1m M)	380	1,138.9
1,039.6	U.S. 22 & 322, Norfolk Southern RR	R (E−1m L; 16m G, L, M, O, D, V)	400	1,139.5
1,036.9	**Clarks Ferry Shelter...** *8.6mS; 6.7mN*	S, w	1,180	1,142.2
1,033.0	Pa. 225 Footbridge	R	1,250	1,146.1
1,031.1	Table Rock View		1,200	1,148.0
1,030.2	**Peters Mtn Shelter...** *6.7mS; 18.3mN*	S, w	970	1,148.9
1,027.4	Kinter View		1,320	1,151.7
1,023.9	Spring	w	700	1,155.2
1,023.5	Pa. 325, Clark's Valley	R, w	550	1,155.6
1,020.2	Stony Mtn; Horse-Shoe Trail		1,650	1,158.9
1,016.8	Yellow Springs Village Site		1,450	1,162.3
1,014.5	Cold Spring Trail		1,400	1,164.6

Miles from Katahdin	Features	Services	Elev.	Miles from Springer
1,012.2	**Rausch Gap Shelter**... *18.3mS; 13.7mN*	E–0.3m S, w	970	1,166.9
1,007.5	Pa. 443, Green Point, Pa.	R (W–2.6m C, M, cl, sh)	550	1,171.6
1,006.1	Pa. 72, Swatara Gap	R (E–2.4m C, G, L, M)	480	1,173.0
1,005.7	I-81 Underpass	R	450	1,173.4
998.8	**William Penn Shelter**... *13.7mS; 4.2mN*	S, w	1,300	1,180.3
996.6	Pa. 645	R	1,250	1,182.5
994.7	Pa. 501, **501 Shelter**... *4.2mS; 15.5mN* **Pine Grove, PA 17963**	R (W–0.1m S, w; 0.5m H; 3.7m PO, G, M, L, D, V, cl, sh) (E–2m PO, V, @)	1,460	1,184.4
994.2	Pilger Ruh Spring Trail	C, w	1,450	1,184.9
991.6	Round Head, Shower Steps	w	1,500	1,187.5
989.1	Hertlein Campsite	C, w	1,200	1,190.0
989.0	Shuberts Gap		1,200	1,190.1
985.7	Fort Dietrich Snyder Marker	W–0.2m w	1,440	1,193.4
985.4	Pa. 183, Rentschler Marker	R	1,450	1,193.7
984.1	Black Swatara Spring	W–0.3m w	1,510	1,195.0
980.3	Sand Spring Trail	E–0.2m w	1,510	1,198.8
979.6	**Eagle's Nest Shelter**... *15.5mS; 15mN*	W–0.3m S, w	1,510	1,199.5
977.7	Shartlesville Cross-Mtn Rd		1,450	1,201.4
975.0	Phillip's Canyon Spring	w	1,500	1,204.1
971.9	**Port Clinton, PA 19549**	R, PO (W–0.3m S, C, L, M, sh, O)	400	1,207.2
970.3	Pa. 61 **Hamburg, PA 19526**	R (E–1m L, M, O, f; 5m PO, L. M, G, D, V, cl)	490	1,208.8
967.7	Pocahontas Spring	C, w	1,200	1,211.4
965.1	Windsor Furnace	E–0.5m C, w	900	1,214.0
964.9	**Windsor Furnace Shelter**... *15mS; 9.3mN*	S, w	880	1,214.2
963.3	Pulpit Rock		1,582	1,215.8

Miles from Katahdin	Features	Services	Elev.	Miles from Springer
961.5	Trail to Blue Rocks Campground	E–1.5m S, C, G, cl, sh, f	1,150	1,217.6
961.1	The Pinnacle		1,615	1,218.0
955.8	Hawk Mtn Rd, **Eckville Shelter...** *9.3mS; 7.6mN*	E–0.2m S, w, sh	535	1,223.3
949.7	Tri-County Corner		1,560	1,229.4
948.4	**Allentown Hiking Club Shelter...** *7.6mS; 10mN*	S, w	1,350	1,230.7
946.5	Fort Franklin Rd	R	1,350	1,232.6
944.3	Pa. 309, Blue Mtn Summit	R, L, M, w	1,360	1,234.8
942.5	New Tripoli Campsite	W–0.2m C, w	1,400	1,236.6
941.5	Knife Edge		1,525	1,237.6
940.8	Bear Rocks		1,604	1,238.3
939.4	Bake Oven Knob Rd	R	1,450	1,239.7
939.0	Bake Oven Knob		1,560	1,240.1
938.4	**Bake Oven Knob Shelter...** *10mS; 6.8mN*	S, w	1,380	1,240.7
936.0	Ashfield Rd, Lehigh Furnace Gap	R (E–0.7m w)	1,320	1,243.1
931.6	**George W. Outerbridge Shelter...** *6.8mS; 16.8mN*	S, w	1,000	1,247.5
931.0	Pa. 873, Lehigh Gap **Slatington, PA 18080**	R (E–2m PO, G, L, M, D, cl, sh, f, @)	380	1,248.1
930.9	Pa. 873, Lehigh River Bridge (east end)	R	380	1,248.2
930.7	Pa. 145 **Walnutport, PA 18088**	R (E–2m PO, G, M, D, V)	380	1,248.4
930.7	Pa. 248 **Palmerton, PA 18071**	R (W–2m PO, H, G, L, M, D, cl, f, @)	380	1,248.4
925.7	Little Gap, Blue Mtn Rd **Danielsville, PA 18038**	R (W–1m w, C, sh, f; 2.5m M) (E–1.5m PO, G, L, M)	1,100	1,253.4
920.9	Delps Trail	E–0.25m w	1,580	1,258.2
919.1	Stempa Spring	E–0.6m w	1,510	1,260.0
918.4	Smith Gap Rd	R (W–1.0m w, sh, f)	1,540	1,260.7

Miles from Katahdin	Features	Services	Elev.	Miles from Springer
914.9	**Leroy A. Smith Shelter**... *16.8mS; 13.9mN*	E–0.1m S; 0.2m, 0.4m, 0.6m w	1,410	1,264.2
911.3	Hahns Lookout		1,450	1,267.8
910.3	Pa. 33 **Wind Gap, PA 18091**	R (E–1m PO, G, L, M, D, V, cl) (W– 0.1m L, w)	980	1,268.8
903.3	Wolf Rocks		1,550	1,275.8
901.7	Pa. 191, Fox Gap	R	1,400	1,277.4
901.1	**Kirkridge Shelter**... *13.9mS; 31.4mN*	S, w	1,480	1,278.0
899.2	Totts Gap		1,300	1,279.9
897.2	Mt. Minsi		1,461	1,281.9
896.2	Lookout Rock		800	1,282.9
895.4	Council Rock		600	1,283.7
894.7	Pa. 611 **Delaware Water Gap, PA 18327**	R (W–0.1m PO, H, M; 0.4m L, M, G, O, f; 5m G, M, L, O, cl)	400	1,284.4
894.5	Delaware River Bridge (west end), Pa.–N.J. State Line		350	1,284.6

Camping regulations vary depending on the type of public land. Be aware of posted notices, and check maps for boundaries. Most water sources are unreliable during summer months.

Pa. 16—East 1.2 miles to **Blue Ridge Summit, Pa. [P.O. ZIP 17214: M–F 8–4:30, Sa 9–11:30; (717) 794-2335].** ■ *Restaurants:* Mountain Shadows, daily, B/L/D, phone; Summit Plaza, daily 7–8, B/L/D, pay phone; Unique Bar and Grill; and fast-food options. ■ *Internet access:* library, M–Th 3–8, Sa 10–4. ■ *Other services:* True Value hardware, denatured alcohol; bank with ATM; JJ's Laundromat; barber; and Blue Ridge Summit Medical Center, M, Tu, Th 8–5, W, F 8–1.

West 2 miles to Rouzerville, Pa., with grocery store, convenience store, bank with ATM, Red Run Grill, and Walmart.

West 2.3 miles to *Groceries:* Food Lion (long-term resupply).

West 5 miles to **Waynesboro, Pa. [P.O. ZIP 17268: M–F 8:30–5, Sa 9–12; (717) 762-1513; pick-up window only, M–F 6–5, Sa 6–12:15]**, with all major services. ■ *Lodging:* Burgundy Lane B&B, (717) 762-8112, phone for shuttle from Trailhead, Internet access, laundry, local shuttles, and slackpacks; Days Inn, (717) 762-9113, call for current rates. ■ *Groceries:* Martin's (long-term resupply); 7–11 (short-term resupply). ■ *Restaurants:* Golden Corral Buffet and Grill, Pizza Hut, Dairy Queen, Domino's Pizza. ■ *Internet access:* library, M–F 9:30–8, Sa 9–4. ■ *Other services:* 24-hour coin laundry; hospital; bank with ATM; Radio Shack; pharmacies; Ace Hardware, denatured alcohol; veterinarian; dentist; K-Mart; and UPS Store.

Deer Lick Shelters (1940s)—Two shelters, each sleeps 4. Privy. Water source is a spring 0.2 mile on a blue-blazed trail to the east of the shelter area (reported dry in Oct '07), or stream 50 feet north of shelter.

Antietam Shelter (1940)—Sleeps 6. Privy. Water source is 0.2 mile north on the A.T. to a springhouse with spigot by the ballfield in Old Forge Park. Southbounders should get their water before reaching the shelter.

Tumbling Run Shelters (1940s)—Two shelters, each sleeps 4. Privy. Located on a short, blue-blazed trail. Water source is 100 yards to the west of the shelter.

 Pa. 233—East 1.2 miles to **South Mountain, Pa. [P.O. ZIP 17261: M–F 8–1 & 2–4:45, Sa 8:30–11:30; (717) 749-5833].** *Restaurant:* Sou-Mont Hotel and Bar, a.k.a. South Mountain Bar and Restaurant (not to be confused with the Old South Mountain Inn on U.S. 40-A at Turners Gap in Maryland); (717) 749-3845, grill-type menu (no lodging), M–Sa 9 a.m.–2 a.m., Su 11 a.m.–midnight.

Rocky Mountain Shelters (1989)—Two shelters, each sleeps 4. Privy. Located 0.2 mile on a steep, downhill, blue-blazed trail; for water, continue on side trail down to a road, then right 75 yards to spring.

 U.S. 30—East 14 miles to historic Gettysburg with many motels and most major services.

West 0.3 mile to *Restaurant:* Taormina's Pizza, with ice cream, Tu–Su 11–10; pay phone.

West 0.7 mile to *Groceries:* Henicle's Grocery (long-term resupply) with deli, pay phone; M–Sa 8–9, Su 8–6.

West 3.5 miles to **Fayetteville, Pa. [P.O. ZIP 17222: M–F 8–4:30, Sa 8:30–12; (717) 352-2022].** ■ *Lodging:* Rite Spot Motel, (717) 352-2144, $55S, $65D, $20 EAP, dog $15; shuttle $5 one-way, call ahead. ■ *Groceries:* convenience store (short-term resupply). ■ *Restaurants:* Flamingo Family Restaurant, Mamma's II. ■ *Other services:* doctor, pharmacy, coin laundry, barber, and ATM.

Caledonia State Park—(717) 352-2161, home to the Thaddeus Stevens Museum, but, more importantly for hot hikers, home to a swimming pool. The pool is visible as the A.T. enters a clearing in the park. Open only weekends from Memorial Day to mid-Jun, then daily to Labor Day; $4 admission. A snack bar with short-order grill opens at 10. Pay phone next to the pool and a second near the office. *Camping:* Campsites, nonelectric, with showers, no pets: F–Sa, $23 Pa. residents/$25 nonresidents; Su–Th, $19 Pa. residents/$21 nonresidents; shower only $3. With pets, add $2 to rates above. Maximum of 5 people/tents per site as long as tents don't extend beyond campsite. U.S. Sen. Thaddeus Stevens, an outspoken abolitionist, owned Caledonia Ironworks during the Civil War. Confederates burned the ironworks *en route* to the battle of Gettysburg. The old blacksmith shop was refurbished and now houses some artifacts.

Quarry Gap Shelters (1935)—Two shelters, each sleeps 4. Privy. Water source is 10 yards in front of the shelter.

Quarry Gap Shelters to Birch Run Shelter—Between these two shelter areas, the A.T. travels through impressive thickets of mountain laurel. Peak bloom is usually late May–early Jun.

Birch Run Shelter (2003)—Sleeps 8. Privy. Shelter located on the east side of the A.T. Water source is a spring 30 yards in front of the shelter.

Toms Run Shelters (1936)—Two shelters, each sleeps 4. Privy. Water source is a spring near old chimney.

Pa. 233/Pine Grove Furnace State Park—(717) 486-7174. ■ *Groceries:* Pine Grove General Store (short-term resupply), open daily 11–7 Memorial Day to Labor Day, weekends 10–6 Apr 15–Memorial Day and Sep–Oct, closed Nov 1–Apr 14. The first opportunity for northbounders to join the traditional "half-gallon club." To belong, you have to eat a half-gallon of ice cream to mark your halfway point. With relocations, the halfway point of the Trail today is now about 2.8 miles south of Pa. 233. ■ *Camping:* Nonelectric, no pets; F–Sa $23 Pa. resident, $25 nonresident; Su–Th $19 resident, $21 nonresident. Nonelectric site with pets is $2 more per night. Hot showers and flush toilets; concession stand with short-order grill, phone, and swimming in Laurel and Fuller lakes. An iron furnace that produced firearms used in the Revolutionary War ceased operation in the 1890s, but its remains are visible from the Trail. ■ *Hostel:* Ironmasters Mansion (Hostelling International), (717) 486-7575, south of the entrance to Pine Grove Furnace State Park. An 1827 mansion that was once a "station" on the Underground Railroad (ask to see the secret room). Hours 7:30–9:30 a.m., 5–10 p.m. Dormitory-style rooms with bunk beds, semiprivate rooms, shower, laundry, linens (sleeping bags not allowed on bunks), and kitchen privileges: $22 for HI members with membership card and for ATC, PATC, AMC members and thru-hikers; $25 for all others; shower only $4, with towel $5. Laundry facilities, wash $2, dry $2. No dogs allowed. Hiker message boards inside and out, as well as a giant outdoor chess board. The hostel holds packages sent to Ironmasters Mansion, 1212 Pine Grove Rd., Gardners, PA 17324.

Mountain Club of Maryland—MCM maintains the 16.2 miles from Pine Grove Furnace State Park to Center Point Knob and the 12.7 miles from the Darlington/Tuscarora Trail junction to the Susquehanna River. Correspondence should be sent to 7923 Galloping Circle, Baltimore, MD 21244; (410) 377-5625; <paulives2@aol.com>.

Midpoint Marker—North of the park, a wooden sign with a register that marked the old midpoint of the Trail has been retired to the new A.T. Museum nearby. ALDHA member Chuck Wood, "Woodchuck" of 1985, from Norristown, built and erected the marker. PATC is making a new one.

Mountain Creek Campground—West 0.7 mile; 349 Pine Grove Rd., Gardners, PA 17324; (717) 486-7681, <www.mtncreckcg.com>; mid-Apr–Oct, tenting $27, cabin w/o heat $45, hot showers, heated pool, camp store, camp supplies, snack shack; pets must be kept on a leash.

James Fry Shelter at Tagg Run (1998)—Sleeps 9. Privy (composting). Called "Tagg Run" in some sources, after the 1930s-vintage shelters it replaced. Tentsites available in the open adjacent field. Water source is 0.4 mile east of the A.T. on a blue-blazed trail; reported dry in Oct 2007.

Pine Grove Road—West 0.4 mile to Cherokee Family Restaurant and Campground, (717) 486-8000, deli 12–6; tentsites with shower $16D, $5EAP; pay phone outside.

Pa. 34—East 0.2 mile to the Green Mountain Store and Deli (short-term resupply), M–Sa 7–8, Su 9–6, Coleman fuel by the pint, pay phone. For southbounders, the first opportunity to join the Half-Gallon Club.

Pa. 94—West 2.5 miles to **Mt. Holly Springs, Pa. [P.O. ZIP 17065: M–F 8–4:30, Sa 9–12; (717) 486-3468].** ■ *Lodging:* Holly Inn and Restaurant, (717) 486-3823, call and will send car to pick up; <www.hollyinn.com>; $55s/ᴅ includes continental B and ride back to the Trail; L/D Su–Su 11:30–9, F-Sa 11:30–10; Internet. ■ *Restaurants:* Cassell's Grill, 5 West Pine St., (717) 486-8800, Tu–Su 11–9; Laura's Family Restaurant; Sicilia Pizza and Subs. ■ *Internet access:* library. ■ *Other services:* Uni-Mart (short-term resupply), with pay phone; coin laundry; pharmacy; dentist; doctor; optometrist; and bank with ATM.

Alec Kennedy Shelter (1991)—Sleeps 7. Privy (composting). Built by the MCM and Tressler Wilderness School. The shelter is 0.2 mile east on a blue-blazed trail. Water source is a spring located on a side trail behind the shelter; prone to go dry during the summer. A second source is a small stream 0.5 mile south of the shelter on the A.T.

Cumberland Valley Appalachian Trail Club—CVATC maintains the 17.2 miles between Center Point Knob and the Darlington/Tuscarora Trail junction. Correspondence should be sent to P.O. Box 395, Boiling Springs, Pa. 17007; <www.cvatclub.org>; <wbohn@paonline.com>.

No camping or fires in the valley—Between Alec Kennedy Shelter and Darlington Shelter, the Boiling Springs campsite (see next entry) is the only place where camping is allowed.

Boiling Springs, Pa. [P.O. ZIP 17007: M–F 8–4:30, Sa 8–12; (717) 258-6668]—Home to ATC's mid-Atlantic regional office, (717) 258-5771. Open weekdays 8–5. Staff members and volunteers can provide information on Trail conditions, weather forecasts, and water availability. Coleman fuel and denatured alcohol are available for a donation; A.T. maps and books for sale. A pay phone, picnic table, and hiker bulletin board are located on the porch. Bursting-at-seams office cannot accommodate packages sent to hikers; please use P.O. across street. *No camping at the office.* Limited parking available at opposite end of lake in township parking lot; obtain permit from ATC office during regular office hours (overnight parking is only allowed with permit that you display on your dashboard). Lodging is limited in Boiling Springs, but a year-round campsite with a portable toilet in season is south of town, before the railroad tracks (toilet Memorial Day–Labor Day). The trains do run past here all night long. The water source for the campsite is a spigot behind the ATC office, next to the oil tank. ■ *Lodging:* Gelinas Manor B&B, (717) 258-6584,

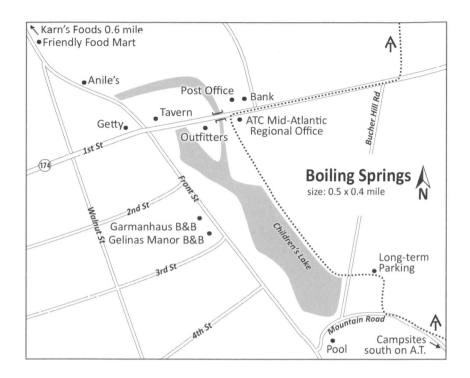

Karn's Foods 0.6 mile
Friendly Food Mart

Anile's

Post Office
Bank
Tavern
ATC Mid-Atlantic
Getty
Regional Office
Outfitters

1st St

Bucher Hill Rd

174

Front St

Boiling Springs
size: 0.5 x 0.4 mile
N

2nd St

Walnut St

Garmanhaus B&B
Gelinas Manor B&B

Children's Lake

3rd St

Long-term
Parking

4th St

Mountain Road

Pool
Campsites
south on A.T.

$69 (one room only) to $129 includes full B, no pets, no packs inside, $5 laundry service, mail drops for guests; Garmanhaus B&B, (717) 258-3980, Su–Th $50S, $60D, F–Sa $75S, $100S for 2 nights or camp in the backyard for $1 (no shower or bathroom privileges); Red Cardinal B&B, (717) 245-0823, <redcardinalbandb@aol.com>, call for reservations and a ride. Check the hiker-information board at ATC for postings of additional camping possibilities in the area.

West on Pa. 174—*Restaurants:* Anile's, L/D; Boiling Springs Tavern, L/D. ■ *Outfitter:* Yellow Breeches Outfitter, (717) 258-6752, closed M, limited hiker supplies, socks, clothing, rain gear, first aid, A.T. maps of Pa., bug spray, water-purification tablets. ■ *Groceries:* Karn's Store (long-term resupply), open daily 7–10; Getty Mart and Friendly Food Mart (both short-term resupply). ■ *Other services:* bank with ATM next to post office; doctor; dentist; veterinarian; Boiling Springs pool, (717) 258-4121, open Memorial–Labor Day, $9.75 admission, $1 hot shower, check ATC hiker bulletin board for coupons; barber; Jumpers Shoe Service, (717) 766-3422, in nearby Mechanicsburg.

East on Pa. 174—Allenberry Inn & Playhouse, (717) 258-3211; hikers' special $25/room, no reservations, first-come/first-served; B/D buffet extra: dinner-and-theater package W–Su, $25PP.

Cumberland Valley—Water is scarce between Boiling Springs and Darlington Shelter, as the A.T. winds along hedgerows and through Pennsylvania farmland. Thanks to an ambitious land-acquisition program, most of the Trail has been taken off roads through this heavily developed area, but it is still a hot walk on steamy summer days. Water can be obtained at one of the restaurants on U.S. 11 (see below) or at Scott Farm, which is 10.3 miles north of Boiling Springs.

U.S. 11—West 0.5 mile to various facilities spread along this busy highway. ▪ *Lodging:* America's Best Inn, (717) 245-2242 or (800) 445-6715, call for 2010 rates, dogs extra, laundry, WiFi; Super 8, (717) 249-7000, call for 2010 rates, laundry, pool, WiFi, accepts mail drops to 1800 Harrisburg Pike, Carlisle, PA 17013; Econolodge, (717) 249-7775, call for 2010 rates, continental B, pets extra and only in smoking rooms, laundry, pool, WiFi; Holiday Inn, (717) 245-2400, call for 2010 rates, pets okay ($10 nonrefundable fee), laundry, pool, Duffy's Restaurant and Pub, WiFi; Pheasant Field B&B, (717) 258-0717, Su–Th $88D, F–Sa $105–$185D, pet-friendly room may be available, laundry, free phone, shuttle to and from Trail with stay; Hotel Carlisle, (717) 243-1717, heated indoor pool, sauna, hot tub, WiFi, call for rates. Other options beyond I-81: Travel Lodge, Rodeway Inn, Howard Johnson, Quality Inn. ▪ *Restaurants:* Trailside Restaurant (limited hours), 24-hour Middlesex Diner, Bob Evans, Dunkin' Donuts, and fast-food restaurants on the other side of I-81. The Flying J Travel Plaza has restaurant (AYCE 6 a.m.–10 p.m., 24-hr. menu service), shower $11.50 (includes refundable $5 towel deposit), laundry, store (short-term resupply).

West—5 miles to Carlisle, a large town with all major services.

Conodoguinet Creek Bridge—An old farmhouse, known as the Scott Farm, is located next to the bridge where the Trail U-turns, passes under the bridge, and heads north. Open May–Oct, the farm has a privy, water, and a picnic table. *No camping.*

Wolf Trail—Water available where the A.T crosses an overgrown dirt road.

Tuscarora Trail—The northern terminus of the blue-blazed Tuscarora Trail, a 260-mile route to its southern terminus on the A.T. in Shenandoah National Park in Virginia. It was blazed when maintainers feared that the A.T. route would be closed by private landowners.

Darlington Shelter (2005)—Sleeps 8. Privy. Built by MCM to replace a 1982 shelter. Campsites available. Water source, an intermittent spring 0.2 mile on a blue-blazed trail in front of the shelter, regularly dries up early in the hiker season. It is recommended that northbounders bring water to the shelter from the Wolf Trail spring at the base of North Mountain; southbounders, from Cove Mountain.

Cove Mountain Shelter (2000)—Sleeps 8. Privy. Built with the help of the Timber Framers Guild using timber salvaged from a barn, some more than 100 years old. Water source is a spring 125 yards away on a steeply graded trail near the shelter.

U.S. 11/Duncannon, Pa. [P.O. ZIP 17020: M–F 8–4:30, Sa 8–12; (717) 834-3332. ID required for mail drops.]—The A.T. passes through the center of town, and all services are within a short walk. ■ *Camping:* Riverfront Campground (south of the Clarks Ferry Bridge), (717) 834-5252, tentsites and shower $3.50PP in designated hiker area, shuttle service, canoe and kayak rentals. ■ *Lodging:* Doyle Hotel, (717) 834-6789, one of the original Anheuser-Busch hotels, more than 100 years old, $25S, $7.50EAP, laundry, free Internet, pets allowed, shower only $7.50, will hold mail drops (ID required) sent to 7 North Market St., Duncannon, PA 17020, free shuttles to Mutzabaugh's, other shuttles available. On U.S. 11/15, 2 miles **north** of the truck stop, Stardust Motel, (717) 834-3191, Su–Th $40S, F–Sa $45S, $5EAP, laundry, no dogs, free shuttles to and from town. ■ *Groceries:* **West** of town 0.5 mile on Pa. 274, Mutzabaugh Market and pharmacy (long-term resupply), M–Sa 6–10, Su 7–10; Uni-Mart Convenience Store (short-term resupply), daily 6–11. ■ *Restaurants:* All-American Truck Plaza, B/L/D with AYCE buffet; Doyle Hotel, L/D full menu and bar; Goodie's Café, B/L M–F, B Sa–Su; The Pub, L/D; Riviera Tavern, L/D; Sorrento's Pizza and Subs, L/D; Zeiderelli's Pizza, L/D, seasonal ice-cream stand. ■ *Outfitter:* Blue Mountain Outfitters, (717) 957-2413, <www.bluemountainoutfitters.net>, 8 miles **south** on U.S. 11 in Marysville, closed M, 10–8 T, 10–6 W–Su; fuel, water bottles, freeze-dried food, canoe and kayak rentals. ■ *Other services:* All-American Truck Plaza (short-term resupply), $8 shower, ATM; laundry; banks with ATM; doctor; dentist; bank; veterinarian; Duncannon Community Library and Education Center at Duncannon Presbyterian Church, 3 N. High St., Duncannon 17020, open W 1–3, Sat 10–12, Internet, a/c, cold drinks & snacks, hiker box, all hikers welcome; Mary Parry (Trail Angel Mary), (717) 834-4706, can answer questions about services in Duncannon.

U.S. 22 & 322—East 1 mile to *Lodging:* Le Ellen Motel, (717) 921-8715, $35S, $40D, $10EAP, no pets, no phone.

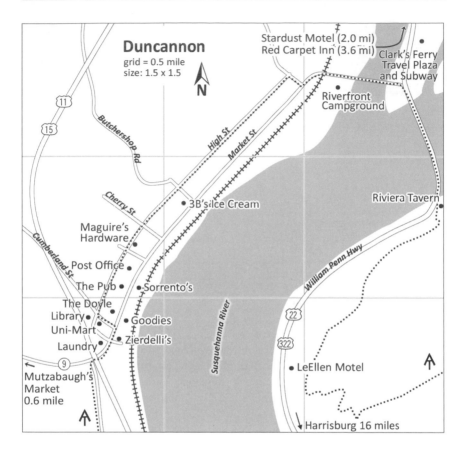

Duncannon
grid = 0.5 mile
size: 1.5 x 1.5

N

Stardust Motel (2.0 mi)
Red Carpet Inn (3.6 mi)

Clark's Ferry
Travel Plaza
and Subway

11

15

Butchershop Rd

High St

Market St

Riverfront
Campground

Cherry St

3B's Ice Cream

Riviera Tavern

Maguire's
Hardware

Cumberland St

Post Office

The Pub • • Sorrento's

William Penn Hwy

The Doyle
Library
Uni-Mart
Laundry

• Goodies
• Zierdelli's

22

322

Susquehanna River

9

Mutzabaugh's
Market
0.6 mile

• LeEllen Motel

Harrisburg 16 miles

East 16 miles to Harrisburg, Pennsylvania's capital city, with all major services, including Wildware Backcountry, (717) 564-8008, backpacking gear and supplies.

York Hiking Club—YHC maintains the 7.2 miles from the Susquehanna River to Pa. 225. Correspondence should be sent to YHC, 2684 Forest Rd., York, PA 17402; (717) 244-6769; <president@yorkhikingclub.com>.

Earl Shaffer—Almost all hikers recognize Earl "Crazy One" Shaffer (1918–2002) from York, Pa., as the first A.T. thru-hiker. In 1948, he completed a northbound thru-hike; in 1965, he completed a southbound thru-hike, becoming the first to accomplish both northbound and southbound hikes. To celebrate the 50th anniversary in 1998 of his first hike, Earl did a northbound thru-hike at the young age of 79. ATC's first "corresponding secretary," he was active in Trail maintenance and promoting trails for the YHC and Susquehanna Appalachian Trail Club for many years.

Clarks Ferry Shelter (1993)—Sleeps 8. Privy. A blue-blazed trail leads 100 yards to the shelter and 100 yards farther to a reliable piped spring.

 Pa. 225—In 2003, a pedestrian bridge was built to avoid a dangerous road-crossing; it offers a good view of Powell Creek Valley, too.

Susquehanna Appalachian Trail Club—SATC maintains the 20.4 miles from Pa. 225 to Rausch Creek. Correspondence should be sent to <hike-hbg@satc-hike.org> or SATC, P.O. Box 61001, Harrisburg, PA 17106-1001.

Peters Mountain Shelter (1994)—Sleeps 20. Privy. The little shelter that Earl Shaffer built years earlier was removed in 2008 for inclusion in the new A.T. Museum. Water source for shelter is down blue-blazed trail in front of shelter on north side of the mountain. The trail is a steep path of almost 300 rock steps installed by SATC and ATC's mid-Atlantic crew between 1996 and 1999.

Clarks Ferry to Rausch Gap—The A.T. passes near the remains of old mining villages dating back to the 1800s. Remnants of Yellow Springs Village are still visible along the Trail, and, in Rausch Gap, near where the A.T. crosses Rausch Creek, a trail leads to a small family cemetery from the 1850s. Between here and Virginia's Sinking Creek Mountain, the Trail is in the Chesapeake Bay watershed.

Blue Mountain Eagle Climbing Club—BMECC maintains the 62.9 miles from Rausch Creek to Tri-County Corner and the 3.1 miles from Bake Oven Knob to Lehigh Furnace Gap. Correspondence can be sent to P.O. Box 14982, Reading, PA 19612; <www.bmecc.org>; <info@bmecc.org>; (610) 326-1656.

Rausch Gap Shelter (1972)—Sleeps 12. Privy. Built by the BMECC; no tenting. Water source is a reliable spring next to the shelter.

Pa. 443—West 2.6 miles to *Camping:* Twin Grove KOA, (717) 865-4602, <info@ twingroveparkcampground.com>, $26–$45 tentsite, laundry, restaurant, ice-cream parlor, Internet, pool, nonguest shower $5.

Pa. 72/Swatara Gap—East 2.4 miles to Lickdale, adjacent to I-81 Exit 90. ■ *Restaurants:* Wendy's, Dairy Queen, Love's truck stop (showers $9) with McDonald's, Chester's Chicken, Sbarro Italian, Subway in Exxon with short-term resupply, Godfather's Pizza, Blimpie, Dunkin' Donuts. ■ *Lodging:* Best Western, (717) 865-4234, $109D, continental B, pool, WiFi; Days Inn, pets $10, laundry, ATM, hot tub, continental B, free Internet access; Quality Inn, (717) 865-6600, continental B, Internet access, laundry, pool. ■ *Camping:* Lickdale Campground and General Store (short-term resupply), with rotisserie chicken and pizza.

William Penn Shelter (1993)—Sleeps 16. Privy. With second-floor loft and windows, 0.1 mile east of the A.T., often visited by summer camping groups. Water source is 200 yards on a blue-blazed trail to the west of the A.T.

Pa. 501—East 2 miles to **Bethel, Pa. [P.O. ZIP 19507: M–F 8–12 & 1:15–4:30, Sa 8:30–10:30; (717) 933-8305].** ■ *Other services:* Bethel Animal Clinic, (717) 933-4916. ■ *Internet access:* Bethel Library, M–Th 10–8, F 10–5, Sa 9–4.

West 0.5 mile to *Hostel:* PAmoneypit, (570) 345-1119 or cell (570) 292-3350, <pamoneypit@yahoo.com>, Amy Lu Holland, $25PP includes hot shower, laundry $2, and continental B. Reservations required; call for availability. Pet-friendly; kennel on premises. Local shuttles to town for P.O., bank, pizza, grocery store, medical or dentist services. Will also shuttle to other stops along the A.T. and airports. Call for shuttle and slackpacking rates.

West 3.7 miles to **Pine Grove, Pa. [P.O. ZIP 17963: M–F 8:30–4:30, Sa 9–12; (570) 345-4955.** *ID required.*]. Most major services but spread out over three miles. ■ *Lodging:* Hampton Inn, (540) 345-4505, indoor pool, laundry, WiFi, continental B; Econo Lodge, (570) 345-4099, weekdays $55S, $60D, weekends $70D, dogs $10, continental B; Comfort Inn, (570) 345-8031, $60–$109D, pets $10, includes continental B, pool; Colony Lodge, (570) 345-8095, $40–$55D, pets $5. ■ *Groceries:* Turkey Hill Market with ATM, pay phone (short-term resupply); BG's Market (long-term resupply), daily 7–9. ■ *Restaurants:* O'Neals Pub, L/D W–Su; McDonald's; Arby's; the Original Italian Pizza Place, L/D; Do's Pizza, L/D, closed Su; Dominick's Pizza,

L/D, closed M; Buddy's Log Cabin Restaurant; Burke's Dairy Bar; Sholl Family Restaurant, (570) 345-8715, B/L/D, AYCE buffets, closed M, smoke-free, return shuttle possible; Gooseberry Farms Family Restaurant, open 24/7, shower $9 with $5 towel deposit; Subway; Dairy Queen; Blimpie. ■ *Other services:* coin laundry, barber, bank with ATM, doctor, podiatrist, dentist, veterinarian, pharmacy (closed Su), movie theater, community pool ($9.50), and bus service to Harrisburg.

501 Shelter (1980s)—Immediately north of paved Pa. 501, go west on the blue-blaze 0.1 mile; always open, no fee. Shelter is fully enclosed, with 12 bunks, table, chairs, skylight (a potter once had her wheel underneath), privy, and solar shower. Tentsites off woods road uphill, beyond fire ring. Water available from faucet at adjacent house of BMECC caretaker, (717) 933-4327, cell (570) 681-5017, <ronh19@yahoo.com>. No smoking inside shelter; no alcoholic beverages allowed. Pets allowed (on leash only) if other shelter guests are willing to share and owner takes care of sanitary needs. Shuttles and motoring visitors park in public lot on paved 501 and walk in *via* blue-blaze.

Eagles Nest Shelter (1988)—Sleeps 8. Privy. Shelter is 0.3 mile from the A.T. on a blue-blazed trail. Intermittent Yeich Spring is crossed *en route* to the shelter.

Port Clinton, Pa. [P.O. ZIP 19549: M–F 7:30–12:30 & 2–5, Sa 8–11; (610) 562-3787]—Port Clinton allows hikers to camp free under the roof of its pavilion. The pavilion, with outhouse, is located 0.3 mile west of the A.T. on Penn Street. Hikers must either check in at Ye Olde Backpacker or call LaVerne Sterner at (570) 366-0489. The pavilion is a drug- and alcohol-free area. Permission is required for a stay of more than two nights; no car camping. Water can be obtained from a spigot outside the Port Clinton Hotel. ■ *Lodging:* Port Clinton Hotel, (610) 562-3354, <www.portclintonhotel.net>, $49PP, $10 deposit for room key and towel, shower only $5, closed M, limited rooms available, laundry, no reservations, WiFi; Union House Bed & Bath, (610) 562-4076, (610) 562-3155, offers bedroom, bath, and sitting room for hikers $65s, call to ask about double rooms and pets. ■ *Restaurants:* Port Clinton Hotel, L/D, closed M; 3-C's Restaurant, B/L, M–F 5–3, Sa–Su 6–2; Union House B&B, D. ■ *Outfitter:* Ye Olde Backpacker, <www.yeoldepackpacker.com>, 45 Penn St., (610) 562-2322; M–Sa 9–8, Su 10–5; backpacking and other supplies, fuel, cold drinks, ice cream; nominal fee for shuttles to Hamburg, shuttles for section-hikers available south to Duncannon and north to Delaware Water Gap; mail drops accepted and shipped UPS, photo ID required. ■ *Other services:* The Port Clinton Peanut Shop, open M–Th 10–7, F–Sa 10–8, Su 10–6, with home-made goodies and snacks, cold drinks, ATM. ■ *Bus service:*

Bieber Trailways, (800) 333-8444, <www.capitoltrailways.com>, flag the bus on the road in front of Peanut Shop for connections to Pottsville, Hamburg, Reading, Harrisburg, and Philadelphia; Schuykill Transportation System, (570) 429-2701 or (800) 832-3322 in Pa., <www.go-sts.com>, service from Pottsville to Cabela's.

East on Pa. 61 1 mile to ■ *Lodging:* Microtel Inn, <www.microtelinn.com>, (610) 562-4234, $66–$135D, continental B, pet-friendly ($10 nonrefundable fee), free long-distance phone, laundry, WiFi. ■ *Restaurants:* Cabela's Restaurant, B/L/D; Wendy's; Burger King; Cracker Barrel; Pappy T's in Microtel Inn, L/D; Dunkin' Donuts–Baskin Robbins; Shell with food mart (short-term resupply), pay phone; Subway; Taco Bell/Long John Silver's; McDonald's; Pizza Hut/Wings Street. ■ *Outfitter:* Cabela's Superstore, <www.cabelas.com>, (610) 929-7000, M–Sa 8–9, Su 9–8, a 250,000-square-foot outfitter (nation's largest), mostly for hunting and fishing, fuel (Esbit, propane/butane, Coleman Powermax), ATM. ■ *Bus service:* M–Sa from Cabela's to Hamburg to Reading with connections to Philadelphia; (610) 921-0601, <www.bartabus.com>.

East on Pa. 61 3 miles, then left on State Street to **Hamburg, Pa. [P.O. ZIP 19526; M–F 9–5, Sa 9–12; (610) 562-7812].** ■ *Lodging:* American House Hotel near center of town, (610) 562-4683. ■ *Groceries:* Weis Supermarket, open daily 6–11, one block east of the town center. In town are laundry, pharmacy, movie theater, doctor, dentist, bakery, medical center, veterinarian, banks with ATM. Near Pa. 61 are Redner's Market Warehouse (open 24 hrs., long-term resupply), Dollar General, Family Dollar, Rite Aid, Arby's, Xiang Shan, Loue's, Subway.

Hamburg Reservoir—A parking area 0.3 mile **East** of the A.T. requires permits for overnight parking, available at no charge. Call the Borough of Hamburg, (610) 562-7821, for permission.

Windsor Furnace Shelter (1970s)—Sleeps 8. Privy. Shelter is located on a blue-blazed trail near the reservoir. Tentsites available. Water source is the creek south of the shelter. *No campfires except at shelter. No swimming in streams or reservoir.*

Blue Rocks Campground— **East** 1.5 miles to campground, (866) 478-5267, <www.bluerockscampground.com>, *via* a blue-blazed trail from Pulpit Rock and a yellow-blazed trail from The Pinnacle. Tentsites $30 M–F, 50% discount for thru-hikers M–Th, showers, swimming (nonguest) $4, laundry, pay phone. Camp store (short-term resupply), M–Th 9–7, F 9–11, Sa 8–11, Su 8–7, with Coleman fuel and limited hiker supplies. Will hold packages mailed to 341 Sousley Rd., Lenhartsville, PA 19534. Hiker-friendly.

The Pinnacle—A panoramic view of Pennsylvania farmland from an elevation of 1,635 feet, said to be the best view on the A.T. in the state. Below the viewpoint lies a sheer cliff and a few caves. *No camping or fires are permitted.*

Hawk Mountain Road—**East** 0.2 mile to Eckville Hikers Center, an enclosed bunkroom that offers space for 6. No fee. Water from a spigot at the back of the caretaker's house. Solar shower, flush toilet, and tent platforms with picnic table available. Open year-round.

Hawk Mountain Sanctuary—Atop the Kittatinny Ridge sits the Hawk Mountain Visitors Center, <www.hawkmountain.org>, accessible *via* a 2.5-mile blue-blazed trail from the A.T. Located within the visitors center are a bookstore, gift shop, and interpretive exhibits on raptors that fly by the mountain during the migratory seasons. Rosalie Edge founded the sanctuary in 1934. Prior to that time, instead of birders, hunters flocked to the mountain each fall to shoot the raptors. Several species other than raptors can be seen; 16 species of hawks, falcons, and eagles have been spotted over the mountain. Peak viewing months are Sep–Nov, with $7 entrance fee; rest of year, $5 entrance fee.

Allentown Hiking Club—AHC maintains the 10.7 miles from Tri-County Corner to Bake Oven Knob. Correspondence should be sent to P.O. Box 1542, Allentown, PA 18105; <www.allentownhikingclub.org>; <info@allentownhikingclub.org>.

Allentown Hiking Club Shelter (1997)—Sleeps 8. Privy. Tentsites. Water source is a spring 0.2 mile downhill in front of shelter; if dry, try one 0.1 mile more downhill.

Pa. 309—*Lodging:* Blue Mountain B&B, (570) 386-2003, <www.bluemountainsummit.com>, $95–$125 per night when available. Restaurant open Th–Sa 11–10, Su 11–8; live music all year on F 7–10, on Su Jun–Sep Su 5–8 on the patio; hiker register. Possible camping near restaurant if you ask first. Water available from outside spigot.

Bake Oven Knob Shelter (1937)—Sleeps 6. No privy. One of the original Pennsylvania shelters. The first water source on the blue-blazed trail is often dry; continue 200 yards to the second, more dependable spring, although both may be intermittent.

Philadelphia Trail Club—PTC maintains the 10.3 miles from Lehigh Furnace Gap to Little Gap. Correspondence should be sent to 741 Golf Rd., Warrington, PA 18976; <pauls@deperjico.com>.

George W. Outerbridge Shelter (1965)—Sleeps 6. No privy. The surrounding area suffers from heavy-metal contamination from the zinc plant at Palmerton (see Superfund entry below). Water source is a piped spring north 150 yards on the A.T.

Pa. 873/Lehigh Gap—East 2 miles on Pa. 873 to **Slatington, Pa. [P.O. ZIP 18080: M–F 8:30–5, Sa 8:30–12; (610) 767-2182].** ■ *Lodging:* Fine Lodging, (610) 760-0700, <finelodging@aol.com>; call ahead; rooms $39 and up depending on availability; no dogs and no alcoholic beverages; Internet access for guests; shower without stay $4. When available, owner Ira Fine will shuttle guests to and from the A.T. and other locations. Call from the office phone at D & J Auto on Pa. 873. Will hold packages mailed to Fine Lodgings, 700 Main St., Slatington, PA 18080. ■ *Restaurants:* The Shack, L/D; Mama's Pizza; Sal's Pizza; Slatington Diner B/L/D. ■ *Internet access:* Slatington Library, M, W 9–7, Tu 9–3, F 9–5, Sa 8–2. ■ *Other services:* coin laundry, ATM, convenience stores, A.F. Boyer Hardware store, doctor, dentist, pharmacy, bowling alley, and bus service to Walnutport and Allentown.

East 2 miles on Pa. 145 to **Walnutport, Pa. [P.O. ZIP 18088: M–F 8:30–5, Sa 8:30–12; (610) 767-5191].** ■ *Groceries:* Super Fresh Supermarket (long-term resupply). ■ *Restaurants:* Valley Restaurant and Pizza, $5.75 L AYCE; King Palace Chinese, $4.95 L AYCE; Great Wall Chinese; d'Sopranos Pizza; Burger King; McDonald's; Subway; Pizza Hut. ■ *Other services:* ATM, doctor, dentist, pharmacy, veterinarian, K-Mart.

West 2 miles on Pa. 248 or 2-mile blue-blaze to **Palmerton, Pa. [P.O. ZIP 18071: M–F 8:30–5, Sa 8:30–12; (610) 826-2286].** *Blue-blaze directions:* **West** 1.5 miles from the gravel lot on the northwest side of the Lehigh River over the Aquashicola Creek Bridge to the back road leading to Delaware Ave. in Palmerton. ■ *Hostel:* The city allows hikers to sleep in the basement of the borough hall, (610) 826-2505, 443 Delaware Ave.; showers. Hikers (unassisted-by-vehicles only) should check in before 4:30; the town police (located at 401 Delaware Ave.) admit hikers after 4:30 weekdays and Sa–Su. You will need to provide an ID, name, address, and Trail name. No pets. *No alcoholic beverages or intoxicated persons are permitted.* ■ *Lodging:* The Palmerton Hotel, (610) 826-5454, $55S, $65 efficiency unit. ■ *Groceries:* IGA, Country Harvest (both long-term resupply). ■ *Restaurants:* Bert's Steakhouse, B/L/D; One Ten Tavern, L/D, closed M; Simply Something Café, B/L/D; Tony's Pizzeria; Joe's Place, deli sandwiches; Palmerton Pizza and Restaurant; Subway; Hunan House Chinese. ■ *Internet access:* library M 10–8, T–F 10–5, Sa 9–4 (Sa Jul–Aug 9–1). ■ *Other services:* coin laundry; ATM; shuttle back to the Trail, Duane Masonheimer, (610) 767-7969; Shea's Hardware and Sporting Goods, Heet, Coleman fuel, and denatured alcohol; bowling alley; pharmacy; doctor; dentist; and hospital.

Palmerton EPA Superfund Site—The devastation along Blue Mountain near Lehigh Gap is the result of nearly a century of zinc smelting in Palmerton. In 1980, the Environmental Protection Agency shut down the furnaces and, in 1982, put the affected area on the Superfund clean-up list. Revegetation efforts are underway, and the mountain is slowly coming back to life. A product called Ecoloam—municipalwaste sludge, fly ash, lime, fertilizer, and seeds—has been spread on the slopes. Before you curse the zinc manufacturers, consider that zinc is likely one of the metals in the grommets and eyelets on your backpack. It is used in everything from face powder to zippers. The scramble up the denuded rocks is among the most challenging on the A.T. south of New Hampshire.

Appalachian Mountain Club–Delaware Valley Chapter—AMC–Delaware Valley maintains the 15.4 miles from Little Gap to Wind Gap. Correspondence should be sent to 1180 Greenleaf Dr., Bethlehem, PA 18017; <www.amcdv.org>.

 Little Gap, Blue Mountain Drive—**West** 2.5 miles to Little Gap and *Restaurant:* Covered Bridge Inn.

East 1.5 miles to **Danielsville, Pa. [P.O. 18038: M–F 8–12 & 1–5, Sa 8–12; (610) 767-6822].** ■ *Lodging:* Filbert B&B, (610) 428-3300, <www.filbertbnb.com>, starting at $100D, reservations required; full, hearty, country B; will pick up and drop off hikers and possibly shuttle. ■ *Restaurants:* Blue Mountain Family Restaurant, Mama's Pizza, Como Pizza. ■ *Groceries:* Millers Market. ■ *Other services:* Carl and Judy Rush, (610) 765-6007, <crush@ptd.net>, will shuttle and provide help to hikers as needed.

Smith Gap Road—For northbounders, it is the first road after the Stempa Spring side trail, on which it's **West** 1 mile to a water spigot at the rear of the house of Linda "Crayon Lady" and John "Mechanical Man" Stempa, (610) 381-4606; camping in yard, free cold shower, hiker's register. Pets welcome. Homemade alcohol stoves, windscreens, and methyl fuel available; shuttles to area Trailheads by arrangement; ask about safe parking.

Leroy A. Smith Shelter (1972)—Sleeps 8. Privy (composting). Built by the AMC–Delaware Valley Chapter, shelter is located 0.2 mile down a blue-blazed trail. Water sources can be intermittent; the first, 0.2 mile down the blue-blazed trail; a second, on a yellow-blazed trail 0.2 mile farther; a third, even farther, may be running when the first two are not.

Batona Hiking Club—BHC maintains the 8.6 miles from Wind Gap to Fox Gap (Pa. 191). Correspondence should be sent to BHC, 6651 Eastwood St., Philadelphia, Pa. 19149; <www.batonahikingclub.org>.

Pa. 33—East 1 mile to **Wind Gap, Pa. [P.O. ZIP 18091: M–F 8:30–5, Sa 8:30–12; (610) 863-6206].** ■ *Lodging:* Travel Inn, (610) 863-4146, $50S, $60D, $10EAP, holidays and weekends higher, dogs $10, soda machine inside. ■ *Groceries:* Giant Food Store located in K-Mart Plaza (long-term resupply); Turkey Hill Mini Market, Sunoco Mini Mart (both short-term resupply). ■ *Restaurants:* Tony's Pizza; Beer Stein; McDonald's; Wendy's; Burger King; Subway; Hong Kong Restaurant; diners serving

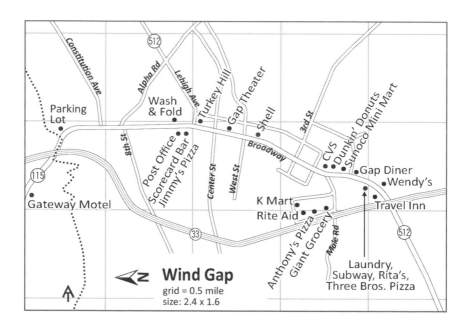

B/L/D; Dunkin' Donuts; Rita's Ices; other fast-food outlets. ■ *Other services:* coin laundry, K-Mart, hardware store, doctor, dentist, pharmacy, veterinarian, bank with ATM, and movie theater.

West 0.1 mile to *Lodging:* Gateway Motel, (610) 863-4959, $59S, $65D, $75T, nice dogs allowed $10, sodas for sale. Pete, the owner, allows hikers to fill water bottles, provides free shuttles when available.

Wilmington Trail Club—WTC maintains the 7.2 miles from Fox Gap to the Delaware River Bridge. Correspondence should be sent to P.O. Box 1184, Wilmington, DE 19899; <www.wilmingtontrailclub.org>.

Kirkridge Shelter (1948)—Sleeps 8. Privy. Shelter is on a blue-blazed trail with excellent views south. Water source is an outside tap to rear of shelter before the Kirkridge Retreat facility parking lot. Tap is secured when frost is possible.

Pa. 611/Delaware Water Gap, Pa. [P.O. ZIP 18327: M–F 8:30–12 & 1–4:45, Sa 8:30–11:30; (570) 476-0304]—The A.T. doesn't go through the town center, but services are within a mile of where it crosses Pa. 611. ■ *Hostel:* The Presbyterian Church of the Mountain Hostel, with overflow lean-to in backyard, has been overwhelmed with hikers in the past; please respect the good-will of the pastor and her parishioners. Space with shower limited to long-distance hikers—no car or van parking or support vehicles permitted in parking lot. Two-night limit, donations suggested, *absolutely no drugs or alcohol.* ■ *Lodging:* Deer Head Inn, (570) 424-2000, restaurant and upscale rooms available. ■ *Restaurants:* DWG Diner, (570) 476-0132, B/L/D; Doughboy Pizza; Deer Head Inn for fine dining F–Su, pizza, and live entertainment, notably jazz; Sycamore Grille, L/D, closed Su–M, D by reservation; Castle Inn, on Trail at Mountain Road, old-fashioned ice cream. ■ *Groceries:* BP Mini Mart with ATM, Gulf Mini Mart (both short-term resupply); Farmer's Market with fruits, vegetables, lots of baked goods, and ice cream. ■ *Outfitters:* The Pack Shack, (570) 424-8533: backpacking gear, supplies, and a special rate for tubing the Delaware River. Owner John Greene gives thru-hikers discounts, repairs poles, sells Coleman fuel and denatured alcohol by the ounce, and holds packages mailed from manufacturers only, no regular mail drops; contact the outfitter for an address. Daily shuttle $2.25/mi for slackpacking 2 people, $5EAP; must be back by 6 p.m. Edge of the Woods Outfitters, 110 Main St. (Rt. 611), (572) 421-6681, maps, bike rentals, outerwear, activewear, footwear, national park info, all brands; will hold UPS packages for thru-hikers, shuttle $1.50/mi, very hiker-friendly. ■ *Other services:* hair salon,

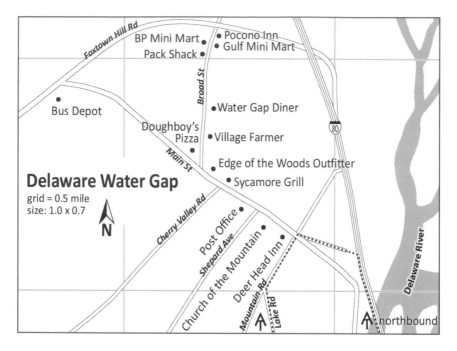

run by Paulette, (570) 421-8218, Tu–F 10–7, Sa 10–3. ■ *Bus service:* Martz Trailways, (570) 421-4451 or (570) 421-3040, to New York, Philadelphia, and Scranton, and local service to Stroudsburg.

West 5 miles to East Stroudsburg and Stroudsburg, Pa., full-service towns. *Outfitter:* Dunkelberger's Sports Outfitter, (570) 421-7950, with backpacking equipment, supplies, and clothing, is located at 6th and Main streets.

New Jersey

Miles from Katahdin	Features	Services	Elev.	Miles from Springer
894.5	Delaware River Bridge (west end), N.J.–Pa. State Line		350	1,284.6
893.5	DWG Nat'l Rec. Area Visitors Center	R, w	350	1,285.6
891.5	Holly Springs Trail	E–0.2m w	950	1,287.6
889.9	Backpacker Campsite	C, nw	1,300	1,289.2
888.6	Sunfish Pond		1,382	1,290.5
888.5	Spring	w	1,400	1,290.6
886.8	Herbert Hiller plaque		1,450	1,292.3
884.2	Camp Rd; Mohican Outdoor Center	R, w (W–0.3m C, L, w, f)	1,150	1,294.9
881.8	Catfish Fire Tower		1,565	1,297.3
881.2	Rattlesnake Spring	W–50ft w	1,260	1,297.9
880.8	Millbrook-Blairstown Rd-CR 602	R (W–1.1m w)	1,350	1,298.3
876.9	Blue Mtn Lakes Rd	R, w (W–0.8m C, w)	1,350	1,302.2
874.9	Crater Lake	E–0.5m w	1,360	1,304.2
872.1	Rattlesnake Mtn		1,492	1,307.0
869.9	**Brink Rd Shelter**... *31.4mS; 6.9mN*	W–0.2m S, w	1,110	1,309.2
866.3	U.S. 206, Culvers Gap **Branchville, NJ 07826**	R, M (E–0.8m G; 1m M; 1.6m G, M; 2.5m G, M, L; 3.4m PO) (W–1.8m L, M)	935	1,312.8
864.4	Culver Fire Tower		1,550	1,314.7
863.3	**Gren Anderson Shelter**... *6.9mS; 5.9mN*	W–0.1m S, w	1,320	1,315.8
860.9	Sunrise Mtn	R, nw	1,653	1,318.2
857.5	**Mashipacong Shelter**... *5.9mS; 3.3mN*	S, nw	1,425	1,321.6
854.6	**Rutherford Shelter**... *3.3mS; 4.8mN*	E–0.4m S, w	1,345	1,324.5
852.0	N.J. 23; High Point State Park HQ	R, w (E–0.9m C, sh; 1.5m L; 2.6m G, M) (W–4.4m G, L, M)	1,500	1,327.1

Miles from Katahdin	Features	Services	Elev.	Miles from Springer
850.3	**High Point Shelter...** *4.8mS; 12.5mN*	E–0.1m S, w	1,280	1,328.8
849.0	County 519	R (E–2.5m L)	1,100	1,330.1
846.4	Gemmer Rd	R	740	1,332.7
845.4	Goodrich Rd	R	610	1,333.7
845.0	Trail to Jim Murray property	W–0.2m w, S, C, sh	660	1,334.1
844.9	Goldsmith Rd	R	600	1,334.2
844.1	Unionville Rd	R	610	1,335.0
843.2	Lott Rd **Unionville, NY 10988**	R (W–0.4m PO, C, G, M)	590	1,335.9
842.2	N.J. 284	R (W–0.4m G, M, @)	420	1,336.9
841.7	Oil City Rd	R	400	1,337.4
840.7	Wallkill River	R	410	1,338.4
838.4	Lake Wallkill Rd (Liberty Corners Rd)	R, w	440	1,340.7
837.9	**Pochuck Mtn Shelter...** *12.5mS; 11.6mN*	S, nw	840	1,341.2
836.4	Pochuck Mtn		985	1,342.7
835.2	County 565	R	720	1,343.9
833.7	County 517 **Glenwood, NJ 07418**	R (W–1.1m PO, G, L)	440	1,345.4
833.0	Pochuck Creek Footbridge		410	1,346.1
832.3	Canal Rd	R	410	1,346.8
831.4	N.J. 94 **Vernon, NJ 07462**	R (E–1.8m L; 2.4m PO, C, H, G, L, M, V, cl, f, @; 3.5m D) (W–0.1m G)	450	1,347.7
830.0	Wawayanda Mtn		1,340	1,349.1
828.3	Barrett Rd	R	1,140	1,350.8
827.2	Iron Mtn Rd Bridge		1,060	1,351.9
826.6	Wawayanda Rd	R	1,150	1,352.5
826.4	**Wawayanda Shelter...** *11.6mS; 12.2mN*	W–0.1m S; 0.4m w	1,200	1,352.7
825.9	Warwick Turnpike	R (E–1.9m G, M) (W–2.7m G, M)	1,140	1,353.2

Miles from Katahdin	Features	Services	Elev.	Miles from Springer
824.5	Long House (Brady Rd)	R	1,080	1,354.6
823.4	Long House Creek		1,085	1,355.7
822.3	State Line Trail; N.J.–N.Y. State Line		1,385	1,356.8

Bear boxes are provided at several New Jersey shelters; please use them! Bears are extremely active in this area. One pair destroyed a hiker's tent. Never feed bears or leave food unattended. Do not bury or scatter excess food; avoid eating or preparing food in your tent. It is now estimated that the New Jersey counties where bears range have one per square mile.

Campfires are prohibited in New Jersey. Camping in areas other than those designated by signs also is prohibited in New Jersey.

Hitchhiking is illegal in New Jersey.

New Jersey has the highest population of bears per square mile and a one-mile boardwalk. Southbounders are at the end of their deli-to-deli hike, whereas northbounders hungrily look forward to theirs. Thru-hiker legs are operating at machine level by now, which is good, because you may have to walk farther to find water.

New York–New Jersey Trail Conference—The NY–NJ TC maintains the 160.6 miles from Delaware Water Gap to the New York–Connecticut state line. Correspondence should be sent to NY–NJ TC, 156 Ramapo Valley Rd., Mahwah, NJ 07430; (201) 512-9348; <www.nynjtc.org>; <info@nynjtc.org>.

Delaware Water Gap National Recreation Area—The information center, visible from the Trail, closed due to major flooding of the Delaware River in April 2005, reopened in mid-2007. Restrooms and pay phone are available for use. Water is available from a spigot to the left of the building. The Trail on Kittatinny Ridge runs through the NRA and state parks and forests, where regulations are different. The history of the recreation area is linked to a controversial 1960s plan to dam the Delaware, defeated by local opponents and the Trail community. Thru-hikers (defined by DWG as those who are hiking for two or more consecutive days) are permitted to camp along the Trail in the NRA with the following restrictions: one night per campsite, no more than ten persons per campsite, hiker camping allowed only within 100 feet of the A.T., no camping within 0.5 mile of an established roadway, no camping within 200 feet of another camping party, no camping from 0.5 mile south of Blue Mountain Lakes Road to a point 1 mile north of Crater Lake, no camping within 100 feet of any water source. Self-contained stoves are permitted; ground fires and charcoal stoves and grills are prohibited.

Worthington State Forest—Camping in Worthington State Forest is only permitted at the Backpacker Campsite 4.6 miles north of I-80 on the A.T. and at the campground on Old Mine Road. Rangers patrol the area and issue fines for those violating camping restrictions.

Sunfish Pond—The southernmost glacial pond on the A.T. and one of seven protected natural areas in the state of New Jersey, the pond also has several unique man-made features and is a beauty to behold. *No camping or swimming is allowed at the pond.*

Herbert Hiller plaque—The 23rd A.T. 2,000-miler and a longtime Trail booster in New Jersey is memorialized on a plaque off the A.T. on Kittatinny Mountain.

AMC Mohican Outdoor Center—West, on a dirt road, 0.3 mile, (908) 362-5670, operated by the Appalachian Mountain Club (AMC) as a retreat center. Thruhikers can stay overnight for $25PP in a cabin with bunk, stove, shower, and towel. Tent-camping free to thru-hikers. Camp store with deli (Memorial to Labor Day), sodas, candy, and limited hiker supplies, including Coleman and denatured alcohol by the ounce. The center accepts packages sent *via* UPS to 50 Camp Mohican Rd., Blairstown, NJ 07825. Check in at the lodge, entrance on the left. Water available at the lodge or a spigot near the garage across the road.

Rattlesnake Spring—Located 0.6 mile north of the Catfish Fire Tower on a dirt road about 50 feet west of the A.T. Extremely dry years may cause the spring to fail.

Millbrook–Blairstown Road, CR 602—West 1.1 miles to Millbrook Village, a historical park with flush toilets and picnic area. The water supply in the picnic area is cut off from the end of Oct until mid-Apr or May, and the restrooms are closed except for the unisex, handicap-accessible bathroom.

Blue Mountain Lakes Road—Camping needs to be 0.5 mile from this road in the NRA. For northbounders, the hand pump for water is on the west side of the Trail before crossing the paved road. Southbounders can get water here and, in 0.5 mile, reach several grassy areas for tenting. Those open lots were sites of former homes and cottages, acquired in the course of Trail preservation.

West 0.8 mile is Camp Ken-Etiwa-Pec, a former Boy Scout camp on Long Pine Pond now managed by the NPS that offers two screened shelters to thru-hikers May–Sep. No fee, but donations accepted; outdoor pay phone.

Crater Lake—Located 0.5 mile east of the A.T. on a dirt road 2 miles north of Blue Mountain Lakes Road. The dirt road leads to a parking area and beach. North of the dirt road (50 yards) leading to Crater Lake is an orange-blazed trail that leads west 1.5 miles to Hemlock Pond, which offers good swimming.

Brink Road Shelter (1970)—Sleeps 5. Privy. Bears are especially active here. Water source is a spring 100 yards to the right of the shelter.

U.S. 206/Culvers Gap—*Restaurants:* Kevin's Steak House, (973) 948-3007, open W–Su, D, no pay phone but hikers may use restaurant phone for local calls, hiker-friendly; Gyp's Tavern, located on nearby Kittatinny Lake, serves L/D (no credit cards).

East 0.8 mile to a farmer's market with fresh fruit and vegetables.

East 1 mile to *Restaurant:* Jumboland, B/L/D.

East 1.6 miles to ■ *Groceries:* Dale's Market with ATM (long-term resupply). ■ *Restaurants:* Dairy Queen, Jimmy's Pasta and Pizza, Stewarts Root Beer.

East 2.5 miles to ■ *Lodging:* Cobmin Ridge Motel, (973) 948-3459, $55S, $65D, EAP's not allowed. ■ *Groceries:* Yellow Cottage Deli & Bakery (short-term resupply), pay phone outside. ■ *Restaurant:* Pizza/Pasta, open daily, pay phone.

East 3.4 miles to **Branchville, N.J. [P.O. ZIP 07826: M–F 8:30–5, Sa 8:30–1; (973) 948-3580].**

West 1.8 miles to ■ *Lodging:* Forest Motel, (973) 948-5456, $50S, $60D. ■ *Restaurant:* Rosie's Pizza, W–Su 11–9, L/D.

Gren Anderson Shelter (1958)—Sleeps 8. Privy. Built by the now disbanded New York section of the Green Mountain Club. Water source is a spring to left of the shelter.

Sunrise Mountain—*No camping allowed at pavilion.* Nearby parking lot for day-use visitors. No water.

Mashipacong Shelter (1936)—Sleeps 8. Privy. High bear activity in this area. A stone shelter with wooden floor. No water is available at this shelter.

Rutherford Shelter (1967)—Sleeps 6. Privy. High bear activity in this area. Water source is an intermittent spring located 100 yards before the shelter on the connecting trail. Extremely dry years may cause the spring to fail.

 N.J. 23—High Point State Park Headquarters, (973) 875-4800, on the A.T., has pay phone, indoor restroom, and outside water spigot. Rangers hold packages sent to High Point State Park, 1480 State Route 23, Sussex, NJ 07461. Offices are open year-round. Day-use area 0.9 mile to the east of the park office has a swimming area at spring-fed Lake Marcia, a concession stand, grill, and no charge to walk-ins for hot showers; available Memorial Day–Labor Day. High Point Monument, on a short side trail from A.T., marks the highest point in the state, 1,803 feet. *Camping:* Sawmill Lake Campground is located in the park; $20/night, 6 people per site.

East 1.5 miles to *Lodging:* High Point Country Inn; Lee and Mike Hauck, (973) 702-1860, $69S, $79D, includes shuttle to/from Trail and shuttle into town for shopping, laundry service $7, soda machine, pool.

East 1 mile to ■ *Restaurant:* Elias Cole Family Restaurant, (973) 875-3550, B/L/D, 7 a.m.–8 p.m., daily home-made pie, bread, country food. ■ *Groceries:* 2.6 miles to convenience store.

West 4.4 miles to the town of Port Jervis, N.Y. ■ *Lodging:* Comfort Inn, (845) 856-6611, call for current rates (ask sales manager for 10% thru-hiker discount). ■ *Groceries:* Shop-Rite supermarket (long-term resupply). ■ *Restaurants:* Dairy Queen, McDonald's, and a pizzeria. ■ *Other services:* pharmacy; bank, ATM located at gas station next to Comfort Inn.

High Point Shelter (1936)—Sleeps 8. Privy. CCC-built stone shelter with wooden floor. Water sources for this shelter are two streams located on the trail to the shelter; both may fail in dry years. Potable water may be found 1.5 miles south at High Point State Park headquarters.

 N.J. 519—East 2.5 miles to *Lodging:* High Point Country Inn (see listing above).

Trail to Jim Murray Property (0.4 mile north of Goodrich Road)—**West** 0.2 mile to well water. For the past 12 years, Jim Murray (AT '89) has cordially allowed long-distance hikers year-round use of a heated hiker cabin, with hot-water shower and privy, on his private property adjacent to the Trail; no groups. Tenting allowed. Follow the "well water" sign. This is a privately owned cabin. Be responsible, and please do not abuse this privilege.

 Lott Road—West 0.4 mile to the town of **Unionville, N.Y. [P.O. ZIP 10988: M–F 8–12 & 1–5, Sa 8–12; (845) 726-3535]**. Lott Road is also known as Jersey Avenue. ■ *Camping:* Hikers may use Unionville Memorial Park, with water and toilet facility, to pitch a tent; fill out permission slip at Horler's General Store. A phone is located north of the post office on N.Y. 284. ■ *Groceries:* Horler's Store with ATM (long-term resupply), M–Sa 6–9, Su 7–7. ■ *Restaurants:* Backtrack Inn, open daily 12–9 (also has a hostel, $3PP, no shower); bagel shop.

 N.J. 284—West 0.4 mile to *Groceries:* End of the Line Grocery (short-term resupply), M–F 5–9, Sa 6–9, Su 6–7, with deli sandwiches, ATM, and free Internet access for thru-hiker customers.

Pochuck Mountain Shelter (1989)—Sleeps 6. Privy. "Pochuck" is Lenape for "out-of-the-way place." Water source is a spigot on the north side of a vacant white house at the foot of Pochuck Mountain. No camping is allowed at the house (owned by the N.J. Department of Environmental Protection). A 200-foot connecting trail located approximately 0.6 mile south (steeply downhill) from the shelter and 150 feet north of the Liberty Corners Road crossing leads to that source. Southbounders can find water at a stream south of N.Y. 565.

 N.J. 517—West 1.1 miles to **Glenwood, N.J. [P.O. ZIP 07418: M–F 7:30–5, Sa 6:30–2; (973) 764-2616]**. ■ *Lodging:* Apple Valley Inn and B&B, (973) 764-3735, M–Th $125–$140, F–Su $135–$150 includes full B. ■ *Groceries:* Pochuck Valley Farm Market & Deli (short-term resupply) with pay phone, outside water spigot, ATM, and restroom. Open M–F 5–6:30, Sa–Su 5–5.

 N.J. 94—East 1.8 miles to *Lodging:* Appalachian Motel, (973) 764-6070, Su–Th $75D, F–Sa $89D, $10EAP.
   East 2.4 miles to **Vernon, N.J. [P.O. ZIP 07462: M–F 8:30–5, Sa 9:30–12:30; (973) 764-9056]**. ■ *Camping:* Firehouse offers camping for no charge, water, and restrooms; no shower available; call first, (973) 764-6155. ■ *Hostel:* St. Thomas Episcopal Church,

(973) 764-7506, <stthomas@warwick.net>, <www.st-thomas-vernon.org>, offers space for 12. Stay limited to one night; absolutely no dogs, alcohol, or smoking permitted; Internet, laundry, shower, towels, refrigerator, microwave, and cooking in kitchen by permission; $10PP donation requested. Coleman, denatured alcohol, and butane canisters available for purchase. Hikers may have to share space with other groups, are expected to pitch in and keep the hostel clean, and must be out of the hostel by 9 a.m. on Sunday. ■ *Groceries:* A&P Supermarket (long-term resupply) and a natural-foods store. ■ *Restaurants:* Little Anthony's Pizzeria; Mixing Bowl, B/L; Pizza Station; Dairy Queen. ■ *Other services:* bank with ATM, dentist, coin laundry, veterinarian, pharmacy, Camera Shop, R.J. Mars Department Store, and amusement park.

   East 3.5 miles to *Medical:* Vernon Urgent Care, (973) 209-2260, M–F 8–8, Sa–Su 9–5.

   West 0.1 mile to *Groceries:* Heaven Hill Farm, fresh fruit and ice cream (short-term resupply), (973) 764-5144, M–Sa 9–8 Su 9–7, Easter to Sep. Hikers are requested to keep packs outside on left side of building.

Wawayanda Mountain—Near the summit, a blue-blazed side trail leads 0.1 mile to Pinwheel's Vista. The vista provides views to the west of Pochuck Mountain and High Point Monument. "Wawayanda" is Lenape for "winding waters."

Wawayanda Shelter (1990)—Sleeps 6. Privy. The A.T. route was changed recently in the area around the shelter; it now passes compass-south of the shelter. The blue-blazed trail to the shelter turns Trail-west to it, not Trail-east as some guides describe the route. The park office is reached by going north on the blue-blazed trail 0.25 mile; pay phone outside. Water source is a faucet on the maintenance building near the entrance to the fenced-in work yard.

 Warwick Turnpike—East 1.9 miles to *Groceries:* Mt. Jug Deli (short-term resupply); deli, grill, ice cream, ATM.

   West 2.7 miles to a grocery store (long-term resupply) with ATM, pizzeria, bagel shop, and pharmacy.

New York

Miles from Katahdin	Features	Services	Elev.	Miles from Springer
822.3	State Line Trail; N.Y.–N.J. State Line		1,385	1,356.8
821.9	Prospect Rock		1,433	1,357.2
819.1	Village Vista Trail **Greenwood Lake, NY 10925**	E–0.9m PO, G, M, L	1,180	1,360.0
816.4	N.Y. 17A **Greenwood Lake, NY 10925; Bellvale, NY 10912; Warwick, NY 10990**	R (E–2m PO, G, M, L, f) (W–0.2m w, M; 1.6m PO, G; 4.6m PO, G, M, L, D, cl)	1,180	1,362.7
815.1	Eastern Pinnacles		1,294	1,364.0
814.6	Cat Rocks		1,080	1,364.5
814.3	**Wildcat Shelter...** *12.2mS; 14.3mN*	S, w	1,180	1,364.8
812.8	Lakes Rd	R	680	1,366.3
812.5	Fitzgerald Falls	w	800	1,366.6
810.5	Mombasha High Pt.		1,280	1,368.6
809.3	West Mombasha Rd	R	980	1,369.8
808.4	Buchanan Mtn		1,142	1,370.7
807.6	East Mombasha Rd	R	840	1,371.5
806.9	Little Dam Lake		720	1,372.2
806.2	Orange Tpk	R (E–0.5m w)	780	1,372.9
805.5	Arden Mtn, Agony Grind		1,180	1,373.6
804.4	N.Y. 17 **Southfields, NY 10975**	R (E–2.1m PO, G, L, M) (W–3.7m G, L, M, cl)	550	1,374.7
804.2	NYS Thruway (I-87)		560	1,374.9
804.0	Arden Valley Rd	R	680	1,375.1
802.7	Island Pond Outlet	w	1,350	1,376.4
802.1	Lemon Squeezer		1,150	1,377.0
801.4	Long Path Jct		1,160	1,377.7
801.0	Surebridge Mtn		1,200	1,378.1
800.0	**Fingerboard Shelter...** *14.3mS; 5.3mN*	S, nw	1,300	1,379.1
798.9	Arden Valley Rd	R (E–0.3m w, sh)	1,196	1,380.2

Miles from Katahdin	Features	Services	Elev.	Miles from Springer
796.7	Seven Lakes Dr	R	850	1,382.4
795.9	Goshen Mtn		1,180	1,383.2
794.7	**William Brien Memorial Shelter**... *5.3mS; 3.7mN*	S, nw	1,070	1,384.4
793.3	Black Mtn		1,160	1,385.8
792.6	Palisades Interstate Pkwy	R (W–0.4m w)	680	1,386.5
792.4	Beechy Bottom Brook	w	660	1,386.7
791.6	**West Mtn Shelter**... *3.7mS; 31.6mN*	E–0.4m w; 0.6m S, nw	1,240	1,387.5
790.0	Seven Lakes Dr	R	610	1,389.1
788.4	Bear Mtn	R, w	1,305	1,390.7
786.6	**Bear Mtn, NY 10911**	R, w, L, M (E–0.3m PO)	220	1,392.5
785.9	Bear Mtn Museum/Zoo		124	1,393.2
785.8	U.S. 9W, Bear Mtn Circle **Ft. Montgomery, NY 10922**	R (W–0.7m PO, G, M, L, @)	150	1,393.3
785.8	Bear Mtn Bridge	R	200	1,393.3
785.1	N.Y. 9D	R	230	1,394.0
784.6	Camp Smith Trail to Anthony's Nose	E–0.6m	700	1,394.5
783.6	Hemlock Springs Campsite	C, w	550	1,395.5
783.4	Manitou Rd, South Mtn Pass	R	460	1,395.7
780.0	U.S. 9, N.Y. 403 **Peekskill, NY 10566**	R, G (E–4.8m PO, G, M, L, D, V, cl, @) (W–6.7m G, L, M, O)	400	1,399.1
779.4	Graymoor Spiritual Life Center–Franciscan Way	R, w, C, sh	550	1,399.7
778.1	Denning Hill		900	1,401.0
776.7	Old Albany Post Rd– Chapman Rd	R	607	1,402.4
775.0	Canopus Hill Rd	R (E–1.6m G, M)	420	1,404.1
774.0	South Highland Rd	R	570	1,405.1
771.3	Dennytown Rd	R, C, w	860	1,407.8
769.7	Sunk Mine Rd	R	800	1,409.4

Miles from Katahdin	Features	Services	Elev.	Miles from Springer
767.6	N.Y. 301, Canopus Lake, Clarence Fahnestock State Park	R (E–1m C, sh, w)	920	1,411.5
763.4	Shenandoah Mtn		1,282	1,415.7
763.0	Long Hill Rd	R	1,100	1,416.1
761.9	Shenandoah Tenting Area	C, w	900	1,417.2
760.6	Hortontown Rd, **RPH Shelter**... *31.6mS; 9mN*	R, S, w	360	1,418.5
760.3	Taconic State Pkwy	R	650	1,418.8
757.1	Hosner Mtn Rd	R	500	1,422.0
755.5	N.Y. 52 **Stormville, NY 12582**	R (E–0.3m G, M) (W–1.7m PO, G, M)	800	1,423.6
754.1	Stormville Mtn Rd, I-84 Overpass	R	950	1,425.0
751.7	Mt. Egbert		1,329	1,427.4
751.6	**Morgan Stewart Shelter**... *9mS; 7.8mN*	S, w	1,285	1,427.5
750.5	Depot Hill Rd	R	1,230	1,428.6
748.6	Old Route 55	R	750	1,430.5
748.3	N.Y. 55 **Poughquag, NY 12570**	R (W–1.5m M; 2.1m G, M; 3.1m PO, G, M, D)	720	1,430.8
747.1	Nuclear Lake		750	1,432.0
744.3	West Mtn		1,200	1,434.8
743.8	**Telephone Pioneers Shelter**... *7.8mS; 8.7mN*	S, w	910	1,435.3
743.1	County 20, West Dover Rd, Dover Oak **Pawling, NY 12564**	R, w (E–w, f; 3.1m PO, C, G, M, O, cl, @)	650	1,436.0
740.7	N.Y. 22, Appalachian Trail RR Station, Metro North RR	R, M, C, sh, w (E–0.6m G, M) (W–2.6m G, L; 2.8m M; 4m PO, G, L, M)	480	1,438.4
740.5	Hurds Corner Rd	R	480	1,438.6
735.5	Leather Hill Rd	R	750	1,443.6

Miles from Katahdin	Features	Services	Elev.	Miles from Springer
735.1	**Wiley Shelter...** *8.7mS; 4mN*	S, w	740	1,444.0
734.9	Duell Hollow Rd	R	620	1,444.2
733.9	Hoyt Rd, N.Y.–Conn. State Line **Wingdale, NY 12594**	R (W–1.5m M; 3.3m PO, G, M, L, f)	400	1,445.2

In New York, campfires are prohibited except in designated fire rings and fireplaces at established campsites and shelters. Camping itself is limited to designated sites.

Hitchhiking is illegal in New York.

The first miles specifically intended for the A.T. were built here through Harriman–Bear Mountain state parks in 1922–23. With many parks, roads, and a railroad station right on the Trail, many hikers are thinking, what happened to my wilderness experience? You may find this stretch to be a uniquely multicultural experience. The Trail drops to its lowest elevation point—124 feet—after, or just before, you pass through the Trailside Museum and Zoo at Bear Mountain. Hydration becomes an issue in this area. Don't pass up an opportunity for water.

Prospect Rock—At 1,433 feet, this is the highest point on the A.T. in New York (Bear Mountain is 1,305 feet). This and other rock faces along this ridge provide views of Greenwood Lake to the east.

Village Vista Trail—This blue-blazed trail leads **East** 0.9 mile to Greenwood Lake without the fast traffic of N.Y. 17A; from the vista, you can see Lion's Field below, the terminus of the trail. A water fountain on the outside of the little green building next to the softball field can be used by hikers. **Greenwood Lake, N.Y. [P.O. ZIP 10925: M–F 8–5, Sa 9–12; (845) 477-7328].** ■ *Lodging:* Breezy Point, (845) 477-8100, rates begin at $85 plus tax, ATM; Linden Motel, (845) 477-0851, $70 plus tax. ■ *Groceries:* Delicious Deli; Country Grocery; Kwik Mark; BG Bagles; and Cumberland Farms, with deli sandwiches (all short-term resupply). ■ *Restaurants:* Ashley's Pizza; Napoli Restaurant; Murphy's Tavern; Side Street Café; Sing Loong Kitchen; O'Hare's Pub, 112 Windemere Ave. ■ *Other services:* one-hour photo shop, some camping supplies; pharmacy; Long Pond Marina, with boat rentals; and Greenwood Lake Taxi, M–Th, (845) 477-3291 (call ahead).

N.Y. 17A—Public phone. **East** 2 miles to **Greenwood Lake** (see above).
West 0.2 mile to Bellvale Creamery, daily 12–9, ice cream and water.
West 1.6 miles to **Bellvale, N.Y. [P.O. ZIP 10912: M–F 8–12 & 1–4:30, Sa 8–12; (845) 986-2880]**. P.O. inside Mama's Boy Pizzeria with deli sandwiches (short-term resupply), open 7 days.
West 4.6 miles to the larger town of **Warwick, N.Y. [P.O. ZIP 10990: M–F 8:30–7, Sa 9–4; (845) 986-0271]**. Hitchhikers have been cited leaving Warwick on 17A. ■ *Lodging:* Warwick Motel, (845) 986-4822, $80 weekdays, $86 weekends. ■ *Groceries:* ShopRite (long-term resupply) is 1.4 miles south of town on N.Y. 94. ■ *Other services:* hospital, restaurants, drug store, coin laundry, ATM, fresh fruit and ice cream at market, and hardware store.

Wildcat Shelter (1992)—Sleeps 8. Privy. Water source is a spring at the entrance of the side trail leading to the shelter.

Mombasha High Point—On a clear day, you can see the New York City skyline, including the Empire State Building.

Sterling Forest—Between Greenwood Lake and Arden, 6 miles of the A.T. pass through the northern portion of a 20,000-acre tract called Sterling Forest. It was the center of a decade-long struggle between a corporate private landowner and a coalition of conservation groups, state agencies in New York and New Jersey, and such organizations as the NY–NJ TC and ATC. All told, more than 30 environmental groups, along with foundations, individuals, states, and Congress, combined to contribute $55 million toward the 1998 purchase and protection of 14,500 acres. The last unprotected parcel was acquired in late 2006.

 N.Y. 17—Pay phone at road crossing. **East** 2.1 miles to **Southfields, N.Y. [P.O. ZIP 10975: M–F 8–12 & 1–5, Sa 8:30–11:30; (845) 351-2628]**. ■ *Lodging:* Tuxedo Motel, (845) 351-4747, $44.50S, $49.50D, $10EAP, WiFi available. ■ *Restaurant:* Take-out Chinese delivered to Tuxedo Motel, (845) 351-4428. ■ *Groceries:* Corner Deli (short-term resupply) with ATM.
West 0.7 mile to Arden, N.Y.
West 3.7 miles to the town of **Harriman, N.Y.**, for lodgings, groceries, restaurants, and coin laundries.

Bear Mountain/Harriman State Parks—Home to the first completed section of the A.T. Dry conditions and forest fires have forced the closure of the A.T. in the park for days or even weeks in the summer. In 1994, Harriman State Park instituted a policy under which, even if other trails in the park are closed, the A.T. remains open to thru-hikers.

Major William A. Welch—General manager of Palisades Interstate Park from 1912 to 1940, Major Welch, along with volunteers from the NY–NJ TC, was responsible for bringing together the framework for completion of the first section of Trail in Harriman and Bear Mountain state parks. The first chairman of ATC, he also is credited with designing the original A.T. marker that became "the diamond" and remains the most-recognized symbol for the Trail.

Fingerboard Shelter (1928)—Sleeps 8. No privy. A stone structure. The closest dependable water source is the spigot at Lake Tiorati, 0.5 mile east on the blue-blazed Hurst Trail. Southbounders can get their water at Tiorati Circle, 1.1 miles north of the shelter.

Arden Valley Road—East 0.3 mile to Tiorati Circle, with restroom; free showers in bath house for walk-ins; open Memorial Day to Labor Day, M–F 10–5:45, Sa–Su 9–7; vending machines, ice-cream sandwiches, candy, water, and public beach on Lake Tiorati.

William Brien Memorial Shelter (1933)—Sleeps 8. No privy. A stone shelter built by the CCC and named in memory of the first president of the New York Ramblers. Rumored resident rattlesnake; one killed in 2007 (which could violate the Endangered Species Act in some Trail places; please don't do it.). Water source is a spring-fed well that is prone to go dry. This spring is 80 yards down a blue-blazed trail to the right of the shelter. An alternative for northbounders is to stop at Tiorati Circle, swim, cook at one of the picnic tables, and hike to the shelter for the evening. However, the shortcut back to the A.T. has been removed. Southbounders can get water at the park visitors center 0.4 mile west, on the Palisades Interstate Parkway.

Palisades Interstate Parkway—West 0.4 mile to park visitors center with restroom, pay phone, soda and snack machines. From here, it is a mere 34 miles to NYC on the Palisades Interstate Parkway. Hikers heading to West Mountain Shelter may want to pick up water at stream north of the parkway.

West Mountain Shelter (1928)—Sleeps 8. No privy. Water may be available from an unreliable spring 0.4 mile down steep Timp-Torne Trail or alternately at a seasonal stream 0.2 mile before the shelter. Resident rattlesnake at this shelter (at least in past). Located 0.6 mile on the Timp–Torne Trail, this shelter provides views of the surrounding countryside and the NYC skyline.

Bear Mountain—At 1,305 feet, this is one of the highest points on the Trail in New York and offers views of the Hudson River Valley and the New York City skyline. In the early 1900s, the state was considering a site near the base of Bear Mountain for a prison, but Mary Avcrell Harriman, widow of railroad magnate Edward Harriman and primary landholder in the area, had other plans. In 1910, Mrs. Harriman agreed to donate 10,000 acres for the development of a park with the condition that the state discontinue its plans for a prison. What was then known as Sing Sing Prison was eventually built on the Hudson River 20 miles south of the A.T., its location giving birth to the phrase, "sent up the river." No water available at the summit. Do not rely on the seasonally stocked soda vending machine. NY–NJ TC and ATC are near the end of a major, multiyear relocation and rehabilitation project on the Trail and associated trails on the mountain, so expect to see crews on either side of the summit, and, of course, follow the white blazes.

Bear Mountain, N.Y.—**[P.O. ZIP 10911: M–F 8–12, closed Sa; (845) 786-3747].** P.O. may close early (and there's talk of closing it altogether—call ahead). Located across the street from the park administration building on Seven Lakes Drive. Fort Montgomery (see below) may be a better option. *Lodging:* Bear Mountain Inn (on the A.T.), (845) 786-2701, <www.bearmountaininn.com>. Merry-go-round, open Sa–Su 11–5.

Trailside Museums and Zoo—North of the inn and south of Bear Mountain Bridge, the Bear Mountain Zoo contains many native species, including black bears, and offers a unique, and sometimes emotional, experience for thru-hikers. Within the park is also a much-photographed statue of Walt Whitman. Admission $1; A.T. hikers admitted free. The portion of the A.T. leading through the zoo to the bridge—an original section from 1923—descends to 124 feet above sea level; it's the Trail's lowest elevation between Maine and Georgia. *Dogs are not allowed in the museum/zoo section.* After 5 p.m., the gate is closed; the southern gate opens at 10:30 a.m. If you arrive when the gate is closed or are hiking with a dog, hike around on U.S. 9W, which becomes the official route for the time period/circumstances.

Bear Mountain Circle—West 0.7 mile to **Ft. Montgomery, N.Y. [P.O. ZIP 10922: M–F 8–1 & 2:30–5, Sa 9–12; (845) 446-8459].** ■ *Lodging:* Bear Mountain Bridge Motel, (845) 446-2472, $65–$69 weekdays, higher on weekends, with shuttle back to the Trail; Holiday Inn Express, (845) 446-4277, thru-hiker rate $120 for 1 or 2 people, add $10 for third person, Internet and computer/office for guests, laundry, indoor pool, continental B; Victorian River View B&B, (845) 446-5479, $110–$160. ■ *Groceries:* Mobil Mini Mart (short-term resupply). Key Foods supermarket (long-term resupply) is two miles north in Highland Falls. ■ *Restaurants:* Trading Post Restaurant, open M–Th 3–midnight, F 3 p.m.–1 a.m., Sa noon–2 a.m., Su noon–midnight; Bagel Café with ATM, open M–F 5–3, Sa 6–2, B/L; Fox's Deli; M&R Deli. Additional services are located beyond Fort Montgomery, near the U.S. Military Academy at West Point.

Bear Mountain Bridge—Built at a cost of $5 million in 1923–24 by a private company run by the Harriman family. When Earl Shaffer arrived at the bridge in 1948, he had to pay a nickel to cross. Today, only vehicles must pay.

Anthony's Nose—Where the A.T. turns west on a dirt road, 0.5 mile north of N.Y. 9D, a turn east on this road, blazed as the Camp Smith Trail, leads 0.6 mile to the top of the mountain known as Anthony's Nose. This rock outcropping, 900 feet above the river, offers outstanding views of the Hudson River Valley. The state Office of Parks, Recreation, and Historic Preservation now owns the property; please stay on the trail. Originally, the A.T. climbed steeply to the summit but was rerouted when World War II broke out. The Nose remained closed until 1993, when the New York State Division of Military and Naval Affairs, managers of the adjacent National Guard camp, gave permission for hikers to once again walk to the summit.

U.S. 9—*Groceries:* Appalachian Equities, Shell station/convenience store just to west at U.S. 9/N.Y. 403 junction, full-service, food-to-go, 24 hours, (845) 424-6241.

East 4.5 miles to **Peekskill, N.Y. [P.O. ZIP 10566: M–F 9–5, Sa 9–4; (914) 737-1340].** If you plan to go into Peekskill, take Highland Avenue into town, rather than U.S. 9, where the two roads fork about 3 miles from the A.T. Highland Avenue leads directly to downtown. Services in town include several motels and restaurants, supermarkets, pharmacy, laundry, banks with ATM, hospital, doctor, dentist, and veterinarian. The post office is on South St., 4.5 miles from the A.T. Services are spread out over a large, bustling area, and some hikers feel it is too spread out to easily maneuver on foot. Free Internet access at the Field Library, 4 Nelson Ave., M, Tu, Th 9–9, W 11–9, F 9–5, Sa 10–2.

West 6.7 miles *via* Route 403 to N.Y. 9D to **Cold Spring, N.Y.** ▪ *Lodging:* Countryside Motel, 3577 Route 9, Cold Spring, NY 10516, (845) 265-2090, $65S, $74D, $80 3 or 4 people, WiFi, will receive mail drops for guests; Pig Hill Inn, (845) 265-9247, $130 and up. ▪ *Restaurants*: McGuires on Main, Cold Spring Pizza, Whistling Willies. ▪ *Groceries:* Food Town Supermarket (long-term resupply). ▪ *Outfitter:* Hudson Valley Outfitters, (845) 265-0221, <www.hudsonvalleyoutfitters.com>, 63 Main St., M–F 11–6, Sa–Su 9–6, caters to kayakers and day-hikers; clothing, boots, Leki poles and parts, MSR canisters. ▪ *Shuttle:* Highland Transit Taxi, (845) 265-8294. ▪ *Train:* Daily commuter service to NYC.

Graymoor Spiritual Life Center—Hikers are permitted to sleep at the monastery's ball-field picnic shelter, which has water, a cold-water shower during warm months, and a privy. The shelter is open all season long. *Directions:* North of U.S. 9, the A.T. climbs uphill and crosses a second paved road leading to the center. Here, northbounders should follow the blue blazes: Turn east on Franciscan Way, turn left on St. Anthony Way, and turn left on St. Joseph Drive to the ballfield. Southbounders will cross unpaved Old West Point Road onto the Graymoor driveway; continue straight on driveway, then north where the driveway forks. Pizza and deli food may be ordered for delivery to the picnic shelter.

Canopus Hill Road—**East** 1.6 miles to the Putnam Valley Market (short-term resupply), (845) 528-8626, with pizza, hot food from the grill, ATM, pay phone, and phone cards. Open daily 6:30–9 (closes at 7 on Su). *Directions:* east on Canopus Hill Road 0.3 mile to intersection with Canopus Hollow Road. Continue 0.1 mile south on Canopus Hollow Road, turn west on Sunset Hill Road 1.2 miles to store. Sunset Hill Road is a steep, winding road that climbs about 400 feet from Canopus Hill Road.

Dennytown Road—Water available from spigot on the side of the pump building. Opens third F of Apr, closes last Su of Oct. Camping area located 500 feet west on Dennytown Road, then south onto a dirt road to top of hill.

N.Y. 301/Clarence Fahnestock State Park—**East** 1 mile to the park's campground, (845) 225-7207. The beach area can be reached from the A.T. 2.3 miles north of N.Y. 301 *via* an unmarked downhill gully trail that begins a quarter of a mile south of the viewpoint on the A.T. at the northern end of Canopus Lake. The beach area

is visible from the overlook. Campground open Apr 2–second week of Dec, tentsites $13 Su–Th, $16 F–Sa. A free tenting area provided for thru-hikers with hot showers, flush toilets, and water; inquire at the park entrance. The beach-area concession stand, (845) 225-3998, and grill (open Memorial Day–Labor Day, Su–F 9–5, Sa 9–6, grill closes one hour earlier) has grilled sandwiches, soda, ice cream, supplies, pay phone. The beach area closes Labor Day.
West 7.2 miles to Cold Spring (see above).

Shenandoah Tenting Area—0.1 mile west. Group camping is permitted. Water is available from a hand pump.

RPH Shelter (1982)—Sleeps 6. Privy. Available for hikers from Apr until hunting season begins in mid-Nov; closed the remainder of the time, but the grounds are available year-round. Formerly a closed cabin, it was renovated as a three-sided shelter with a front porch to meet NPS building codes. Caretaker Joe Hrouda, (845) 221-9014, does not accept mail drops but will accept postcards and letters sent to 18 Memory Lane, Hopewell Junction, NY 12533; note your ETA. Joe stops by the shelter each day during the thru-hiker season to deliver mail and check on the shelter. Water source is the hand pump to the left of the shelter.

N.Y. 52—**East** 0.3 mile to ■ *Groceries:* Mountain Top Market Deli, (845) 221-0928, (short-term resupply), open daily 6 a.m.–8 p.m., daily specials and hot sandwiches, water for hikers on faucet at side of building, pay phone. ■ *Restaurant:* Danny's Pizzeria, open daily at 11, cheaper soda.
   West 1.9 miles to **Stormville, N.Y. [P.O. ZIP 12582: M–F 8:30–5, Sa 9–12; (845) 226-2627].**
■ *Groceries:* Citgo Mini Mart (short-term resupply). ■ *Restaurants:* Stormville Pizza, M–Sa 11–9:30, Su 12–9.

Morgan Stewart Shelter (1984)—Sleeps 6. Privy. Water source is a well with a pump located downhill and in front of the shelter.

N.Y. 55— Look to the east. If a school bus is parked at the intersection, it is really a deli /hot dog stand. **West** 1.5 miles to ■ *Restaurant:* Pleasant Ridge Pizza, pay phone, serving L/D, closed M. ■ *Other services:* Pleasant Ridge Shopping Center, pharmacy, and deli.
   West 2.1 miles to ■ *Groceries:* Beekman Corner's ShopRite & Cumberland Farms.
■ *Restaurant:* 7 Stars, Tailgates Grill, The Square, Luciano's Pizza Café.
   West 3.1 miles to **Poughquag, N.Y. [P.O. ZIP 12570: M–F 8:30–5, Sa 8:30–12:30; (845)**

724-4763], a larger town with pharmacy, doctor, bank with ATM. ■ *Restaurants:* Great Wall Chinese Restaurant, La Contadina Pizzeria. ■ *Groceries:* convenience store with deli (short-term resupply).

Nuclear Lake—The site of a nuclear fuels-processing research facility until 1972. After the Park Service acquired the lands for the A.T., the buildings were razed, and the area was tested extensively and given a clean bill of health, dispelling fears that the lake was contaminated and allowing the Trail to be rerouted along the shore.

Telephone Pioneers Shelter (1988)—Sleeps 6. Privy. Built with the assistance of the White Plains Council of the Telephone Pioneers of America. Water source is the stream crossed by the side trail leading to the shelter. Alternative water source is 0.7 mile north at the Champion residence (see next entry).

County 20/West Dover Road—Ron and Holly Champion, who live in the purple house east of the Trail, have Coleman fuel for sale. Water is available from a tap at the end of their lower walk. *Please do not knock at door.*

    East 3.1 miles to **Pawling, N.Y. [P.O. ZIP 12564: M–F 8:30–5, Sa 9–12; (845) 855-2669].** Northbound hikers might want to hike 2.4 miles more to N.Y. 22 for easier access to Pawling. ■ *Camping:* The town allows hikers to camp in its Edward R. Murrow Memorial Park, 1 mile from the center of town on West Main Street. The park offers lake swimming, restroom, and pay phone. No dogs permitted. Two-night maximum. ■ *Groceries:* Hannaford, 2 miles south from town center on Rt. 22 (long-term resupply); CVS (short-term resupply); Latinos Mini-Market Family Quick Stop. ■ *Restaurants:* Vinny's Deli & Pasta; Chris's Deli; Mama's Pizza; Gaudino Pizzeria; Great Wall Chinese; Pawling Tavern; McKeene's Restaurant; McKinney & Doyle. ■ *Outfitters:* Pawling Cycling and Sports, (845) 855-9866, small full-service outfitter, possible shuttle service, in the Village Center at 12 West Main St. ■ *Other services:* coin laundry, banks with ATM, pharmacy, and Metro-North station with train service to NYC [call (800) METRO-INFO for fare and schedule]. ■ *Internet access:* Pawling Free Library, 11 Broad St., Tu–Th 10–8, F–Sa 10–4. *Please leave packs and trekking poles outside or in the hallway.*

Dover Oak—Located on the north side of West Dover Road, is reportedly the largest oak tree on the A.T. Its girth four feet from the ground is more than 20 feet, 4 inches, and it is estimated to be more than 300 years old.

N.Y. 22/Appalachian Trail Railroad Station—West, within view of the Trail, a hotdog stand. *Other services:* Native Landscapes & Garden Center; owner Pete Muroski, a hiker, is very hiker-friendly. Allows camping on site, use of restrooms, shower, kitchen, seasonal short-term employment, shuttle to village for supplies. Will hold mail drops sent to 991 Route 22, Pawling, NY 12564. Center is open daily, 7–5, year-round.

East 0.6 mile to *Groceries:* Tony's Deli (short-term resupply), open daily 5 a.m.–midnight. ■ *Restaurants:* Strada's Italian Restaurant, Pizza Express, Big W's Roadside Bar B Que; all might deliver to Dutchess Motor Lodge.

West 2.6 miles to ■ *Lodging:* Dutchess Motor Lodge, (845) 832-6400, Rt. 22, Wingdale, N.Y., $65D including weekends, $7 laundry, pets allowed, Internet access. ■ *Groceries:* Village Deli & Market, Ben's Store (both short-term resupply).

West 4 miles to the village of Wingdale (see Hoyt Road entry below).

Commuter Train—On the south side of N.Y. 22, the Trail passes the A.T. station of a New York City commuter train (Metro-North). Trains leave the platform every Sa and Su at 2:41 p.m., 4:41 p.m., and 6:35 p.m. and arrive at Grand Central Terminal at 4:35 p.m., 6:35 p.m., and 8:20 p.m. Trains leave Grand Central at 7:48 a.m. and 9:50 a.m. on Sa and Su and arrive at the A.T. platform at 9:37 a.m. and 11:37 a.m. Fares are one-way $11.50 off-peak, $15.25 peak, and round-trip $23 off-peak, $30.50 peak. Weekday and additional weekend services are available to New York from stations in nearby Pawling and Wingdale.

Wiley Shelter (1940)—Sleeps 6. Privy. Water source is a pump 0.1 mile north of the shelter on the A.T. beyond tent platform; water should be treated.

Hoyt Road—West 1.5 miles to *Restaurant:* Buttonwood Café with bakery, serving B/L and ice cream; M, W 9–3, Th–F 9–5, Sa–Su 10–9.

West 3.3 miles *via* Hoyt and Webatuck roads to **Wingdale, N.Y. [P.O. ZIP 12594: M–F 8–5, Sa 8–12:30; (845) 832-6147].** To reach Wingdale Metro-North Station, continue south on N.Y. 22 for about one mile. ■ *Lodging:* Dutchess Motor Lodge (see above). ■ *Groceries:* Wingdale Super Market with ATM and Food Market (both long-term resupply). ■ *Restaurants:* Ben's Deli; Pizza Express; Adams Diner, open 24 hours; Cousin's Pizza; Peking Kitchen; Cousin's Café, deli and ice cream. ■ *Other services:* Wingdale Hardware.

Connecticut

Miles from Katahdin	Features	Services	Elev.	Miles from Springer
733.9	Conn. State Line– Hoyt Rd, N.Y. **Wingdale, NY 12594**	R (W–1.5m M; 3.3m PO, G, M, L, f)	400	1,445.2
734.1	Conn.55 **Gaylordsville, CT 06755**	R (E–2.5m PO, G)	580	1,445.0
732.1	Ten Mile Hill		1,000	1,447.0
731.1	**Ten Mile River Lean-to...** *4mS; 8.4mN*	S, w	290	1,448.0
730.9	Ten Mile River	C, w	280	1,448.2
730.2	Trail to Bulls Bridge Parking Area	E–0.2m R; 0.5m G, @	450	1,448.9
729.5	Schaghticoke Rd	R	320	1,449.6
727.8	Schaghticoke Mtn		1,331	1,451.3
726.6	Conn.–N.Y. State Line		1,250	1,452.5
726.2	Indian Rocks		1,290	1,452.9
725.6	Schaghticoke Mtn Campsite	C, w	950	1,453.5
723.7	Thayer Brook		900	1,455.4
722.7	**Mt. Algo Lean-to...** *8.4mS; 7.3mN*	C, S, w	655	1,456.4
722.4	Conn. 341, Schaghticoke Rd **Kent, CT 06757**	R (E–0.8m PO, G, M, L, O, D, f, cl, sh, @; 3.3m L)	350	1,456.7
719.6	Skiff Mtn Rd	R	850	1,459.5
718.2	St. Johns Ledges		900	1,460.9
717.7	River Rd	R	480	1,461.4
715.4	**Stewart Hollow Brook Lean-to...** *7.3mS; 10mN*	C, S, w	425	1,463.7
715.0	Stony Brook Campsite	C, w	440	1,464.1
713.0	River Rd	R	460	1,466.1
712.2	Silver Hill Campsite	C, nw	1,000	1,466.9
711.3	Conn. 4 **Cornwall Bridge, CT 06754**	R (E–0.9m PO, G, L, O, V, f, @; 1.9m C, sh)	700	1,467.8
711.2	Guinea Brook		650	1,467.9
711.1	Old Sharon Rd	R	750	1,468.0

Miles from Katahdin	Features	Services	Elev.	Miles from Springer
709.9	Hatch Brook		880	1,469.2
709.2	Pine Knob Loop Trail	E–0.9m C, sh	1,150	1,469.9
708.8	Caesar Rd, Caesar Brook Campsite	C, w	760	1,470.3
706.6	Carse Brook	w	810	1,472.5
706.5	West Cornwall Rd **West Cornwall, CT 06796; Sharon, CT 06069**	R (E–2.2m PO, G, M, O) (W–4.7m PO, G, M, L, D, cl)	800	1,472.6
705.4	**Pine Swamp Brook Lean-to**... *10mS; 12.8mN*	S, w	1,075	1,473.7
704.5	Sharon Mtn Rd	R	1,150	1,474.6
704.2	Mt. Easter		1,350	1,474.9
703.0	Sharon Mtn Campsite	C, w	1,200	1,476.1
700.2	Belter's Campsite	C, w	770	1,478.9
699.8	U.S. 7, Conn. 112	R	520	1,479.3
699.2	U.S. 7, Housatonic River Bridge	R	500	1,479.9
699.1	Mohawk Trail	E–0.2m L, M	500	1,480.0
687.3	Water Street, Hydroelectric Plant **Falls Village, CT 06031**	R, w, sh (E–0.5m PO, L)	530	1,491.8
697.2	Iron Bridge, Housatonic River **Falls Village, CT 06031**	R	510	1,481.9
696.6	Housatonic River Rd, Great Falls	R	650	1,482.5
696.1	Spring	w	750	1,483.0
693.8	Prospect Mtn		1,475	1,485.3
693.1	**Limestone Spring Lean-to**... *12.8mS; 8mN*	W–0.5m C, S, w	980	1,486.0
693.0	Rand's View		1,250	1,486.1
692.2	Billy's View		1,150	1,486.9
689.7	U.S. 44 **Salisbury, CT 06068**	R (W–0.4m PO, G, L, M, @; 2.4m M, L, D, cl, f)	700	1,489.4
689.0	Conn. 41, Undermountain Rd **Salisbury, CT 06068**	R (W–0.8m PO, G, L, M, @; 2.8m M, L, D, cl, f)	720	1,490.1
686.3	Lions Head		1,738	1,492.8
685.6	**Riga Lean-to**... *8mS; 1.2mN*	C, S, w	1,610	1,493.5

Miles from Katahdin	Features	Services	Elev.	Miles from Springer
685.0	Ball Brook Campsite	C, w	1,650	1,494.1
684.4	Brassie Brook (south branch), **Brassie Brook Lean-to**... *1.2mS; 8.8mN*	C, S, w	1,705	1,494.7
683.9	Undermountain Trail, Riga Jct		1,820	1,495.2
683.7	Bear Mtn Rd		1,920	1,495.4
683.0	Bear Mtn		2,316	1,496.1
682.3	Conn.–Mass. State Line		1,800	1,496.8

Campfires are prohibited on the Trail in Connecticut, and camping is permitted only at designated sites. Ridgerunners patrol the state's 52 A.T. miles and serve as caretakers at Sages Ravine campsite.

Southbounders and northbounders pass each other regularly now, each with a determined mindset. Take a moment to hear each direction's viewpoint. For a while, you'll be following a wheelchair-accessible trail. How apropos after experiencing the hiker shuffle. Lodging becomes pricier, but hospitality abounds. Southbounders should consider the hunting seasons and the need to wear bright "blaze" orange. If hiking with a four-footed friend, keep its safety in mind, too.

AMC–Connecticut Chapter—The Trails Committee of the AMC–Connecticut Chapter maintains the 52.3 miles from the New York–Connecticut state line to Sages Ravine, just across the Massachusetts line. The club can be reached at (413) 528-6333; <www.ct-amc.org>.

Conn. 55—East 2.5 miles to **Gaylordsville, Conn. [P.O. ZIP 06755: M–F 8–1 & 2–5, Sa 8–12; (860) 354-9727].** *Groceries:* Gaylordsville Country Store, (860) 350-3802 (short-term resupply), M–F 6–8, Sa 6–6, Su 6–3, with deli, ATM, and pay phone.

Ten Mile River Lean-to (1996)—Sleeps 6. Privy. Tentsites available nearby at a campsite. Water source is a hand pump 0.2 mile north of the lean-to.

Bulls Bridge Road—East 0.5 mile to Country Market (short-term resupply) with fruit, Ben & Jerry's, water, ATM, and Internet access. On the way to the store, you will cross the Housatonic River on Bulls Bridge, one of a handful of covered bridges still standing in Connecticut. A bridge has spanned the river here since the mid-1700s. During the Revolutionary War, George Washington and his army used this crossing on several occasions. The current bridge dates to the early 1800s.

Indian Rocks—Half a mile north of the only place along the entire A.T. where the Trail (briefly) crosses an Indian reservation. Most of the land from here down to the river is claimed by the Schaghticoke tribe, recognized by the state and briefly (January 2004–May 2005) by the federal government. The tribe, actually the remnants of several tribes, played a unique communications role during the Revolutionary War by transmitting signals along the ridges between Long Island Sound in N.Y. and Stockbridge, Mass., a distance of nearly 100 miles, in about 2 hours.

Mt. Algo Lean-to (1986)—Sleeps 6. Privy. Water source is on blue-blaze leading to lean-to, 15 yards in front of shelter.

Conn. 341—East 0.8 mile to **Kent, Conn. [P.O. ZIP 06757: M–F 8–1 & 2–5, Sa 8:30–12:30; (860) 927-3435].** ■ *Lodging:* Fife 'n Drum Inn & Restaurant, (860) 927-3509, restaurant M–Th (closed Tu) 11:30–9:30, F–Sa 11:30–10, Su 11:30–8:30, hiker rate $106D weekdays, $138D weekends, $25EAP, no dogs, call for reservations; Gibb House B&B, (860) 927-1754; Starbuck Inn, (860) 927-1788, $175D-$235D plus tax, includes full B, check-in 4 p.m., check-out 11 a.m., <frontdesk@starbuckinn.com>, <www.starbuckinn. com>. ■ *Groceries:* Davis IGA (long-term resupply); Kent Market (short-term resupply), with deli sandwiches, M–Sa 6–8, Su 7–7. ■ *Restaurants:* Wasabi Japanese; Shanghai Chinese; Kent Pizza Garden, L/D, 11–10; Kent Coffee and Chocolate Co.; Kent Pharmacy, ice cream; The Villager; Blue Grille; North End Restaurant; Panini Café, ice cream, free Sa-night concerts 7–8 Memorial Day–Labor Day. ■ *Outfitters:* Backcountry Outfitters, (860) 927-3377, <info@bcoutfitters.com>, backpacking gear and supplies; holds packages shipped to 5 Bridge St., Kent, CT 06757; white gas, Esbit, canisters, denatured alcohol by the ounce; open M–Sa 9–6, Su 10–4; will shuttle; Annie Bananie ice cream inside. Sundog Shoe and Leather, 25 N. Main St., <sundogshoe@ aol.com>, (860) 927-0009, boots, socks, insoles, M–Sa 10–5, Su 12–5. ■ *Internet access:* Kent Memorial Library, M–F 10–5:30, Sa 10–4. ■ *Other services:* banks with ATM; Kent Laundromat with CATV, WiFi, storage-locker area for hikers, open 6 a.m. –11 p.m., last wash at 10; doctor; dentist; pharmacy; House of Books, with guides, maps, fax, UPS and FedEx services, open daily.

North 2.5 miles *via* U.S. 7 to *Lodging:* Rosewood Meadow B&B, (860) 927-4334, shuttle provided to and from town.

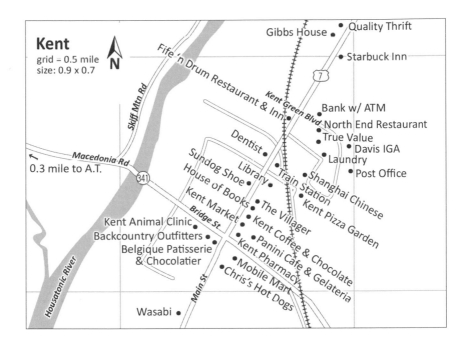

Kent

grid = 0.5 mile
size: 0.9 x 0.7

N

Fife 'n Drum Restaurant & Inn

Skiff Mtn Rd

Kent Green Blvd

Gibbs House

Quality Thrift

Starbuck Inn

7

Bank w/ ATM

North End Restaurant

True Value

Dentist

Davis IGA

Library

Laundry

Shanghai Chinese

Post Office

Macedonia Rd

0.3 mile to A.T.

341

Sundog Shoe

House of Books

Kent Market

Bridge St

Kent Animal Clinic

Backcountry Outfitters

Belgique Patisserie & Chocolatier

Main St

Train Station

The Villager

Kent Pizza Garden

Kent Coffee & Chocolate

Panini Cafe & Gelateria

Kent Pharmacy

Mobile Mart

Chris's Hot Dogs

Wasabi

Housatonic River

Red-pine plantation—The pines along the "river walk" north of Kent have seen hard times due to an insect blight. Most of the trees are now dead. The Connecticut Chapter of AMC harvested some of the dying trees to build new shelters, including the one at Ten Mile River.

Stewart Hollow Brook Lean-to (1980s)—Sleeps 6. Privy. Water source is reliable Stony Brook, 0.4 mile north of the lean-to on the A.T.

Silver Hill Campsite—Campsite, with privy, swing, and pavilion sheltering two picnic tables, are what's left of the Silver Hill Shelter that burned down in 1991. No water. Water pump is broken. Northbounders can get water from stream 0.5 mile south or spring 1.1 miles south. Southbounders can get water from Guinea Brook 1.2 miles north.

Mohawk Trail—The former route of the A.T. starts north of Guinea Brook on the A.T., passes through Cornwall Bridge, and returns to the A.T. near Falls Village.

Conn. 4—East 0.9 mile to **Cornwall Bridge, Conn. [P.O. ZIP 06754: M–F 8–1 & 2–5, Sa 9–12; (860) 672-6710].** ■ *Lodging:* Hitching Post Motel, (860) 672-6219, $65D and up weekdays, $85D and up weekends, $15EAP, laundry service $5 and up, shuttle available depending on staffing; Housatonic Meadows Lodge B&B, (860) 672-6067, $110; Cornwall Inn & Restaurant, open year-round, (800) 786-6884, <www.cornwall-inn.com>, hiker rate $125D, $150 for 4 in room with 2 queen beds; includes continental B, pool, hot tub, Internet access, restaurant and lounge open Th–Su, L/D $8–$30. ■ *Groceries:* Baird's General Store (short-term resupply), with deli, full B, ice cream. ■ *Outfitter:* Housatonic River Outfitters, (860) 672-1010, <hflyshop@aol.com>, open 7 days 9–5, limited hiker gear, canister fuel and fuel by ounce, will accept UPS and FedEx sent to 24 Kent Rd., Cornwall Bridge, CT 06754, but not responsible for packages. Shuttle available by appointment only, $20 and up depending on distance. ■ *Other services:* hardware store; Housatonic Veterinary Care, (860) 672-4948. ■ *Camping:* Housatonic Meadows State Park, (860) 672-6772, 1 mile north of town on U.S. 7. Campsite $36 per night, up to 6 per site; open mid-Apr to Jan 1, water shut off Oct 15. The park may be self-service in midweek; registration information at the main cabin by the gate. Showers free but check with registration desk; pay phone; no pets, no alcoholic beverages allowed. Accessible from the A.T. *via* Pine Knob Loop Trail (see below).

Guinea Brook—The AMC Connecticut Chapter installed stepping stones in the brook. In heavy rain, you may want to take the bypass: Northbounders should turn east on Conn. 4 and go downhill to unpaved Old Sharon Road on the north, which rejoins the A.T. on the other side of the stream. Southbounders should turn east on the dirt road that the Trail crosses before the brook, then follow it to Conn. 4, and turn south.

Pine Knob Loop Trail—Housatonic Meadows State Park (see above) can be reached from the A.T. by taking the blue-blazed Pine Knob Loop Trail 0.5 mile to U.S. 7, then following the highway north for 0.4 mile. You can return to the A.T. *via* the Pine Knob Loop Trail.

West Cornwall Road—East 2.2 miles to **West Cornwall, Conn. [P.O. ZIP 06796: M–F 8–1 & 2–4:30, Sa 9–12; (860) 672-6791]**, site of a historical covered bridge spanning a whitewater section of the Housatonic River. ■ *Groceries:* Berkshire Country Store (short-term resupply), deli, picnic benches, M–F 7–7, Sa 8–6, Su 8–5; West Cornwall Market (short-term resupply), M–Th 6–7, F–Sa 6–8. ■ *Other services:* restaurants and gift shops. ■ *Outfitter:* Clarke Outdoors, (860) 672-6365,

<www.clarkeoutdoors.com>, is located on U.S. 7 south of the village, with tube, canoe, and kayak rentals; limited outdoor gear and sportswear. **West** 4.7 miles to **Sharon, Conn. [P.O. ZIP 06069: M–F 8:30–4:30, Sa 9:30–1:30; (860) 364-5306]**, with a supermarket, restaurant serving B/L/D, laundry, motel, bank with ATM, pharmacy, and hospital.

Pine Swamp Brook Lean-to (1989)—Sleeps 6. Privy. Water is available on the blue-blazed trail.

Hang Glider View—Occasionally still used as a hang-glider launch site, the view is toward Lime Rock Park, where the late Paul Newman and other celebrities have sped their cars around a classic 1.53-mile racecourse. Hikers staying at nearby Sharon Mountain Campsite on Jul 4 can stroll to the viewpoint for a huge fireworks show.

U.S. 7/Mohawk Trail—*Restaurant* and *Lodging:* Mountainside Café, (860) 824-7886, M–Th 6:30 a.m.–3 p.m., F 6:30–8, Sa 7–8, Su 6:30–8; cabin rental $75 (hiker rate), no restrictions on number in room; call for reservations. Not available in winter. *Directions:* At bridge over Housatonic River 0.2 mile north on U.S. 7, or stay on A.T. and take blue-blazed Mohawk Trail 0.2 mile east to U.S. 7.

Wheelchair-accessible trail—South of Falls Village, the A.T. hooks up with the River Trail, converted to create a handicap-accessible loop trail using part of the A.T. and an old racetrack. Also nearby is a nature trail that provides insight into the area's history. The stone ruins near the Trail were part of a pre-Civil War plan to turn the town into a giant industrial city. A stone canal would have channeled water from the Housatonic to power the village's dreams of grandeur. When crowds gathered for the opening of the canal in 1851, the walls leaked; builders had failed to place mortar between its rocks, and the project eventually died, leaving Falls Village the quiet backwater it is today.

Water Street—**East** 0.5 mile to **Falls Village, Conn. [P.O. ZIP 06031: M–F 8:30–1 & 2–5, Sa 8:30–12; (860) 824-7781]**. ■ *Lodging:* Horsetail Farm B&B, 61 S. Canaan Rd., 2 miles from junction of Rtes. 7 & 112, (860) 824-2490, $75PP cash, includes B, D (when available), laundry, shower, shuttle to & from A.T., wireless; Alisha Cleckenger, proprietor. ■ *Restaurants:* Toymakers Café, (860) 824-8168, B/L, Th–F 7–2, Sa–Su 7–4, free tentsites; Pizza Restaurant; Mountainside Café (one mile south on Route 7, see Mohawk Trail entry above); Sweet William's Bakery, open M–Sa 10–3. ■ *Other services:* Liquor store has sodas and hiker snacks; Jacob's Garage has snack machines, but please remove your pack so that the dog won't be alarmed; bank with ATM at corner of Rtes. 7 & 126.

Hydroelectric Plant—Cold shower and water are available outside the small, vine-covered building past the transformer. Look for silver shower head poking through ivy, with a small concrete pad below. Water faucet is below shower head.

Iron Bridge over Housatonic—Built by the Berlin Construction Co. of Connecticut in 1903. The same company built the iron bridge that now takes hikers over Swatara Creek in Pennsylvania.

Picnic Area—North of bridge along the river, opposite the power plant, are picnic tables (no water), fire pits, a privy, trash cans, and parking area.

Great Falls Dam—North 0.5 mile on the A.T. are the Great Falls that gave Falls Village its name. Because the power plant below draws most of the river's water, the falls appear "great" only during heavy rains or snowmelt. In 1996, Falls Village played host to a most unusual visitor from the north. A bull moose that wandered down the Trail tried to negotiate the sluiceway near the dam, but fell in. Workers from the power plant managed to rescue the bewildered beast. For a few days, it attracted throngs of villagers and day-hikers as it munched on river plants and other vegetation. The animal eventually died, but not from a broken leg, as first believed; the cause was attributed to a brain disease that affects moose.

Limestone Spring Lean-to (1986)—Sleeps 6. Privy is uphill to the right. Follow the stream to where a spring comes out of a small limestone cave.

Rand's View—The A.T. passes by this vista, which offers views of the Taconic Range from Lion's Head to Mt. Everett and Jug End. *No camping allowed.*

U.S. 44—West 0.4 mile to **Salisbury, Conn. [P.O. ZIP 06068: M–F 8–1 & 2–5, Sa 9–12; (860) 435-5072]**. Revolutionary War leader Ethan Allen, famous in Vermont history, studied here for a short time in preparation for entrance to Yale University (which he never attended). Allen moved to the New York area that later became Vermont. For northbounders, turn west on U.S. 44 to town. For southbounders, it is best to follow Conn. 41, Undermountain Road, 0.8 mile into town. Water is available from a fountain at town hall and also from a spigot in the cemetery on Lower Cobble Road. ■ *Lodging:* White Hart Inn, (860) 435-0030, <www.whitehar-

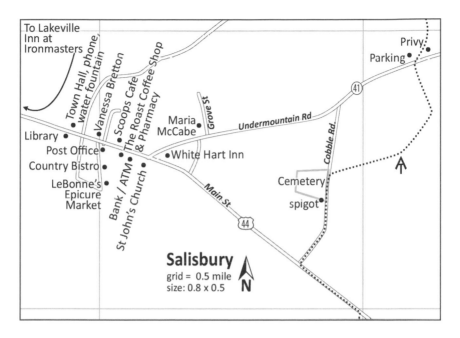

tinn.com>, $89 hiker rate up to 4 depending on room, pets $25, restaurant B/L/D, mail drops accepted for guests, UPS or FedEx to 15 Undermountain Road, Salisbury, CT 06068, or USPS to P.O. Box 545, Salisbury, CT 06068; Maria McCabe offers rooms in her home to hikers, (860) 435-0593, $35PP, includes shower, use of living room, cooking outside, pets outside (no fee), no visitors in home, cash only, mail drops accepted for guests at 4 Grove Street, Salisbury, CT 06068; Vanessa Breton offers 3 rooms in her home, each with 2 single beds, to hikers, (860) 435-9577, $35PP, includes shower, laundry $5, use of living room, cooking outside, pets outside (no fee), no visitors in home, cash only, mail drops accepted for guests at 7 The Lockup Road, Salisbury, CT 06068. ■ *Groceries:* LaBonne's Epicure Market, (860) 435-2559 (long-term resupply), M–Sa, open 8–7, Su until 6. ■ *Restaurants:* White Hart Inn, (860) 435-0030, B M–Sa 7–10, Su 8–10, L M–Su 11:30–3, D M–Su 5–9; The Roast Coffee House & Internet Café, (860) 435-0600, B/L, with fruit and vegetable juices, M–Sa 7–2, Su 8–12. ■ *Internet access:* Scoville Memorial Library and The Roast. ■ *Other services:* pay phone; pharmacy, M–Sa 8–6, Su 8–4; bank with ATM. When open, town hall offers restroom inside.

West 2.4 miles to Lakeville, Conn. ▪ *Lodging:* Inn at Ironmasters, (860) 435-9844, $115S, $125D weekdays, $180 weekends, $15EAP, continental B, dogs allowed in certain rooms without fee, pool. ▪ *Other services:* hardware store, pizza restaurant, laundromat 7–9, doctor, bank with ATM.

 Conn. 41 (Undermountain Road)—West 0.8 mile to Salisbury (see previous entry).

Riga Lean-to (1960s)—Sleeps 6. Privy. The only shelter in Connecticut with a view. Trail to the shelter reported overgrown and not marked, shelter sign missing; without a map, the shelter is easy to miss. The shelter opens to the east, providing sunrise views. Tentsites are also available. Water is a spring on a blue-blazed trail to the left of the clearing at the A.T. A second source is where the trail to the lean-to crosses a small stream. Spring may not run in dry years.

Brassie Brook Lean-to (1980s)—Sleeps 6. Privy. A log lean-to with tentsites available. Water is available from a stream on the A.T. 50 feet north of the side trail to the lean-to.

Bear Mountain—At 2,316 feet, this is the highest peak in Connecticut but not the highest ground, which instead falls on the flank of nearby Mt. Frissel, the peak of which is in Massachusetts. The northbound descent into Sages Ravine is rocky and steep. In foul weather, an alternative route for northbounders is east on the Undermountain Trail for 0.8 mile, then north on the Paradise Lane Trail for 2.1 miles, reconnecting with the A.T. near Sages Ravine, a net 1.7-mile detour.

Massachusetts

Miles from Katahdin	Features	Services	Elev.	Miles from Springer
682.3	Mass.–Conn. State Line		1,800	1,496.8
682.2	Sages Ravine Brook Campsite	C, w	1,360	1,496.9
681.6	Sages Ravine	w	1,340	1,497.5
680.3	Laurel Ridge Campsite	C, w	1,750	1,498.8
678.5	Race Mtn		2,365	1,500.6
677.4	Race Brook Falls Trail	E–0.4m C, w	1,950	1,501.7
676.7	Mt. Everett	R	2,602	1,502.4
676.0	Guilder Pond Picnic Area	R	2,050	1,503.1
675.6	**The Hemlocks Lean-to...** 8.8mS; 0.1mN	S, w	1,880	1,503.5
675.5	**Glen Brook Lean-to...** 0.1mS; 14.3mN	S, w	1,885	1,503.6
674.9	Elbow Trail		1,750	1,504.2
673.2	Jug End		1,750	1,505.9
672.1	Jug End Rd	R (E–0.1m w)	890	1,507.0
671.2	Mass. 41; ATC Kellogg Center/ New England Office **South Egremont, MA 01258**	R (W–1.2m PO, G, M, L, @)	810	1,507.9
669.4	South Egremont Rd, Shays' Rebellion Monument	R	700	1,509.7
667.6	U.S. 7 **Sheffield, MA 01257; Great Barrington, MA 01230**	R (E–3.2m PO, G, M, L; 6m C, M) (W–0.1m C, G, sh; 1.5m G; 1.8m PO, G, M, L, O, D, V, cl, f)	700	1,511.5
666.7	Housatonic River	R	720	1,512.4
664.7	Homes Rd	R	1,150	1,514.4
663.3	East Mtn	w	1,800	1,515.8
661.2	**Tom Leonard Lean-to...** 14.3mS; 5.3mN	S (E–0.2m w)	1,540	1,517.9
660.1	Lake Buel Rd	R	1,150	1,519.0
659.2	Mass. 23 **Monterey, MA 01245**	R (E–4.3m PO, G, M, @) (W–1.6m H; 2.7m M; 4m PO, G, M, L, O, D, V, cl, f)	1,050	1,519.9
658.0	Blue Hill Rd (Stony Brook Rd)	R	1,550	1,521.1

Miles from Katahdin	Features	Services	Elev.	Miles from Springer
657.2	Benedict Pond	W–0.5m C, w	1,620	1,521.9
656.6	The Ledges		1,820	1,522.5
655.9	**Mt. Wilcox South Lean-to...** *5.3mS; 2.1mN*	S, w	1,720	1,523.2
654.1	**Mt. Wilcox North Lean-to...** *2.1mS; 14.8mN*	E–0.3m S, w	1,950	1,525.0
653.5	Beartown Mtn Rd	R, w	1,800	1,525.6
650.3	Fernside Rd	R, w	1,200	1,528.8
650.0	Shaker Campsite	C	1,000	1,529.1
648.2	Jerusalem Rd **Tyringham, MA 01264**	R, w (W–0.6m PO, L; 0.9m C)	930	1,530.9
645.2	Webster Rd	R, w	1,800	1,533.9
642.8	Goose Pond Rd	R	1,650	1,536.3
640.9	Upper Goose Pond		1,500	1,538.2
640.1	**Upper Goose Pond Cabin...** *14.8mS; 9.3mN*	W–0.5m C, S, w	1,483	1,539.0
638.9	Mass. Turnpike (I-90)		1,400	1,540.2
638.8	Greenwater Brook	w	1,400	1,540.3
638.5	U.S. 20 **Lee, MA 01238**	R (E–0.1m L) (W–5m PO, G, L, M, D, V, cl, f)	1,400	1,540.6
637.7	Tyne Rd	R	1,750	1,541.4
637.2	Beckett Mtn		2,180	1,541.9
635.4	Finerty Pond	w	1,900	1,543.7
633.1	County Rd	R	1,850	1,546.0
632.9	Bald Top		2,040	1,546.2
631.3	**October Mtn Lean-to...** *9.3mS; 9mN*	S, w	1,930	1,547.8
630.6	West Branch Rd	R	1,960	1,548.5
629.1	Washington Mtn Rd, Pittsfield Rd **Becket, MA 01223**	R (E–0.1m C, w; 5m PO, D, V)	2,000	1,550.0
627.1	Stream	w	1,950	1,552.0
625.9	Blotz Rd	R	1,850	1,553.2
625.2	Warner Mtn		2,050	1,553.9
622.5	**Kay Wood Lean-to...** *9mS; 17.1mN*	E–0.2m S, w	1,860	1,556.6
622.2	Grange Hall Rd	R	1,650	1,556.9

Miles from Katahdin	Features	Services	Elev.	Miles from Springer
620.1	CSX Railroad		1,199	1,559.0
619.5	Mass. 8, Mass. 9 **Dalton, MA 01226**	R, PO, G, M, L, D, cl, f, @	1,200	1,559.6
618.5	Gulf Rd	R	1,180	1,560.6
614.8	Crystal Mtn Campsite	E–0.2m C, w	2,100	1,564.3
614.4	Gore Pond		2,050	1,564.7
611.9	The Cobbles		1,850	1,567.2
610.8	Church St, Hoosic River **Cheshire, MA 01225**	R, PO, M, O, G, w	950	1,568.3
610.7	Hiker Kiosk	R	970	1,568.4
610.2	Mass. 8 **Adams, MA 01220**	R (E–0.8m L, cl; 2.4m O, f; 4m PO, G, L, M, D, V, cl) (W–0.2m G)	990	1,568.9
609.4	Outlook Ave	R	1,350	1,569.7
606.7	Old Adams Rd	R	2,350	1,572.4
605.8	**Mark Noepel Lean-to…** *17.1mS; 7.1mN*	E–0.2m S, C, w	2,750	1,573.3
605.2	Jones Nose Trail, Saddle Ball Mtn		3,150	1,573.9
603.0	Notch Rd; Rockwell Rd	R	3,290	1,576.1
602.5	Mt. Greylock, Bascom Lodge, Summit Rd	R closed	3,491	1,576.6
599.3	Notch Rd	R, w	3,400	1,579.8
599.2	**Wilbur Clearing Lean-to…** *7.1mS; 10.4mN*	W–0.3m S, w	2,325	1,579.9
597.1	Pattison Rd	R, w	900	1,582.0
596.2	Mass. 2 **North Adams, MA 01247; Williamstown, MA 01267**	R (E–0.6m G, M, cl; 1m sh; 2.5m PO, G, L, M, D, V, cl) (W–0.4m G, L, M; 1.4m G, L, M; 2.9m PO, C, G, L, M, O, D, V, cl, sh, f)	660	1,582.9
594.4	Sherman Brook Primitive Campsite	w (W–0.1 m C)	1,300	1,584.7
593.4	Pine Cobble Trail		2,010	1,585.7
592.7	Eph's Lookout		2,254	1,586.4
592.1	Mass.–Vt. State Line, Long Trail (southern terminus)		2,330	1,587.0

The state line is south of Sages Ravine, near the junction with Paradise Lane Trail. The painted state abbreviations on a tree are so faded they're almost invisible.

From the peaks of Mt. Greylock to Mt. Everett, over hills and valleys, through towns and hamlets of the Berkshires, one is reminded of the cultural mecca of New England's famous writers, artists, and performers. Juicy, sweet blueberries abound in season near Becket. Water and mosquitoes seem to be everywhere—you've been warned!

Sages Ravine—Tent platforms and campsites available, staffed by ridgerunners who take turns as caretakers. No fires permitted. No fees charged. More than 100 acres of forest in the Sages Ravine area have never been cut.

Berkshire Chapter of the Appalachian Mountain Club—The A.T. Committee of the AMC–Berkshire Chapter maintains 89.5 miles from the Sages Ravine area to the Massachusetts–Vermont state line. Correspondence should be sent to Berkshire A.T. Committee, 964 South Main St., Great Barrington, MA 02130; <www.outdoors. org>; (413) 528-8003.

Berkshire Bus Service—The Berkshire Regional Transit Authority, (413) 499-2782 or (800) 292-2782, <www.berkshirerta.com>, serves the Trail towns of Great Barrington, Lee, Dalton, Cheshire, Adams, North Adams, and Williamstown. The buses run M–F 5:45 a.m.–7:20 p.m. and Sa 7:15–7; no service Su or holidays. Schedules may be posted in stores and post offices, but, to be sure, call for accurate, up-to-date information. The buses can be flagged down anywhere along Mass. 2 or 8 or U.S. 7, but there are designated bus stops. Popular trips for hikers include rides from Dalton west into Pittsfield, the region's hub with all major services, and from Cheshire south to the Berkshire Mall, with 103 shops and a 10-screen cinema. Maximum fare one way is $4.40 ($1.10 per community crossed, cash; drivers cannot make change); ask for free transfers.

Peter Pan Bus Lines—(888) 751-8800, <www.peterpanbus.com>. Buses run daily each way between NYC and Williamstown, Mass., stopping at towns near the A.T., including Canaan and Danbury in Connecticut and Great Barrington, Lee, Pittsfield, and Williamstown in Massachusetts. Call for schedules and rates.

Laurel Ridge Campsite—0.1 mile south of Bear Rock Falls, four campsites with single and double tent platforms and one group site with double tent platforms. Privy (composting). Water source is a spring off a short side trail south of campsites. *No fires permitted in this area.*

Race Mountain—A spectacular walk on a clear day; spooky when foggy. It's a steep drop-off to the east.

Mt. Everett—This range is the second-highest on the A.T. in Massachusetts.

Guilder Pond—At 2,042 feet, the short side trail to the west leads to this highest body of water in Massachusetts. Picnic table and privy. For conservation reasons, please, no camping, swimming, or fishing.

The Hemlocks Lean-to (1999)—Sleeps 10. Privy (composting). Nestled in a hemlock grove, the lean-to offers a sleeping loft with overhang. Water source is on the blue-blazed access trail. If you cannot find water here, Glen Brook crosses the A.T. 50 yards north of the access trail to the lean-to.

Glen Brook Lean-to (1960s)—Sleeps 6. Privy. Tent platforms. Water source is a reliable stream to the left of the lean-to.

Jug End Road—**East** 0.1 mile to a reliable, piped spring, off the road to the right.

Mass. 41—**West** 0.1 mile to the Appalachian Trail Conservancy's Kellogg Conservation Center (KCC) at the old April Hill farm, opened in May 2007. Initially solely an office for one ATC and one Appalachian Mountain Club staff member, both of whom are frequently in the field, it became in spring 2009 the New England regional office of ATC (formerly in Lyme, N.H.). For the moment, no visitor or hiker services are available, but the conservation work done out of this office helps ensure that beautiful and serene places like the farmland here are preserved as part of the A.T. experience forever. The property is insured for that business use only, and no public parking is allowed. Trailhead parking is available at Sheffield/Egremont Road, 1.8 Trail miles north. For more information, contact Adam Brown at (413) 528-8002 or <abrown@appalachiantrail.org>.

    West 1.2 miles to **South Egremont, Mass. [P.O. ZIP 01258: M–F 8:15–12 & 12:30–4, Sa 9–11:30; (413) 528-1571].** ■ *Lodging:* The Egremont Inn, (413) 528-2111, <www.egremontinn.com>, <theinn@vgernet.net>, a building dating back to 1780; $75s/D,

$20EAP, B included, call for availability, free WiFi, no pets, pool, shuttle back to the Trail, mail drops accepted for guests if sent to 10 Old Sheffield Road, or P.O. Box 418, South Egremont, MA 01258; Weathervane Inn, (413) 528-9580, (800) 528-9580, <www. weathervaneinn.com>, 11-room B&B, each with private bath, full B, afternoon tea, a/c, $135–$250D, $30EAP, several rooms accommodate 3–4 people, prior arrangements for shuttle to and from Trail, outdoor pool, on-site massage services and yoga, walk to town services, packages accepted with stay and prior arrangements, no pets. ■ *Groceries:* Country Market, (413) 528-8081, with deli and lunch counter, 7 days 6–8, hiker-friendly. ■ *Restaurants:* Egremont Inn, W–Su; Mom's Country Café, with pizza and ice cream. ■ *Internet access:* library. ■ *Other services:* bank with ATM.

Shays' Rebellion Monument—Stone marker commemorates the last skirmish of a bloody farmers' revolt led by Revolutionary War veteran Daniel Shays against government taxes and tactics in 1787. The incident assisted Federalists in making their case for a strong central government with powers to tax and maintain a standing army.

U.S. 7—East 3.2 miles to **Sheffield, Mass. [P.O. ZIP 01257: M–F 9–4:30, Sa 9–12; (413) 229-8772].** ■ *Lodging:* Race Brook Lodge, (413) 229-2916, <www.rblodge. com>, a restored 1790s barn open Su–Th $95–$150, F–Sa $125–$275, $20EAP, pets allowed in same room $15, Th–Sa D, mail drops accepted for guests at Route 41, Sheffield, MA 01257. ■ *Groceries:* Sheffield Market Place (long-term resupply), 6–9, hot foods, deli, and ice cream. ■ *Restaurant:* Village on the Green Restaurant and Pizzeria, M–F 10–9, Sa–Su 8–9. ■ *Other services:* bank, hardware store, ATM, and bus service.

East 6 miles to *Work for Stay:* Moon in the Pond Organic Farm, (413) 229-3092, <dom@moninthepond.com>, 816 Barnum St., Sheffield, MA 01257. Organic meat-and-vegetable farmer Dominic Palumbo offers tentsites, an outdoor shower, and organic meals for a day or two to a week, in exchange for farm work. Transportation can be arranged to and from the Trail. Keep trying to call; not always next to the phone.

West 0.1 mile to the Corn Crib, (413) 528-4947, with fresh fruit, vegetables, ice cream, cold drinks, snacks, water, phone, shower, tenting, long-term parking.

West 1.5 miles to Guido's, with organic produce and deli.

West 1.8 miles to **Great Barrington, Mass. [P.O. ZIP 01230: M–F 8:30–4:30, Sa 8:30–12:30; (413) 528-3670].** ■ *Lodging:* Lantern House Motel, (413) 528-2350, $55S, $65D, higher on weekends, $10EAP, call for reservations, free WiFi, continental B, one room available for pets $10 additional; Travelodge, (413) 528-2340, $55S, $65D, higher on weekends and during special events, pets allowed in some rooms for $10 fee, laundry, free WiFi but no computers available for guests, continental B, outdoor pool; Mountain View Motel, (413) 528-0250, $65S, $75D, higher on weekends, $5EAP, call for reservations, pets $20, free WiFi, some rooms with CATV, phone, refrigerator, microwave, continental B; Holiday Inn Express, (413) 528-1810, 20% discount on current rates, extended continental B, no pets, free WiFi and computers available for guests; Comfort Inn, (413) 644-3200, <www.berkshirecomfortinn.com>, 25% discount on current rates, deluxe continental B, laundry, no pets, indoor and outdoor pools, free WiFi and computers available for guests; Monument Mountain Motel, (413) 528-3272, <www.monumentmountainmotel.com>, $50S, $60D, $10EAP, higher on weekends and during special events, pets allowed $10, laundry, pool, coffee and tea when office is open, mail drops accepted for guests at U.S. 7, 247 Stockbridge Road, Great Barrington, MA 01230; The Seven Stones, <www.thesevenstones.com>. ■ *Groceries:* Big Y Foods, open 7 days 7–9, and Price Chopper, M–Sa 6–midnight, Su 7–midnight (both long-term resupply). ■ *Restaurants:* numerous, in town center and north along U.S. 7. ■ *Other services:* K-Mart, ice-cream store, banks with ATM, hardware store, shoe repair, hospital, dentist, optician, pharmacy, veterinarian, movie theater, coin laundry, and taxi, (413) 528-0911. ■ *Bus service:* Bus tickets at Bill's Pharmacy, cash only.

Tom Leonard Lean-to (1970)—Sleeps 10. Privy. Located just south of Ice Gulch, a deep cleft in the landscape; the lean-to is visible from the A.T. Water source is a very cold stream 0.2 mile down a ravine to the left of the lean-to.

Mass. 23—East 4.3 miles to **Monterey, Mass. [P.O. ZIP 01245: M–F 8:30–1 & 2–4:30, Sa 9–11:30; (413) 528-4670].** ■ *Groceries:* Monterey General Store (long-term resupply), with café, Internet, and pay phone; open M–Sa 7:30–6, Su 8–12.

West 1 mile to Lake Buel Road, turn left, first right driveway 0.6 mile uphill or, 0.5 mile downhill from Tom Leonard Shelter, follow private trail blazed in white circles to *Hostel:* East Mountain Retreat Center, (413) 528-6617, <emrc@bcn.net>, $10 donation, with shower; laundry $3; use of the library; 10 p.m. quiet curfew (no guests admitted after this hour) and prompt 8:30 a.m. checkout.

West 2.7 miles to *Restaurant:* Panda West, L/D.

West 4 miles to Great Barrington (see above).

Benedict Pond—West 0.5 mile on a blue-blazed side trail to a sandy beach with picnic tables, pay phone, tentsites $10.

Mt. Wilcox South Lean-to (1930/2007)—Old lean-to sleeps 6. Privy. Built as a CCC project; approach trail was part of the original A.T. in Massachusetts. New shelter just beyond old one, completed in 2007. Water source is the spring crossed *en route* to the lean-to.

Mt. Wilcox North Lean-to (1930s)—Sleeps 10. Privy. Lean-to is on a 0.3-mile blue-blazed trail. Water source, stream in front of the privy, may go dry in late summer.

Shaker Campsite—Tent platforms and privy available. Water is located north on the A.T.

Tyringham Cobble—Formed by a geological event that separated this hill from the mountain behind it, the cobble rises 400 feet above the village below. The hill and nearly 200 acres around it are owned by a conservation trust.

Jerusalem Road—West 0.6 mile to **Tyringham, Mass. [P.O. ZIP 01264: M–F 9–12:30 & 4–5:30, Sa 8:30–12:30; (413) 243-1225]**. May also be reached from Tyringham Main Road 1.1 mile north on A.T. Water fountain outside post office; pay phone next to library (no Internet). ■ *Lodging:* Cobble View B&B, (800) 467-4136, call for rates; no pets, no visitors; across from P.O.; drinks and snacks available.

  West 0.9 mile to *Camping:* tenting allowed at outdoor pavilion next to the firehouse; Porta-potty.

Jerusalem Road Spring—West several yards to short path on left that leads to a piped spring (if you pass the first house on the right, you've gone too far).

Upper Goose Pond Cabin—AMC–Berkshire Chapter A.T. Committee maintains this cabin on a 0.5-mile side trail north of the pond. The cabin offers bunks, fireplace, covered porch, privy, swimming, and tent platforms. Open daily Memorial Day–Labor Day, then weekends through Columbus Day. During summer months, the resident volunteer caretaker brings water by canoe from a spring across the pond; otherwise, the pond is the water source. When the caretaker is not in residence, or when the cabin is closed for the season, hikers may camp on the porch or tent platforms. Privy behind the cabin and near tentsites. There is no fee for staying at this site; donations appreciated.

Upper Goose Pond Cabin by Isaac Wiegmann

U.S. 20—East 0.1 mile to *Lodging:* Southern Comfort Lodge, (413) 243-9907, $49–$99; pets allowed, no fee; beach on Greenwater Pond; use of outside grill, canoes, kayaks, and rowboats; mail drops accepted for nonguests, no fee, 3949 Jacob's Ladder Road, Becket, MA 01223; was for sale in 2009, so check on availability.

West 5 miles to **Lee, Mass. [P.O. ZIP 01238: M–F 8:30–4:30, Sa 9–12; (413) 243-1392]**, home of the famous Tanglewood Festival at Tanglewood Performing Arts Center, an outdoor theater that hosts a series of rock, jazz, and country concerts throughout the summer. ■ *Lodging:* Sunset Motel, (413) 243-0302, $85s/D weekdays to $190 weekends, WiFi; Rodeway Inn, (413) 243-0813, Su–Th $55–$85, F–Sa $79–$185, WiFi, continental B; Pilgrim Inn, (413) 243-1328, Su–Th $79–$95, F–Sa $95–$195, $10 EAP, continental B, coffee in room, pool, WiFi, microfridge, laundry; Super 8, (413) 243-0143, $95s/D weekdays, $107 weekends, microfridge, WiFi, accepts mail drops at 170 Housatonic St., Lee, MA 01238. ■ *Groceries:* Price Chopper Supermarket (long-term resupply). ■ *Restaurants:* Joe's Diner, Athena's Pizza House, Rose's Restaurant (B/L 7–2), and several fast-food chains. ■ *Other services:* Lee Coin-Op Laundromat, banks, hardware store, doctor, dentist, pharmacy, health clinic, veterinarian, and taxi.

October Mountain Lean-to (1980s)—Sleeps 12. Privy. Food-hoist cables available. Do not leave packs unattended. A large lean-to with porch. Water source is a stream just south of the lean-to on the A.T.

Washington Mountain Road—East 0.1 mile to the "Cookie Lady," Marilyn Wiley, (413) 623-5859, who lives on a blueberry farm on the left of Washington Mountain Road. Water spigot near the garage door is for hikers. A.T. signs are posted; please sign register on the steps. Homemade cookies are often available to munch on as you watch hummingbirds buzz her feeder; pick your own blueberries at reasonable rates during season. Camping is allowed on the property if you ask permission first. Will also hold packages and provide shuttles. Roy and Marilyn Wiley, 47 Washington Mountain Rd., Becket, MA 01223.

East 5 miles to **Becket, Mass. [P.O. ZIP 01223: M–F 8–4, Sa 9–11:30; (413) 623-8845]**, where the A.T. is listed as a historical site in a town settled more than 300 years ago. ■ *Lodging:* Becket Motel, 29 Chester Rd., Becket, MA 01223, (413) 623-8888, $70–$120, free shuttles to/from Trail, WiFi, mail drops accepted. ■ *Groceries:* Becket General Store, (413) 623-5700, M–Sa 6-8, Su 7-2, small grocery, del;i, counter. ■ *Other services:* doctor, veterinarian.

Kay Wood Lean-to (1980s)—Sleeps 10. Privy, bear box. Lean-to is named for Kay Wood, a 1972 thru-hiker. Ms. Wood is now in her 80s and continues to work as a Trail maintainer in the area. Water source is the stream in front of the lean-to.

Dalton, Mass. [P.O. ZIP 01226: M–F 8:30–4:30, Sa 9–12; (413) 684-0364]—The A.T. goes through the eastern side of town, where most services are available. Depot Street, which the A.T. follows into town from the south, offers a pharmacy and restaurants. Other services are within 0.5 mile of the A.T. ■ *Lodging:* Thomas Levardi, 83 Depot St., , (413) 684-3399, cell (413) 212-9691, allows hikers to use a water spigot outside his home and provides the hospitality of his front porch and back yard for tenting (get permission first); Shamrock Village Inn, (413) 684-0860, S–Th $75S, $79D, F–Sa $99S/D, hiker box, well-behaved pets allowed. ■ *Groceries:* Cumberland Farms with ATM, Dalton General Store with deli (both short-term resupply). ■ *Restaurants:* Jacob's Pub, (413) 684-9766, 51 Daly Ave., L/D M–Sa 11:30–1, Su 12–8, great Reubens, very hiker-friendly, hiker box; Mill Tavern, L/D; Duff & Dell's Variety, B/L, closed Su; Pizza Palace; Angelina's Subs with veggie burgers; Dalton Restaurant, serves D daily, Th–Sa with live entertainment; Shamrocks Restaurant and Pub, L/D, M–Sa 11:30–9, Su 11:30–8, closed M, WiFi. ■ *Internet access:* library, 1-hour limit. ■ *Other services:* Dalton Laundry, M–F 8:30–6, Sa 8:30–4, Su 8:30–12; banks; L.P. Adams sells denatured alcohol and Coleman fuel; doctor; dentist; pharmacy. ■ *Bus service:* Connections to Pittsfield, with all major services and various AYCE options.

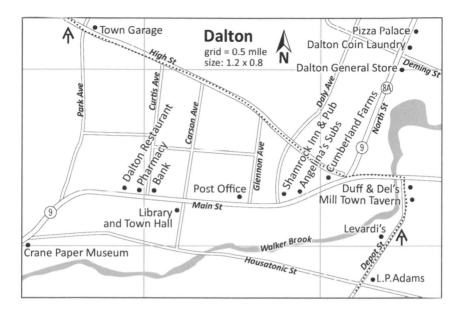

Crystal Mountain Campsite—0.2 mile east. Privy. Water is north on Trail.

The Cobbles—These outcroppings of marble overlook the Hoosic River Valley and offer views of the town of Cheshire and Mt. Greylock. The Hoosic River, which is crossed south of Cheshire, flows north and empties into the Hudson River in New York.

Cheshire, Mass. [P.O. ZIP 01225: M–F 7:30–1 & 2–4:30, Sa 8:30–11:30; (413) 743-3184]—The Trail skirts the center of town to the east and crosses Mass. 8 0.4 mile east of the main stoplight at Church Street. St. Mary of the Assumption Church allows hikers to get water and use the restroom, but no tenting. Church may allow hikers to stay in parish hall and use parking lot, but speak to Father David Raymond first. ■ *Lodging:* Mason Hill, 195 West Mountain Rd., <wwwmasonhilllife.com>, (413) 743-2492, 5 miles from P.O., west of Church St. and Mass. 8, four bunks and single bed $25 in restored barn, large common room and kitchen, two private cabins $50s $90D, tentsites near brook $15s/D, bath and shower in barn, outdoor shower, laundry $5, shuttles. No drugs or alcohol, no mail drops. Open May 1–Oct 31. ■ *Groceries:* H.D. Reynolds, a general store, hiker snacks, denatured alcohol, and Coleman fuel. ■ *Restaurants:* Cobbleview Pub & Pizzeria, L/D Su–W 10–10, Th–Sa

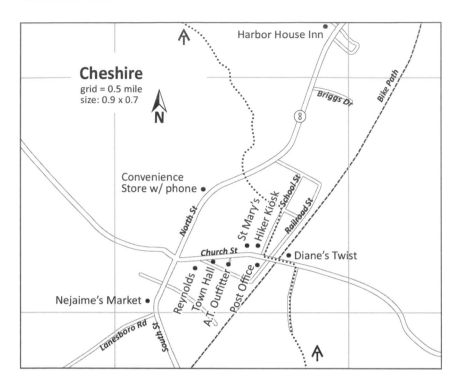

10–11, home-made desserts, restrooms with amenities to clean up with; Bass Water Grill, B/L/D, closed M; Diane's Twist, M–Su 11–6, mid-Apr–mid-Oct, outdoor spigot, deli sandwiches, soda, and ice cream. ■ *Other services:* bank with ATM; AT Bicycle Works & Outfitters, owned by "Dragon" of '05, across from church in back, emergency backpacking supplies, all fuels, call (413) 743-2453 if no one in shop. ■ *Bus service:* Stop across the street from the post office, connections to the Berkshire Mall and Adams, Mass.

Hiker kiosk—A detailed town map with hiker services marked.

Mass. 8—East 0.8 mile to *Lodging:* Harbour House Inn, (413) 743-8959, <www.harbourhouseinn.com>, provides rooms midweek $85. Rate includes B, Internet access, shuttle to the Trail; laundry available. Hiker-friendly.

   East 2.4 miles to *Outfitter:* Berkshire Outfitters, (413) 743-5900, <www.berkshireoutfitters.com>, M–Sa 10–5, Th until 8, Su 11–4, with hiker supplies, Coleman fuel, minor equipment repairs.

East 4 miles to **Adams, Mass. [P.O. ZIP 01220: M–F 8:30–4:30, Sa 10–12; (413) 743-5177]**, an alternative to the smaller town of Cheshire. Adams is accessible by the Berkshire Bus Service. ■ *Lodging:* Mount Greylock Inn, (413) 743-2665, <mountgreylockinn. com>, $89–$159, includes B. ■ *Groceries:* Big Y Foods supermarket (long-term resupply). ■ *Restaurants:* Pizza Jim's, (413) 743-9161, will deliver; CJ's Pub and Daily Grind Coffee; many fast-food outlets. ■ *Other services:* Thrifty Bundle Laundromat, banks, hardware store, doctor, dentist, Rite Aid, veterinarian, and Western Union.

West 0.2 mile to *Groceries:* Convenience store (short-term resupply), deli sandwiches, pay phone.

Mark Noepel Lean-to & Bassett Brook Campsite (1985)— Sleeps 10. Privy is on a 0.1-mile, blue-blazed trail. Porcupines make regular appearances at this lean-to with tent platforms. Water source is from a spring to the right of the lean-to.

Saddle Ball Mountain—At 3,238 feet and located at the A.T. junction with the Jones Nose Trail, Saddle Ball is the A.T.'s first 3,000-footer north of North Marshall in Shenandoah National Park.

Mt. Greylock—Topped by a war memorial, paved road, and Bascom Lodge, Greylock is Massachusetts' highest peak (3,491 feet). A stone tower, crowned by a globe lit at night, is a tribute to the state's war dead. You can climb the 89 steps to the top for views of the Green, Catskill, and Taconic mountains and surrounding towns. The mountain has inspired literary giants from Thoreau to Hawthorne. *Thunderbolt Shelter on Mt. Greylock is an emergency-only warming hut. No camping or fires on the summit.*

Bascom Lodge—Now operated by Bascom Lodge Group, (413) 743-1591, <www.bascomlodge.net>, open 7 days, B/L/D, showers and towel $5, bunk $35, private rooms $100D–$125, $25EAP.

Wilbur Clearing Lean-to (1970)—Sleeps 8. Privy. Located 0.3 mile down the Money Brook Trail; very popular during the summer months. Tentsites available. Water source is an intermittent stream to the right of the lean-to.

Mass. 2/North Adams—BRTA hourly bus service is available on this road (see page 194). *Note: The town of North Adams extends one mile west and several miles east of the Trail; the Williamstown line is 1.4 miles west of the Trail.*

East 0.6 mile to ■ *Groceries:* Price Chopper Supermarket (long-term resupply), open M–Sa 6 a.m.–midnight, Su 6–10, with deli, pay phone, Western Union, ATM; West's Variety (short-term resupply). ■ *Restaurants:* Chinese Buffet, AYCE L/D; Friendly's. ■ *Other services:* Thrifty Bundle Laundromat.

East 1.0 mile to YMCA, shower $2.

East 2.5 miles to **North Adams, Mass. [P.O. ZIP 01247: M–F 8:30–4:30, Sa 10–12; (413) 664-4554]**. Large, spread-out city with most major services, including motels. ■ *Groceries:* Big Y Foods and Convenience Plus (both long-term resupply); Cumberland Farms (short-term resupply). ■ *Restaurants:* Boston Seafood Restaurant, Freight Yard Pub, other fast-food chains. ■ *Other services:* banks with ATM, hospital, shoe repair, hardware store, doctor, dentist, veterinarian, Radio Shack, and movie theater. ■ *Shuttles:* between Hudson (Bear Mountain Bridge) and Connecticut (Hanover, N.H.) rivers; Dave Ackerson, 82 Cherry St., North Adams, MA 01247, (413) 346-1033, <daveackerson@yahoo.com>.

West 0.4 mile to ■ *Groceries:* Super Shop & Stop (long-term resupply), ATM, pharmacy, Western Union, bank, and pay phone. ■ *Lodging:* Redwood Motel, (413) 664-4351, $70–$149, CATV.

West 1.4 miles to town border with **Williamstown** and ■ *Lodging:* Williamstown Motel, (413) 458-5202, $59S, $109D, pick-up from Mass. 2 and Phelps Rd.; Howard Johnson, (413) 458-8158, <www.howardjohnson.com>, $59–$149 rate based on season and day of week, no pets, continental B, outdoor pool, satellite TV; Maple Terrace Motel, (413) 458-9677, <www.mapleterrace.com>, $75–$160 includes B, DVD, WiFi, CATV, heated pool, picnic area, all rooms nonsmoking; Willows Motel, (413) 458-5768, <www.willowsmotel.com>, Su–Th $69–$119, F–Sa $89–$129, accepts packages for guests if notified in advance to 480 Main St., Williamstown, MA 01267. ■ *Restaurants:* Angelina's Subs, Chopsticks Asian, Colonial Pizza, Desperado's Mexican Grille, Dunkin' Donuts, Happy Star Chinese, Michael's Greek & Italian, Moonlight Diner & Grille. ■ *Groceries:* Wild Oats Whole Foods Market (long-term resupply). ■ *Other services:* Alcaro Rent-A-Car, (413) 458-1620, M–Sa; American Cab & Livery, (413) 662-2000.

West 2.6 miles to **Williamstown, Mass. [P.O. ZIP 01267: M–F 8:30–4:30, Sa 9–12; (413) 458-3707]**, home of Williams College. ■ *Lodging:* Williams Inn, (413) 458-9371; although $120S and $175D and up is out of the price range of most hikers, $7 gets you a towel, shower, swim, and sauna; free WiFi; parking $2/day. ■ *Restaurants:* Papa

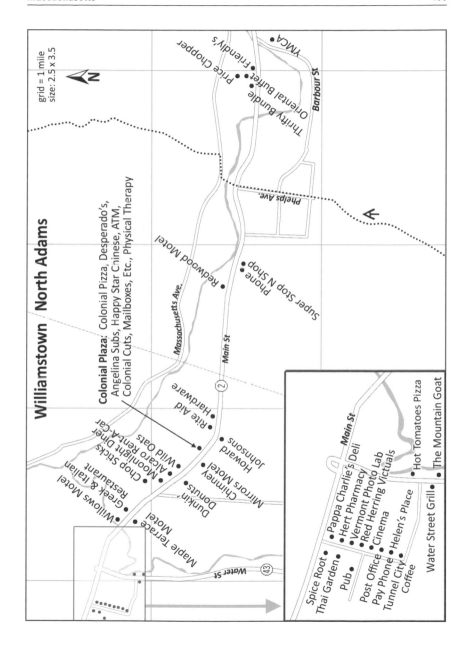

Williamstown / North Adams

grid = 1 mile
size: 2.5 x 3.5

N

YMCA
Barbour St
Price Chopper
Friendly's
Oriental Buffet
Thrifty Bundle
Phelps Ave

Colonial Plaza: Colonial Pizza, Desperado's, Angelina Subs, Happy Star Chinese, ATM, Colonial Cuts, Mailboxes, Etc., Physical Therapy

Redwood Motel
Massachusetts Ave.
Main St
Phone
Super Stop N Shop

Rite Aid
Hardware
Howard Johnsons
Chimney Mirrors Motel
Dunkin' Donuts
Chop Sticks Diner
Moonlight Diner
Alcaro Rent-A-Car
Wild Oats
Greek & Italian Restaurant
Willows Motel
Maple Terrace Motel
Water St
43
2

Main St
Pappa Charlie's Deli
Hert Pharmacy
Vermont Photo Lab
Red Herring Victuals
Cinema
Helen's Place
Hot Tomatoes Pizza
The Mountain Goat
Water Street Grill
Spice Root
Thai Garden
Pub
Post Office
Pay Phone
Tunnel City Coffee

Charlie's, Helen's Place, Hot Tomatoes Pizza, Red Herring Victuals, Thai Garden, Tunnel City Coffee (with extensive selection of homemade pastries), Spice Root (Indian), Water Street Grill (L buffet, M–F). ■ *Other services:* banks with ATM; doctor; dentist; health clinic; pharmacy; veterinarian; movie theater; bookstore; American Cab Co., (413) 662-2000; and Bonanza Peter Pan bus line, (888) 751-8800, (800) 343-9999, <www.peterpanbus.com>.

Sherman Brook Campsite—Tent platforms available. A blue-blazed trail lets you bypass a boulder field north of the campsite in bad weather. Water at Pete's Spring.

Vermont

Miles from Katahdin	Features	Services	Elev.	Miles from Springer
592.1	Vt.–Mass. State Line, Long Trail (southern terminus)		2,330	1,587.0
591.7	Brook	w	2,300	1,587.4
589.3	**Seth Warner Shelter**... *10.4mS; 7.4mN*	W–0.2m S, C, w	2,180	1,589.8
589.0	County Rd	R	2,290	1,590.1
587.9	Ed's Spring	E–100ft w	2,890	1,591.2
586.3	Roaring Branch	w	2,470	1,592.8
582.1	**Congdon Shelter**... *7.4mS; 5.9mN*	S, w	2,060	1,597.0
579.6	Harmon Hill		2,325	1,599.5
577.8	Vt. 9 **Bennington, VT 05201**	R, w (W–5m PO, G, M, L, O, D, cl, f, @; 7m G, L, M, @))	1,360	1,601.3
576.2	**Melville Nauheim Shelter**... *5.9mS; 8.5mN*	E–250ft S, w	2,330	1,602.9
574.6	Hell Hollow Brook	w	2,350	1,604.5
572.0	Little Pond Lookout		3,060	1,607.1
570.2	Glastenbury Lookout		2,920	1,608.9
567.7	**Goddard Shelter**... *8.5mS; 4.3mN*	S, w	3,540	1,611.4
567.4	Glastenbury Mtn		3,748	1,611.7
563.4	**Kid Gore Shelter,** Caughnawaga Tentsites... *4.3mS; 4.6mN*	S, C, w	2,795	1,615.7
559.1	Lydia's Rest		3,300	1,620.0
559.7	South Alder Brook	w	2,600	1,619.4
558.8	**Story Spring Shelter**... *4.6mS; 10.4mN*	S, w	2,810	1,620.3
555.2	Stratton-Arlington Rd (Kelley Stand Rd)	R, w	2,230	1,623.9
551.4	Stratton Mtn		3,936	1,627.7
548.4	+**Stratton Pond Shelter** *via* Stratton Pond Trail ... *10.4mS; 5.4mN*	W–450ft S, w	2,565	1,630.7
548.2	Stratton Pond, North Shore Trail to +North Shore Tenting Area	w (W–0.5m C, w)	2,555	1,630.9

Miles from Katahdin	Features	Services	Elev.	Miles from Springer
546.3	Winhall River	w	2,175	1,632.8
543.5	**William B. Douglas Shelter** *via* Branch Pond Trail... *5.4mS; 3.6mN*	W–0.5m S, w	2,210	1,635.6
542.6	Old Rootville Rd, Prospect Rock	R (W–150ft w)	2,150	1,636.5
540.5	**Spruce Peak Shelter**... *3.6mS; 5mN*	W–0.1m C, S, w	2,180	1,638.6
540.1	Spruce Peak	W–300ft	2,040	1,639.0
537.7	Vt. 11 & 30 **Manchester Center, VT 05255**	R, w (E–2.1m L, M; 2.5m G; 2.7m L, M; 3m L) (W–5.8m PO, G, M, L, O, D, V, cl, f, @)	1,840	1,641.4
535.7	**Bromley Shelter**... *5mS; 8.2mN*	E–0.1m C, S, w	2,560	1,643.4
534.7	Bromley Mtn		3,260	1,644.4
532.2	Mad Tom Notch, USFS 21	R, w	2,446	1,646.9
530.6	Styles Peak		3,394	1,648.5
528.9	Peru Peak		3,429	1,650.2
527.6	**+Peru Peak Shelter**... *8.2mS; 4.7mN*	C, S, w	2,605	1,651.5
527.1	Griffith Lake, +Griffith Lake Tenting Area	C, w	2,600	1,652.0
526.9	Griffith Lake	w	2,600	1,652.2
524.9	Baker Peak		2,850	1,654.2
522.9	**Lost Pond Shelter**... *4.7mS, 2.5mN*	W–100ft C, S, w	2,150	1,656.2
521.4	**Old Job Shelter** *via* Old Job Trail ... *2.5mS; 1.2mN*	E–1m C, S, w	1,525	1,657.7
521.2	**Big Branch Shelter**... *1.2mS; 3mN*	C, S, w	1,460	1,657.9
519.9	Danby—Landgrove Rd, USFS 10, Black Branch **Danby, VT 05739**	R, w (W–3.2m PO, G, M, L, f; 5.5m C)	1,500	1,659.2
518.2	**+Lula Tye Shelter**... *3mS; 0.7mN*	E–100ft S, nw; N–0.4m w	1,920	1,660.9
517.9	+Little Rock Pond Tenting Area	C; N–0.1m w	1,854	1,661.2
517.8	Spring	w	1,854	1,661.3

Miles from Katahdin	Features	Services	Elev.	Miles from Springer
517.6	Green Mtn Trail to Homer Stone Brook Trail		1,854	1,661.5
517.5	+**Little Rock Pond Shelter**... *0.7mS; 4.6mN*	E–100ft S, nw; S– 0.3m w	1,885	1,661.6
513.6	Trail to White Rocks Cliff vista	W–0.2m	2,400	1,665.5
513.1	**Greenwall Shelter**... *4.6mS; 5.3mN*	E–0.2m S, w	2,025	1,666.0
511.7	Sugar Hill Rd	R	1,260	1,667.4
511.6	Vt. 140 **Wallingford, VT 05773**	R, w (W–2.7m PO, G, M, L)	1,160	1,667.5
509.5	Bear Mtn		2,220	1,669.6
508.0	**Minerva Hinchey Shelter**... *5.3mS; 3.8mN*	E–200ft C, S, w	1,605	1,671.1
505.4	Clarendon Gorge, Mill River Suspension Bridge	w	800	1,673.7
505.3	Vt. 103	R (W–0.5m M, V; 1m G)	860	1,673.8
504.3	**Clarendon Shelter**... *3.8mS; 5.9mN*	E–0.1m C, S, w	1,190	1,674.8
503.8	Beacon Hill		1,740	1,675.3
503.4	Lottery Rd	R	1,720	1,675.7
501.4	Lower Cold River Rd	R	1,400	1,677.7
500.6	Gould Brook (ford)	w	1,480	1,678.5
499.9	Upper Cold River Rd	R, w	1,630	1,679.2
498.5	**Governor Clement Shelter**... *5.9mS; 4.3mN* (see text)	S, w	1,900	1,680.6
494.2	Trail to Killington Peak	E–0.2m	3,900	1,684.9
494.2	**Cooper Lodge**... *4.3mS; 3mN*	C, S, w	3,900	1,684.9
491.7	Jungle Jct; Sherburne Pass Trail to **Pico Camp** ... *3mS; 2.5mN*	E–0.5m S, w	3,480	1,687.4
489.8	**Churchill Scott Shelter**... *2.5mS; 3.4mN*	W–0.1m C, S, w	2,560	1,689.3
487.9	U.S. 4 **Rutland, VT 05701**	R, w (E–0.9m L, M; 2.2m PO, G) (W–0.9m L, M; 1.5m L, M; 8.9m PO, H, L, G, M, O, D, V, cl, f, @)	1,880	1,691.2

Miles from Katahdin	Features	Services	Elev.	Miles from Springer
486.9	Willard Gap, Maine Junction, Long Trail, **Tucker Johnson Shelter...** *3.4mS; 9.5mN*	W–0.4m S, w	2,300	1,692.2
486.0	Sherburne Pass Trail	E–0.5m L, M	2,440	1,693.1
484.6	Vt. 100, Gifford Woods State Park **Killington, VT 05751; Pittsfield, VT 05762**	R, w, C, S, sh (E–0.6m PO, G, L, M) (W–6m P.O., G, L, M)	1,660	1,694.5
483.9	Thundering Brook Rd, Kent Pond	R, L, M, @ (E–0.3m O)	1,450	1,695.2
482.7	River Rd	R	1,214	1,696.4
482.2	Quimby Mtn		2,550	1,696.9
477.9	**Stony Brook Shelter...** *9.5mS; 10.2mN*	E–0.1m S, w	1,760	1,701.2
473.2	Chateauguay Rd	R	2,000	1,705.9
472.5	Lakota Lake Lookout		2,640	1,706.6
470.4	Trail to the Lookout	W–0.2m	2,320	1,708.7
468.0	**Wintturi Shelter...** *10.2mS; 11.9mN*	W–0.2m S, w	1,910	1,711.1
464.2	Vt. 12, Gulf Stream Bridge **Woodstock, VT 05091**	R, w (E–4.4m PO, G, L, M, D, @) (W–0.2m G)	882	1,714.9
462.7	Woodstock Stage Rd (Bartlett Brook Rd) **South Pomfret, VT 05067**	R, w (E–0.9m PO, G)	820	1,716.4
460.5	Pomfret–South Pomfret Rd	R, w	980	1,718.6
458.7	Cloudland Rd	R (W–0.2m S, G)	1,370	1,720.4
456.7	Thistle Hill		1,800	1,722.4
456.4	**Thistle Hill Shelter...** *11.9mS; 9mN*	E–0.1m S, w	1,480	1,722.7
454.9	Joe Ranger Rd	R	1,280	1,724.2
451.6	Iron Bridge, White River, Vt. 14 **West Hartford, VT 05084**	R, G, M (E–0.3m PO, C, G, M, @; 6m H, G, M, L)	390	1,727.5
451.0	Tigertown Rd, Podunk Rd	R	540	1,728.1
450.2	Podunk Brook, Podunk Rd	R, w	860	1,728.9
447.6	**Happy Hill Shelter...** *9mS; 7.4mN*	E–0.1m C, S, w	1,460	1,731.5

Miles from Katahdin	Features	Services	Elev.	Miles from Springer
443.3	U.S. 5 **Norwich, VT 05055**	R (E 0.25m PO, G, L, M, @)	537	1,735.8
442.3	Connecticut River, Vt.–N.H. State Line	R	380	1,736.8

+ Fee charged

Avoid Vermont trails in "mud season," mid-Apr to Memorial Day. Hiking there in wet, sloppy conditions leads to serious Trail erosion.

Green Mountain Club—GMC maintains the 127.9 miles from the Massachusetts–Vermont border to Vt. 12. Correspondence should be sent to GMC at 4711 Waterbury–Stowe Rd., Waterbury Center, VT 05677; (802) 244-7037; fax, (802) 244-5867; <gmc@greenmountainclub.org>, <www.greenmountainclub.org>.

GMC Shelter Fees—Fees are collected at high-use campsites to help defray the costs of field programs and shelter and Trail maintenance along the A.T. in Vermont. The fee is $5PP per night. This fee applies to anyone camping within 0.5 mile of a fee site. In addition, all hikers who pay the $5 fee in cash at one of the three southern-pond fee sites (Stratton Pond, Griffith Lake, and Little Rock Pond—see chart for details) will receive a dated receipt that they can then use for one free night at either or both of the other two fee sites. The receipt must be used within 7 days. No receipt, no free nights; no exceptions. This offer does not extend north of Maine Junction on the Long Trail. This deal only works if you pay cash; it does not apply to folks who promise to pay later.

Fee Site	Includes (listed S to N)
Stratton Pond	Stratton Pond Shelter North Shore Tenting Area
Griffith Lake	Peru Peak Shelter Griffith Lake Tenting Area
Little Rock Pond	Lula Tye Shelter Little Rock Pond Campsite Little Rock Pond Shelter

Caretakers are present throughout the season, May–Oct, at several locations. Through conversation and example, caretakers educate hikers about Leave No Trace practices and perform Trail and shelter maintenance. Most importantly, caretakers compost sewage at high-use fee sites and a few no-fee shelter sites in southern Vermont.

A ridgerunner may be found along the Coolidge Range at the following locations, although a fee is not charged: Clarendon Shelter, Governor Clement Shelter, Cooper Lodge, Pico Camp, and Churchill Scott Shelter.

Long Trail—At the Vermont–Massachusetts state line, the A.T. joins the Long Trail (L.T.) for 105.2 miles, to "Maine Junction" at Willard Gap. At Maine Junction, the A.T. leads toward Maine, and the L.T. continues north, reaching the Canadian border in another 167.8 miles. Completed in 1930, the L.T. served as one inspiration for the A.T. The L.T. and A.T. are seeing increased traffic in Vermont. Please use only designated shelters and campsites, and make use of privies and wash pits to protect water quality and greatly reduce the visible and permanent impact of greater use of the Trail.

Public transportation—Amtrak to Rutland and White River Junction, (800) 872-7245; Green Mountain Express–Green Mountain Chapter of the American Red Cross community bus from Bennington to Manchester and Bennington to Williamstown, (802) 447-0477, M–F 8–5; Marble Valley Regional Transit community bus serves Manchester, Rutland, and Killington, (802) 773-3244, no Sunday bus service between Rutland and Manchester; local taxi service is also available.

Bears—To prevent future problems and costly interventions, please hang all food from tree limbs at least 12 feet off the ground, and practice Leave No Trace camping.

Seth Warner Shelter (1965)—Sleeps 8. Privy, bear box. Tentsites available. Water source, a brook 150 yards to the left of the shelter, is known to fail in dry years.

Congdon Shelter (1967)—Sleeps 8. Privy. Tentsites available behind the shelter on the ridge. Water source is a brook in front of the shelter. If the brook is dry, follow downstream to larger Stamford Stream.

Vt. 9— East 2.5 miles to *Groceries:* Tift's Trading Post, (802) 442-5222, M–F 7–7, Sa–Su 7-5 (short-term resupply), deli, Heet.
West 5.1 miles to **Bennington, Vt. [P.O. ZIP 05201: M–F 8–5, Sa 9–2; (802) 442-2421]**. Note: Aug 1, 2010, BTown ChowDown for hikers at Merchants Park; free food, free beer, and music by local artists; hosted by local merchants. ■ *Lodging:* Samuel Safford Inne, 722 Main St., (802) 442-5934; Kirkside Motor Lodge, (802) 447-7596, totally smoke-free facility; Bennington Motor Inn, 143 Main St., (802) 442-5479; Paradise Motor Inn, 141 West Main St., (802) 442-8351; Autumn Inn, 924 Main St., (802) 447-7625, $60S, $65D, $10 pick-up at Vt. 9 Trailhead, WiFi, laundry, will hold packages for guests. ■ *Groceries:* Henry's Market; Spice and Nice Natural Foods. ■ *Restaurants:* Rattlesnake Café, open Tu–Su, L/D, Mexican fare; Izabella's B/L; Blue Benn Diner, B/L/D; South Street Café, B/L, WiFi; Your Belly's Deli; Full Bellies;

Bennington
grid = 1 mile
size: 2.4 x 2.4
N

Friendly's. ■ *Internet access:* Bennington Free Library. ■ *Other services:* Town-wide, free use of yellow bikes to ride to area businesses: must be over 18, sign release, and return bike to business from which it was originally borrowed; Family Dollar; coin laundry; banks with ATM; hospital; shoe repair; doctor; dentist; pharmacy; veterinarian; hardware store; and free showers available at Town Recreation Center on Gage Street. ■ *Shuttles:* Bennington Taxi, (802) 442-9052; Green Mountain Express, (802) 447-0477, <www.greenmtncn.org>, M–F, 7:30–5:30, call to arrange $2 shuttle to Route 9 Trailhead and, M–F, four trips daily, $2 service between Bennington and Manchester (see above under "Public transportation").

West 7 miles to **North Bennington, Vt.**, Routes 67 and 7A, and ■ *Lodging:* Knotty Pine Motel, (802) 442-5487, <kpine@knottypinemotel.com>, 130 Northside Dr. , occasional shuttle back to the A.T., rates $79–$96D, $8EAP, pets accepted on limited basis, WiFi, laundry, pool, holds packages only for guests; Best Western, (802) 442-6311, 200 Northside Dr.; Hampton Inn, (802) 440-9862, 51 Hannaford Square. ■ *Groceries:* Price Chopper, Hannaford, ALDI supermarkets (long-term resupply). ■ *Restaurants:* McDonald's, Wendy's, KFC, Taco Bell. ■ *Other services:* Walmart, movie theater.

Melville Nauheim Shelter (1977)—Sleeps 8. Privy. Water source is a stream just north of the spur to the shelter.

Vt. 9 to Kelley Stand Road—Please note: *This section of the Trail is receiving heavy use and experiencing resource damage as a result. GMC encourages hikers to use the designated shelters and campsites. If you must camp between shelters, please follow Leave No Trace practices, and camp 200 feet away from the Trail and all water sources.*

Goddard Shelter (2005)—Sleeps 10. Privy. The shelter has a front porch with a view to the south. Please tent above the shelter, to the west of the A.T. Water source is a spring 50 yards south on the A.T. *To preserve the pristine nature of the spring, no tenting is allowed east of the trail up the mountain.*

Glastenbury Mountain (3,748 ft.). The original firetower was built in 1927 and renovated once in 1970 and again in 2005 by the Long Trail Patrol, USFS, and volunteers from the GMC. The nearby ridges seen from the observation deck are the Berkshires to the south, the Taconics to the west, Mt. Equinox and Stratton Mountain to the north, and Somerset Reservoir, Mt. Snow, and Haystack Mountain to the east. Remains of the old firewarden's cabin and woodstove can be seen to the west of the

Trail, south of the summit. Porcupines are active in this area; take precautions with your gear.

Kid Gore Shelter (1971)—Sleeps 8. Privy. Ecologically fragile area. Tentsites available north on Trail at the former Caughnawaga Shelter site. Water source is a brook near Caughnawaga. An unreliable spring is north of Kid Gore Shelter.

Caughnawaga Tentsites—Tenting only. A 1930s-era shelter was torn down in July 2008.

Story Spring Shelter (1963)—Sleeps 8. Privy. Tentsites. Water source is a spring north on the A.T. 50 yards.

Stratton Mountain—Although he offered a number of variations on the story about how he first thought of the A.T., many believe it was on the slopes of Stratton Mountain that Benton MacKaye first imagined a long-distance trail that would link the high peaks of the Appalachian Mountains. A firetower tops the summit and is open to hikers. A GMC summit caretaker is in the area during the day to interpret the area's cultural and natural history for hikers. No camping or fires on the summit. A side trail at the summit leads east 0.8 mile to a ski gondola at the top of Stratton Ski Area; this hut is not available for hiker use. The gondola has operated in past years, allowing hikers to ride down to Stratton Village, which has a grocery store and restaurants. Please check with the GMC summit caretakers or Stratton Mountain staff to see if the gondola is available for hiker use.

Stratton Pond Shelter (1999)—Sleeps 16. Privy. Overnight fee. Go 0.2 mile west *via* Stratton Pond Trail. No tenting is available at this shelter, but you may tent on platforms at the nearby North Shore Tenting Area; otherwise, within 0.5 mile of the pond, camping is permitted only at designated sites. Shelter has an open first floor, table, bunks, and an enclosed loft. Water source is Bigelow Spring at Stratton Pond about 0.1 mile down the Lye Brook Trail. *No fires at this shelter.*

William B. Douglas Shelter (1956, renovated 2005)—Sleeps 10. Privy. Go 0.5 mile west *via* the Branch Pond Trail. Water source is a spring located south of the shelter.

Spruce Peak Shelter (1983)—Sleeps 14. Privy. This shelter, 0.1 mile west on a spur trail, was constructed by GMC, USFS, and a work crew from the Rutland Community Correctional Center. Water source is a boxed spring 35 yards to the right of the shelter.

Vt. 11 & 30—East 2.1 miles to *Lodging:* Bromley Sun Lodge, (800) 722-2159, rooms starting at $85s/D, tavern fare, indoor pool, game room, WiFi, laundry, Rt. 11 & 30 Trailhead shuttle, and mail drops (nonguest mail-drop fee, $5) to 4216 Vt. 11, Peru, VT 05152.

East 2.5 miles *via* Vt. 11 to *Groceries:* Bromley Market, (802) 824-4444, short-term resupply, open M–Sa 6:30–6, Su 7–2, Ben & Jerry's, home-baked goodies, some hiker supplies, mail drops accepted, 3776 Vt. 11, Peru, VT 05152.

East 2.7 miles *via* Vt. 11 to *Lodging:* Johnny Seesaw's Lodge, (802) 824-5533, <www.johnnyseesaw.com>, $50D, restaurant B/D, lounge, Rt. 11 & 30 Trailhead shuttle, WiFi, pets $10 based on room availability, mail drops accepted at P.O. Box 68 or 3574 Vt. 11, Peru, VT 05152.

East 3.0 miles *via* Vt. 30 to *Lodging:* Bromley View Inn, (877) 633-0308, <www.bromleyviewinn.com>, $85D weekends higher, includes B, pet-friendly, WiFi, call for shuttle to and from Rt. 11 & 30 Trailhead only, mail drops accepted at 522 Vermont 30, Bondville, VT 05340.

West 5.5 miles to **Manchester Center, Vt. [P.O. ZIP 05255: M–F 8–4:30, Sa 9:30–12; (802) 362-3070]**. Pick up mail at the post office on the way into town to avoid an extra walk. The Mountain Goat and EMS are good resources for hiker services in town. *Note:* During the Manchester Horse Show, Jul 9–Aug 15, affordable lodging will be difficult to find in the area. ■ *Hostel:* Gren Mountain House; Jeff and Regina Taussig host hikers at their residence; reservations required, (330) 388-6478; open Jul 5–Sep 7. Bed, shower with towel, laundry, Internet, hiker kitchen, shuttles from town and to Trail; suggested donation, $15/night. No drugs or alcohol. ■ *Lodging:* Sutton's Place, (802) 362-1165, <www.suttonsplacevermont.com>, $55S, $68D, $84T plus tax, WiFi, within walking distance of all services; Avalanche Motel, (802) 362-2622, $75–$95 seasonal rates, pet-friendly, WiFi, Bob's Diner next door for B/L/D; Carriage House Motel, (802) 362-1706, <www.carriagehousemotel.com>, $58–$125PP, no pets, opens in May; Chalet Motel, (800) 343-9900; Red Sled Motel, (802) 362-2161, smoke-free facility; Toll Road Inn, (802) 362-1711. ■ *Groceries:* Price Chopper, Shaw's supermarkets (both long-term resupply). ■ *Restaurants:* Manchester Pizza House, Sirloin Saloon, Mrs. Murphy's Doughnuts and Coffee Shop, Friendly's, Up For Breakfast, Christo's Pizza, Ben & Jerry's Scoop Shop, and several fast-food outlets. ■ *Internet access:* library, Tu–Sa; I Ship Express (below). ■ *Outfitters:* The Mountain Goat, (802)

362-5159, open M–Sa 10–6, Su 11–5, full-service outfitter, fuel by the ounce, custom footbeds and orthotics, mail drops (USPS, UPS & FedEx) accepted at 4886 Main Street, Manchester, VT 05255; Eastern Mountain Sports (EMS), (802) 366-8082, open Su–Th 10–6, F–Sa 10–7, Coleman and alcohol fuel by the ounce. Both are authorized Leki repair firms. ■ *Other services:* coin laundry; bank with ATM; doctor; dentist; pharmacy; veterinarian; movie theater; Manchester Taxi, (802) 362-4118 and (802) 362-0062; Leonard's Taxi, (802) 362-7039; Joe LeBlanc Taxi, (802) 362-7094; Green

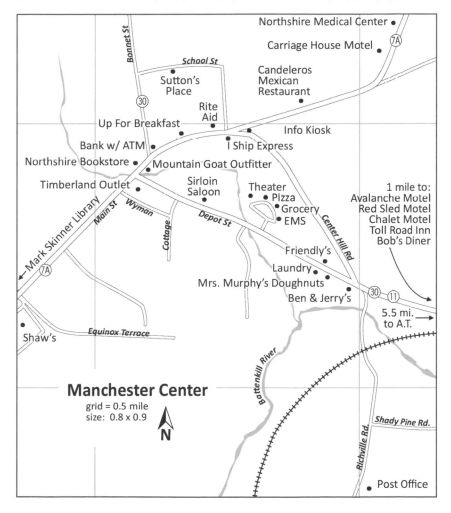

Mountain Express, (802) 447-0477, <www.greenmtncn.org>, $2 bus service between Manchester and Bennington, flag stop across from RiteAid and Shaw's; I Ship Express, 5018 Main St., (802) 362-1652, M-F 9:30–5, Sa 9:30–noon, packing and shipping services; Marble Valley Regional Transportation, $2 bus service between Manchester and Rutland/Killington, with stops along the U.S. 7 corridor (Danby, Wallingford, North Clarendon).

Bromley Shelter (2003)—Sleeps 12. Privy (composting). Tent platforms and campsite are north 0.1 mile. Water is a brook at the end of the spur trail.

Bromley Mountain—An observation tower offers a five-state view. Ski trails lead to Bromley Base Lodge area.

Peru Peak Shelter/Griffith Lake Campsite (1935/1980/2000)—Sleeps 10. Privy. Overnight fee. Originally built by the CCC and renovated twice. Camping permitted only at designated sites within 0.5 mile of Griffith Lake. Water source is a brook near the shelter.

Lost Pond Shelter (2009)—Sleeps 8. Privy. Shelter burned down in 2001, was rebuilt in 2002, burned down again in Nov 2006, rebuilt last year. Tentsites. Water source is nearby stream.

Old Job Shelter (1935/2009)—Sleeps 8. Privy. Built by the CCC. Water source is in front of the shelter at Lake Brook.

Big Branch Shelter (1963)—Sleeps 8. Privy. This site is close to USFS 10 and receives heavy weekend use. Good soaking pools. Water source is Big Branch, located in front of the shelter.

Danby–Landgrove Road—*Light traffic, may be a difficult hitch.* **West** 3.5 miles to **Danby, Vt. [P.O. ZIP 05739: M–F 7:15–12 & 1:15–4, Sa 7:30–10:30; (802) 293-5105].** ■ *Lodging:* Silas Griffith Inn, (802) 293-5567, <www.SilasGriffith.com>, <stay@SilasGriffith.com>, 1891 inn owned by hiker-friendly Brian and Cathy Preble; $149 and up, call for specials, B included; pool, spa, WiFi; laundry service (fee); pet-friendly; shuttle for guests to USFS 10 Trailhead; other shuttles for fee, only if time available; mail drops for guests accepted at 178 South Main St., Danby, VT 05739; Emma's Restaurant on premises, Th–Su 9–9, reservations required, will accommodate dietary restrictions and other meals by prior arrangement. ■ *Groceries:* Mt. Tabor Country

Store, Nichols Store (both short-term resupply). ■ *Restaurants:* Alice's Someday Café, M–F 6:30–3, Sa–Su 7:30–5, closed Tu; Emma's; White Dog Tavern, D, W–Su. **West** 5.5 miles *via* U.S. 7 to *Campground:* Otter Creek Campground, (802) 293-5041; Geogre and Alice Araskiewicz, owners. Tentsites $16, coin showers, camp store with Coleman fuel; possible shuttle service and long-term parking, call for rates. Will hold UPS and USPS packages addressed to the campground at 1136 U.S. 7, Danby, VT 05739.

Note: In 2010, both Lula Tye and Little Rock Pond shelters are scheduled to be torn down and rebuilt as a single shelter at the present Little Rock Pond Tenting Area. Watch for notices on the Trail, and plan accordingly.

Lula Tye Shelter (1962)—Sleeps 8. Privy. Overnight fee. Within 0.5 mile of Little Rock Pond, camping is permitted only at designated sites. Water source (shared with Little Rock Pond Shelter) is a spring 0.3 mile north on the A.T.

Little Rock Pond Tenting Area—Platforms. Privy. Overnight fee.

Little Rock Pond Shelter (1962)—Sleeps 8. Privy. Overnight fee. Within 0.5 mile of the pond, tenting is restricted to designated sites. Water source (shared with Lula Tye Shelter) is a spring 0.3 mile south on the A.T.

Greenwall Shelter (1962/2009)—Sleeps 8. Privy 0.2 mile east on spur trail. Water source is a spring, prone to fail in dry seasons, 200 yards along a trail behind the shelter.

Vt. 140—West 2.8 miles to **Wallingford, Vt. [P.O. ZIP 05773: M–F 8–4:30, Sa 9–12; (802) 446-2140].** ■ *Restaurants:* Mom's Restaurant, B/L, open 'til 2; Sal's Pizza, L/D, Su D only. ■ *Groceries:* Wallingford Country Store & Deli, Cumberland Farms, Midway Mobil Mart (all short-term resupply). ■ *Internet access:* Gilbert Hart Library, Tu–Sa. ■ *Other services:* hardware store (closed Tu), ATM, dentist.

Minerva Hinchey Shelter (1969/2006)—Sleeps 10. Privy. Water source is a spring 50 yards south of shelter; follow "Wada" signs. Tenting area.

Clarendon Gorge—A suspension bridge 0.1 mile from Vt. 103 overlooks a favorite swimming hole for residents. Built in 1974, this bridge is dedicated to the memory of Robert Brugmann, who drowned while trying to cross the swollen Mill River. Swimming in the gorge is hazardous during high water. Watch for broken glass. *No camping permitted in the gorge.*

Vt. 103—West 0.5 mile to *Restaurant:* Whistle Stop Corner Restaurant, B/L/D, closed M. ■ *Other services:* veterinarian; commuter bus MVRT, (802) 773-7244, <www.thebus.com>, Bellows Falls to Rutland, $3, flag stop M–F at approximately 6:30 a.m., 8:30 a.m., 4:30 p.m., 7:30 p.m. (leaves Rutland about 75 minutes before).

West 1 mile to *Groceries:* East Clarendon General Store, (802) 786-0948, short-term resupply, M–Sa 7:30–7, Su 7:30–6, Ben & Jerry's, pay phone, call for mail-drop information.

Clarendon Shelter (1952)—Sleeps 10. Privy. Located near the old Crown Point Military Road that was built during the French and Indian Wars. Water source is a stream 25 yards from the shelter.

Lower Cold River Road—East 1 mile to Pierces' Store, reopened as a community co-operative; short-term resupply, sandwiches and specials, open 10 a.m.; closed M.

Governor Clement Shelter (1929/2009)—Sleeps 12. Privy. Named for former Vermont Governor Percival W. Clement. *Due to its close proximity to a public road, this shelter has a long history of visits by local revellers creating serious problems with vandalism and hiker harassment. For the safety of all hikers, ATC strongly discourages any overnight use of the Gov. Clement Shelter site.* ATC and the Green Mountain Club are working toward a long-term solution for the site. GMC is working with the USFS and the town of Shrewsbury to limit inappropriate use. A forest road leading up to the shelter will be closed between Apr 15 and Sep 15, but the shelter will be accessible by motorized vehicles after then. Move on if you encounter problems. Water source is a stream across the road and north of the shelter.

Cooper Lodge (1939)—Sleeps 16. Privy. This enclosed stone cabin was built by the Vermont Forest Service. Behind the shelter is a 0.2-mile side trail to Killington Peak. Water source is a spring north of shelter on A.T. Tent platforms.

Killington Peak—Reached by a steep 0.2-mile side trail from Cooper Lodge. At 4,235 feet, this is the highest point near the Trail in Vermont and the second-highest peak in the state. The open, rocky summit offers panoramic views, and, on a clear day, you can see the White Mountains of New Hampshire and the Adirondacks of New York. A short side trail leads from the summit to a snack bar and ski lift operated by the Killington ski resort; shops are located at the village reached by the gondola. Gondola operates Jun 27–Sep 1, 10–5, then weekends only, 10–5, until Oct 3; full operation during fall-foliage season. A GMC ridgerunner patrols the Coolidge Range (including Killington and Pico) and may be available to answer natural-history and Trail questions.

Jungle Junction–Sherburne Pass Trail—Named after a 1938 hurricane left behind a "jungle" of blowdowns (and essentially broke the A.T. as a continuous footpath a year after it opened as such). The blue-blazed Sherburne Pass Trail (former A.T.) leads 3.1 miles north to Sherburne Pass on U.S. 4, directly to the Inn at Long Trail (opened in 1938, ironically), and continues north of the inn 0.5 mile to reconnect with the A.T.

Pico Camp (1959)—Sleeps 12. Privy. An enclosed shelter located 0.5 mile east on the Sherburne Pass Trail, the former A.T. Water source is 45 yards north on the Sherburne Pass Trail.

Rutland city watershed: The western flanks of the Coolidge Range comprise a significant portion of the city of Rutland's watershed. Fires are not permitted. Please camp only at designated sites and use facilities provided.

Churchill Scott Shelter (2002)—Sleeps 8. Privy (composting). Tent platform available; water on spur trail downhill behind shelter.

U.S. 4—East 0.9 mile uphill along a busy thoroughfare to ■ *Lodging:* The Inn at Long Trail, (802) 775-7181, closed for innkeeper vacation mid-Apr to mid-Jun. The inn offers discount rooms for hikers with full B; no dogs in the lodge. McGrath's Irish Pub serves L/D. Amenities include laundry facilities, hiker box, outside water spigot, WiFi. Only accepts UPS or Fed Ex packages; send to The Inn at Long Trail, 709 Route 4, Sherburne Pass, Killington, VT 05751. Bus service daily from inn to Rutland. *A safer alternative to the roadwalk in heavy traffic is to cross Route 4 and continue on the A.T. north 1.9 miles to the northern terminus of the Sherburne Pass Trail, which will lead you 0.5 mile south directly to the inn.*

West 0.9 mile to *Lodging:* Edelweiss Motel, (802) 775-5577, on bus route, $59D with B.

West 1.5 miles to *Lodging:* Mendon Mountain View Resort Lodge & Restaurant, (802) 773-4311, on bus route, $45PP, $65D with B, seven hiker rooms available, shuttle to Trail in morning and pick-up from the Trailhead if available, free Internet, WiFi, laundry services, will hold packages mailed to 78 U.S. 4, Killington, VT 05751.

West 7.5 miles to the city of **Rutland, Vt. [P.O. 05701: M–F 8–5, Sa 8–12; (802) 773-0222]**, with all major services and chain motels. ■ *Hostels:* Back Home Again Café, (802) 775-9800 or (802) 773-0160, <www.twelvetribes.com>, check-in at restaurant, closed Sa, call to reach a member to gain access, work for stay or donation, common room with kitchen facilities, separate bunk rooms for men and women, pets stay outside, located near downtown Rutland Transit Center, mail drops accepted at 23 Center Street, Rutland, VT 05701; A-Towns Place, work for stay or suggested donation $20 (bunk), $5 (tenting space), short-term resupply, shuttles to/from all A.T. and L.T. trailheads (free for guests), laundry (free for guests), Internet access, mail drops accepted at 335 Grove St., Brandon, VT 05733, (803) 465-0136, <azchipka@mac.com>. ■ *Restaurants:* Back Home Again Café, L/D, only organic food, closed Sa; Applebee's; A Crust Above; Pizza Hut; Sal's Italian Restaurant; Sirloin Saloon; Tokyo House; Kong Chow; Gill's Delicatessen. ■ *Outfitters:* Mountain Travelers Outdoor Shop, (802) 775-0814, <www.mtntravelers.com>, 147 Woodstock Ave., with backpacking equipment and supplies, fuel by the ounce, open M–S 10–6, Su 12–5; The Great Outdoors, (802) 775-9989, <www.joejonessports.com>, 219 Woodstock Ave., general sporting-goods store with backpacking equipment; Simon the Tanner, (802) 282-4016, <www.simonthetanner.com>, 21 Center St., M–Th 11–9, F 11–3, closed Sa, Su 12–7, footwear, clothing, fuel, backpacking items. Dick's Sporting Goods at Green Mountain Shopping Plaza and Eastern Mountain Sports at Diamond Run Mall both can be reached *via* local MVRT bus. ■ *Internet access:* Rutland Free Library. ■ *Bus service:* MVRT bus ($2 per ride) is available from Killington to Rutland; the bus can be flagged anywhere along U.S. 4. The bus travels from downtown Rutland Transit Center to Killington and back approximately once every 2 hours, leaving Rutland beginning at 7:15 a.m. until 5:15 p.m. No bus service on Sundays, and no service to White River Junction. ■ *Train service:* Amtrak provides daily train service on the Ethan Allen Express, (800) USA-RAIL, from Rutland to Albany and New York City. Call for reservations and to confirm arrival and departure times, as they are constantly changing. Amtrak service on the Vermonter is also available at White River Junction, 35 miles east. ■ *Other services:* Walmart; Rutland Regional Medical Center Hospital; veterinarian; Rutland Taxi, (802) 236-3133; All Occasion Transportation, (802) 236-1966.

The Rutland Long Trail Festival will be held Aug 7, 2010, at the Vermont Fair-grounds; <www.longtrailfestivalvt.com>.

Maine Junction–Willard Gap. The L.T. continues north 167.8 miles to Canada, while the A.T. diverges to the east toward New Hampshire and Maine.

Tucker-Johnson Shelter (1969/2009)—Sleeps 8. Privy. Located on the L.T. 0.4 mile north of Maine Junction. Water source is nearby Eagle Square Brook.

Vt. 100—The A.T. passes through Gifford Woods State Park, (802) 775-5354, with shelters, tentsites, and bathhouse visible from the Trail; office has ice cream and soda machines inside. ■ *Camping:* shelters $21–$23; tentsites $14–$16 up to 4 people, cabin $42 for 4 people, limited primitive sites $4, coin-operated showers 50¢, water spigot, pay phone, restroom located at the park. Space fills up quickly during the fall "leaf season."

East 0.6 mile to **Killington, Vt. [P.O. ZIP 05751: M–F 8:30–4:30, Sa 8:30–12; (802) 775-4247].** ■ *Lodging:* Sherburne-Killington Motel, (802) 773-9535, summer rates Su–F $62D, Sa $72D, fall-foliage and winter rates higher, WiFi, Internet access. ■ *Groceries:* Deli at Killington Corners (short-term resupply), 6:30 a.m.–7 p.m. daily, excellent sandwiches, daily hot-meal specials, and ATM.

West 6 miles to **Pittsfield, Vt. [P.O. ZIP 05762: M–F 8–12 & 2–4:30, Sa 8:30–11:30; (802) 746-8953].** ■ *Hostel:* Amee Farm Hostel, (419) 277-3070, $20PP/night, farm work for stay optional (milking cows, weeding garden, *etc.*); shower; laundry; Internet access; package pick-up from P.O.; shuttle to/from Trail; common room with kitchen included; no pets or illegal drugs. ■ *Groceries:* Original General Store (short-term resupply), daily hot-meal special, great food and large portions, WiFi, ATM; Pittstop Gas Station and Market, soft-serve ice cream. ■ *Other services:* yoga studio; kayak and tubing rentals.

Kent Pond—on A.T. *Lodging:* Mountain Meadows Lodge, (802) 775-1010, <www.mountainmeadowslodge.com>, hikers welcome, owner is a hiker; $59 includes B, reasonably priced L/D; laundry (fee); free use of computer, dogs permitted outside; hikers not staying at the lodge can have a reasonably priced B/L/D; outdoor pool, hot tub, sauna, kayaking; hiker box inside; mail drops to 285 Thundering Brook Rd., Killington, VT 05751.

East 0.3 mile on side cross-country ski trail. *Outfitter:* Base Camp Outfitters, (802) 775-0166, on bus route; <www.basecambvt.com>; backpacking euipment, clothing, and supplies, freeze-dried food, fuel, inside hiker box; accepts mail drops to 2363 U.S. 4, Killington, VT 05751. Owners provide safe pack storage for hikers taking the bus into Rutland.

Thundering Falls—This 2007-8 relocation, which took 30 years from conception to complete, eliminated the road walk on Thundering Brook Road and River Road and added views of Thundering Falls and the Ottauquechee River. The new path in the woods descends through northern-hardwood forest to the base of high Thundering Falls and then passes through the open Ottauquechee River floodplain. A new wheelchair-accessible bridge built by the Green Mountain Club and financed by ATC and the National Park Service crosses the river.

Stony Brook Shelter (1997)—Sleeps 8. Privy. Water source is brook 100 yards north of shelter on A.T.

Side Trail to the Lookout—One of the few views between Killington Peak and New Hampshire. Follow side trail 0.2 mile west from A.T. to a private cabin. Use care on ladder that leads up to an observation deck. No water available. The owners permit its use *as a viewpoint* by hikers; please be responsible to ensure that this privilege continues.

Wintturi Shelter (1994)—Sleeps 8. Privy. Frame shelter. Water source is a spring to the right of the shelter.

 Vt. 12—Please respect landowners at this road crossing by not camping in woods or fields near Vt. 12.

East 4.4 miles to **Woodstock, Vt. [P.O. ZIP 05091: M–F 8:30–5, Sa 9–12; (802) 457-1323].** Services include several motels and inns, grocery (long-term resupply), restaurants, bank with ATM, doctor, dentist, pharmacy, and movie theater open F–Su. *Internet access:* library, M–Sa.

West 0.2 mile to *Groceries:* On the Edge farm stand, open daily in summer 10–6, Su 10–5; seasonal veggies, fruit, cold drinks, ice cream, pies, cheese, smoked meat, jerky.

Dartmouth Outing Club—DOC maintains the 75.2 miles from Vt. 12 to Kinsman Notch in New Hampshire. Correspondence should be sent to DOC, P.O. Box 9, Hanover, NH 03755; (603) 646-2428; <www.dartmouth.edu/student/doc>. The DOC no longer uses orange-and-black paint for blazes, although many are still visible. The DOC does continue to use orange and black on trail signs.

 Woodstock Stage Road (Bartlett Brook Road)—East 1 mile to **South Pomfret, Vt. [P.O. ZIP 05067: M–F 8–1 & 2–4:45, Sa 8:30–11:30; (802) 457-1147].** *Groceries:* Teago General Store (short-term resupply), M–Sa 7–6, Su 8–4, with deli sandwiches and P.O. inside the store.

 Cloudland Road—West 0.2 mile to *Groceries:* Cloudland Farm Country Market, <www.cloudlandfarm.com>; water, cold drinks, beef jerky, ice cream. This operating farm is run by Bill and Cathy Emmons. Tenting and overnight stays may be available on a work-for-stay or donation basis. The Old Cloudland Shelter on their property is always available.

Thistle Hill Shelter (1995)—Sleeps 8. Privy. The Cloudland privy was moved to Thistle Hill, partly with ALDHA's help. Water source is a stream near the shelter.

 Vt.14—*Groceries:* West Hartford Village Store and snack bar, (802) 280-1713, short-term resupply, is on the A.T., full B/L, M–Sa 7–7, Su 8–5, information about nearby camping.

East 0.3 mile to **West Hartford, Vt. [P.O. ZIP 05084: M–F 7:30–11:30 & 1–4:45, Sa 7:30–10:15; (802) 295-6293].** Window at post office closes 15 minutes before lobby. *Internet access:* library.

East 6 miles to White River Junction, a large town with all services. Amtrak provides daily train service on the Vermonter, (800) USA-RAIL. *Hostel:* Hotel Coolidge (Hostelling International), (802) 295-3118, (800) 622-1124, <www.hotelcoolidge.com>, <info@hotelcoolidge.com>, 39 South Main St., White River Junction, VT 05001; nonmember rates: twin bed $35s $55D, full bed $55s/D; member rates: twin bed $25s, full bed $45s $55D; private rooms available; laundry, WiFi; walk to restaurants, banks, and stores.

Happy Hill Shelter (1998)—Sleeps 8. Privy. The oldest A.T. shelter (built in 1918, before the A.T.) was torn down, then burned; the debris was carried out. In 1998, a new shelter was built about 0.2 mile north of the original. ALDHA members worked on this project after the 1997 Gathering. Water source is the brook near the shelter.

U.S. 5/Norwich, Vt. [P.O. ZIP 05055: M–F 8:30–5, Sa 9–12; (802) 649-1608]—East 0.25 mile to *Lodging:* Norwich Inn, (802) 649-1143, <www.norwichinn.com>, under reconstruction and only partially open; call for rates. Built in 1791 as a stage-coach inn, reportedly the inspiration for the "Newhart" TV show. ■ *Restaurants:* Norwich Inn, Tu–Su B/L/D, Su brunch. ■ *Groceries:* Dan & Whits (long-term resupply), open daily 7–9, a sprawling, eclectic general store; Allechante Bakery and Café, M–F 7:30–6, Sa 7:30–5. ■ *Internet access:* library. ■ *Other services:* bank with ATM.

New Hampshire

Miles from Katahdin	Features	Services	Elev.	Miles from Springer
442.3	Connecticut River, N.H/–Vt. State Line	R	380	1,736.8
441.8	N.H. 10, Dartmouth College **Hanover, NH 03755**	R, PO, C, G, M, L, O, D, V, f, @ (E–2m L, cl; 16m H, f) (W–1.5m cl; 2.5m L)	520	1,737.3
441.1	N.H. 120	R	490	1,738.0
440.3	**Velvet Rocks Shelter...** *7.4mS; 9.5mN*	S (N–0.2m w)	1,040	1,738.8
439.8	Ledyard Spring	W–0.4m w	1,200	1,739.3
437.3	Trescott Rd	R	490	1,741.8
435.9	Etna-Hanover Center Rd	R (E–0.7m G, H)	845	1,743.2
433.4	Three Mile Rd	R	1,350	1,745.7
433.2	Mink Brook	w	1,320	1,745.9
431.6	Moose Mtn (South Peak)		2,290	1,747.5
430.8	**Moose Mtn Shelter...** *9.5mS; 5.9mN*	S, w	1,850	1,748.3
428.9	South Fork, Hewes Brook	w	1,100	1,750.2
427.6	Goose Pond Rd	R	952	1,751.5
425.6	Holts Ledge		1,930	1,753.5
425.1	**Trapper John Shelter...** *5.9mS; 6.9mN*	W–0.2m S, C, w	1,345	1,754.0
424.2	Dartmouth Skiway, Lyme-Dorchester Rd **Lyme, NH 03768**	R (W–3.2m PO, G, M, L)	880	1,754.9
422.2	Lyme–Dorchester Rd	R, w	850	1,756.9
418.5	Smarts Mtn Tentsite	C, w	3,200	1,760.6
418.4	**Firewarden's Cabin** and Fire Tower... *6.9mS; 5.6mN*	S, w	3,230	1,760.7
414.5	South Jacob's Brook		1,450	1,764.6
413.1	**Hexacuba Shelter...** *5.6mS; 7.5mN*	w (E–0.3m S)	1,980	1,766.0
411.5	Side trail to Mt. Cube (north summit)		2,911	1,767.6
408.2	N.H. 25A **Wentworth, NH 03282**	R (E–4.3m PO, G, L) (W–1.9m C, G)	900	1,770.9

Miles from Katahdin	Features	Services	Elev.	Miles from Springer
406.6	Cape Moonshine Rd	R (E–1m C, sh)	1,480	1,772.5
406.0	**Ore Hill Shelter**... *7.5mS; 8.7mN*	E–0.1m S, w	1,720	1,773.1
403.4	N.H. 25C **Warren, NH 03279**	R (E–4m PO, G, M, D, cl, @)	1,550	1,775.7
400.9	Mt. Mist		2,200	1,778.2
398.5	N.H. 25 **Glencliff, NH 03238**	R (E–0.4m PO, H, sh, cl, f)	1,000	1,780.6
397.4	**Jeffers Brook Shelter**... *8.7mS; 6.9mN*	S, w	1,350	1,781.7
392.8	Mt. Moosilauke		4,802	1,786.3
390.5	**Beaver Brook Shelter/ Campsite**... *6.9mS; 9mN*	C, S, w	3,750	1,788.6
389.0	N.H. 112, Kinsman Notch **North Woodstock, NH 03262; Lincoln, NH 03251**	R (E–0.3m w; 5m PO, G, M, L, cl, f; 6m PO)	1,870	1,790.1
384.4	Mt. Wolf (East Peak)		3,478	1,794.7
381.5	**Eliza Brook Shelter/ Campsite**... *9mS; 4.1mN*	C, S, w	2,400	1,797.6
379.0	South Kinsman Mtn		4,358	1,800.1
378.1	North Kinsman Mtn		4,293	1,801.0
377.5	+**Kinsman Pond Shelter/ Campsite**... *4.1mS; 15.3mN*	E–0.1m C, S, w	3,750	1,801.6
375.6	+Lonesome Lake Hut	L, M, w	2,760	1,803.5
372.7	I-93, U.S. 3, Franconia Notch, Lafayette Place Campground **North Woodstock, NH 03262; Lincoln, NH 03251**	R (E–0.7m sh; 0.8m M, ph; 5.8m, 7.3m PO, G, M, L, cl, f) (W–2.1m C, G, sh; 8m G, L, M, sh, @)	1,450	1,806.4
370.1	+Liberty Springs Tentsite	C, w	3,870	1,809.0
368.0	Little Haystack Mtn		4,800	1,811.1
367.3	Mt. Lincoln		5,089	1,811.8
366.3	Mt. Lafayette, +Greenleaf Hut *via* Greenleaf Trail	(W–0.2m w; 1.1m L, M, w)	5,260	1,812.8
363.5	Garfield Pond		3,860	1,815.6
362.8	Mt. Garfield		4,500	1,816.3

Miles from Katahdin	Features	Services	Elev.	Miles from Springer
362.4	+**Garfield Ridge Shelter/ Campsite**... *15.3mS; 6.4mN*	W–0.1m C, S, w	3,900	1,816.7
359.7	+Galehead Hut	L, M, w	3,800	1,819.4
358.9	South Twin Mtn, North Twin Spur		4,902	1,820.2
356.9	Mt.Guyot; +**Guyot Shelter/ Campsite** *via* Bondcliff Trail... *6.4mS; 9.8mN*	E–0.8m C, S, w	4,580	1,822.2
353.9	Zeacliff		4,084	1,825.2
352.7	+Zealand Falls Hut	L, M, w	2,630	1,826.4
347.9	+**Ethan Pond Shelter/ Campsite**... *9.8mS; 20.5mN*	C, S, w	2,860	1,831.2
345.0	U.S. 302, Crawford Notch **Bartlett, NH 03812**	R (E–1.8m C, cl, sh; 3m C, G, L, sh; 10m PO) (W–1m M; 3.7m L, M, sh; 8.4m G, L, @)	1,277	1,834.1
344.9	Saco River		1,277	1,834.2
343.1	Webster Cliffs		3,350	1,836.0
341.7	Mt. Webster		3,910	1,837.4
340.3	Mt. Jackson		4,052	1,838.8
338.6	+Mizpah Spring Hut, +Nauman Tentsite	C, L, M, w	3,800	1,840.5
337.8	Mt. Pierce (Mt.Clinton)		4,312	1,841.3
336.9	Spring	w	4,350	1,842.2
335.6	Spring	w	4,480	1,843.5
335.0	Mt. Franklin		5,004	1,844.1
333.9	+Lakes of the Clouds Hut /0 /.⁰⁰	L, M, w	5,012	1,845.2
332.5	Mt. Washington, Mt. Washington Auto Rd **Mt. Washington, NH 03589 (not recommended)**	R, PO, M (8m *via* Auto Road to N.H. 16)	6,288	1,846.6
332.5	Tuckerman Ravine Trail to +**Hermit Lake Shelter** and Pinkham Notch	(E–2m S; 4.2m R, G, M, L, sh, f)	6,288	1,846.6
329.0	Edmands Col	w	4,938	1,850.1

Miles from Katahdin	Features	Services	Elev.	Miles from Springer
328.3	Israel Ridge Path to +**The Perch Shelter/ Campsite**... *20.5mS; 23.5mN*	W−0.9m C, S, w	4,313	1,850.8
327.7	Thunderstorm Jct, Trail to +RMC Crag Camp Cabin; Lowe's Path to Mt. Adams & +RMC Gray Knob Cabin	W−1.1m, 1.2m C, S, w	5,500	1,851.4
326.8	+Madison Spring Hut *20.00*	L, M, w	4,800	1,852.3
328.6	Valley Way Tentsite	W−0.6m C, w	3,900	1,850.5
326.3	Mt. Madison		5,366	1,852.8
323.8	Osgood Tentsite	C, w	2,540	1,855.3
323.0	West Branch, Peabody River	w	2,300	1,856.1
321.1	Low's Bald Spot		2,860	1,858.0
319.0	N.H. 16, Pinkham Notch, Pinkham Notch Visitor Center +Joe Dodge Lodge *58.00*	R, G, M, L, sh, f (E−16m L, O; 18m G, M, L, O, D) (W−4m AMC Camp Dodge; 11m Gorham, N.H., see below)	2,050	1,860.1
316.0	Wildcat Mtn, Peak D Tower		3,990	1,863.1
314.0	Wildcat Mtn, Peak A		4,422	1,865.1
313.1	Carter Notch, +Carter Notch Hut	E−0.2m L, w	3,350	1,866.0
312.4	Spring	w	4,700	1,866.7
311.9	Carter Dome		4,832	1,867.2
310.5	Zeta Pass	w	3,890	1,868.6
309.7	South Carter Mtn		4,458	1,869.4
308.4	Middle Carter Mtn		4,610	1,870.7
307.8	North Carter Mtn		4,539	1,871.3
305.9	+**Imp Shelter/Campsite**... *23.5mS; 6.3mN*	W−0.2m C, S, w	3,250	1,873.2
303.8	Mt. Moriah		4,049	1,875.3
299.8	**Rattle River Shelter/ Campsite**... *6.3mS; 13.7mN*	S, w	1,260	1,879.3
297.9	U.S. 2 **Gorham, NH 03581**	R, w (W−1.8m H, C, M, cl, sh; 3.6m PO, H, G, M, L, O, cl, f, @; 8m D)	780	1,881.2

Miles from Katahdin	Features	Services	Elev.	Miles from Springer
297.6	Androscoggin River	R	750	1,881.5
297.4	Hogan Rd	R	760	1,881.7
296.4	Brook	w	1,350	1,882.7
294.3	Mt Hayes, Mahoosuc Trail		2,555	1,884.8
292.1	Cascade Mtn		2,631	1,887.0
291.0	Trident Col Tentsite	W–0.1m C, w	2,020	1,888.1
288.3	Dream Lake	w	2,600	1,890.8
286.8	Moss Pond	w	2,630	1,892.3
286.1	**Gentian Pond Shelter/ Campsite...** 13.7mS; 5.5mN	C, S, w	2,166	1,893.0
283.3	Mt. Success		3,565	1,895.8
281.4	N.H.–Maine State Line		2,972	1,897.7

+ Fee charged   *RMC = Randolph Mountain Club*

At Hanover, southbounders will have already experienced the White Mountains. Northbounders should gear up for the conditions ahead.

Although this is considered one of the most challenging states, it is also one of the most rewarding. As the trees get shorter and the views get longer, you've entered the krummholz zone, where trees are stunted with flag-like tops due to stress from the wind and cold. Boreal bogs are home to local carnivorous plant species, sundew and pitcher plants. Hardy, yet delicate alpine flowers—Labrador tea, bunchberry, mountain sandwort, and cloudberry—may be in bloom when you pass through. Spruce grouse, winter wren, dark-eyed junco, and the white-throated sparrow will greet you along the way.

Much of the Trail is above timberline, where the temperature may change very suddenly; snow is possible in any season. Snow falls on Mt. Washington during every month of the year. High winds and dense fog are common. Most shelters and campsites charge a fee.

Tenting is prohibited within 200 feet of the A.T. from the Connecticut River (Vermont state line) to the summit of Mt. Moosilauke.

Many water sources in southern New Hampshire are not always reliable, including sources at, or adjacent to, shelters.

Hanover, N.H. [P.O. ZIP 03755: M–F 8:30–5, Sa 8:30–12, package pick-up opens at 7 a.m.; (603) 643-4544]—Home of Dartmouth College. The A.T. passes through the center of Hanover, and most services are along the route of the Trail (see map). At the center of town and the Dartmouth Green, a blue-blazed side trail leads (Trailwest) to Robinson Hall and the office of the Dartmouth Outing Club (DOC) in Room 113, (603) 646-2428, <www.dartmouth.edu/~doc/>. DOC has student volunteers (DOCtours), Su–Th 2–6, phone, and Internet access. This is a good place to begin in town. The college does not allow nonstudents to stay in student housing. Dartmouth College security has reported problems with improper use of college facilities and buildings by hikers; hikers must not enter dormitories, offices, laundry rooms, _etc._, without permission or try to sleep overnight in those locations, including the DOC building. The locker rooms and showers in the DOC basement are not public. Neither the college nor the DOC is responsible for hikers who leave their packs or other belongings unattended on college property. Public (on-street) consumption of alcohol is illegal in the downtown area. ■ _Camping:_ Tenting is permitted in the woods, past the soccer fields, _if you are 200 feet from the Trail and on Forest Service land._ ■ _Groceries:_ Hanover Food Co-op (long-term resupply), bulk and natural foods; Irvings, CVS Pharmacy/Food Shop, and Stinson's Village Store (all short-term resupply). ■ _Restaurants:_ 5 Olde Nugget Alley Restaurant; Ramunto's Pizza; Everything But Anchovies, B/L/D; Lou's Bakery & Restaurant, B/L; Thayer Hall, the Dartmouth dining hall, B/L/D; C&A Pizza; Quizno's; Gusano's Mexican Restaurant; Ben & Jerry's Scoop Shop; Boloco; Bagel Basement; India Queen; Dirt Cowboy Café; The Canoe Club Restaurant; Murphy's on the Green. ■ _Internet access:_ Howe Public Library and the DOC. ■ _Outfitters:_ Mountain Goat, 68 S. Main St., (603) 676-7240; Hanover Outdoors, (603) 643-1263, <www.hanoveroutdoors.com>, M–Sa 9–6, Su 10–4, clothing, outdoor equipment, and flyfishing, accepts hikers' packages mailed to 17½ Lebanon St.; Zimmermann's, sells primarily North Face clothing and packs; Omer and Bob's Sport Shop. EMS, (603) 298-7716, and L.L.Bean Outlet, (603) 298-6975, both in West Lebanon—take "Orange" bus route, switch to "Red," and ask the driver to let you off at the Powerhouse Mall. ■ _Other services:_ True Value Hardware, Coleman fuel, denatured alcohol; College Cleaners on Allen Street offers "wash, dry, and fold"; One Clean Place, 1.5 miles north on N.H. 10 on "Brown" bus route, has self-service laundry; bookstores; dentist; doctor; hospital; movie theater; optician; banks with ATM; pharmacy; barber shop; Hanover Veterinary Clinic, (603) 643-3313, (603) 643-4829 after hours; Hanover Hot Tubs. ■ _Bus service:_ Advance Transit is a

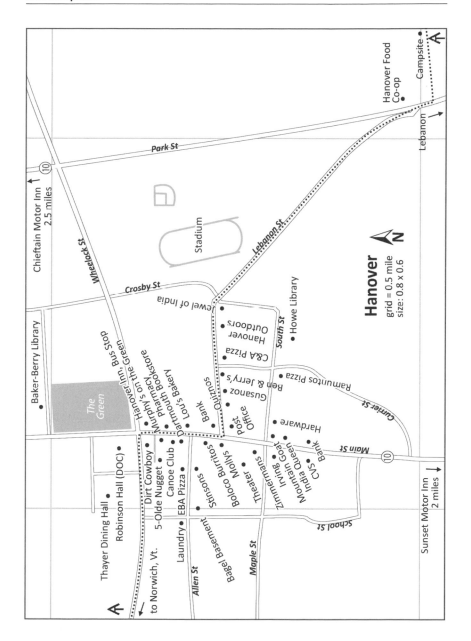

Hanover
grid = 0.5 mile
size: 0.8 x 0.6

local bus service, 6 a.m. to 6 p.m., M–F only. Most routes are free; can be picked up outside the Hanover Inn; offers transportation throughout Hanover and to White River Junction, Vt. (where there is an Amtrak station), Lebanon, and West Lebanon, with all major services. Bus to West Lebanon leaves from bookstore on Main Street. Bus schedules available in the bookstore. Vermont Transit Bus, (800) 552-8737, provides service from Hanover to Boston. ■ *Long-term parking:* available for hikers in "A" lot, east of campus. Call parking operations, (603) 646-2204, for directions and to make arrangements. ■ *Shuttles:* Big Yellow Taxi, (603) 643-8294; Apex Transportation, "Stray Kat" '96 & '06, (603) 252-8294.

East (south)—2.0 miles to *Lodging:* Sunset Motor Inn, (603) 298-8721, on N.H. 10, on the "Orange" bus route, $65–$95, no pets, no smoking, CATV, continental B, shuttle and laundry may be available if you ask the owners; Super 8 Motel in White River Junction, Vt., (802) 295-7577, on the "Orange" bus route; Days Inn in Lebanon, N.H., (603) 448-5070, on the "Blue" bus route.

West (north)—2.5 miles to *Lodging:* Chieftain Motor Inn, (603) 643-2550, on the "Brown" bus route (bus stops within 0.5 mile), $75–$100, pets $35, no smoking, CATV, continental B.

East 16 miles to Canaan, N.H., and *Hostel:* A.T. Hillton, (603) 252-8295 (hostel/ shuttle), <apexlake@hotmail.com>, 365 Choate Rd., Canaan, NH 03741, owned by "Stray Kat." Hostel open Jun 1–Sep 30 with year-round shuttle services; bunkhouse $30PP includes bed with linens, shower with towel, and round-trip shuttle; please call ahead to make arrangements for either 11:30 a.m. or 4:30 p.m. shuttle in front of DOC/Robinson Hall at Dartmouth; other Trailhead shuttles available. Amenities include TV, radio, taped movies, BBQ grill, microwave, refrigerator, meals, pizza, soft drinks, Coleman and denatured alcohol. Pets are welcome but not allowed inside. Laundry $3. Fee for additional shuttles to town for movie theaters, P.O., groceries, and health club with pool and hot tub. Limit 15 people per night with three-day limit unless there is a medical problem or injury. Mail drops accepted. Parking $3/ day, $15/week, $50/month.

Velvet Rocks Shelter (1980s/2006)—Sleeps 6. Privy. On blue-blazed loop trail with access from the north and south. Water source is Ledyard Spring, located along the northern access trail. During dry periods, hikers may want to bring water from town.

Etna–Hanover Center Road—East 0.7 mile to ■ *Groceries:* Etna General Store (limited resupply), (603) 643-1655, M–F 6 a.m.–7 p.m., Sa 8–7, Su 8–6, snacks, sandwiches, cold drinks, stove fuels, hot food weekdays. ■ *Hostel:* Tigger's Treehouse

Hostel, (603) 643-9213. Please call at least one day in advance. Showers and laundry available, shuttle into town for restaurants and resupply, dogs welcome. "Not a party place; this is our home and not a business." Donations welcomed.

Moose Mountain Shelter (2004)—Sleeps 8. Privy. New log shelter built entirely with hand tools by DOC. Water source is on the A.T. north of the shelter—follow loop trail to end.

Trapper John Shelter (1990s)—Sleeps 6. Privy uses an old chair. Tentsites. Water source is a brook 15 yards to the left of the shelter.

 Lyme–Dorchester Road—Water and ice cream at blue house just west of trail; sign on Trail after road intersection.

West 3.2 miles to **Lyme, N.H. [P.O. ZIP 03768: M–F 8–12 & 2:30–4:45, Sa 8–11:30; (603) 795-4421]**. ■ *Lodging:* Dowd's Country Inn B&B, (603) 795-4712; weekdays $95S, $125D; weekends $115S, $145D; $105S weekdays includes B and afternoon tea. One or two rooms are pet-friendly. Internet access. Reservations and a minimum two-night stay most likely are required for weekends (F and Sa). Ask about possible weekday discounts. Trail pick-up may be possible. ■ *Restaurant:* Stella's Italian Kitchen & Market, L/D M–Sa, closed Su. ■ *Other services:* Country store and deli (short-term resupply), open daily; banks with ATM; Nichols Hardware store; and pay phone.

Smarts Mountain Tentsites—Maintained by DOC; cleared area for three tents; privy; water from Mike Murphy Spring (see next entry).

Smarts Mountain Firewarden Cabin—Sleeps 8. Privy. The cabin, built by the N.H. Forest Service, is now maintained as shelter by DOC. Panoramic views from the abandoned firetower on Smarts Mountain summit. Water source is Mike Murphy Spring 0.2 mile north of cabin on blue-blazed Daniel Doan Trail.

Hexacuba Shelter (1989)—Sleeps 8. Privy (penta-style). Constructed by DOC. Tentsites. Water source is an unreliable stream at the blue-blaze junction to the shelter. Alternative source is 0.3 mile south on the A.T. at North Jacobs Brook.

 N.H. 25A—**East** 0.1 mile to lake with beach for swimming; 4.8 miles to **Went-worth, N.H. [P.O. ZIP 03282: M–F 7:15–1 & 3–5, Sa 7:15–12; (603) 764-9444]**. ■ *Groceries:* Shawnee's General Store (long-term resupply), (603) 764-5553, M–Th 5 a.m.–8 p.m., F 5–9, Sa 6–9, Su 7–8; outside pay phone.

West 1.9 miles to *Groceries:* Mt. Cube Sugar House & Farm House, (603) 353-4814, owned and operated by the Thomson family. Fruit stand open 8:30–dusk; home-made snacks, maple products, cold drinks, seasonal fruits and vegetables. Hikers may be allowed to stay in the hay barn, known as the Governor's Mansion. No cooking or open flames allowed in hay barn; Sugar House facilities available in bad weather, with permission.

Cape Moonshine Road—East 1 mile to *Work for stay:* Dancing Bones Village, an independent community that offers hikers tentsites, showers, and sometimes meals in exchange for light work.

Ore Hill Shelter (2000)—Sleeps 8. Privy (medieval-style). Water source is a spring on the path 100 yards in front of the shelter.

N.H. 25C—East 4 miles to **Warren, N.H. [P.O. ZIP 03279: M–F 7:30–1 & 2:30–5, Sa 8–11:30; (603) 764-5733].** ■ *Groceries:* Warren Village Market (long-term resupply), open daily and 6:30 a.m.–8 p.m. (7 on Su), ATM, pay phone. ■ *Restaurant:* Calamity Jane's, B/L/D, (603) 764-5288, open M 6 a.m.–2 p.m., Tu–F 6 a.m.–8 p.m., Sa 6–11 p.m., Su 8–7. ■ *Other services:* hardware store, doctor, and laundry. See Warren's "Mystery Missile"—according to the *Boston Globe,* it is one of New England's eight most bizarre roadside attractions.

N.H. 25—East 0.4 mile to **Glencliff, N.H. [P.O. ZIP 03238: M–F 7–10 & 2–5, Sa 7–1; (603) 989-5154],** with pay phone located on south side of white building at driveway entrance to P.O. This is a prudent mail drop for northbounders to pick up cold-weather gear before entering the high country of the White Mountains. ■ *Hostel:* The Hikers Welcome Hostel, (603) 989-0040, P.O. Box 25, 1396 N.H. Route 25, located at the base of Mt. Moosilauke, across the street from the post office; $21 hostel/bunks includes shower and laundry; $15s/$23D tenting includes shower and laundry; hot outdoor shower $2.50; laundry, $2.50 wash, $2.50 dryer; hiker snacks, denatured alcohol and Coleman fuel by the ounce, free wireless Internet, and shuttles. Resupply, ATM, and restaurants in Warren (5 miles; see above).

Oliverian Brook—The brook can be a difficult ford after rain. Be careful.

Jeffers Brook Shelter (1970s)—Sleeps 10. Privy. Located on a spur trail. Water source is Jeffers Brook, located in front of the shelter.

The White Mountains—One of the most impressive sections of the A.T., the Whites offer magnificent views with miles of above-treeline travel. Extra caution should be exercised while above treeline, due to rapidly changing weather and the lack of protection from it. Carry cold-weather gear, even in the middle of summer. Winter weather, including sleet, snow, and ice, is possible on these high ridges year-round. Each year, carelessness ends in death for a few visitors to the Whites. Pay close attention at Trail intersections. The Appalachian Mountain Club (AMC) maintains many trails that cross the A.T., and the A.T. route is commonly referred to on signs and in guidebooks by the name of the local trail it follows, such as "Franconia Ridge Trail." (And, to add to the confusion, sections above treeline from Mizpah Hut to Madison Hut are often marked with yellow blazes on rock cairns, to stand out in the snow.) When above treeline, stay on the Trail. This alpine zone is home to very fragile plants. One misplaced bootstep can destroy them.

Backcountry regulations—Each summer, AMC serves tens of thousands of backpackers and campers at its backcountry shelters and campsites in the White Mountain National Forest. To prevent the Whites from being "loved to death," the USFS, in conjunction with AMC and the New Hampshire state parks agency, established a strict set of backcountry rules and regulations for the White Mountains. Please follow the rules. Hikers should be aware of all pertinent rules and regulations pertaining to camping in these areas and should not be surprised if they are rigorously enforced by ridgerunners and rangers. This especially applies to those who choose to camp immediately adjacent to huts, shelters, caretaker campsites, and road crossings. Hikers who ignore posted warnings may well receive hefty tickets. You will encounter forest protection areas (FPAs), where camping and fires are prohibited. The following regulations apply in those areas: no camping above treeline (where trees are less than eight feet high); no camping within 0.25 mile of huts, shelters, or tentsites except at the facility itself; no camping within 200 feet of the Trail. Groups of 6 or more should contact AMC Group Notification System, <www.outdoors.org>, (603) 466-2721 x8150, so it can effectively manage all large groups that stay at AMC sites. AMC-managed sites can accommodate groups of up to 10. USFS parking fees are established throughout the Whites; be prepared to pay if you park at Forest Service trailheads.

Mt. Moosilauke—The north side of Mt. Moosilauke is slick, particularly in rain. Be careful! Sections use rebar, rock steps, and wooden blocks for footing. For northbounders, it is the first mountain above treeline. For southbounders, the meadow at the base of the southern side is the first pastureland they encounter on the A.T. From the summit, Franconia Ridge, as well as the rest of the Whites, can be seen to the northeast; the Green Mountains are visible to the west. The remnants of the 1860 Prospect House, a popular tourist spot that burned to the ground in 1942, can still be seen at the summit.

Beaver Brook Shelter (1980s)—Sleeps 10. Privy (composting). Completed by DOC and ALDHA members, site includes tentsites and a nice view of Franconia Ridge. Water source is Beaver Brook on the spur trail to the shelter.

Appalachian Mountain Club—AMC maintains most of the A.T. and many of the surrounding trails between Kinsman Notch and Grafton Notch in Maine, a total of 122.1 miles; (603) 466-2721; <www.outdoors.org>.

AMC Tentsites, Shelters, and Campsites—"Tentsites" have designated tenting areas and platforms or pads. "Shelters" are three- or four-sided structures. "Campsites" have designated tenting areas *and* a shelter. See below for description of "huts," where reservations are required. Tentsites, shelters, and campsites are on a first-come, first-served basis. USFS parking fees are established throughout the Whites; be prepared to pay if you park at a Forest Service trailhead. Caretakers are in residence at the following tentsites, shelters, and campsites, where a $8 overnight fee is charged: Kinsman Pond Campsite, Liberty Spring Tentsite, Garfield Ridge Campsite, 13 Falls Tentsite, Guyot Campsite, Ethan Pond Campsite, Nauman Tentsite, Imp Campsite, and Speck Pond Campsite (Maine). A caretaker works at those sites due to the locations' popularity and the fragility of their resources. The remaining tentsites, shelters, and campsites, except those operated by the Randolph Mountain Club (see below), are available to backcountry travelers at no charge.

A *work-for-stay option* is possible for thru-hikers at the tentsites and shelter sites that have caretakers. This is at the discretion of the caretaker and may not always be available. A maximum of two thru-hikers per night can be accommodated in that way at each site, and each will be expected to contribute an hour of work.

AMC Huts—These large, enclosed lodges sleep from 36 to 90 people and are open with full service from Jun 3 to Sep 11 or Oct 16, depending on the hut. All huts are closed May 31–Jun 2. Rates range from $88 to $116, depending on the day, AMC membership, and the hut. Lonesome Lake, Carter Notch, and Zealand Falls huts are self-service from fall to the following Jun; Mizpah, Galehead, and Greenleaf are self-service May 7–30. A crew ("croo") staffs these facilities during the full-service season. An overnight stay includes bunk space, pillow, blanket, bathroom privileges (no showers), and potable water. If you plan to stay three consecutive nights, there is a discounted package rate, available all summer. Rates for self-service seasons are significantly less ($32–$35) than full-service seasons. Each hut has trained wilderness EMT and wilderness first-responders, and the facilities' crews give natural- and cultural-history evening programs. The huts also contain excellent libraries and displays on cultural and natural history.

If you plan to pay for a stay in one of the huts, make reservations, (603) 466-2727, especially for the weekends, when bunk spaces fill quickly. Call AMC or check <www. outdoors.org> to verify the huts' opening and closing dates as well as rates. You may also be able to make a reservation by having a caretaker at one of the other huts or campsites radio ahead for you. The huts cater mainly to families and weekend hikers. AMC had wells drilled at all the huts, so you can look forward to water that meets state health standards. During the self-service season, a caretaker is at Lonesome Lake, Zealand, and Carter huts. Schedules vary from hut to hut; check individual listings for specific dates.

Work exchange at the huts—Thru-hikers can sometimes arrange with the croo to work off their stays at the full- or self-service huts on the A.T. Most huts can accommodate one or two working thru-hikers each night—except for Lakes of the Clouds Hut, which takes up to four thru-hikers—but availability of work is never guaranteed. Work-for-stay is at the discretion of the hut croo. When work is available, thru-hikers are asked to put in two hours either at night or in the morning; when work is not available, the full fee may be charged. Please give other thru-hikers a chance to work off their stay, and limit your use of the work-for-stay option to no more than three huts.

The AMC *Thru-Hiker's Guide to AMC-Maintained Trails & Facilities in the White Mountains & Mahoosucs* is a resource written for those who plan to stay at the fee sites (both backcountry and hospitality). It is not a tool for thru-hikers who correctly follow backcountry regulations and camp through this area; see <www.outdoors.org/thru-hikers>.

AMC Shuttle—603-466-2727, <www.outdoors.org/lodging/lodging-shuttle.cfm>, daily Jun 3–Sep 11, weekends only Sep 18–Oct 17; $16 AMC members ($18 nonmembers), reservations strongly recommended; walk-ons accepted on a space-available basis, see driver; drop-offs on route between scheduled stops may be arranged with driver. Stops include trailheads at Liberty Spring/A.T. on I-93, Lafayette Place Campground, Old Bridle Path, Gale River, Zealand Falls, Ammonoosuc Ravine, Highland Center at Crawford Notch, Webster Cliff/A.T. at U.S. 302, Pinkham Notch Visitors Center, 19-Mile Brook Trail, Gorham Irving Gas Station, Valley Way/Appalachia. Check Web site for further details.

N.H. 112/Kinsman Notch—East 0.3 mile to Lost River Gorge and Boulder Caves, a series of streams, caves, and waterfalls owned by the Society for the Protection of New Hampshire Forests. Self-guided tour of gorge, ecology trail, and nature garden, $14, daily 9–5, from mid-May to mid-Oct, last ticket sold at 4 p.m. Snack bar. Phone available during business hours, with permission and a phone card.

East 5 miles to **North Woodstock, N.H. [P.O. ZIP 03262: M–F 8:30–12:30 & 1:30–4:30, Sa 9–12; (603) 745-8134]**, which also is accessible from Franconia Notch (below). ■ *Lodging:* Woodstock Inn, (603) 745-3951 or (800) 321-3985, shared bath $94PP, private bath $104PP, rates vary on weekends and holidays, no pets permitted, includes B, nonsmoking rooms, pool at Alpine Village, restaurant L/D; Autumn Breeze, (603) 745-8549, $68–$90, no dogs, rooms have kitchenettes; Carriage Motel, (603) 745-2416, $68–$82, game room, gas grills, picnic tables, pool, hiker box, deli, laundry, P.O. across street. ■ *Groceries:* Wayne's Market (long-term resupply), deli and excellent grinders. ■ *Restaurants:* Truants Taverne, Landmark II Family, Peg's, and Woodstock Station. ■ *Other services:* ATM, barber shop and beauty salon, Handy Wash Laundry, Fadden's General Store, ice cream, fudge shop, and Cascades town beach. ■ *Shuttles:* The Hiker Shuttle Connection, (603) 745-3140, 6 a.m.–2 a.m. year-round; from A.T. in Franconia Notch, follow Rt. 3 south to Exit 34A for shuttle pick-up on Rt. 3.

East—6 miles to **Lincoln, N.H.** (see below).

Eliza Brook Campsite (1963)—Shelter sleeps 8. Privy (composting). Two hardened tent pads. Water source is Eliza Brook.

Kinsman Pond Campsite and Shelter (2007)—Shelter sleeps 15, replaces one built in 1966. Privy (composting). Two single and two double tent platforms. Overnight fee $8PP, caretaker on site. Water source is Kinsman Pond; treat your water.

Lonesome Lake Hut—This southernmost hut offers swimming in Lonesome Lake. Full service Jun 3–Oct 16. Self-service the rest of the year except May 31–Jun 2.

I-93/U.S.3/Franconia Notch—East 0.7 mile to *Shuttle via* Whitehouse Brook Trail to hiker parking lot on U.S. 3 and AMC hiker shuttle stop.

East—0.8 mile to Flume Visitor Center, with snack bar/restaurant, and ice cream. Open daily early May to late Oct, 9–5. Call about mail drops; (603) 745-8391. Pay phone 24 hours; cell phones should work. Admission to see The Flume itself is $13.

East 5.8 miles to North Woodstock (see above).

East 7.3 miles to **Lincoln, N.H. [P.O. ZIP 03251: M–F 8–5, Sa 8–12; (603) 745-8133].** *Hostel:* One Step At A Time, (603) 745-8196, 197 Pollard Rd., owned by former hiker Chet West, bunk space for 6; work for stay, barter, donation; laundry (small fee), dogs okay; central to supermarket, outfitters, restaurants, movie theater, medical center, pharmacy, bus service, and Whale's Tale Water Park. Please call ahead.

West 2.1 miles to *Camping:* Lafayette Place Campground, (603) 823-9513, with tentsites $25D, coin-operated hot showers $1, store (short-term resupply), Coleman fuel by the quart, outside soda vending machine. Park rangers hold packages mailed to Franconia Notch State Park, Lafayette Place Campground, Franconia, NH 03580. Write the date you expect to arrive on the package. Open mid-May to Columbus Day. Campground is usually filled by noon on weekends.

West 8 miles to Franconia; I-93 North at N.H. 18. ■ *Lodging:* Gale River Motel, 1 Main St., Franconia, N.H. 03580, (603) 823-5655 or (800) 255-7989, <www.galeriver-motel.com>, <info@galerivermotel.com>, $90–$99 Jun–Sep, $95–$180 foliage season, $45–$95 in between and ski season, shuttle to and from Trail when available, seasonal pool, hot tub, Internet access, laundry, call ahead for mail drops; White Mountain Best Western, $90–$110, indoor pool, hot tub, Internet access, restaurant on site. ■ *Groceries:* Mac's Market (long-term supply), pay phone. ■ *Internet access:* library. ■ *Other services:* pizza, restaurant, bank, ATM, Concord Coach bus service, and AMC hiker shuttle stop at Lafayette Place Campground.

Liberty Springs Tentsite—Privy (composting). Seven single and three double tent platforms. Overnight fee $8PP, caretaker on site. Water source is the spring.

Franconia Ridge—In any kind of weather, this ridge walk will leave you awestruck. Beautiful views from the summit of Mt. Liberty can be reached from the A.T. *via* a side trail.

Greenleaf Hut—Visible from the summit of Mt. Lafayette, it is 1.1 miles on the Greenleaf Trail to the hut. Self-service May 7–30. Full service Jun 3–Oct 16.

Garfield Ridge Campsite (1971)—Shelter sleeps 12. Privy (composting). Two single and five double tent platforms. Overnight fee $8PP, caretaker on site. Water source is a spring at the junction to the campsite.

Galehead Hut—Rebuilt 1999–2000, with wheelchair-accessible design. Self-service May 7–30. Full service Jun 3–Oct 16.

Guyot Campsite (1977)—Shelter sleeps 12. Privy (composting). Four single and two double tent platforms. Located 0.7 mile east on Bondcliff Trail. Overnight fee $8PP, caretaker on site. Water source is a spring at the campsite.

Zealand Falls Hut—Next to beautiful falls. Full service Jun 3–Oct 16. Self-service the rest of the year except May 31–Jun 2.

Ethan Pond Campsite (1957)—Shelter sleeps 10. Privy (composting). Three single and two double tent platforms. Metal bear box. Overnight fee $8PP, caretaker on site. Water source is the inlet brook to the pond.

U.S. 302/Crawford Notch—East 1.8 miles to ■ *Camping:* Dry River Campground, (603) 374-2272, $27.25D, pay phone, coin laundry, and showers 25¢. Trail access to A.T. ■ *Shuttle:* AMC shuttle stop at Webster Cliff/A.T. Trailhead.

East 3 miles to *Camping:* Crawford Notch Campground and General Store, 1138 U.S. 302, Harts Location, NH 03812, <www.crawfordnotch.com>, (603) 374-2779; bunkhouse (hostel) $24PP includes coin-operated shower; no dogs; campsites $24D, additional fee for up to 4 people; laundry for overnight guests only; long-term resupply; white gas and denatured alcohol; shower $2 plus tokens 8 a.m.–9 p.m.; mail drops accepted, call for information; open daily mid-May–mid-Oct. Camp store (short-term resupply) has hot and cold sandwiches, limited camping supplies including bug spray and sunscreen, cold drinks, ice cream, ATM, pay phone.

East 10 miles to the small town of **Bartlett, N.H. [P.O. ZIP 03812: M–F 8:30–1 & 1:30–4:45, Sa 8:30–12; (603) 374-2351].**

West 1 mile to the Wiley House, with snack bar (ice cream, cold drinks, fudge, sandwiches) and pay phone, hiker message board, tent repair and seam sealer, open daily mid-May to mid-Oct, 9–5.

West 3.7 miles to ■ *Lodging:* AMC's Highland Center, (603) 278-4453, <www. outdoors.org>, limited hiker supplies, AYCE B $11, 6:30–8:30; *a la carte* L $8–$10, 10–4; 4-course D $22, reserve seat by 6; bunk room in lodge $71PP, includes B/D; private room in lodge $120–$168PP, includes B/D; Shapleigh Bunkhouse, $30PP AMC member, $40PP nonmember, includes bunk, shower, towel, and B. Facilities generally are for overnight guests only. Mail drops accepted sent to AMC Highland Center at Crawford Notch, Route 302, Bretton Woods, NH 03575. ■ *Shuttle:* AMC shuttle stop. ■ *Other services:* Showers at the visitors center, 9–5 Memorial Day–Columbus Day, coin-operated; towel rental, $2.

West 8.4 miles to *Lodging:* Above the Notch Motor Inn, (603) 846-5156, <www.abovethenotch.com>, rooms with phones, bath, TV, microwave, refrigerator, coffee/tea/condiments, WiFi, $78–$88 weekdays, $83–$93 weekends, $10EAP, call about mail drops; no pets, no smoking. Grocery store (short-term resupply) nearby.

Presidential Range—The highest part of the Trail in New Hampshire, with 25 miles of ridge-walking between Crawford Notch and Pinkham Notch, most of which is above treeline (about 4,400 feet). The A.T. skirts many peaks, which can be reached by short side trails leading to, and often over, the summits.

Mizpah Spring Hut & Nauman Tentsite—Constructed in 1964 and 1965. Self-service May 7–30; full-service Jun 3 to Oct 16. Tentsite, five single and two double tent platforms, composting privy, metal bear box. Overnight fee $8PP. Water source for tentsite is a stream or potable water from hut (if open).

Lakes of the Clouds Hut—Constructed in 1915 at an elevation of 5,050 feet, the highest, largest, and most popular hut. Full-service Jun 3 to Sep 11, with no self-service operation. "The Dungeon," a small basement shelter, is available to hikers for $10, with access to hut restroom and the common area; it sleeps only 6, first-come/first-served, no reservations. "The Dungeon" is an emergency-only shelter when the hut is closed; must not be used as a destination.

Mt. Washington Auto Road/Mt. Washington—The highest peak in the Northeast (6,288 feet). Since it is also accessible by the Auto Road and a cog railroad, more touristy services are here than one might expect to find. *Note: In 2007, 8 hikers were arrested for mooning said cog railroad, with newspapers around the world running the story; take heed.* The summit building is operated by the New Hampshire Division of Parks and Recreation and houses Mt. Washington Observatory, <www.mountwashington.org>; Mt. Washington Museum ($2 admission); a snack bar; a post office; and pay phones. The state park is open daily 8–8 early May–early Oct, weather permitting. A hiker room is downstairs, with a table, restroom, and a space to rest. (Absolutely no overnight stays are allowed.) Over the years, many buildings have come and gone on the summit, including a 94-bedroom hotel completed in

1873 and destroyed by fire in 1908. The summit is under cloud cover about 55 percent of the time. Average summertime high is 52 degrees, and the average wintertime high is 15 degrees. On April 12, 1934, an on-land wind speed of 231 mph was recorded, which still stands as the world's record. If you see a staff meteorologist, ask about the "Century Club." The upper plateau is home to large grassy areas, strewn with rocks but known as "lawns." These lawns hold many species of plants and animals otherwise found only on high mountain peaks and in tundra areas hundreds of miles to the north.

Mt. Washington, N.H. [P.O. ZIP 03589: (603) 466-3347]—The post office in the summit building is *not* recommended as a mail drop. Its hours are limited, and it caters to those who visit the summit and desire to have the distinguished Mt. Washington postmark; since there is little space for storing mail drops, they may be redirected to other New Hampshire post offices, well off the Trail.

East 8 miles *via* Auto Road to N.H. 16.

Tuckerman Ravine Trail—A steep, 4.2-mile route from Mt. Washington to Pinkham Notch. In bad weather, you may wish to use this trail to get below treeline and bypass the exposed northern loop of the Presidential Range, but this precarious route is no picnic in icy conditions.

Hermit Lake Shelters—At the base of the Tuckerman Ravine bowl, 2 miles downhill, with some steep rock- and boulder-scrambling from the summit; 8 lean-tos, 3 tent platforms, $10PP; pets are not permitted overnight in the shelters; caretaker year-round.

Edmands Col—Just down to the east in the col is a reliable spring and the site of the former Edmands Col emergency shelter. Also, look for a bronze tablet in memory of J. Rayner Edmands, who was instrumental in the construction of most of the graded paths through the northern Presidentials.

Crag Camp/Randolph Mountain Club (RMC) Cabins and Shelters—Randolph Mountain Club, Randolph, NH 03570. RMC maintains a network of 100 miles of hiking trails, principally on the northern slopes of Mounts Madison, Adams, and Jefferson in the Presidential Range of the White Mountain National Forest and on the Crescent Range in the town of Randolph. Its trails are maintained through the joint efforts of volunteers, two seasonal trail crews, and one Student Conservation Association crew. The RMC maintains several cabins and shelters below treeline in the Presidential Range that are often used by A.T. hikers seeking shelter from the exposed ridgeline. Crag Camp (capacity 15) and Gray Knob (capacity 15) are cabins. The Perch is a lean-to with tent platforms. Another lean-to, the Log Cabin (capacity 10), is on Lowe's Path, 1 mile below Gray Knob. All camps are available to the public on a first-come, first-served basis. If a site is full, the caretaker may ask visitors to move to another RMC facility, if space is available. Groups are limited to 10. To maintain serenity, cellular phones may not be used at any of the camps. Since it is insulated and outfitted with a woodstove for cold-months use, Gray Knob has a caretaker year-round. Although fall and winter hikers are asked to bring up a couple of hardwood sticks, only its caretaker operates Gray Knob's woodstove. In Jul and Aug, Crag Camp has a caretaker. In those months, gas stoves at both camps are available to the public; at all other times, users must bring their own stoves. The Log Cabin, located at a lower elevation than the other RMC camps, is well suited to families with younger children and hikers making a late-in-the-day start. Year-round, the weather is far harsher and colder here than "below the notches." RMC relies on visitors to carry out their trash and help keep the cabin and woods clean. To support the caretakers' wages and maintain the camps, fees are charged on a per-night basis: Crag Camp and Gray Knob, $12; The Perch, Log Cabin, and tent platforms, $7. If the caretaker is absent, please mail fees to: Treasurer, RMC, Randolph, NH 03570.

The Perch (1948)—Shelter sleeps 8. Privy. Four tent platforms, $7PP fee. Water source is crossed *en route* to the shelter.

Madison Spring Hut—Located in a col 0.5 mile south of the summit of Mt. Madison. Full service Jun 3–Sep 5, with no self-service operation.

Valley Way and Osgood Tentsites—These two no-fee U.S. Forest Service tentsites, below treeline on Mt. Madison, are often used by hikers starting or finishing the traverse of the Presidential Range. Valley Way Tentsite is off the A.T., 0.6 mile west of Madison Springs Hut, with two large tent platforms and a privy. Osgood Tentsite is 3 miles north of the hut, along the A.T., and has three tentsites, privy, and spring.

N.H. 16/Pinkham Notch—Pinkham Notch Visitors Center; front desk, (603) 466-2721. AMC's New Hampshire headquarters, located on the A.T., offers a store with limited hiker supplies, restroom, coin-operated showers (open 24 hours), AMC shuttle stop, and Concord Coach bus service (see below). The center holds packages sent to AMC Visitors Center, c/o Front Desk, N.H. 16, Gorham, NH 03581.

■ **Restaurant:** Cafeteria with AYCE $9.50 B, deli L (not AYCE) 9:30–4, trail L $9, $19 D (thru-hikers get member rates). ■ **Lodging:** Joe Dodge Lodge, (603) 466-2727, $61 includes B/D. Prices can change; contact AMC for the most current rates.

East 13–16 miles to Intervale, N.H. ■ **Outfitter:** Ragged Mountain Equipment, (603) 356-3042, open daily with backpacking gear and repair service. ■ **Lodging:** Cranmore Mountain Lodge, (603) 356-2044, $30–$38 includes B, shower, bed, $5 fee for bed linens, heated pool, spa, mail drops accepted at 859 Kearsage Rd., Kearsarge, NH 03847. ■ **Other services:** Peter Limmer & Sons Shop, (603) 356-5378, located on N.H. 16A, home of legendary hand-made hiking boots, will repair many brands of boots and hiking gear with priority to thru-hikers; closed Su.

East 18 miles to North Conway, N.H., a tourist town with most major services, including several outfitters, a supermarket, cobbler, laundry, bank, ATM, hospital, veterinarian, pharmacy, one-hour photo, movie theater, hotels, and restaurants.

West 2 miles to the Wildcat Mountain Gondola, operates daily mid-Jun to mid-Oct, 10–4:45, and offers rides to and from the A.T. on the top of Wildcat Mountain; $15 round-trip, $8 down only; special round-trip with lunch (deli) available.

West 11 miles to Gorham, N.H. (see below).

Concord Coach Bus Service—Provides service between Boston and Pinkham Notch, as well as Gorham, Berlin, and Conway, (800) 639-3317, <www.concordtrailways. com>. The bus leaves Pinkham Notch daily at 8:12 a.m. and arrives at Boston South Station at 12:20 p.m. The bus to Pinkham Notch leaves Boston at 5:15 p.m. and arrives at Pinkham Notch at 9:10 p.m. One-way, $32; round-trip, $60.

Carter Notch Hut—The northernmost hut, located on the banks of two small lakes in Carter Notch. It is the original hut, built in 1914. Full service Jun 3–Sep 11; self-service rest of year except May 31–Jun 2.

Imp Campsite (1981)—Shelter sleeps 16. Privy (composting). Four single and one double tent platform. Overnight fee $8PP, caretaker on site. Water source is the stream near shelter.

Rattle River Shelter (1980s)—Sleeps 8. Privy. Shelter built by USFS. Water source is Rattle River.

U.S. 2—West 1.8 miles to *Hostel:* White Birches Camping Park, owners Bob/ Janet Langlands; (603) 466-2022, <www.whitebirchescampingpark.com>, <whbirch@ncia.net>; 218 State Rt. 2, Shelburne, NH 03581, May 1–end of Oct, tent-

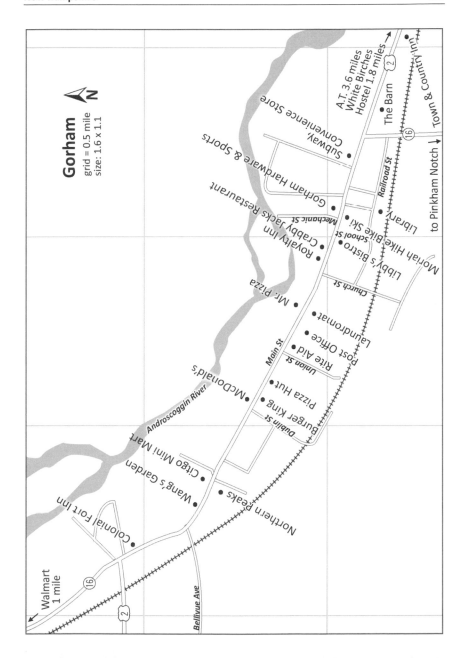

Gorham
grid = 0.5 mile
size: 1.6 x 1.1

N

A.T. 3.6 miles
White Birches
Hostel 1.8 miles

The Barn

Town & Country Inn

Subway, Convenience Store

Railroad St

to Pinkham Notch

Gorham Hardware & Sports

Mechanic St

Library

Moriah Hike/Bike/Ski

Crabby Jacks Restaurant

Royalty Inn

Libby's Bistro

School St

Mr. Pizza

Church St

Laundromat

Post Office

Main St

Rite Aid

Union St

McDonald's

Androscoggin River

Pizza Hut

Burger King

Dublin St

Wang's Garden

Citgo Mini Mart

Northern Peaks

Colonial Fort Inn

Walmart
1 mile

Bellvue Ave

sites $11S, hostel $15S per night, private cabins available, inquire. Hot showers and laundry for guests only, limited resupply, microwave, refrigerator, coin laundry, dogs welcome, local restaurants deliver, swimming pool, mail drops accepted for guests, limited shuttle to town/trailhead for guests only, Visa/MasterCard.

West 3.6 miles to **Gorham, N.H. [P.O. ZIP 03581: M–F 8:30–5, Sa 8:30–12; (603) 466-2182].** The postmaster requests that all packages include your legal name and ETA; use bold letters/colors and have ID; can knock on door inside lobby to pick up mail drops after hours. ■ *Hostels:* Hikers Paradise Hostel at Colonial Fort Inn, 370 Main St., (603) 466-2732, <www.hikersparadise.com>, <paradise@ncia.net>; owners Mary Ann and Bruno Janicki offer three hostel units, $19PP, each with bath, kitchen, phone, linen, and heat; motel rooms available; pool; no pets, no mail drops; limited shuttle service to Trailhead, coin laundry, Coleman fuel and denatured alcohol; special hikers' B at motel restaurant. The Barn Hostel, (603) 466-2271, <theskilift@aol.com>, at Libby House B&B offers room in the hostel, $20PP; microwave, TV, coin laundry, shower, occasional shuttle, no pets, $5 laundry; will hold mail drops, for guests only, mailed to 55 Main Street, Gorham, NH 03581. ■ *Lodging:* Libby House B&B, (603) 466-2271, beginning at $70S, $85D, includes B; Royalty Inn, (603) 466-3312, $78S, $85D, <www.royaltyinn.com>, <innkeeper@royaltyinn.com>: Northern Peaks, (603) 466-3374, $46 up to 3 hikers, dogs welcome, a/c, pool; Town & Country Inn, (603) 466-3315, $50–60S, $74–84D, $6EAP, pets welcome, mail drops accepted at U.S. 2, Gorham, NH 03581. ■ *Groceries:* Shaw's and Super Walmart (both long-term resupply) are located 1.5 miles north of town on N.H. 16. ■ *Restaurants:* Mr. Pizza, J's Steak and Seafood, and various fast-food opportunities. ■ *Outfitters:* Altitude Sport-Hike-Bike-Ski, (603) 466-5050, owned and run by Steve Jackson, hiker gear, Coleman fuel and alcohol by the ounce; Gorham Hardware/Sports Center, (603) 466-2312, boots and hiker gear, Coleman fuel and alcohol by the ounce. ■ *Internet access:* public library, M, W, F, 10–7, Tu, Th 10–8, closed weekends, located near railroad, nominal fee. ■ *Other services:* coin laundry, bank with ATM, dentist, free concerts on the common Tu evenings.

West 8 miles to the small city of Berlin, N.H., and the Androscoggin Valley Hospital.

Trident Col Tentsite—Four tent pads. Privy (composting). Water source is an intermittent spring on a side trail.

Gentian Pond Shelter/Campsite (1974)—Shelter sleeps 14. Privy (composting). Three single and one double tent platform. Water source is the inlet brook of Gentian Pond.

Maine

Miles from Katahdin	Features	Services	Elev.	Miles from Springer
281.4	Maine–N.H. State Line		2,972	1,897.7
280.9	**Carlo Col Shelter/Campsite**... *5.5mS; 4.7mN*	W–0.3m C, S, w	2,945	1,898.2
280.5	Mt. Carlo		3,565	1,898.6
278.7	Goose Eye Mtn (East Peak)		3,790	1,900.4
277.5	Goose Eye Mtn (North Peak)		3,675	1,901.6
276.5	**Full Goose Shelter/Campsite**... *4.7mS; 5.1mN*	C, S, w	3,030	1,902.6
276.0	Fulling Mill Mtn (South Peak)		3,395	1,903.1
275.0	Mahoosuc Notch Trail Mahoosuc Notch (west end)	w	2,400	1,904.1
273.9	Mahoosuc Notch (east end)	w	2,150	1,905.2
272.3	Mahoosuc Arm		3,770	1,906.8
271.4	**+Speck Pond Shelter/ Campsite**... *5.1mS; 6.9mN*	C, S, w	3,500	1,907.7
270.3	Old Speck Trail, Grafton Loop Trail		3,985	1,908.8
267.9	Brook	w	2,500	1,911.2
266.8	Maine 26, Grafton Notch	R (E–4.7m H, M, cl, sh, f; 5.5m C; 12.7m C, f; 17m G, L, M, O, f; 20m H, C, cl)	1,495	1,912.3
264.5	**Baldpate Lean-to**... *6.9mS; 3.5mN*	S, w	2,645	1,914.6
263.7	Baldpate Mtn(West Peak)		3,662	1,915.4
262.8	Baldpate Mtn (East Peak), Grafton Loop Trail		3,810	1,916.3
261.0	**Frye Notch Lean-to**... *3.5mS; 10.4mN*	S, w	2,280	1,918.1
257.3	Dunn Notch and Falls	w	1,350	1,921.8
256.5	East B Hill Rd **Andover, ME 04216**	R (E–8m PO, H, G, L, M, f, cl, @; 11m H)	1,500	1,922.6
254.7	Surplus Pond	w	2,050	1,924.4
251.8	Wyman Mtn		2,920	1,927.3

Miles from Katahdin	Features	Services	Elev.	Miles from Springer
250.5	**Hall Mtn Lean-to...** *10.4mS; 12.8mN*	S, w	2,635	1,928.6
249.1	Sawyer Notch, Sawyer Brook (ford)	w	1,095	1,930.0
248.2	Moody Mtn		2,440	1,930.9
246.4	South Arm Rd, Black Brook (ford) Andover, ME 04216	R (E–9m PO, H, G, L, M, f, @; 12m H) (W–3.5m C, G, cl)	1,410	1,932.7
243.6	Old Blue Mtn		3,600	1,935.5
240.4	Bemis Stream Trail		3,350	1,938.7
239.4	Bemis Range (West Peak)		3,580	1,939.7
237.7	**Bemis Mtn Lean-to...** *12.8mS; 8.3mN*	S, w	2,790	1,941.4
233.9	Bemis Stream (ford)	w	1,495	1,945.2
233.1	Maine 17 **Oquossoc, ME 04964**	R (W–11m PO, G, M, cl, f)	2,200	1,946.0
231.5	Moxie Pond	w	2,400	1,947.6
229.7	Long Pond	w	2,330	1,949.4
229.4	**Sabbath Day Pond Lean-to...** *8.3mS; 11.2mN*	S, w	2,390	1,949.7
224.8	Little Swift River Pond Campsite	C, w	2,460	1,954.3
222.1	South Pond	w	2,174	1,957.0
220.0	Maine 4 **Rangeley, ME 04970**	R (W–9m PO, H, G, L, M, O, D, cl, f, @; 15m G, M, cl; 23m H)	1,700	1,959.1
219.9	Sandy River		1,595	1,959.2
218.2	**Piazza Rock Lean-to...** *11.2mS; 8.9mN*	S, C, w	2,080	1,960.9
216.3	Eddy Pond	w	2,616	1,962.8
214.3	Saddleback Mtn		4,120	1,964.8
212.7	The Horn		4,040	1,966.4
212.0	Redington Stream Campsite	C, w		1,967.1
210.7	Saddleback Junior		3,655	1,968.4
210.3	Stream	w	3,200	1,968.8
209.3	**Poplar Ridge Lean-to ...** *8.9mS; 8mN*	S, w	2,920	1,969.8
206.6	Orbeton Stream (ford)	w	1,550	1,972.5

Miles from Katahdin	Features	Services	Elev.	Miles from Springer
203.5	Lone Mtn		3,260	1,975.6
202.4	Mt. Abraham Trail		3,184	1,976.7
201.3	**Spaulding Mtn Lean-to...** *8mS; 18.6mN*	S, w	3,140	1,977.8
200.5	Spaulding Mtn		4,000	1,978.6
198.4	Sugarloaf Mtn Trail	E−0.3m w; 0.6m to summit	3,540	1,980.7
196.2	South Branch Carrabassett River (ford)	w	2,100	1,982.9
196.1	Caribou Valley Rd	R	2,220	1,983.0
195.1	Crocker Cirque	E−0.2m C, w	2,710	1,984.0
194.0	South Crocker Mtn		4,040	1,985.1
193.0	North Crocker Mtn		4,228	1,986.1
187.8	Maine 27 **Stratton, ME 04982**	R (E−2m G) (W−5m PO, H, G, L, M, cl, f, @; 10m H)	1,450	1,991.3
187.0	Stratton Brook Pond Rd	R	1,250	1,992.1
186.8	Stratton Brook	w	1,230	1,992.3
185.9	Cranberry Stream	C, w	1,350	1,993.2
184.6	Bigelow Range Trail, Cranberry Pond	W−0.2m w	2,400	1,994.5
182.9	Horns Pond Trail		3,200	1,996.2
182.7	**Horns Pond Lean-tos...** *18.6mS; 10.2mN*	S, w	3,160	1,996.4
182.2	South Horn		3,831	1,996.9
180.1	Bigelow Mtn (West Peak)		4,145	1,999.0
179.8	Bigelow Col, Avery Memorial Campsite, Fire Warden's Trail	C, w	3,850	1,999.3
179.6	Spring	w	3,900	1,999.5
179.4	Bigelow Mtn (Avery Peak)		4,090	1,999.7
177.5	Safford Brook Trail		2,260	2,001.6
177.4	Safford Notch	E−0.3m C, w	2,230	2,001.7
174.2	Little Bigelow Mtn (east end)		3,010	2,004.9
172.5	**Little Bigelow Lean-to...** *10.2mS; 7.3mN*	S, C, w	1,760	2,006.6
171.1	East Flagstaff Rd	R	1,200	2,008.0
171.0	Bog Brook Rd, Flagstaff Lake (inlet)	R, w	1,150	2,008.1

Miles from Katahdin	Features	Services	Elev.	Miles from Springer
168.7	Long Falls Dam Rd	R	1,225	2,010.4
167.0	Roundtop Mtn		1,760	2,012.1
165.9	West Carry Pond	w	1,320	2,013.2
165.2	**West Carry Pond Lean-to...** *7.3mS; 10mN*	S, w	1,340	2,013.9
164.5	West Carry Pond	w	1,320	2,014.6
162.6	Sandy Stream, Middle Carry Pond	w	1,229	2,016.5
161.1	East Carry Pond	w	1,237	2,018.0
159.4	Logging Rd	R	1,300	2,019.7
158.7	North Branch Carrying Place Stream	w	1,200	2,020.4
155.2	**Pierce Pond Lean-to...** *10mS; 9.7mN*	S, w	1,150	2,023.9
154.8	Trail to Harrison's Pierce Pond Camps	R (E–0.3m L, M, w)	1,100	2,024.3
151.5	Kennebec River	w	490	2,027.6
151.2	U.S. 201 **Caratunk, ME 04925**	R (E–0.3m PO; 16.5m G, L, M, cl) (W–2m C, L, M, sh, cl; 7m PO, G; 21m D, L, G, M, cl, O, f)	520	2,027.9
148.5	Holly Brook	w	900	2,030.6
145.9	Boise-Cascade Logging Rd	R	1,400	2,033.2
145.5	**Pleasant Pond Lean-to...** *9.7mS; 9mN*	S, w	1,320	2,033.6
144.2	Pleasant Pond Mtn		2,470	2,034.9
139.3	Moxie Pond	R, w	970	2,039.8
136.5	**Bald Mtn Brook Lean-to...** *9mS; 4.1mN*	S, w	1,280	2,042.6
134.5	Moxie Bald Mtn		2,629	2,044.6
132.4	**Moxie Bald Lean-to...** *4.1mS; 8.9mN*	S, w	1,220	2,046.7
130.3	Bald Mtn Pond	w	1,213	2,048.8
126.6	W Branch Piscataquis River (ford)	w	900	2,052.5
123.5	**Horseshoe Canyon Lean-to...** *8.9mS; 12mN*	S, w	880	2,055.6

Miles from Katahdin	Features	Services	Elev.	Miles from Springer
121.2	E Branch Piscataquis River (ford)	w	650	2,057.9
120.8	Shirley-Blanchard Rd	R	850	2,058.3
117.8	Blue-blaze to Monson	E−0.3m R; 2m PO, G, M, L, cl, sh, f, @	900	2,061.3
114.5	**Maine 15 Monson, ME 04464**	R (E−4m PO, G, M, L, cl, sh, f, @) (W− 8m G, M, L, O, D, f, @)	1,215	2,064.6
114.4	Spectacle Pond-outlet	w	1,163	2,064.7
113.3	Bell Pond	w	1,278	2,065.8
112.6	Lily Pond	w	1,130	2,066.5
111.5	**Leeman Brook Lean-to**... *12mS; 7.4mN*	S, w	1,070	2,067.6
110.7	North Pond (outlet)	w (W−0.4m H, M, sh, f)	1,000	2,068.4
107.9	Little Wilson Falls		850	2,071.2
107.7	Little Wilson Stream (ford)	w	750	2,071.4
104.8	Big Wilson Stream (ford)	w	600	2,074.3
104.5	Montreal, Maine & Atlantic RR		850	2,074.6
104.1	**Wilson Valley Lean-to**... *7.4mS; 4.7mN*	S, w	1,000	2,075.0
100.2	Long Pond Stream (ford)	w	620	2,078.9
99.4	**Long Pond Stream Lean-to**... *4.7mS; 4.4mN*	S, w	930	2,079.7
96.3	Barren Mtn		2,660	2,082.8
95.4	**Cloud Pond Lean-to**... *4.4mS; 7.3mN*	E−0.4m S, w	2,420	2,083.7
93.3	Fourth Mtn		2,380	2,085.8
90.8	Third Mtn, Monument Cliff		1,920	2,088.3
90.2	West Chairback Pond Trail	w	1,770	2,088.9
88.9	Columbus Mtn		2,325	2,090.2
88.5	**Chairback Gap Lean-to**... *7.3mS; 9.9mN*	S, w	2,000	2,090.6
88.0	Chairback Mtn		2,180	2,091.1
85.8	East Chairback Pond Trail	W−0.2m w	1,630	2,093.3
84.6	Katahdin Iron Works Logging Rd	R (E−20m C, G)	750	2,094.5

Miles from Katahdin	Features	Services	Elev.	Miles from Springer
84.1	West Branch Pleasant River (ford)	w	680	2,095.0
83.8	The Hermitage	W–8m L	695	2,095.3
82.8	Gulf Hagas Trail	w	950	2,096.3
82.1	Gulf Hagas Cut-off Trail	w	1,050	2,097.0
78.6	**Carl A. Newhall Lean-to...** *9.9mS; 7.2mN*	S, w	1,840	2,100.5
77.7	Gulf Hagas Mtn		2,683	2,101.4
76.8	Sidney Tappan Campsite	C (E–0.2m w)	2,425	2,102.3
76.1	West Peak		3,178	2,103.0
74.5	Hay Mtn		3,244	2,104.6
73.9	White Brook Trail		3,125	2,105.2
72.8	White Cap Mtn		3,650	2,106.3
71.4	**Logan Brook Lean-to...** *7.2mS; 3.6mN*	S, w	2,530	2,107.7
69.8	W Branch Ponds Rd	R	1,650	2,109.3
67.8	**East Branch Lean-to...** *3.6mS; 8.1mN*	S, w	1,240	2,111.3
67.5	East Branch Pleasant River (ford)	w	1,200	2,111.6
65.9	Mtn View Pond	w	1,597	2,113.2
65.6	Spring	w	1,580	2,113.5
64.3	Little Boardman Mtn		1,980	2,114.8
62.9	Kokadjo-B Pond Rd	R	1,380	2,116.2
62.0	Crawford Pond	w	1,240	2,117.1
59.7	**Cooper Brook Falls Lean-to...** *8.1mS; 11.4mN*	S, C, w	910	2,119.4
56.0	Jo-Mary Rd	R, w (E–6m C, G, cl, sh; 20m G)	625	2,123.1
53.1	Mud Pond (outlet)	w	508	2,126.0
51.8	Antlers Campsite	C, w	500	2,127.3
50.1	Sand Beach, Lower Jo-Mary Lake	w	580	2,129.0
48.3	**Potaywadjo Spring Lean-to...** *11.4mS; 10.1mN*	S, w	620	2,130.8
47.7	Pemadumcook Lake	w	580	2,131.4
46.0	Maher Trail, Maher Tote Rd	E–1.2m G, L, M, sh, f	580	2,133.1

Miles from Katahdin	Features	Services	Elev.	Miles from Springer
44.0	Nahmakanta Stream Campsite	C, w	600	2,135.1
42.5	Tumbledown Dick Trail			2,136.6
40.8	Nahmakanta Lake	R, w	650	2,138.3
38.2	**Wadleigh Stream Lean-to**... *10.1mS; 8.1mN*	S, w	685	2,140.9
36.3	Nesuntabunt Mtn		1,520	2,142.8
33.9	Crescent Pond	w	980	2,145.2
32.5	Pollywog Stream	w	682	2,146.6
30.1	**Rainbow Stream Lean-to**... *8.1mS; 11.5mN*	S, w	1,005	2,149.0
28.1	Rainbow Lake (west)	w	1,080	2,151.0
26.3	Rainbow Spring Campsite	C, w	1,100	2,152.8
22.9	Rainbow Lake (east)	w	980	2,156.2
21.1	Rainbow Ledges		1,517	2,158.0
18.6	**Hurd Brook Lean-to**... *11.5mS; 13.7mN*	S, w	715	2,160.5
15.1	Golden Rd, Abol Bridge, West Branch/Penobscot River	R, w, C, G, sh (E– 20m PO, G, M, L, D, cl)	588	2,164.0
14.4	Abol Stream, Baxter Park Boundary		620	2,164.7
14.0	Katahdin Stream	w	620	2,165.1
11.0	Pine Point	w	640	2,168.1
10.5	Lower Fork Nesowadnehunk Stream (ford)			2,168.6
9.6	Upper Fork Nesowadnehunk Stream (ford)			2,169.5
8.8	Big Niagara Falls	w	900	2,170.3
7.6	+Daicey Pond Campground	E–0.1m L, w	1,100	2,171.5
5.3	Pack Tote Rd	R	1,080	2,173.8
5.2	+Katahdin Stream Campground, **+The Birches**... *13.7mS*	C, w (E–0.25m S)	1,080	2,173.9
4.0	Katahdin Stream Falls	w	1,550	2,175.1
1.0	Thoreau Spring	w	4,620	2,178.1
0.0	Katahdin (Baxter Peak)		5,268	2,179.1

+ Fee charge, ~ Northbound long-distance hikers only at The Birches

Hikers in Maine encounter approximately 281 miles of lakes, bogs, moose, loons, hand-over-hand climbs, and a 100-mile wilderness that is neither 100 miles nor truly a wilderness. It is a mystical, magical place to begin or end your A.T. journey.

No camping is allowed above treeline on the A.T. in Maine.

Carlo Col Shelter and Campsite (1976)—Shelter sleeps 8. Off trail 0.3 mile west. Privy (composting). Two single and one double tent platforms. Water source is a spring left of the lean-to.

Full Goose Shelter and Campsite (1978)—Shelter sleeps 8. Privy (composting). Many hikers choose to stay here before or after Mahoosuc Notch. Three single and one double tent platforms. Water source is stream behind shelter.

Mahoosuc Notch—Famous for ice found in deep crevices throughout the year. Many call this scramble under, around, over, and between the boulders the most difficult mile on the Trail.

Speck Pond Shelter and Campsite (1968)—Shelter sleeps 8. Privy (composting). Three single and three double tent platforms. Cookstoves only. Overnight fee $8PP. Speck Pond is the highest body of water in Maine. Water source is a spring on the blue-blazed trail behind the caretaker's yurt.

Maine 26/Grafton Notch—Difficult hitch, very light traffic. **East** 4.7 miles to *Hostel*: Mahoosuc Mountain Lodge, 1513 Bear River Rd (Rt. 26), Newry, ME 04261, (207) 824-2073, <www.mahoosucmountainlodge.com>, 2 bunk rooms with shower, $35 (with towel and wash cloth, no bed linen), $45 with bed linen, $50 with B; full kitchen; mail drops accepted; no dogs; fuel by the ounce (white gas, alcohol); prepared meals available with advance notice; call from Old Spec/Baldpate for shuttle from parking lot (fee).

    East 5.5 miles to *Camping:* Grafton Notch Camp Ground, 1471 Bear River Rd., Newry, ME 04261, (207) 824-2292, <www.campgrafton.com>, shower only $5.

    East 12 miles to junction of Maine 26 and U.S. 2: Bear River Trading Post, (207) 824-2327, soda, Heet.

    East 12.7 miles to *Camping:* Stony Brook Recreation Camping Area, (207) 824-2836 or (207) 824-2789, <www.stonybrookrec.com>, tentsite $22 for 4, $4EAP; lean-to $28 for 4; includes shuttle to Grafton Notch, shower, laundry, pool, miniature golf, rec room, and convenience store (short-term resupply) with Coleman fuel, plus RV sites with hook-ups available. Mail drops held if sent c/o SBRCA, Route 2, 42 Powell Place, Hanover, ME 04237.

East 17 miles to the town of Bethel, offering most major services. ■ *Lodging:* Chapman Inn, (877) 359-1498 or (207) 824-2657, <www.chapmaninn.com>, $30 for bunk in hiker dorm with shower, B, kitchen privileges, $4 laundry, and possible shuttle back to A.T.; mail drops accepted at 2 Church St., P.O. Box 1067, Bethel, ME 04217. ■ *Restaurant:* Moose's Tale Food and Ale, Sunday River Brewery. ■ *Groceries:* Bethel IGA Food Liner (long-term resupply), Irving Mainway convenience store with Subway & Dunkin' Donuts. ■ *Outfitter:* True North Adventurewear, (207) 824-2201, M–Sa 10–6, Su 10–5, full-service backpacking outfitter, stove fuel. ■ *Camping:* Bethel Outdoor Adventure & Campground, (800) 533-3607, (207) 824-4224, <www.betheloutdooradventure.com>; tentsites $20D, $3EAP; showers; restaurant nearby, phone, mail drops accepted if sent to 121 Mayville Rd., U.S. 2, Bethel, ME 04217-4410; canoe trips on the Androscoggin River from Shelburne, N.H., to Bethel, Maine. ■ *Other services:* bank with ATM.

East 20 miles to *Hostel:* Bethel Outdoor Adventure's "Bethel International Hostel–Snowboarding House," (800) 533-3607, (207) 824-4224, <www.snowboardinghouse.com>, $22PP, coin laundry, kitchen, microwave, shuttle available, mail drops accepted to 646 W. Bethel Rd., Bethel, ME 04217.

Maine Appalachian Trail Club—MATC maintains the 266.9 miles from Grafton Notch to Katahdin. Correspondence should be sent to MATC, P.O. Box 283, Augusta, ME 04332-0283; <www.matc.org>.

Baldpate Lean-to (1995)—Sleeps 8. Privy. Lean-to replaced Grafton Notch Lean-to, which was too close to a road. Water source is a spring behind the lean-to.

Frye Notch Lean-to (1983)—Sleeps 6. Privy. Water source is Frye Brook in front of the lean-to.

East B Hill Road/Andover—**East** 8 miles to **Andover, Maine [P.O. ZIP 04216: M–F 8:30–1:30 & 2–4:30, Sa 8:30–11:30; (207) 392-4571].** Andover also can be reached *via* South Arm Road, 9.5 miles north on the A.T. Neither road has much traffic. ■ *Hostel:* Pine Ellis Hiking Lodge, (207) 392-4161, <www.pineellislodging.com>; hiker-firendly hosts Ilene Trainor and David Rousselin; located near P.O. and stores; large shared room in house or bunkhouse in backyard $20PP, private rooms $35S, $50D, $60T, includes house privileges, Internet, CATV, use of kitchen, guest phone line.For a fee: shuttle to/from Trailhead, laundry, slackpacking from Grafton Notch to Rangeley, denatured alcohol, and Coleman. Credit cards accepted; will hold packages mailed to 20 Pine St., P.O. Box 12, Andover, ME 04216. ■ *Groceries:* Andover General Store, 4:30 a.m.–9 p.m., B/L/D, ATM, Heet; Mill's Market, with deli and homemade pizza (both short-term resupply). ■ *Internet access:* Andover Public Library, Tu–Th, Sa 1–4:30. ■ *Other services:* Pete's Hardware, Coleman; massage therapist Donna Gifford, (207) 357-5686.

East 11 miles to East Andover and *Lodging:* The Cabin, (207) 392-1333, <thecabin@ megalink.net>, <www.thecabininmaine.com>; owned by Margie and Earle Towne (Honey and Bear); log cabin with bunkroom and private room. Call to see if they are home and for reservations. Alumni always welcome.

Surplus Pond—See and hear an abundance of wood warblers during spring and summer.

Hall Mountain Lean-to (1978)—Sleeps 6. Privy. Water source is a spring south of the lean-to on the A.T.

South Arm Road—East 9 miles to Andover, Maine (see above).

West 3.5 miles to *Camping:* South Arm Campground, (207) 364-5155, open mid-May to mid-Sep; $15 per site, up to 4. Campstore (short-term resupply); showers 25¢; coin laundry; canoe, kayak, and boat rentals. No credit cards. Packages accepted at P.O. Box 310, Andover, ME 04216.

Bemis Mountain Lean-to (1988)—Sleeps 8. Privy. Water source is a small spring to the left of the lean-to.

Maine 17—West 11 miles to **Oquossoc, Maine [P.O. ZIP 04964: M–F 8–1 & 1:30–4:15, Sa 9–12; (207) 864-3685].** ■ *Lodging:* Oquossoc's Own B&B, (207) 864-5584, $60S, $90D, includes B. ■ *Groceries:* Carry Road Country Store (short-term resupply), with deli and bakery. ■ *Restaurants:* Gingerbread House, B/L/D with vegetarian specials; Four Seasons Café, daily 11–11, serves Mexican and vegetarian specialties, L/D. ■ *Other services:* pay phone and swimming area.

Sabbath Day Pond Lean-to (1993)—Sleeps 8. Privy. A sandy beach, 0.3 mile south on the A.T., provides an excellent swimming opportunity. Water source is Sabbath Day Pond in front of the lean-to.

Little Swift River Pond Campsite (1975)—Privy. Water is available from piped spring near pond.

Maine 4—West 9 miles to **Rangeley, Maine [P.O. ZIP 04970: M–F 9:30–12:30 & 1:30–4:15, Sa 9:30–12; (207) 864-2233]**, where services are spread along Maine 4. ■ *Hostel:* Gull Pond Lodge, (207) 864-5563, owned by Bob O'Brien, call ahead; bunkroom $20PP, private room $30S, $50D, includes linens, fuel refill; use of kitchen and grill, TV, phone, laundry, slackpacking, shuttles in and out of town and back to Trail. Packages accepted if mailed to P.O. Box 1177, Rangeley, ME 04970. ■ *Lodging:* Rangeley Inn, (800) MOMENTS or (207) 864-3341, $84–$99; Saddleback Motor Inn, (207) 864-3434, $90D, WiFi; Town and Lake Motel, (207) 864-3755, $85S, $99D. ■ *Groceries:* IGA Supermarket (long-term resupply). ■ *Restaurants:* Parkside Main Café, L/D; Sarge's Pub & Grub, L/D; Red Onion, L/D; BMC Diner, B/L. ■ *Outfitter:* Alpine Shop, (207) 864-3741, Coleman fuel and alcohol by the ounce; Ecopelagicon 7 Pond St., (207) 864-2771, freeze-dried meals, backpacker supplies, fuel, ATC publications. ■ *Internet access:* Rangeley Public Library. ■ *Other services:* banks with ATM; Village Scrub Board laundry; doctor; Rangeley Region Health Center, (207) 864-4397; dentist; pharmacy; bookstore.
West 15 miles to Oquossoc (see entry above).

Piazza Rock Lean-to (1993)—Sleeps 8. Privy. Constructed by MATC's team of maintainers from L.L.Bean, this lean-to and tent platforms are home to a two-seat privy and cribbage board. Water source is the stream that passes through the campsite.

Saddleback Mountain—One of the most spectacular above-treeline stretches of the Trail in Maine; you may not notice the ski resort on one side. For many years, Saddleback was the controversial "missing link" in Maine during federal attempts to buy lands along the Trail to protect it from encroaching development. In late 2000, a deal was struck to sell a Trail corridor across Saddleback to the government, but it does permit future development of the resort, which was sold in 2003 to a local family that is investing heavily in lakeside facilities downslope.

Redington Stream Campsite—0.9 mile north of Saddleback's Horn, at the east base of the Horn (middle peak of the Saddleback mountain range), right where the descent from the Horn levels off and the Trail heads for Saddleback Junior. The blue-blazed side trail (marked with a temporary sign) leads 1,100 feet to a reliable water source. It is about 400 feet along this side trail from the A.T. to the privy. Before you reach the privy, side trails branch off to tent pads, with a current capacity of about two tents each. Open fires are *absolutely prohibited* at this campsite as it is in a very vulnerable softwood stand. Stoves are allowed, as usual.

Poplar Ridge Lean-to (1961)—Sleeps 6. Privy. This shelter uses the increasingly rare "baseball bat" design for its sleeping platform. No tentsites. Water source is the brook in front of lean-to.

Spaulding Mountain Lean-to (1989)—Sleeps 8. Privy. Water source is a small spring to right of lean-to.

Sugarloaf Mountain—A 0.6-mile side trail to the east leads to the summit of Sugarloaf, where, on clear days, panoramic views include glimpses of Katahdin and Mt. Washington. Cool spring water can be found at 0.3 mile. This side trail was the last section of the original A.T. to open, in August 1937. The summit building of the Sugarloaf Ski Resort is now closed to the hiking public. *No camping.*

Crocker Cirque Campsite (1975)—Privy. Numerous campsites; east on a 0.2-mile side trail, one large group platform, 2 small platforms. Water source is the spring.

 Maine 27—East 2 miles to *Groceries:* Mountainside Grocers (long-term resupply), (207) 237-2248, at the base of Sugarloaf access road; open 7:30–6.
 West 5 miles to **Stratton, Maine [P.O. ZIP 04982: M–F 9–1 & 1:30–4, Sa 9–11:30; (207) 246-6461].** ■ *Hostel:* Stratton Motel & Hostel, (207) 246-4171, <www.thestrattonmotel.com>, owned by Susan Smith; hostel $20PP includes hiker kitchen, free Internet and long-distance phone; motel rooms $45S, $50D, $10EAP; free shuttle to Trail at Maine 27, local shuttles available; $5 laundry for nonguests; send mail drops to P.O. Box 284, Stratton, ME 04982. ■ *Lodging:* Spillover Motel, (207) 246-6571, $55S, $72D, pets okay with a $20 deposit and $5 charge, continental B, located south of town; White Wolf Inn, (207) 246-2922, closed Tu, $50S, $55D, dogs $5, accepts packages mailed to Main St., P.O. Box 590, Stratton, ME 04982; Diamond Corner B&B, (207) 246-2082, <www.bbonline.com/me/diamondcorner>, rooms $70–$100, includes B, shuttle to Trail, accepts mail drops at 8 Rangeley Road, P.O. Box 176, Stratton, ME 04982. ■ *Groceries:* Fotter's Market (long-term resupply), with deli, Coleman fuel and denatured alcohol by the ounce, M–Sa 8–8 Su 9–5; Northland Cash Supply (short-term resupply), pizza, daily 5–9, hiker box, accepts packages sent to 152 Main St., Stratton, ME 04982. ■ *Restaurants:* Stratton Diner B/L/D, Th–Tu, B only on W; White Wolf Café, L/D (closed Tu, D-only W); Stratton Plaza, Tu–Sa 11–9, Su 12–5, pizza, L/D; The Looney Moose Café, B/L/D, W–Su 7–8. ■ *Internet access:* library.

■ *Other services:* Old Mill Laundromat; bank; ATM; Mt. Abram Regional Health Center, (207) 265-4555, located in Kingfield. ■ *Shuttles:* Susan at Stratton Motel, (207) 246-4171.

West 10 miles *via* Route 16 to *Hostel:* The Maine Roadhouse, (207) 246-2060, <www.maineroadhouse.com>, owned by Susan Smith; bunk room $20PP, semiprivate rooms $40S, $50D, $10EAP; includes free laundry, free long-distance phone, satellite TV, hiker kitchen and grill, free shuttle to Trail (Route 27) and post office. Mail drops can be sent c/o Stratton Motel and Hostel, P.O. Box 284, Stratton, ME 04982.

Cranberry Stream Campsite (1995)—Privy. Stream is the water source.

Horns Pond Lean-tos (1997)—Two lean-tos; each sleeps 8. Privy. Located on a clear pond at which fishing is permitted. A MATC caretaker is in residence in this heavily used area. Water source is an often-dry spring on the A.T., north of the lean-tos, or Horns Pond.

Bigelow Mountain—Known as Maine's "Second Mountain," the Bigelow Range might look very different today had it not been for the efforts of many conservation groups, including MATC. During the 1960s and '70s, land developers had plans to turn the Bigelow Range into the "Aspen of the East," but opponents forced a state referendum on the issue. In 1976, the citizens of Maine decided, by a 3,000-vote margin, to have the state purchase the land and create a 33,000-acre wilderness preserve.

Bigelow Col/Avery Memorial Campsite—This deep cleft between West Peak and Avery Peak is a beautiful (although often cold) place to spend the night. You can catch the sunset or sunrise views from either peak. Avery Memorial Campsite, with tent platforms, privy, and spring, is located in the col. The spring is unreliable in dry years (2007); one maintained water site is behind the red maintenance shack, to left down unblazed trail.

Safford Notch Campsite—Privy. Located 0.3 mile east. Tent pads and platforms. Water source is Safford Brook, downhill from the campsite.

Little Bigelow Lean-to (1986)—Sleeps 8. Privy. Plenty of tentsites at this lean-to. Swimming in "the Tubs" along the side trail. Water source is a spring 50 yards in front of the lean-to.

West Carry Pond Lean-to (1989)—Sleeps 8. Privy. Swimming in pond. Water source is a spring house located to the left of the lean-to or West Carry Pond.

Arnold Trail—From West Carry to Middle Carry Pond, the A.T. follows the route of the historic Arnold Trail. In 1775, Benedict Arnold and an army of 1,150 men used this trail *en route* to Quebec, where they hoped to mount a surprise winter attack on the British. Like so many hikers, the army literally bogged down in the streams and swamps of the area, and, as a result, the remaining 650 men were so weakened by the passage that the attack was unsuccessful. Prior to Arnold's transit, the Abenaki Indians used the route as a portage around rapids on the Dead River, the waters of which now fill artificial Flagstaff Lake.

Pierce Pond Lean-to (1970)—Sleeps 6. Privy (moldering). Located on the east bank of Pierce Pond, with swimming, sunsets, and wildlife. Water source is the pond. A trail near here leads to Harrison's Pierce Pond Camps (see below).

Harrison's Pierce Pond Camps (1934)—Traditional Maine camp on blue-blazed trail across Pierce Pond Stream. Tim Harrison caters primarily to vacationers and anglers; summer radio phone, (207) 672-3625. Twelve-pancake lumberjack breakfast with juice, $8; eggs, $9; bacon, $10; hiker cabin, shower, towel, $30PP. If staying at Pierce Pond Lean-to, make reservations for B the night before. Water spigot; no credit cards; pets must be on leash. Hikers may use phone for emergencies.

Kennebec River Ferry—Over the last 21 years, canoes have ferried in excess of 18,000 hikers across the Kennebec River. For the 2010 hiker season, Fletcher Mountain Outfitters, David P. Corrigan/Registered Maine Master Guide, 82 Little Houston Brook Rd., Concord Township, ME 04920, (207) 672-4879, <maineguide@liv.com>, will handle this monumental task. The ferry will operate daily, at no cost to hikers, tentatively from:

Mid-May–mid-Jul	9–11 a.m.
Mid-Jul–Sep 27	9–11 a.m. and 2–4 p.m.
Sep 28–Oct 12	9 a.m.–11 a.m.

Exact hours and dates will be posted at Pierce Pond and Pleasant Pond lean-tos and on line at <www.matc.org>.

Kennebec River—The most formidable unbridged water-crossing on the Appalachian Trail. Ironically, the Indian word "Kennebec" means "long, quiet water." A thru-hiker drowned in 1985 trying to ford the river, and many other hikers have had close calls. Dangers include rocks, strong currents, and unpredictable water levels due to releases from the dams upstream. ATC and MATC strenuously urge hikers not to attempt to ford the river. Purists also should note that a ferry is the official "white-blaze" route, as well as the original, historical route of the A.T. across the Kennebec. This is a free service funded by ATC and MATC. Hikers need to arrive a half-hour before the ferry ceases operation. If late, be prepared to wait, and note that camping and fires are prohibited on both banks of the river. You will be required to sign a release form before crossing, wear a life jacket during the crossing, and follow the instructions of the ferry operator; please cooperate in these matters. If river conditions or weather make the crossing dangerous, the service will be discontinued until conditions improve. The ferry is for hiker and pack—the operator will not carry your pack so you can attempt to ford.

U.S. 201—East 0.3 mile on Main Street to **Caratunk, Maine [P.O. ZIP 04925: M–F 7:30–11:30 & 12–3:45, Sa 7:30–11:15; (207) 672-3416]**. The post office accepts credit and debit cards with limited cash back. Pay phone.

East 1 mile on U.S. 201 to *Lodging:* The Sterling Inn, (207) 672-3333, <maineskeptsecret@yahoo.com>, <www.mainesterlinginn.com>, 1041 U.S. 201, P.O. Box 129, Caratunk, ME 04925. Private rooms, continental B, $50–$65 includes pick-up at P.O.

East 16.5 miles to the small town of Bingham, with restaurants, laundry, pharmacy, and three grocery facilities (all long-term resupply). *Lodging:* Bingham Motor Inn, (866) 806-6120, <www.binghammotorinn.com>, $60S, $75D, $85T.

West 2 miles to *Lodging:* Northern Outdoors Resort, (800) 765-7238, rates begin at $57.252/room for lodge rooms (max 4 persons, subject to availability), cabin tents at $10.70PP, tent sites at $6.42PP; include all taxes; B/L/D, Kennebec River Pub & Brewery, shuttle to the A.T. (ask ahead), coin laundry, free showers, free Internet access, hot tubs, Kennebec River rafting trips (class IV) start at $79, accepts hiker mail/packages sent to Northern Outdoors, 1771 U.S. 201, The Forks, ME 04985. The Inn by the River, (207) 663-2181, <www.innbytheriver.com>, rooms with whirlpools and private porches start at $79–$129, B/L/D.

West 7 miles to Berry's General Store and Hardware, (207) 663-4461, <www.theforksarea.com>, accepts credit and debit cards; short, Heet-term resupply; in same building as West Forks P.O.

West 25 miles to Jackman, Maine, Regional Health Center, (207) 668-2691, 24-hour ER. The busy town of Jackman has coin laundry, pharmacy, and many moderately priced markets, motels, pubs, and restaurants. Bishop's Store (long-term resupply), (207) 668-3411, <www.bishopsstore.com>, has hiking and camping supplies, canister stove fuel, pizza, hot subs, beer, and liquor. *Lodging:* Bishop's Motel, (207) 668-3231, <www.bishopsmotel.com>, $89D.

Pleasant Pond Lean-to (1958, renovated 1991)—Sleeps 6. Privy. Sandy beach on Pleasant Pond is 0.2 mile from the lean-to. Water source is a small brook crossed on the path to the lean-to or pond.

Bald Mountain Brook Lean-to (1994)—Sleeps 8. Privy. Water source is Bald Mountain Brook, in front of the lean-to.

Moxie Bald Lean-to (1958)—Sleeps 6. Privy. Many moose in the area. Water source is Bald Mountain Pond in front.

West Branch of Piscataquis River—Normally knee-deep, this ford can be dangerous during periods of heavy rain. Do not attempt to cross in high water.

Horseshoe Canyon Lean-to (1991)—Sleeps 8. Privy. Lean-to is located on a blue-blaze. Water source is a spring at the A.T. junction or the river in front of, and below, the lean-to.

East Branch of the Piscataquis River—Like its West Branch, the 50-foot-wide East Branch of the Piscataquis can be tricky fording during periods of heavy rain.

Blue-blaze to Monson—Northbounders have an alternative route to Monson (see below), 3.3 miles south of Maine 15, near Lake Hebron; signs will point you in the right direction. This route leads a short distance to Pleasant St., where you will go left 2 miles into town.

Maine 15—East 4 miles to **Monson, Maine [P.O. ZIP 04464: M–F 7:30–11:30 & 12:30–4, Sa 7:30–11; (207) 997-3975].** No ATM, but post office accepts debit cards with *limited* cash back. ■ *Lodging:* Lake Shore House Lodging & Pub, (207) 997-7069, <www.lakeshore-house.com>, <thelakeshorehouse@yahoo.com>, open year-round; owner Rebekah Santagata. Bunks $25, private rooms $40S $55D, check-out anytime, packs out of rooms by 11 a.m.; advance reservations appreciated; laundromat open

24 hours; coin-op shower for nonguests; mail drops to P.O. Box 215, Monson, ME 04464; use of house phone with credit card; kayaks and paddleboats free for guests; occasional work-for-stay(3 hours' work); WiFi for guests; shuttle, slackpack, and food-drop arrangements anywhere; pub hours Tu–Sa 12–9, Su 12–8, bar open later, closed M; Lake Shore House guests welcome at Shaws' for breakfast, $7; well-behaved dogs welcome; floating bonfire weekends. Shaws' Lodging, (207) 997-3597, P.O. Box 72, Monson, ME 04464, <www.shawslodging.com>, <info@shawslodging.com>; owners Dawn MacPherson-Allen and Sue Stevens continue the Shaws' tradition of hospitality; open May to Oct, no credit cards; tenting $12PP, bunkhouse and bunkroom $21.50PP, guest rooms $32S $53.50D, semiprivate $26.75PP; advance reservations accepted; famous AYCE B $6.50, D Su–W $12; please sign up for meals in advance; dogs welcome in bunkhouse; nonguest showers $6; shuttles and laundry facilities available; mail drops accepted free for guests, small fee for nonguests; camp store open for 2009 season, long-term resupply and gear. ■ *Groceries:* Tim's Monson General Store (long-term resupply), debit/credit cards accepted, Coleman fuel by

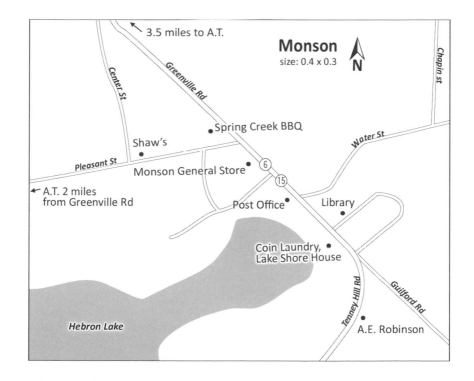

the ounce, alcohol-stove fuel; Friday nights, an old-fashioned bluegrass jam session fills the store with locals and hikers; be sure to sign the famous register. A.E. Robinson Mobil Mart (short-term resupply), pizzas, hiker-sized calzones, hot sandwiches. ■ *Restaurants:* Spring Creek BBQ, open Th–F 10–8 or until food runs out, Su 8–4 (food runs out at 3); work-for-food offered to thru-hikers, one hour of work for lunch, two hours for dinner. ■ *Internet access:* Monson Public Library, closed Sa–Su. ■ *Other services*: Monson Laundromat. ■ *Shuttles:* Buddy Ward, cell (207) 343-2564, home (207) 997-3792, <Buppyx4@midmaine.com>, provides shuttles in and out of the 100-Mile Wilderness, food drops, and emergency pick-ups, and will help set up slackpacking trips across the A.T. in Maine; Shaw's Lodging provides full-service shuttles throughout Maine and along A.T. between Caratunk and Baxter State Park.

West 8 miles to Greenville, Moosehead Lake's major tourist town and gateway to Maine's North Woods. ■ *Lodging:* Indian Hill Motel, (207) 695-2623, <indianhill-motel@gmail.com>, $68S/D, $10EAP. ■ *Groceries:* Village Food Mart (excellent bakery) and Indian Hill Trading Post (both long-term resupply). ■ *Restaurants:* Kelly's Landing, AYCE B on Su; Auntie M's Family Restaurant; The Stress-Free Moose Pub; Blue Frog Pub; Flatlanders Rod and Reel. ■ *Outfitter:* Northwoods Outfitters, (207) 695-3288, <www.maineoutfitter.com>, daily 7–7, Internet (fee), and coffee at the Hard Drive Café inside store. ■ *Other services:* Indian Hill Trading Post, <www.indianhill.com>, (800) 675-4487; banks with ATM; Harris Drug Store, (207) 695-2921; Charles A. Dean Memorial Hospital, 24-hour ER, (207) 695-5200; Greenville Veterinary Clinic, (207) 695-4408.

"100-Mile Wilderness"—Signs at each end of this section proclaim this area's remoteness and warn the unprepared hiker to stay away, but don't be intimidated. For those who don't think they can go 100 miles without resupply, supplies can be shuttled in at Jo-Mary, Kokadjo-B, and Katahdin Iron Works roads. There is a $10 fee for out-of-state residents to pass through the forest-road gates in vehicles. A local resupply provider is Kathy Preble, (207) 965-8464, <chair_back_mtn@yahoo.com>, P.O. Box 284, Brownville, ME 04442. The White House Landing Wilderness Camp, (207) 745-5116, is 32.3 miles south of Abol Bridge and 73.5 miles north of Monson; accepts MasterCard and Visa; no longer accepts mail drops but does have limited short-term resupplies. Hikers should remember to bring cash for Baxter State Park.

Leeman Brook Lean-to (1987)—Sleeps 6. Privy. Water source is the stream in front of the lean-to.

North Pond (outlet)   **West** 1.0 mile to *Hostel*: North Pond Haven, (207) 343-2787, hot showers, some food and beverages, transportation to town, propane stove and lights, woodstove with firewood, outhouse, $20 (1 or 2), $30 (3 or 4), $40 (5 or 6).

Wilson Valley Lean-to (1993)—Sleeps 6. Privy. Located north of Big Wilson Stream. Water source is a small spring in front of the lean-to, on the opposite side of the A.T.

Long Pond Stream Lean-to (1991)—Sleeps 8. Privy. Swimming in the scenic Slugundy Gorge and falls located 0.1 mile south, on a side trail 150 yards off the A.T. Water source is a small stream to the left of the lean-to.

Cloud Pond Lean-to (1992)—Sleeps 6. Privy 0.4 mile east. Water source is Cloud Pond, in front of the lean-to, or a spring to the north of the side trail to the lean-to.

Chairback Gap Lean-to (1954)—Sleeps 6. Privy. Water source, a small spring downhill and north of the lean-to 25 yards, is prone to go dry in drier years.

 Katahdin Iron Works (KIW) Road/West Branch of Pleasant River—Just east of the A.T., on the KIW logging road, is a parking lot for Gulf Hagas.
　　East 20 miles to Maine 11 and Brownville Junction. ■ *Groceries:* The Junction General Store and Trackside Café (short-term resupply), (207) 965-8876, <www. thejunctiongeneral.com>, deli, live outdoor music on summer weekends, primitive camping available. ■ *Other services:* Kathy Preble provides food drops and shuttles on the Jo-Mary, Kokadjo-B, and Katahdin Iron Works roads. Contact her well in advance: (207) 965-8464, <svivor@midmaine.com>, 191 Main St., Brownville, ME 04414.

The Hermitage—Camping is not allowed inside this protected area, a national landmark owned by The Nature Conservancy. Look for the plaque to learn the meaning of its name. Home to magnificent old-growth white pines. *Camping:* Maine North Woods campgrounds and $7 tentsites available near the Hermitage area. Maine North Woods, P.O. Box 425, Ashland, ME 04732, (207) 435-6213, <www.northmainewoods.org>, <info@northmainewoods.org>; contact it at the gatehouses; advance reservations are strongly recommended.
　　West 8 miles to *Lodging:* AMC Little Lyford Pond Camps, (603) 466-2727; $92 for bunkroom space, two-night minimum, B/L/D included.

Gulf Hagas—If you've got the food and the time, you may want to take this side trail. The gulf was formed by water eroding the slate walls of a narrow canyon. The result of this sculpting is a stretch of many spectacular waterfalls nestled in a chasm about 500 feet deep. If you want a taste of the gulf's scenery, Screw Auger Falls is only 0.2 mile from the A.T. on Gulf Hagas Brook. A 5.2-mile loop hike is possible using the Rim and Gulf Hagas trails. MATC stations a ridgerunner in the area, which receives a tremendous amount of day use. *No camping allowed.*

Carl A. Newhall Lean-to (1986)—Sleeps 6. Privy. Lean-to is north of Gulf Hagas Brook, the water source.

Sidney Tappan Campsite—Privy. Follow the blue-blaze 0.2 mile east to water; trail begins just north of the campsite.

Logan Brook Lean-to (1983)—Sleeps 6. Privy. Water source is Logan Brook behind the lean-to; cascades are farther upstream.

East Branch Lean-to (1996)—Sleeps 8. Privy. Water source is the East Branch of the Pleasant River, in front.

Cooper Brook Falls Lean-to (1956)—Sleeps 6. Full-moon privy. Tentsite on trail to lean-to. A waterfront lean-to with numerous pools and falls. Water source is Cooper Brook in front of the lean-to.

Jo-Mary Road—East 6 miles to *Camping:* Smith's Jo-Mary Lake Campground, (207) 723-8117, <www.campmaine.com/jo-mary>, mid-May–Oct 1, campsites $18.50, campstore B/L, showers, laundry, bean-hole suppers W after Jul 4, shuttle, dogs welcome. For those wishing to resupply, Jo-Mary Road sees some traffic, thanks to the campground; 20 miles to Maine 11 and Brownville Junction.

Antlers Campsite—Campsites are on the edge of Lower Jo-Mary. Fort Relief privy to the west of the Trail. Water source is Jo-Mary Lake.

Potaywadjo Spring Lean-to (1995)—Sleeps 8. Privy. Water source is the 15-foot-wide Potaywadjo Spring, to the right of the lean-to.

Maher Trail/Maher Tote Road/White House Landing Wilderness Camp—East 1.2 miles to *Lodging:* White House Landing, (207) 745-5116. *Northbound directions:* Follow A.T. 2.8 miles north of Potaywadjo Spring Lean-to to third road north of lean-to, go east 0.2 mile on Maher Trail/Maher Tote Road to Pemadumcook Lake, follow lake shoreline south 1.0 mile to boat dock. *Southbound directions:* Follow A.T. 1.5 miles south of Nahmakanta Stream Campsite, go east 0.2 mile on Maher Trail/Maher Tote Road to Pemadumcook Lake, follow lake shoreline south 1.0 mile to boat dock. At boat dock, sound airhorn one short blast for ferry ride to camp; no ferry after dark. Owners Bill, Linda, and Ben Ware offer bunkhouse $35PP, private rooms $45PP, includes AYCE B and shower for guests only. Open year-round; L and grill menu 11–1 (try Linda's famous one-pound burger); D for all, but, if you're not staying, be packed up and ready for the boat ride immediately afterward. Ben & Jerry's, cold drinks, campstore (short-term resupply), butane/propane canister fuel, denatured alcohol, white gas, and canoes. *No* mail drops. Shuttle service may be available with advance notice, but not every day. Round-trip shuttle to Millinocket takes 3 hours. Visa and MasterCard accepted; fee may be charged.

Nahmakanta Stream Campsite—Privy. Water is a stream in front of the campsite.

Wadleigh Stream Lean-to (1981)—Sleeps 6. Privy. Located 0.5 mile north of Nahmakanta Lake, which has a sandy beach. Water source is a spring on the beach.

Rainbow Stream Lean-to (1971)—Sleeps 6. Privy. Home of the A.T.'s best totem pole; often crowded with hiker groups. Good tenting and hammocking above and behind the lean-to. Water source is Rainbow Stream, in front.

Rainbow Spring Campsite—Privy. Water source is a flowing spring at the shore of Rainbow Lake.

Hurd Brook Lean-to (1959)—Sleeps 6. Privy. During high water, Hurd Brook, 50 feet south of the lean-to, can be deep and swift, and the ford dangerous. Area is frequented by hunters. Water source is Hurd Brook. Southbounders might want to tank up at the spring 0.7 mile north of the lean-to.

"Golden Road"/Abol Bridge. ■ *Camping:* Abol Bridge Campground, open May 15–Sep 30, privately run and located along the road on the West Branch of the Penobscot River, campsites $10PP, coin-op showers for guests only, all visitors must register; Abol Pines, seasonal, tentsite or space in one of two six-person lean-tos,

$8PP plus tax for out-of-state residents, reached by following a dirt road 75 yards east in front of the camp store. ■ *Groceries:* Linda's Store at Abol Bridge (short-term resupply), deli, microwave foods, ice cream, A.T. souvenirs, cellular pay phone ($1 per 3 minutes for out-of-state calls, even toll-free; 50¢ local); credit cards accepted. **East** 20 miles to Millinocket, Maine (see page 275).

Baxter State Park—The northern terminus of the Appalachian Trail is Baxter Peak on Katahdin, Maine's highest mountain. Katahdin, along with the surrounding landscape, is part of a 209,501-acre wilderness sanctuary and forest preserve, Baxter State Park; <www.baxterstateparkauthority.com>. The lands were donated in perpetual trust to the people of Maine by former Governor Percival Proctor Baxter, who served from 1921 to 1924. BSP is self-supporting, in large part due to Baxter's trust funds and by his design, and is administered separately from any other agency or state park in Maine. Baxter's goal was to place preservation of natural resources as a priority over their recreational use, so some of BSP's regulations and policies are distinct from what may be encountered elsewhere along the A.T. They were created to address protection of the park's natural features and wilderness, protection of the visitor's wilderness experience, and promotion of an attitude of personal responsibility and safety. No other entity is comparable to BSP along the Trail corridor. All visitors here are recipients of a very special gift, so please work with park authorities to honor the intent of such generosity by upholding its policies and regulations.

Most of Baxter's A.T-related rules stem from the weather. Unlike the surrounding landscape south, Katahdin is exposed to extreme weather, including high winds, and has gotten snow during every month of the year. No shelters are located above treeline (north of Katahdin Stream Campground), and all trails to the summit are completely exposed. On humid, unsettled, late-summer days, for example, it is wise to start down by 1 p.m. to avoid electrical storms.

Dogs—Dogs are not allowed in the park. See Millinocket and Medway entries for kennels.

Katahdin—The translation of the Indian word is "greatest mountain." Maine Indians considered the mountain a holy place and believed in Pamola, the deity of Katahdin, who purportedly would destroy any man who ventured too close to the mountain. The first recorded ascent of Katahdin by Euroamericans came on Aug 13, 1804, when a party led by Charles Turner, Jr., reached the summit by the same rocks-and-roots route used by the A.T.—the Hunt Trail (named after the Hunt family that

Katahdin by Scott Gamble

had a homestead below). Since then, the mountain has captured the imagination of many, including Henry David Thoreau, who explored the area in 1846. Thoreau Spring on the Tableland bears his name, although he never made it there. From Katahdin Stream Campground, it is a 10.4-mile trip to the summit and back. The ascent packs an elevation gain of 4,000 feet into 5 miles. Backpacks may be left at the ranger station at the campground, where you can borrow a daypack and obtain information on weather conditions. The park posts "cut-off" times for beginning your climb: In Aug, you must start before 11 a.m.; in Sep, 10 a.m.; in Oct, 9 a.m. Park rules require that you sign in at the campground before your climb and sign out on your return. Don't forget to make your final, or first, register entry on the ranger station's front porch.

Weather—Baxter State Park posts daily weather reports during the hiking season at 7 a.m. The categories tell you what to expect for your hiking day:

- *Class I*—Recommended for hiking above treeline.

- *Class II*—Not recommended for hiking above treeline.

- *Class III*—Not recommended for hiking above treeline, with the following trails closed (specified trails will follow).

- *Class IV*—All trails closed at the trailheads. A hiker who climbs Katahdin on a Class IV day is subject to a court summons, a fine, seizure of equipment, and revocation of park privileges.

Register—Every hiker must register with a ranger upon entering BSP. An information kiosk is located on the A.T. 1 mile north of Abol Bridge. The 12 hikers using The Birches (see below) must sign up at the Abol Stream kiosk and also with the ranger at Katahdin Stream Campground. A MATC/Baxter Park ridgerunner patrols the area to help hikers with information on the A.T. and the park.

Reservations—A "rolling reservations" policy is available four months in advance of the day you wish to stay within the park. If you want Jun 3, you need to know your reservation will not be processed before Feb 3. The traditional opening day to make walk-in reservations is Jan 17. More information, and a chart outlining when reservations can be made, is at <www.baxterstateparkauthority.com>.

The overnight camping season is May 15–Oct 15 each year. After Oct 15, overnight camping is prohibited anywhere within the park. You may camp at the private Abol Bridge campground or the Maine DOC Abol Pines Campground downriver of Abol Bridge. Both charge fees. Your hike to the summit is then 15 miles one way from this area outside the park. Another option when BSP is closed for camping is to stay in Millinocket and hire a taxi or shuttle in and out of Baxter on the day of your hike. Southbounders should note that the A.T. from Katahdin Stream Campground to Baxter Peak might not be open until Jun 1. Northbounders should note that they can phone the park about openings at the campground and mail in their reservations request. Campsite reservations may be made *via* phone no sooner than 14 days before the desired date, if available, with a credit card. If you can't get camping space at one of the reservation-only campgrounds or the 12-slot Birches (see below), a very fit and fast thru-hiker, with 2,000 miles under her (or his) belt, might try leaving from and returning to Abol Bridge *via* the Blueberry Ledges Trail, a 19.2-mile round-trip to Katahdin's summit that includes the most challenging ascent and descent on the entire A.T. It wouldn't be a very leisurely way to end your thru-hike.

Pamphlet—*Long-Distance Hiking in Baxter State Park*, a pamphlet, is available on request from BSP. It has a map of the A.T. and the Blueberry Ledges Trail, a wealth of information about the park, and a message from park management.

Mail and Messages—BSP does not accept mail or packages. Mail drops should be arranged through the Millinocket post office.

Trail closings at Katahdin—It is advised to plan to reach BSP by Oct 1. A.T. hikers must arrange to climb Katahdin before Oct 15; park officials emphasize that this is the cut-off date for climbing Katahdin. It also coincides with the end of the summer/fall camping season in the park. Statistics show that, in this northerly climate, chances are slim that you will be able to successfully finish your hike at Katahdin's summit after this date. Winter hiking season is Dec 1–Mar 31; you must obtain a permit from the park to climb Katahdin then, and you must have a minimum of four people in your climbing party.

In some years, access to the park road and trails up Katahdin can be closed by snowstorms for up to two weeks *before* Oct 15. On those days, the A.T. up to Baxter Peak is open only when weather permits (see above). Each day at 7 a.m., park rangers post the weather forecast and determine the "class" for trails above treeline. Class III and IV days, which involve trail closures, are common in late Sep–Oct. When the day has been classified as a Class IV, anyone hiking beyond the Trailhead at Katahdin Stream toward the summit of Katahdin is subject to a summons and fine, seizure of equipment, and permanent revocation of park privileges. If you must be rescued, assistance will be delayed until the rescuers can proceed safely; you could be found negligent and liable for all costs of search and rescue.

After Oct 15, Baxter State Park is open for day use only (sunrise to sunset) for all hiking, conditions permitting. Vehicular access to the park usually ends completely by Nov 1 or whenever conditions that pose a threat to personal safety or to the resources have locked in for the season.

Beginning at Katahdin—Thru-hikers beginning their trek at Katahdin should make reservations for campsites well in advance of their starting dates. During July and Aug, campsites normally are booked to maximum levels.

Ending at Katahdin—Northbounders who plan to have family and friends meet them at the park should reserve campsites in advance. Labor Day weekend is especially packed, with a traditional Indian festival reserving the entire Katahdin Stream Campground. If driving into the park, there is a $13 fee at the gate for out-of-state residents. Advise those who are meeting you to be waiting in line when the south gate, Togue Pond, opens at 5 a.m. between July 1 and Labor Day. When parking lots fill, visitors will be directed to open lots and alternate trailheads by the rangers at the gatehouse. Plan ahead!

Southbounders, it is suggested you reserve a site for the nights before and after climbing Katahdin. For reservations and information, contact BSP, 64 Balsam Dr., Millinocket, ME 04462, (207) 723-5140.

Camping in Baxter State Park—Two 4-person lean-tos and tenting space for 4 additional people are available at a site called **The Birches**, not far from Katahdin Stream Campground. Advance reservations are not required; the fee to stay there is $10PP. At reservation campgrounds, the fee is $30 for either lean-to or tentsite. *Cash only inside park.*

The Birches is 9.8 miles from Abol Bridge *via* the A.T. or 4.4 miles from Abol Bridge *via* the Blueberry Ledges Trail. Use of the The Birches facilities is limited strictly to 12 long-distance or thru-hikers (must be hiking, at a minimum, the "100-Mile Wilderness") *and is limited to one night.* Park authorities have posted a sign-up sheet for long-distance hikers at the information kiosk just north of Abol Bridge. If all 12 spaces are claimed for the night that you planned to stay at The Birches, you will need to stay elsewhere. Your choices include the Abol Bridge private campground; the nearby Department of Conservation Abol Pines site on the West Branch of the Penobscot (both are fee sites); standard-reservation campsites at Katahdin Stream Campground, Foster Field Group Campsite, or any other available site of your choice in the park, if they are not already full; or staying in a campground or motel near Millinocket, if available. In Jul and Aug, and on all fall weekends, it is difficult to get a site at Katahdin Stream or elsewhere in the park, because sites are often reserved months in advance. However, Labor Day–Oct 15, it is possible (although not certain) that you will find vacant sites at Katahdin Stream during the week.

2,000-Miler Certificate Applications—ATC has asked rangers at Katahdin Stream Campground to hand out forms to all northbounders who are about to finish the Trail, in an effort to expedite the processing of 2,000-miler certificates. See requirements on page ix.

Reaching Baxter State Park—No public transportation is available to and from BSP. Unless you have someone meeting you at the park, you'll need to hitch 24 miles from the Trail to Millinocket. Rides are usually easy to find, since almost everyone headed out of the park must go through Millinocket.

Baxter State Park Road—BSP Togue Pond Visitors Center, M–Th 7–3, F–Su 7–6; maps, guidebooks, additional information; beach, and picnic area (no camping).

East 2 miles from the park's south gate to *Lodging:* Maine Timberland Company's Katahdin Forest Cabins, (877) 622-2467, log cabin on Sunday Pond, spectacular view of Katahdin, $87 per night, sleeps 6, with gas heat, stove, and privy; advance reservations necessary.

East 2.6 miles to *Camping:* Penobscot Outdoor Center on Pockwockamus Pond, (207) 723-3580, tentsites, showers, sauna, hot tub, restaurant, and lounge; call for rates.

East 7 miles to Golden Road junction (8 miles from here to Abol Bridge).

East 8.3 miles to ■ *Groceries:* Northwoods Trading Post (short-term resupply), (207) 723-4326, open 7–9, last gas station, pay phone, and ATM before entering BSP. A.T. maps, books, trail guides, patches, and souvenirs. ■ *Lodging:* Big Moose Inn, (207) 723-8391, <www.bigmoosecabins.com>, inn room with shared bath weekday $40, weekend $44; camping $10PP; lean-to $13PP; cabins, call for rates; restaurant and bar open W–Su, B available Sa–Su, no pets.

East 15.6 miles to *Camping:* Hidden Springs Campground, (888) 685-4488 or (207) 723-6337, <www.hiddenspring.com>, tentsites $10PP/night, shower without stay $3.

East 17 miles from the park's south gate to **Millinocket, Maine [P.O. 04462: M–F 9–4, Sa 9–11:30; (207) 723-5921]**. BSP Headquarters, (207) 723-5140, 64 Balsam Dr., park reservations, publications, maps, and general information. ■ *Camping:* Rice Farm Campgrounds, (207) 723-8475, tentsites $10–$12PP, canvas tents $22–$28PP, showers included. ■ *Lodging:* Appalachian Trail Lodge and Café, (207) 723-4321, <www.appalachiantraillodge.com>, your one-stop hiker service, owners Paul (Ole-Man) & Jaime (NaviGator) Renaud, $25 bunkroom, $35S, $55D, furnished apartment call for rates; other hiker specials; parking $1/day; showers for nonguests $3; WiFi, fuel, some hiking supplies; licensed and insured shuttle service to and from bus in Medway, into 100-mile wilderness or Monson, free daily shuttle from Baxter in Sep; food drops in 100-mile wilderness; other shuttles by prearrangement; one private room available for hikers with pets; accepts mail drops at 33 Penobscot Ave., Millinocket, ME 04462; credit cards accepted for lodge at café. Econolodge Inn & Suites, (207) 723-4555, $69S, $89D, $10EAP, dogs okay, continental B, indoor pool, hot tub, restaurant/lounge on premises. Best Value Heritage Motor Inn, (207) 723-9777, $79S, $89D, $10EAP, dogs welcome $10, continental B. Katahdin B&B, (207) 723-5220, 96 Oxford St., <katahdinbandb@yahoo.com>, e-mail for reservations, hosts Mary Lou and Rodney (a Maine guide), $60–$75, laundry available, accepts mail drops; hiker supplies, hot tubs, no pets; call ahead for shuttles; no credit cards accepted. Pamola

Motor Lodge, (800) 575-9746, (207) 723-9746, <wwwpamolamotorlodge.com>, $59S, $67D, dogs okay, continental B, Internet access, outdoor pool, hot tub, lounge, laundry service; call ahead for shuttles. Hotel Terrace, (207) 723-4525, $47S, $56D, $5EAP. The Young House B&B, (207) 723-5452, <www.theyounghousebandb.com>, 193 Central Ave., $80, credit cards accepted, WiFi, accepts mail drops. ■ *Restaurants:* Appalachian Trail Café, open 5–8, owned by Paul and Jaime Renaud, home of the Sundae Summit Challenge, home-made food, free Internet access, one-of-a-kind countertop of A.T.; Hotel Terrace, L/D, AYCE only on weekends; Hang Wong at Pamola Inn, (207) 723-6084, M–Sa AYCE L; Mountain Village Company, with bakery, deli, and Internet access ($3.50 for 20 minutes); Central Street; Scootic Inn Restaurant, (207) 723-4566; Blue Ox Saloon; Neoc River Drivers Restaurant, with coffee shop, bakery, deli, and Internet access ($3.50 for 30 minutes). ■ *Other services:* Most major services are available in town, including supermarkets, coin laundries, and banks with ATM; Town Taxi, (207) 723-2000, provides service to the bus station ($15) in Medway and ($55) to Baxter State Park; Millinocket Regional Hospital, (207) 723-5161. ■ *Kennel services:* Connie McManus, (207) 723-6795, will pick up at Abol Bridge and house dogs for thru-hikers. There is no bus service in Millinocket, but Cyr Bus Lines of Old Town, Maine, serves nearby Medway (see below).

Medway—*Lodging:* Katahdin Shadows Motel, (207) 746-5162, 10 miles east on Maine 157, <www.katahdinshadows.com>, $49S, $54D, $10EAP; Gateway Inn, <www.medwaygateway.com>, (207) 746-3193, $55 and up, dogs welcome; Pine Grove Campground and Cottages, (207) 746-5172, <www.pinegrovecamping.com>, tentsites, fully equipped cottages, dogs welcome, free use of canoe and kayak for guests, will pick up at bus station. ■ *Outfitter:* Nicatau Outfitter, <www.mainecampingtrips.com>, (207) 746-3253 or (207) 746-3251, call ahead for shuttles or boarding pet. ■ *Bus service:* Cyr Bus Lines of Old Town, Maine, serves northern Maine; 10 miles east on Maine 757, (207) 927-2335, (207) 827-2010, or (800) 244-2335, <info@cyrbustours.com>. A bus leaves Bangor at 6:00 p.m. and arrives at Medway at 7:40 p.m.; leaves Medway at 9:30 a.m. and arrives at Bangor at 10:50 a.m.; fee $11.50 one way. ■ *Kennel services:* North Ridge Boarding Kennel, (207) 746-9537, <northridgekennels.com>, owner Jack Misiaszek will pick up and deliver dogs (and packages), $75 each way; hours for drop-off and pick-up are 9–10 a.m. and 6–7 p.m.; $20 per day per dog. Pawprints Resort, (207) 746-3434, <www.pawprintsresort.com>, day care and boarding, pick-up/drop-off services.

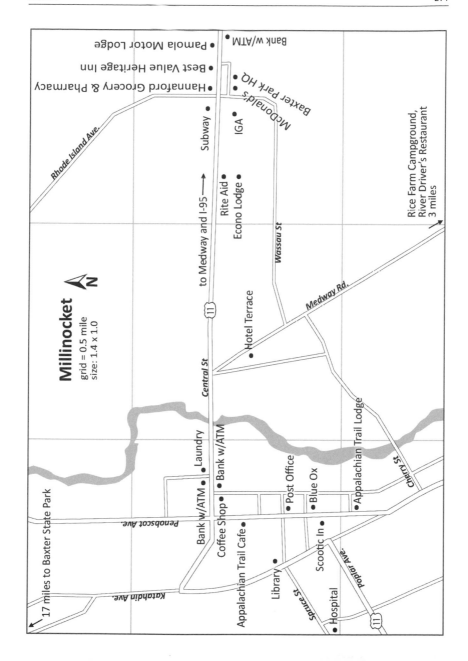

Millinocket

grid = 0.5 mile
size: 1.4 x 1.0

N

Bank w/ATM
Pamola Motor Lodge
Best Value Heritage Inn
Hannaford Grocery & Pharmacy
Baxter Park HQ
McDonald's
Rhode Island Ave.
Subway
IGA
Rite Aid
Econo Lodge
Wassau St.
to Medway and I-95
Medway Rd.
Rice Farm Campground,
River Driver's Restaurant
3 miles
Hotel Terrace
Central St.
Laundry
Bank w/ATM
Appalachian Trail Lodge
Cherry St.
Bank w/ATM
Coffee Shop
Post Office
Blue Ox
Penobscot Ave.
Appalachian Trail Cafe
Library
Scootic In
Poplar Ave.
Spruce St.
Hospital
Katahdin Ave.
17 miles to Baxter State Park

Bangor—A city with all major services, <www.bangorinfo.com>. For those traveling to or returning from BSP, Bangor offers a bus station and airport. The Chamber of Commerce, (207) 947-0307, can provide information as you prepare for your hike or return. For information on local transportation in the Bangor area: BAT Commuter Connection, (207) 992-4670, <www.bangormaine.gov>. ■ *Lodging:* Many motels and a mall are near the airport, including Days Inn, (207) 942-9272; Econo Lodge, (207) 945-0111; Fairfield Inn, (207) 990-0001; Howard Johnson's, (207) 947-3464; Holiday Inn, (207) 947-0101. ■ *Outfitters:* Epic Sports, (207) 941-5670, <www.epicsportsofmaine.com>, 6 Central St., M–Sa 9–8, Su 9–5; Dick's Sporting Goods, (207) 990-5932, located in the Bangor Mall. ■ *Bus service:* Concord Coach, (800) 639-3317; Cyr Bus Lines with daily transportation to Medway, (800) 244-2335 (see above).

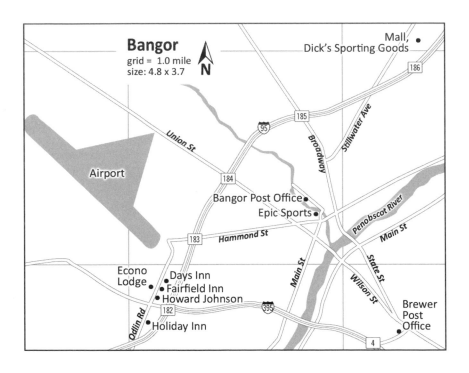

Post Offices along the A.T.

Post offices are listed here in south-to-north order. *Note: Many post offices (perhaps all) have been shaving one hour or more off their daily hours, typically some in the morning, some in the afternoon, and some at lunch time.* Changes we have verified are reflected here, but please take this development into account in your planning for picking up packages—call ahead!

Local post office telephone numbers can be verified by calling (800) 275-8777 (ASK USPS).

Post offices printed in bold are located on, or within one mile of, the Trail.

Town	ZIP Code	Hours Phone
Suches, GA	30572	M–F 7:30–11:30 & 1–4:30, Sa 7:30–11:30 (706) 747-2611
Helen, GA	30545	M–F 9–5, Sa 9–12 (706) 878-2422
Hiawassee, GA	30546	M–F 8:30–5:30, Sa 8:30–12 (706) 896-3632
Franklin, NC	28734	M–F 8:45–12 & 1:15–5, Sa 8:30–10 (828) 524-3219
Bryson City, NC	28713	M–F 8:30–12 & 12:30–4, closed Sa (828) 488-3481
Fontana Dam, NC	28733	M–F 8:30–12 & 12:30–4:30, closed Sa (828) 498-2315
Gatlinburg, TN	37738	M–F 9–5, Sa 10–11 (865) 436-3229
Cherokee, NC	28719	M–F 9–4:30, Sa 10–11:30 (828) 497-3891
Hot Springs, NC	**28743**	M–F 8:30–11:30 & 1–4, Sa 8:30–10:30 (828) 622-3242
Erwin, TN	37650	M–F 8:30–4:45, Sa 10–12 (423) 743-9422
Unicoi, TN	37692	M–F 8–11 & 12–4, Sa 8:30–10:30 (800) 275-8777
Elk Park, NC	28622	M–F 7:30–12 & 1:30–4:15, Sa 7:30–11 (828) 733-5711
Roan Mountain, TN	37687	M–F 8:15–11:30 & 12:30–4:15, Sa 8:15–11 (423) 772-3014

Hampton, TN	37658	M–F 7:30–11:30 & 12:30–4:30, Sa 8–10 (423) 725-2177
Shady Valley, TN	37688	M–F 7:30–11 & 12–3:30, Sa 7:30–9:30 (423) 739-2173
Damascus, VA	**24236**	M–F 8:30–1 & 2–4:30, Sa 9–11 (276) 475-3411
Troutdale, VA	24378	M–F 8:15–12 & 1–4:30, Sa 8:15–11:30 (276) 677-3221
Sugar Grove, VA	24375	M–F 8:15–12 & 1:15–4:45, Sa 8:15–10:30 (276) 677-3200
Marion, VA	24354	M–F 8:30–5, Sa 9:30–12 (276) 783-5051
Atkins, VA	24311	M–F 9–1 & 2:30–4:, Sa 9:30–11 (276) 783-5551
Bland, VA	24315	M–F 8–11:30 & 12–4, Sa 9–11 (276) 688-3751
Bastian, VA	24314	M–F 8–12 & 12:30–4, Sa 8–10:30 (276) 688-4631
Pearisburg, VA	**24134**	M–F 9–4:30, Sa 10–12 (540) 921-1100
Catawba, VA	**24070**	M–F 7:30–12 & 1–5, Sa 8–10:30 (540) 384-6011
Daleville, VA	**24083**	M–F 8–5, Sa 8–12 (540) 992-4422
Cloverdale, VA	24077	M–F 8:30–11 & 11:30–4, Sa 9–12 (540) 992-2334
Troutville, VA	24175	M–F 9–12 & 1–5, Sa 9–11 (540) 992-1472
Buchanan, VA	24066	M–F 8:30–1 & 1:30–4:30, Sa 10–12 (540) 254-2178
Big Island, VA	24526	M–F 8:30–12:30 & 1:30–4:30, Sa 8–10 (434) 299-5072
Glasgow, VA	24555	M–F 8–11:30 & 12:30–4:30, Sa 8:30–10:30 (540) 258-2852
Buena Vista, VA	24416	M–F 8:30–4:30, closed Sa (540) 261-8959
Lexington, VA	24450	M–F 9–5, Sa 10–12 (540) 463-6449
Montebello, VA	24464	M–F 8–12 & 12:30–4:30, Sa 9–12 (540) 377-9218
Waynesboro, VA	22980	M–F 9–5, closed Sa (540) 942-7320

Elkton, VA	22827	M–F 8:30–4:30, Sa 9–11 (540) 298-7772
Luray, VA	22835	M–F 8:30–4:30, closed Sa (540) 743-2100
Front Royal, VA	22630	M–F 8:30–5, Sa 8:30–1 (540) 635-7983
Linden, VA	22642	M–F 8–12 & 1–5, Sa 8–12 (540) 636-9936
Bluemont, VA	20135	M–F 8:30–12 & 1–5, Sa 8:30–12 (540) 554-4537
Harpers Ferry, WV	**25425**	M–F 8–4, Sa 9–12 (304) 535-2479
Boonsboro, MD	21713	M–F 9–1 & 2–5, Sa 9–12 (301) 432-6861
Smithsburg, MD	21783	M–F 8:30–1 & 2–4:30, Sa 8:30–12 (301) 824-2828
Cascade, MD	21719	M–F 8–1 & 2–5, Sa 8–12 (301) 242-3403
Blue Ridge Summit, PA	17214	M–F 8–4:30, Sa 9–11:30 (717) 794-2335
Waynesboro, PA	17268	M–F 8:30–5, Sa 9–12 (717) 762-1513
South Mountain, PA	17261	M–F 8–1 & 2–4:45, Sa 8:30–11:30 (717) 749-5833
Fayetteville, PA	17222	M–F 8–4:30, Sa 8:30–12 (717) 352-2022
Mt. Holly Springs, PA	17065	M–F 8–4:30, Sa 9–12 (717) 486-3468
Boiling Springs, PA	**17007**	M–F 8–4:30, Sa 8–12 (717) 258-6668
Duncannon, PA	**17020**	M–F 8–4:30, Sa 8–12 (717) 834-3332
Bethel, PA	19507	M–F 8–12, 1:15–4:30, Sa 8:30–10:30 (717) 933-8305
Pine Grove, PA	17963	M–F 8:30–4:30, Sa 9–12 (570) 345-4955
Port Clinton, PA	**19549**	M–F 7:30–12:30 & 2–5, Sa 8–11 (610) 562-3787
Hamburg, PA	19526	M–F 9–5, Sa 9–12 (610) 562-7812
Slatington, PA	18080	M–F 8:30–5, Sa 8:30–12 (610) 767-2182

Walnutport, PA	18088	M–F 8:30–5, Sa 8:30–12 (610) 767-5191
Palmerton, PA	18071	M–F 8:30–5, Sa 8:30–12 (610) 826-2286
Danielsville, PA	18038	M–F 8–12 & 1–5, Sa 8–12 (610) 767-6882
Wind Gap, PA	**18091**	M–F 8:30–5, Sa 8:30–12 (610) 863-6206
Delaware Water Gap, PA	**18327**	M–F 8:30–12 & 1–4:45, Sa 8:30–11:30 (570) 476-0304
Branchville, NJ	07826	M–F 8:30–5, Sa 8:30–1 (973) 948-3580
Unionville, NY	10988	M–F 8–12 & 1–5, Sa 8–12 (845) 726-3535
Glenwood, NJ	07418	M–F 7:30–5, Sa 6:30–2 (973) 764-2616
Vernon, NJ	07462	M–F 8:30–5, Sa 9:30–12:30 (973) 764-9056
Greenwood Lake, NY	10925	M–F 8–5, Sa 9–12 (845) 477-7328
Bellvale, NY	10912	M–F 8–12 & 1–4:30, Sa 8–12 (845) 986-2880
Warwick, NY	10990	M–F 8:30–7, Sa 9–4 (845) 986-0271
Southfields, NY	10975	M–F 8–12, 1–5, Sa 8:30–11:30 (845) 351-2628
Bear Mountain, NY	**10911**	M–F 8–12, closed Sa (845) 786-3747
Ft. Montgomery, NY	**10922**	M–F 8–1 & 2:30–5, Sa 9–12 (845) 446-8459
Peekskill, NY	10566	M–F 9–5, Sa 9–4 (914) 737-1340
Stormville, NY	12582	M–F 8:30–5, Sa 9–12 (845) 226-2627
Poughquag, NY	12570	M–F 8:30–5, Sa 8:30–12:30 (845) 724-4763
Pawling, NY	12564	M–F 8:30–5, Sa 9–12 (845) 855-2669
Wingdale, NY	12594	M–F 8–5, Sa 8–12:30 (845) 832-6147
Gaylordsville, CT	06755	M–F 8–1 & 2–5, Sa 8–12 (860) 354-9727

Kent, CT	06757	M–F 8–1 & 2–5, Sa 8:30–12:30 (860) 927-3435
Cornwall Bridge, CT	06754	M–F 8–1 & 2–5, Sa 9–12 (860) 672-6710
West Cornwall	06796	M–F 8–1 & 2–4:30, Sa 9–12 (860) 672-6791
Sharon, CT	06069	M–F 8:30–4:30, Sa 9:30–12:30 (860) 364-5306
Falls Village, CT	06031	M–F 8:30–1 & 2–5, Sa 8:30–12 (860) 824-7781
Salisbury, CT	06068	M–F 8–1 & 2–5, Sa 9–12 (860) 435-5072
South Egremont, MA	01258	M–F 8:15–12 & 12:30–4, Sa 9–11:30 (413) 528-1571
Sheffield, MA	01257	M–F 9–4:30, Sa 9–12 (413) 229-8772
Great Barrington, MA	01230	M–F 8:30–4:30, Sa 8:30–12:30 (413) 528-3670
Monterey, MA	01245	M–F 8:30–1 & 2–4:30, Sa 9–11:30 (413) 528–4670
Tyringham, MA	01264	M–F 9–12:30 & 4–5:30, Sa 8:30–12.30 (413) 243-1225
Lee, MA	01238	M–F 8:30–4:30, Sa 9–12 (413) 243-1392
Becket, MA	01223	M–F 8–4, Sa 9–11:30 (413) 623-8845
Dalton, MA	01226	M–F 8:30–4:30, Sa 9–12 (413) 684-0364
Cheshire, MA	01225	M–F 7:30–1 & 2–4:30, Sa 8:30–11:30 (413) 743-3184
Adams, MA	01220	M–F 8:30–4:30, Sa 10–12 (413) 743-5177
North Adams, MA	01247	M–F 8:30–4:30, Sa 10–12 (413) 664-4554
Williamstown, MA	01267	M–F 8:30–4:30, Sa 9–12 (413) 458-3707
Bennington, VT	05201	M–F 8–5, Sa 9–2 (802) 442-2421
Manchester Center, VT	05255	M–F 8–4:30, Sa 9:30–12 (802) 362-3070
Danby, VT	05739	M–F 7:15–12 & 1:15–4, Sa 7:30–10:30 (802) 293-5105

Wallingford, VT	05773	M–F 8–4:30, Sa 9–12 (802) 446-2140
Rutland, VT	05701	M–F 8–5, Sa 8–12 (802) 773-0222
Killington, VT	**05751**	M–F 8:30–4:30, Sa 8:30–12 (802) 775-4247
Pittsfield, VT	05762	M–F 8–12 & 2–4:30, Sa 8:30–11:30 (802) 746-8953
Woodstock, VT	05091	M–F 8:30–5, Sa 9–12 (802) 457-1323
South Pomfret, VT	**05067**	M–F 8–1 & 2–4:45, Sa 8:30–11:30 (802) 457-1147
West Hartford, VT	**05084**	M–F 7:30–11:30 & 1–4:45, Sa 7:30–10:15 (802) 295-6293
Norwich, VT	**05055**	M–F 8:30–5, Sa 9–12 (802) 649-1608
Hanover, NH	**03755**	M–F 8:30–5, Sa 8:30–12, pkg pick-up open 7 a.m. (603) 643-4544
Lyme, NH	03768	M–F 8–12 & 2:30–4:45, Sa 8–11:30 (603) 795-4421
Wentworth, NH	03282	M–F 7:15–1 & 3–5, Sa 7:15–12 (603) 764-9444
Warren, NH	03279	M–F 7:30–1 & 2:30–5, Sa 8–11:30 (603) 764-5733
Glencliff, NH	**03238**	M–F 7–10 & 2–5, Sa 7–1 (603) 989-5154
North Woodstock, NH	03262	M–F 8:30–12:30 & 1:30–4:30, Sa 9–12 (603) 745-8134
Lincoln, NH	03251	M–F 8–5, Sa 8–12 (603) 745-8133
Bartlett, NH	03812	M–F 8:30–1 & 1:30–4:45, Sa 8:30–12 (603) 374-2351
Mt. Washington, NH	**03589**	Not recommended for mail drop (603) 466-3347
Gorham, NH	03581	M–F 8:30–5, Sa 8:30–12 (603) 466-2182
Andover, ME	04216	M–F 8:30–1:30 & 2–4:30, Sa 8:30–11:30 (207) 392-4571
Oquossoc, ME	04964	M–F 8–1 & 1:30–4:15, Sa 9–12 (207) 864-3685
Rangeley, ME	04970	M–F 9:30–12:30 & 1:30–4:15, Sa 9:30–12 (207) 864-2233

Stratton, ME	04982	M–F 9:00–1 & 1:30–4, Sa 9–11:30 (207) 246-6461
Caratunk, ME	**04925**	M–F 7:30–11:30 & 12–3:45, Sa 7:30–11:15 (207) 672-3416
Monson, ME	04464	M–F 7:30–11:30 & 12:30–4, Sa 7:30–11 (207) 997-3975
Millinocket, ME	04462	M–F 9–4, Sa 9–11:30 (207) 723-5921

Mail Drops

Many thru-hikers use "mail drops" to send themselves supplies. The *Companion* lists U.S. Postal Service (USPS) offices and also establishments that accept packages from shippers such as UPS and FedEx. Mail drops can be sent to both types of locations, but it is important to address them differently. Post offices accept only mail; a post office will not accept a FedEx or UPS package. Only post offices will accept packages addressed to a "General Delivery" address. USPS will forward unopened first-class and "priority" items at no additional fee. **UPS and FedEx packages cannot be sent to "General Delivery"**—you must provide a physical address other than a post office, such as a street number, and (for FedEx) a telephone number for those shipments. Please assist the businesses and post offices by printing legibly and practicing the following labeling instructions:

> Your Full Name (no nicknames or Trail names)
> c/o the business (*General Delivery* if a post office)
> City/State/ZIP Code
> *Please Hold for Thru-hiker or Section-Hiker*
> (and estimated date of arrival)

At the post office, be prepared to show a photo ID when you pick up your package. Postmasters are one of a thru-hiker's best friends on the Trail. Help them help you and other hikers by following the labeling instructions above for all your mail. Send a postcard if you leave the Trail for any reason, to let the post office know what to do with your package.

To ensure that your food parcels don't pick up any "unwanted visitors" before you arrive, we suggest that hikers double-bag and securely seal all parcels.

Hostels, Camping & Showers

The first thing that comes to a hiker's one-track mind when she/he hits town is FOOD and lots of it, followed by a good hot shower and affordable accommodations. In the pursuit of just food, shower, and laundry, some hikers want to minimize the town experience and return to the Trail as soon as possible, usually the same day. This list provides low-cost options and will help you to keep the grunge at bay. Campgrounds were chosen for their proximity to the Trail, and consideration was given if they allowed nonguest showers, while keeping in mind travel by foot. There are many other campgrounds listed in the *Companion* that are best reached by car or require a longer walk.

Establishments printed in **bold** are located on or within one mile of the Trail.
NA=not available
n/c= no charge
S = shelter; H = hostel; C = camping; L = lodging; B = bunk

State	Location; Establishment	Guest Fee	Nonguest Shower-only fee
Ga.	**Amicalola Falls State Park**	C $23, L $75+	
Ga.	Suches; A.T. Hiker Hostel	H $16	
Ga.	**Neels Gap**; Walasi-Yi Center	H $15	$3.50
Ga.	Hiawassee; Blueberry Patch	H donation	
N.C.	Rock Gap; Standing Indian Campground	C $16	$2
N.C.	**Wesser; Nantahala Outdoor Center**	H $17	
N.C.	**Fontana Dam Visitors Center**		n/c
Tenn.	**Green Corner Rd**; Standing Bear Farm	H $20/$15	
N.C.	**Hot Springs**; The Sunnybank Inn	L $20	
Tenn.	Greeneville; Hemlock Hollow	L $48 B $20 C $12	$3
Tenn.	Erwin; Cherokee Adventures	C $5 B $8	$2
Tenn.	Erwin; Nolichucky Hostel and Outfitters	H $15 C $8	$3
Tenn.	**Greasy Creek Gap**; Greasy Creek Friendly	H $10/$16 C $7.50	$3
Tenn.	**U.S. 19E**; Mountain Harbour B&B/Hostel	C $8 B $18	$3
Tenn.	**Roan Mtn**; Abby's Place	H $5/$10	$3

Tenn.	Dennis Cove; Laurel Fork Lodge	B $6 L $12	$2
Tenn.	Dennis Cove; Kincora Hostel	H $4 donation	
Va.	Damascus; The Place	H $4 donation	
Va.	Damascus; Dave's Place, MRO	H $10	$3
Va.	USFS Hurricane Campground	C $16	$2
Va.	Va. 16; Troutdale Baptist Church	H donation	n/c
Va	Groseclose; Happy Hiker Hollow	H, C	
Va.	Va. 606; Trent's Grocery Store	C $6	$3
Va.	Sugar Run Rd; Woodshole Hostel	H donation	
Va.	Pearisburg; Holy Family Church Hostel	H donation	
Va.	Pearisburg; Rendevous Motel	L $41.04	$8
Va.	U.S. 11; Day Stop Inn (Travel Centers of America)		$10
Va.	Va. 614; Middle Creek Campground	C $26/4	$5
Va.	Buena Vista; Glen Maury Campground	C $20	$2
Va.	Montebello; Montebello Camping and Fishing	C $10S/ $3EAP	$3.50
Va.	Tye River; Crabtree Falls Campground	C $23D	n/c
Va.	Lyndhurst; Rusty's Hard Time Hollow	H donation	
Va.	Waynesboro; Grace Evangelical Lutheran Church	H donation	n/c
Va.	Waynesboro; Waynesboro YMCA	C donation	n/c
Va.	SNP; Loft Mountain Campground	C $16	$1
Va.	SNP; Lewis Mountain Campground	C $16	$1
Va.	SNP; Big Meadows Campground	C $19	$1
Va.	Compton Gap Trail/Front Royal Terrapin Hostel	H $19	
Va.	Bears Den Hostel	H $27.50/$15 C $10	$3
Va.	Blackburn Trail Center	H, C donations	
W.Va.	Harpers Ferry; The Town's Inn	H $30	
Md.	Keep Tryst Road; Harpers Ferry Hostel	H $18/$21 C $10	$5
Md.	Gapland Rd. West; Maple Tree Campground	C (ask for rate)	
Md.	Dahlgren Backpack Campground	C	n/c
Md.	Md. 17/ Wolfsville Rd; The Free State Hiker Hostel	H $32	

Pa.	Caledonia State Park	C $19/$21 weekday; $23/$25 weekend	$3
Pa.	**Pa. 233; Pine Grove Furnace State Park, Ironmasters Mansion**	H $22/$25	$4
Pa.	**Boiling Springs**; Boiling Springs Pool		$1
Pa.	**U.S. 11, Carlisle**; Flyin J Travel Plaza		$11.50
Pa.	**Duncannon**; Doyle Hotel	L $25S/$7.50 EAP	$7.50
Pa.	**Duncannon**; All-American Truck Stop		$8
Pa.	**Pa. 501**; PAmoneypit Hostel	H $25	
Pa.	**Port Clinton** pavilion	C n/c	
Pa.	**Hawk Mountain Road**; Eckville Hikers Center; solar shower	B, C n/c	n/c
Pa.	Slatington; Fine Lodging	L $39	$4
Pa.	Palmerton; Borough Hall	H n/c	n/c
Pa.	**DWG; Presbyterian Church of the Mountain Hostel**	H donation	
N.J.	**Mohican Outdoor Center**	L $25 C n/c	
N.J.	**High Point State Park** day-use area		n/c
N.J.	**Sawmill Lake Campground**	C $20	
N.J.	Vernon; St. Thomas Episcopal Church	H $10 donation	
N.Y.	**Arden Valley Rd**; Tiorati Circle		n/c
N.Y.	**Graymoor Spiritual Life Center**	C	n/c
N.Y.	N.Y. 301; Clarence Fahnestock State Park	C $13/$16	n/c
Conn.	**Cornwall Bridge**; Housatonic Meadows State Park	C $36	n/c
Conn.	**Falls Village Hydroelectric Plant**; cold water		n/c
Mass.	**U.S. 7**; Corn Crib	C	n/c
Mass.	East Mountain Retreat	H $10	
Mass.	**Cheshire**; Mason Hill	B $25 C $15	
Mass.	Mass. 2; North Adams YMCA		$2
Mass.	Williamstown; Williams Inn		$7
Vt.	Rutland; Back Home Again Café	H donation	
Vt.	**Vt. 100**; Gifford Woods State Park	S $21 C $14–16/4	50¢

Vt.	Pittsfield; Amee Farm Hostel	H $20 or work for stay	
N.H.	**Etna–Hanover Ctr. Rd East; Tigger's Treehouse**	H donation	
N.H.	**Cape Moonshine Rd;** Dancing Dunes Village	C work for stay	
N.H.	**Glencliff;** Hikers Welcome Hostel	H $21 C $15/$23	$2.50
N.H.	I-93, U.S. 3, Franconia Notch; Lafayette Place Campground	C $25D	$1
N.H.	U.S. 302, Crawford Notch; Dry River Campground	C $27.25D	25¢
N.H.	U.S. 302, Crawford Notch; Crawford Notch Campground	C $24	$2
N.H.	U.S. 302, Crawford Notch; AMC Highland Center	B $37	
N.H.	**N.H. 16;** Pinkham Notch Visitors Center		coin-operated
N.H.	U.S. 2, Shelburne; White Birches Camping Park	H $15 C $11	.
N.H.	Gorham; The Barn	H $20	
N.H.	Gorham; Hikers Paradise Hostel at Colonial Fort Inn	H $19	
Maine	Maine 26, Grafton Notch; Bethel Outdoor Adventure's "Snow-boarding House"	H $22	
Maine	Andover; Pine Ellis Hiking Lodge	B $20	
Maine	Andover; South Arm Campground	C $15/4	25¢
Maine	Rangeley; Gull Pond Lodge	B $20	
Maine	Stratton; Stratton Motel & Hostel	H $20	
Maine	Stratton; Maine Roadhouse	B $20	
Maine	U.S. 201; Northern Outdoors Resort	C $10.70/$6.42 L $57.25/4	n/c
Maine	Monson; Lake Shore House	B $25 C $10	
Maine	Monson; Shaws	B $21.50 C $12PP	$6
Maine	**North Pond** Haven	H $20	
Maine	White House Landing	H $35	
Maine	**Golden Road;** Abol Bridge Campground	C $10	
Maine	**Golden Road;** Abol Pines	C $8	
Maine	Millinocket; A.T. Lodge	B $35S, $55D	$3

Equipment Manufacturers & Distributors

Most manufacturers and distributors stand behind their products. Companies will often replace or repair equipment while you are on the Trail. Usually, it is best to deal directly with the manufacturer rather than going through an outfitter along the Trail (except where noted below). A few telephone calls can save lost time and prevent a lot of headaches.

Arc 'Teryx	(866) 458-BIRD www.arcteryx.com
Asolo	(603) 448-8827, ext. 105 www.asolo.com
Backcountry Gear	(800) 953-5499 www.backcountrygear.com
Campmor	(800) 525-4784 www.campmor.com
Camelbak	(800) 767-8725 www.camelbak.com
Cascade Designs	(800) 531-9531 www.cascadedesigns.com
Cedar Tree Industry	(276) 780-2354 www.thepacka.com
Columbia	(800) 547-8066, (503) 985-4000 www.columbia.com
Dana Design (Marmot)	(888) 357-3262 www.danadesign.com
Danner Shoe Manufacturing	(800) 345-0430, (877) 432-6637 www.danner.com
Eagle Creek	(800) 874-9925 www.eaglecreek.com
Eastern Mountain Sports	(888) 463-6367 www.ems.com
Eureka	(888) 6EUREKA www.eurekacampingctr.com
Ex Officio	(800) 644-7303 www.exofficio.com
Feathered Friends	(206) 292-6292 www.featheredfriends.com
Frogg Toggs	(800) 349-1835 www.froggtoggs.com
General Ecology/First Need Filter	(800) 441-8166 www.generalecology.com
Golite	(888) 546-5483 www.golite.com

Gossamer Gear	(512) 374-0133 www.gossamergear.com
Granite Gear	(218) 834-6157 www.granitegear.com
Gregory Mountain Products	(800) 477-3420 www.gregorypacks.com
Hi-Tec Sports, USA	(209) 545-1111 www.hi-tec.com
Jacks 'R' Better Quilts	(757) 643-8908 www.jacksrbetter.com
JanSport	(510) 614-4000 www.jansport.com
Katadyn	(800) 755-6701 www.katadyn.com
Kelty Pack, Inc.	(800) 423-2320 www.kelty.com
Leki	(800) 255-9982, ext 3 www.leki.com
Peter Limmer & Sons, Inc.	(603) 694-2668 www.limmerboot.com
L.L.Bean	(800) 441-5713 www.llbean.com
Lowe Alpine Systems	(877) 888-8533 www.loweapline.com
Marmot	(888) 357-3262 www.marmot.com
Merrell	(800) 288-3124 www.merrell.com
Mont-bell	(303) 449-5331 www.montbell.com
Montrail	(800) 953-8398 www.montrail.com
Mountain Hardwear	(800) 953-8398 www.mountainhardwear.com
Mountain Safety Research (Cascade Designs)	(800) 531-9531 www.msrcorp.com
Mountainsmith	(800) 426-4075, ext. 2 www.mountainsmith.com
The North Face	(866) 715-3223, ext. 7 www.thenorthface.com
Osprey	(970) 564-5900 cs@ospreypacks.com
Outdoor Research	(888) 467-4327 www.outdoorresearch.com
Patagonia	(800) 638-6464 www.patagonia.com

Peak 1/Coleman	(800) 835-3278 www.coleman.com
Photon	(877) 584-6898 www.photonlight.com
Primus	(888) 546-2267 www.primus.stoves.com
Princeton Tec	(609) 298-9331 www.princetontec.com
REI	(800) 426-4840 www.rei.com
Royal Robbins	(800) 587-9044 www.royalrobbins.com
Salomon	(800) 654-2668 www.salomonsports.com
Sierra Designs	(800) 369-3949 www.sierradesigns.com
Six Moon Designs	(503) 430-2303 www.sixmoondesigns.com
Slumberjack	(800) 233-6283 www.slumberjack.com
Speer Hammocks	(828) 724-4444 www.edspeerhammocks.com
Suunto	(800) 543-9124 www.suunto.com
Tarptent by Henry Shires	(650) 587-1548 www.tarptent.com
Tecnica	(800) 258-3897, ext. 2 www.tecnicausa.com
Teva/Deckers Corporation	(800) FOR-TEVA www.teva.com
The Underwear Guys	(570) 573-0209 www.theunderwearguys.com
ULA-Equipment	(435) 753-5191 www.ula-equipment.com
Vasque	(800) 224-4453 www.vasque.com
Warm Stuff	(570) 573-0209 www.warmstuff.com
Western Mountaineering	(408) 287-8944 www.westernmountaineering.com
ZZManufacturing (Zipztove)	(800) 594-9046 www.zzstove.com

Key Dates to Remember (2010)

January 15–18	Southern Ruck, Nantahala Outdoor Center, Wesser, N.C.
January 29–31	Pennsylvania Ruck, Pine Grove Furnace State Park, Gardners, Pa.
March 5	ALDHA's 27th anniversary
March 20	ALDHA Steering Committee meeting, open to the public, Pine Grove Furnace State Park, Gardners, Pa.
April 25	Appalachian Trail Fest, Hot Springs, N.C.
May 13–16	Appalachian Trail Days, Damascus, Va.
June 5	National Trails Day and dedication of the Appalachian Trail Museum at Pine Grove Furnace State Park, Gardners, Pa.
August 7	Vermont Long Trail Festival, Rutland, Vt.
September	ALDHA West Gathering, California; see <www.aldhawest.org>.
October 15–17	29th ALDHA Gathering, Concord University, Athens, W.Va.

ALDHA 2010 Membership/Registration Form

Membership open to all   **No prerequisites or requirements**   **No need to be a hiker to join**

Name(s)

Current ALDHA member? ☐ Yes ☐ No

Date

Address City, State, ZIP

Phone *(with area code)*

E-mail

Trail name(s)

Home page

Trails completed and years they were hiked

Areas of expertise for the directory

☐ **Membership** (choose one)
   (includes four newsletters & the membership directory):

☐ Enclosed is $10 for my 2010 annual membership in ALDHA. *(It's $10 per family. Memberships run Jan. 1–Dec. 31.)*

☐ Enclosed is $20 for my 2010 and 2011 annual memberships in ALDHA.

☐ Enclosed is $200 for a lifetime membership in ALDHA.
   (Membership is for life but does not include the Gathering fee each year.)

☐ **2010 Gathering registration fee**
   (It's $10 per person; $20 per couple, etc.) _____ registrants

☐ $_____ tax-deductible donation to the **Appalachian Trail Museum**, a 501(c)(3) nonprofit *(separate check payable to **A.T. Museum Society**)*

Send completed form with payment (payable to ALDHA) to:
ALDHA, 10 Benning St., PMB 224, West Lebanon, NH 03784